ESP and Parapsychology: A Critical Reevaluation

C. E. M. Hansel

Prometheus Books
Buffalo, New York 14215

Published by Prometheus Books
1203 Kensington Avenue
Buffalo, New York 14215

Copyright © 1980 by Prometheus Books

Library of Congress Catalog Card Number 79-56361
ISBN 0–87975–119–3 (cloth)
ISBN 0–87975–120–7 (paper)

Printed in the United States of America

Contents

74691

Preface

In 1966, *ESP: A Scientific Evaluation* was published with the aim of evaluating research on ESP and other reputedly psychic phenomena. Since then new experiments have been reported and the feats of men such as Uri Geller have received wide publicity. The aim here is to examine all the experiments and to make a further evaluation in the light of any new features that have emerged.

In the earlier book the material was taken in its historical perspective. It was stressed that this is necessary in order to give understanding of the nature of the research and of the claims that have been made. For this reason much of the original material has been retained, since no reason could be found to change what has already been written. New developments have, however, arisen in the case of some of the earlier experiments and these have been updated where necessary.

I would like to acknowledge my indebtedness again to all those who collaborated with me when I was preparing my earlier book, in particular to Professor Emeritus R. T. Birge and to Mr. Martin Gardner. Thanks are also now due to Mr. Kenneth Heuer, formerly Science Editor at Charles Scribner's Sons, for his expert advice and encouragement.

For assistance when preparing this new volume my thanks are due to Dr. E. G. Dingwall, Dr. Trevor H. Hall, and to Dr. Christopher Scott. In addition I would like to thank Mr. Francis Hitchin for the loan of published material. I am also most grateful to Professor Paul Kurtz for making publication possible.

Finally, I am indebted to my wife, Gwenllian, who has spent many laborious hours correcting the manuscript and proofs, and who has maintained extensive records and reference material.

PART ONE

1
The Origins of Psychical Research

Most persons learn through experience that awareness of objects in the world outside them arises through the use of the senses. Scientific knowledge explains how this comes about—we see an object because light is reflected from it into our eyes—and also makes clear, indirectly, the conditions under which seeing cannot take place—light is necessary for vision; therefore, without it, we cannot see.

Personal experience also tells us that our thoughts remain private unless expressed by voice or action. Another person's thoughts can be guessed, but few would claim to be able to know them as they would if the person were thinking aloud. There are exceptions. On the stage, men appear to see when blindfolded and to read thoughts; but such performances are classified as magic, and it is known that the magician uses tricks that enable him to appear to do what common sense says is impossible.

During the past 50 years, however, the public has become aware of reports that abilities such as clairvoyance and telepathy have been demonstrated in the laboratory by means of rigorously controlled experiments. These claims are puzzling to many persons who are interested in natural processes and scientific experimentation, for the investigators appear to have established, by means of carefully planned experiments and conventional statistical analyses, the reality of phenomena that conflict with well-established principles.

Experimental evidence has been produced for four such processes to date:

1. *Telepathy,* a person's awareness of another's thoughts in the absence of any communication through sensory channels.

2. *Clairvoyance,* knowledge acquired of an object or event without the use of the senses.
3. *Precognition,* knowledge a person may have of another person's future thoughts (*precognitive telepathy*) or of future events (*precognitive clairvoyance*).
4. *Psychokinesis,* a person's ability to influence a physical object or an event, such as the fall of a die, by thinking about it.

Since the first three of these processes involve an act of perception or cognition and also because they are, by definition, independent of activity in the sense organs, each is commonly referred to as a kind of *extrasensory perception,* or ESP.

It will be seen that these four terms are restatements in systematic language of beliefs that have long been a part of folklore and superstition. Telepathy is a new name for mind reading; clairvoyance for second sight; precognition for divination or premonition; and psychokinesis is another name for levitation or for the process whereby a man thinks, for example, that he can get good weather for his holiday by praying for it. For this reason, the experiments, if they can be relied on, would imply that much of what has in the past been regarded as superstition must now be included in the domain of natural science.

The Foundation of the Society for Psychical Research

Preoccupation with these beliefs was responsible for the emergence at the end of the nineteenth century of *psychical research,* in which the study of ESP and other related phenomena became an organized discipline. At that time, there was a great deal of speculation about the possibility of strange new human powers. Stories of extraordinary happenings that seemed to contravene accepted scientific principles were popular, just as they are today. In the latter half of the nineteenth and well into the twentieth century, much publicity was given to *spiritualist mediums,* who supposedly received messages from the dead and whose exploits attracted considerable scientific interest.

But, at that time science displayed a unity in that when a new discipline, such as biology, revealed facts involving new types of processes, they were always consistent with other scientific knowledge. Thus, principles of physics and chemistry operated in the new discoveries of biology. As D'Arcy Thompson (1860–1948), the Scottish biologist, wrote, ". . . no physical law, any more than gravity itself, not even among the puzzles of stereo-chemistry, or of physiological surface-action and osmosis, is known to be transgressed by the bodily mechanism."[1]

In the realm of the senses, the eye was found to employ principles known to optics and the ear to contain mechanisms that might be expected from the study of sound. Messages were transmitted along nerve fibers from the sensory organs to the brain, and the nervous system behaved in a manner that was consistent with knowledge of other physical systems.

While it was not clear at that time whether psychological events would ever be fully explicable in terms of the natural laws already known to science, nothing in human behavior seemed at variance with known processes. The precise changes arising in the brain that were responsible for, say, memory were not known, but remembering displayed no very strange characteristics; similar processes, such as the camera's recording of a photographic image or the creation of a charge in a condenser, were well understood. However, if a man had shown himself to be capable of knowing about things before they happened, that would have involved a process of quite a different order, as if the photograph could emerge before the film had been exposed in the camera.

While telepathy seemed unlikely but not impossible—for it was conceivable that some sixth sense lay undiscovered—precognition displayed characteristics foreign to science, since, in this case, an effect seemed to precede its cause.

Not all the scientists were skeptical about the reports of what appeared to be paranormal happenings. A number of eminent British scientists, including the chemist Sir William Crookes (1832–1919), the physicists Sir William Fletcher Barrett (1844–1925) and Sir Oliver Joseph Lodge (1851–1940), the mathematician Augustus De Morgan (1806–1871), and the biologist Alfred Russel Wallace (1823–1913), thought that there was more in the reports than orthodox science would admit. After some early unsuccessful attempts to bring these matters to the serious attention of the scientific world, a group of scholars at Cambridge University decided that the time had come to set up a learned society to examine those faculties of man, real or supposed, that appeared inexplicable to science. As a result, the Society for Psychical Research was founded in 1882, with Henry Sidgwick (1838–1900), Professor of Moral Philosophy at Cambridge, as its first president. An American Society for Psychical Research was established a few years later, with the distinguished astronomer Simon Newcomb (1835–1909) as its president; today there are similar groups in many countries.

Since those early beginnings, a considerable amount of research has been conducted by the societies, by private individuals, and in universities. Today, psychical research, or *parapsychology* as it is now known, has come to be regarded by many as an accepted field of scientific study; investigations are in progress in some university departments; several laboratories and associations are committed to full-time research; and higher degrees are awarded in the topic. In 1969, the Parapsychological Association was granted affiliation with the American Association for the Advancement of Science.

Attitudes toward ESP

For the student of psychology, the position is extremely puzzling. Most of the leading British psychologists, for example, who have had anything to say on the matter of extrasensory perception, including Sir Cyril Burt, Mrs. Margaret

Knight, Dr. Robert H. Thouless, and Professor H. J. Eysenck, leave no doubt that they regard its existence as proved. For example, Mrs. Knight, formerly lecturer in psychology at Aberdeen University and well known to the British public, wrote: "But as Thouless convincingly argues, it is a waste of time to conduct further laborious experiments merely to demonstrate the occurrence of ESP. This has now been established beyond reasonable doubt."[2]

Professor Eysenck, head of the Department of Psychology at the Maudsley Hospital, London, known as a hard-headed and critical scientist, wrote:

> Unless there is a gigantic conspiracy involving some thirty university departments all over the world and several hundred highly respected scientists in various fields, many of them originally hostile to the claims of the psychical researchers, the only conclusion the unbiased observer can come to must be that there does exist a small number of people who obtain knowlege existing either in other people's minds, or in the outer world, by means yet unknown to science.[3]

The student finds a similar viewpoint expressed by other well-known philosophers and scientists. Yet parapsychology is unlikely to appear in his curriculum, and little reference is made to it in his textbooks.

If he questions his teachers, he will probably find that they know very little about psychical research, or, if they are critical of it, that they have few facts with which to support their criticisms. Thus, the late Dr. Samuel George Soal, a mathematician at London University and Britain's best-known parapsychologist, wrote:

> There is, of course, no shortage of people who feel that, because they are qualified in psychiatry or psychology they are competent to pass judgment on the work of the parapsychologist. The "expert" knowledge of such persons is usually based on some quite elementary books on the subject which omit the essential experimental details without which a proper evaluation of the work is not possible. It would be interesting to meet the psychiatrist or psychologist who has perused every page of the 49 volumes of the *Proceedings* of the Society for Psychical Research, and who remains a sceptic. It is no coincidence that those most sceptical of ESP research are almost invariably those who are least acquainted with the facts.[4]

Even in the beginnings of psychical research, the conflict between skeptic and believer existed. The members of the new Society for Psychical Research thought that a strong a priori case for telepathy and kindred phenomena existed in the numerous reports of inexplicable experiences; many scientists adopted the attitude that any such phenomena were, a priori, so unlikely in view of existing knowledge that there was no point in bothering about them.

Toward the end of the nineteenth century the great German scientist Hermann Ludwig von Helmholtz (1821–1894) expressed this viewpoint when he declared: "Neither the testimony of all the Fellows of the Royal Society, nor even the evidence of my own senses, would lead me to belive in the transmission of thought from one person to another independently of the recognized channels of sense."[5] Helmholtz was speaking with some authority, since he was the greatest living expert on sensory communication. To him, the manner in which information is acquired through the activity of the sense organs and the relationship between bodily processes and mental processes made the idea of telepathy as scientifically untenable as that of a flat earth.

A similar viewpoint has been expressed more recently by D. O. Hebb, Professor of Psychology at McGill University, Canada.

Personally, I do not accept ESP for a moment, because it does not make sense. My external criteria, both of physics and physiology, say that ESP is not a fact despite the behavioral evidence that has been reported. I cannot see what other basis my colleagues have for rejecting it; and if they are using my basis, they and I are allowing psychological evidence to be passed on by physical and physiological censors. Rhine may still turn out to be right, improbable as I think that is, and my own rejection of his views is—in a literal sense—prejudice.[6]

The well-known English author, Aldous Huxley (1894–1963), commented on Hebb's statement in *Life* magazine: "That a man of science should allow a prejudice to outweigh evidence seems strange enough. It is even stranger to find a psychologist rejecting a psychological discovery simply because it cannot be explained. Psi (the process of ESP) is intrinsically no more inexplicable than, say, perception or memory; it is merely less common.[7]

Dr. Thouless, former Reader in Psychology at Cambridge University and a former president of the British Society for Psychical Research, also has attacked those who refuse to accept the findings of research on extrasensory perception. In a paper read to the Royal Institution of Great Britain in 1950, he said:

In all science an unexpected experimental result is a challenge to the basis of our expectations and so becomes a possible starting point of theoretical advance. The failure of the Michelson-Morley experiment to reveal the expected motion of the earth relative to the ether made necessary the reconstruction of the theory on which the expectation of a detectable ether drift was based. By good fortune, this situation also produced the genius of Einstein who was able to take the essential step in the reconstruction of theory which made the Michelson-Morley result explicable.

I would suggest that the discovery of the *psi* phenomena has brought us to a similar point at which we must question basic theories because they lead

us to expectations contradicted by experimental results . . . I can only suggest that we must be ready to question all our old conceptions and to distrust
all our habits of thought.[8]

The case cited by Thouless is perhaps not so apt as it appears at first sight. The
Michelson-Morley experiment—which attempted to measure the velocity of the
earth through the ether (postulated as the medium through which light in space
traveled) through the effect of this velocity on the velocity of light—failed to show
any movement of the earth relative to the ether. Scientists did not, from this result,
conclude that the earth was stationary and that the rest of the solar system moved
around it; this would have contradicted too much of what was known and already
accepted as true. Instead, they looked afresh at the process of measurement and the
assumptions underlying it. The result, of course, was a new concept of the nature
of light and its motion. Parapsychologists, on the other hand, ask critics to accept
ESP as proved and to change the rest of science so that it can include this new
phenomenon.

What Thouless is implying is, however, quite clear. No one can ignore a mass
of empirical data, provided that it conforms with all the safeguards and requirements of science.

In Helmholtz's time, the evidence for telepathy was almost entirely of an
anecdotal nature; but, during the last century, numerous full-scale experiments
have been carried out, and it is claimed that they provide overwhelming evidence
for the existence of ESP. It may be that any a priori theoretical objections must now
be relinquished in the light of empirical evidence; but, before such a drastic step is
taken, it is necessary to be quite certain that the experimental results obtained by
parapsychologists are due to paranormal rather than to normal processes and that
the experiments establish this fact beyond all doubt.

A close inspection of the work of the parapsychologists is, in any case,
important for two reasons: if their claims are justified, a complete revision in
contemporary scientific thought is required at least comparable to that made
necessary in biology by Darwin and in physics by Einstein. On the other hand, if
ESP is merely an artifact, it is then important to understand how conventional
experimental methods can yield results leading to erroneous conclusions.

Notes

1. D'Arcy Thompson, *Growth and Form* (Cambridge, England: Cambridge
   University Press, 1942), p. 13.
2. Margaret Knight, "Theoretical Implications of Telepathy," *Science News*,
   No. 18 (London: Penguin Books Ltd., 1950), p. 20.
3. H. J. Eysenck, *Sense and Nonsense in Psychology* (London: Penguin Books
   Ltd., 1957), p. 13.

4. S. G. Soal and F. Bateman, *Modern Experiments in Telepathy* (London: Faber & Faber Ltd., 1954), p. 24.
5. Quoted in Rosalind Heywood, *Beyond the Reach of Sense* (New York: E. P. Dutton & Co., Inc., 1961), p. 11
6. D. O. Hebb, "The Role of Neurological Ideas in Psychology," *Journal of Personality*, 20 (1952), 45.
7. Aldous Huxley, *Life*, 36, No. 2 (1954), 96.
8. R. H. Thouless, "Thought Transference and Related Phenomena, 1950," from Soal and Bateman, *Modern Experiments in Telepathy*, p. 357.

2
The Subject Matter of Psychical Research

In order to identify more exactly the processes in which parapsychologists are interested, it is necessary to describe the way in which they are investigated in the laboratory. It is not implied, however, that experiments have been conducted in precisely the manner described in this chapter

Sensory and Extrasensory Perception

Most branches of science start by classifying the material and processes being studied and then proceed by a series of definitions to give an agreed usage of words and symbols for descriptive and deductive purposes. A rigid system of definitions is available in the "hard" sciences, but definitions tend to become more vague and less agreed in the "soft" sciences.

The term *perception* is often left undefined owing to the difficulty of encompassing it into a behavioral framework. Its definition in one of the most widely used psychology texts is given as "the process of becoming aware of objects, qualities, or relations *by way of the sense organs.*" This definition assumes first that the process of "becoming aware" is well known and needs no further explanation and second (in the italicized portion) that empirical findings about the nature of perception are correct. If, initially, perception is defined as "the process of becoming aware of objects, qualities, or relations," this does not assume anything about the nature of the mechanisms involved, and it can then cover all forms of perception including ESP if it exists. *Sensory perception* is then a particular form of perception in which the sense organs are involved.

If a man says "I see a chair," further investigation may reveal that he can describe the chair and state its position in space relative to himself. His statements may be verified so that it becomes evident that he is aware of the presence of the chair, i.e., that he has perceived it.

An essential feature of perceiving is that the person involved (the *percipient*) *gains information* about objects or events in his environment. He is then able to make statements about the objects or events with which other people will agree and that can be checked and found to be true.

In the case of the person seeing a chair, a sequence of processes arises, starting with light being reflected from the chair and ending with the percipient perceiving the chair. The stages may be represented as follows:

1. *The stimulus*. The adequate stimulus for vision is light. Light emitted from a luminous source—such as a lamp—falls on the chair. Some of the light is absorbed at the surface of the chair, the remainder is reflected and scattered in all directions. Light of different wavelengths is absorbed to different extents. Thus the reflected light is capable of revealing something about the light absorption characteristics of a particular area of the surface of the chair—or in the present case, the color of the chair.

2. *The detection stage*. An optical image of the chair and its background is projected by the optical system of the eye onto the retina. Light is absorbed in the retina, photochemical action takes place, and nerve impulses are generated according to the amount and characteristics of the light absorbed in different parts of the retina and thence to the distribution of light in the optical image projected onto the retina. These nerve impulses originating from light sensitive cells in the retina (photoreceptors) are transmitted via nerve fibers to the brain. The particular fibers that are transmitting impulses, and the temporal characteristics of these impulses, are related to the distribution of light in the optical image and thence to the corresponding areas of the stimulus (the chair).

3. *Past experience*. The outcomes of previous acts of perception have produced semipermanent changes in the system, or are stored in some manner, so that incoming information from the senses is affected by what has been stored in the past as the result of previous perceptions. Incoming information may not necessarily result in perception, since what is perceived is dependent on set and past experience—thence by what a person expects to perceive. Past experience thus determines and modifies the form that perception will take. The new perception becomes part of past experience and will affect future perceptions.

4. *Perception and awareness*. At the final stage, perception or a state of awareness consists of a gain of information by the percipient about objects or events in the environment. Awareness is of the object and its characteristics, such as its color, shape, and its relationship to the percipient and to other objects in time and space. The amount of information reaching the subject may be limited, e.g.,

by presenting the stimulus for a brief interval of time. Under such conditions, at the earliest stage, with a very brief presentation when very little information is available, the percipient may be aware of "something in the field." He has awareness of something positioned in time and space without identification of the object. At a later stage, particular characteristics of the object may be perceived, and eventually the object is recognized and named. At each stage, perception and awareness result from some gain of information on the part of the percipient. This is implied in the first part of the definition by the words "becoming aware."

The restricted definition does not assume that all perceptions arise in this manner and that stages 1 and 2 are essential. *Extrasensory perception,* defined by J. B. Rhine as "awareness of or response to an external event or influence not apprehended by sensory means," is then within the perview of psychology provided no assumptions are made about the modus operandi as covered in the second part of the initial definition.

Certain other forms of awareness covered by the restricted definition could be regarded as being independent of the sense organs. Thus, if a person becomes aware of a relationship about which he was previously unaware, e.g., if he multiplies 29 by 11 in his head and becomes aware of the fact that the product is 319, or if he sees a pink elephant, awareness arises of a relationship or of an object without there being objects in the environment at the time of the perception. The parapsychologist is, however, concerned with the perception of real *external* events and with the possibility of information being gained about such events without the sensory apparatus being involved. What is perceived can then be verified in the same manner as sensory perception is verified.

Measuring Information Gain

When studying a possible new means of bringing about perception, it is necessary to determine whether there is any measurable information gain on the part of the percipient that could be attributed to this new means when other known sources of information are excluded. Since each of the known forms of sensory perception is dependent on an adequate stimulus—light, acoustic energy, molecules of substances giving chemical change, pressure, etc.—it is a relatively simple matter to exclude any of them by removing the adequate stimulus or by screening it from the subject. Thus, visual perception of an object cannot arise when the illuminant is removed or when light is screened from the eyes.

To establish that information is gained, a stimulus may be present or absent in a random binary series of trials. The subject has to state at each trial whether he perceives the stimulus as being present or not present. If he is perceiving the stimulus on a fraction of occasions, this will result in his giving a report agreeing with the presence or absence of the stimulus on more than 50 percent of occasions in a large number of trials. The subject may be told after each trial whether he was

"correct" or not without this affecting the result. In addition, any process of inference or the adoption of a strategy cannot enable him to display a gain of information if it is not, in fact, occuring. Whatever the subject does, if he consistently obtains an above chance score of responses agreeing with the presence or absence of the stimulus, this indicates that information is being utilized.

If the score is consistently at the chance expectation value, this indicates that information is not being utilized. When testing for ESP, the subject is normally asked to identify a particular stimulus from a number of alternatives that are presented in random order. In this case also, information used by the subject will result in a number of hits greater than the theoretical value. If the experimental conditions are such that the sensory channels cannot receive information, it is then assumed that extrasensory perception is present.

Transmitting a Message

A *message,* containing some form of information, is normally communicated by one person—the sender—through the means of voice, gesture, or some other activity involving the use of his muscles. This generates stimuli that can be detected by another person—the receiver—through the medium of one or more of his senses. The receiver thereby can become aware of what the sender is doing or of the message he is transmitting. Most messages involve the use of *language,* a means whereby sounds are encoded to signify objects or actions; but any other code can be used so long as both the sender and the receiver employ the same system.

The number of methods of communication is limited by the ways in which the sender can, with his muscles, initiate activity detectable by the receiver. An instrument, such as a megaphone or a telescope, may be employed to increase the distance over which messages can be transmitted. The sender may also use apparatus to produce disturbances that cannot be detected by the unaided sense organs but that can be detected by means of suitable apparatus, such as a television set or a telephone receiver. However, in all these cases the sender has to initiate activity by using his muscles, and the receiver ultimately has to detect stimuli by means of his sense organs.

Telepathy

For telepathy to exist, the receiver, or *percipient,* must learn, without the use of his sense organs, what the sender, or *agent,* is thinking about. It is also usually implied that there is no special activity on the part of the agent. That is, his thoughts become known to the percipient, whether he wishes it or not and without his making any effort at communication.

Furthermore, in telepathic communication, information passes from one person to another without the use of any special apparatus. It does not involve the

setting up of disturbances, such as those created by voice or movements, and it does not require any activity of the known senses. Telepathy, therefore, implies abilities of human beings thus far unknown to psychology and physiology and properties of matter unknown to physics.

To read someone's thoughts does not necessarily involve the idea of telepathy. Any normal person may at times have some idea of another's thoughts by utilizing cues such as facial expression, skin color, and posture. He will not know the verbal content, but he may obtain some idea of the other person's emotional state and from this deduce the type of thought the other person is having.

In experiments carried out to demonstrate telepathy, the percipient tries to guess the nature of a symbol about which the agent is thinking. If the percipient could invariably guess correctly, or even could know when he had done so, there would be no difficulty in demonstrating telepathy. The experimenters themselves have, however, admitted the inability of their subjects to do either of these things.

The task of the percipient is made easier as the number of possible things about which the agent may be thinking is reduced. Thus, when the agent has complete freedom of choice, the percipient's job is at its most difficult; if he knows that the agent has been instructed to think of a digit between 0 and 10, then this task is greatly simplified. But even under the simplest conditions—namely, when the agent is instructed to think of one of two possible symbols—no percipient has ever guessed correctly all the time. The experimenters merely claim that some persons, while they do make mistakes, produce more correct guesses than are likely to arise by chance.

Most investigators of telepathy have preferred to use five symbols, and the percipient is informed that when he makes his guess the agent will be thinking about one of these five. An experiment consists of a number of *trials,* or guesses; during each, while the agent looks at a card bearing one of the five symbols, the percipient tries to guess which symbol the agent is seeing. A subject might be tested by giving him 200 trials, broken up into eight *runs* of 25 trials each. If the symbols are presented to the agent in random order, a person with no telepathic ability would be expected to guess correctly an average of one-fifth of the trials. If he made 200 guesses, he would therefore be expected to obtain about 40 successes.

It is claimed that, under such conditions, subjects sometimes obtain scores that are highly unlikely to arise by chance. If, for example, a subject obtains 60 successes in 200 trials and then goes on achieving similar scores on further runs, it soon becomes clear that something other than chance is responsible for his scores.

Clairvoyance

Clairvoyance differs from telepathy in that only one person is involved; the percipient can become aware of an event or the characteristics of an object without the involvement of a second person acting as transmitter.

If clairvoyance is possible, the agent in a telepathy experiment might appear to play a minor role, since there would be little point in his transmitting a message,

giving the symbol on a card, to a percipient who can identify it by clairvoyance. In the United States, investigators have obtained high scores as easily in clairvoyance experiments when no agent is employed as in telepathy experiments. In Great Britain, many efforts to demonstrate clairvoyance have been made with subjects who have been successful in telepathy experiments; however, these attempts have not succeeded.

In the majority of the clairvoyance experiments, a subject attempts to guess the identities of symbols depicted on cards. One such experiment is similar to the telepathy study described above, except that the agent, instead of looking at the symbol displayed on the face of a card, merely touches its back and does not see the symbol; the percipient then attempts to guess it. In a more ambitious type of experiment, a pack of cards is shuffled and placed on a table in front of the percipient. He attempts to guess the identity of the cards in their order in the pack while it is left undisturbed.

Precognition

In a variation of the last experiment, the pack is shuffled after the subject has guessed at the identities of the cards. If scores above the chance level are observed when the subject's guesses are checked against the cards as they exist *after the shuffle,* he is said to display precognitive clairvoyance.

In another test, the percipient takes part in a telepathy experiment in which he has to guess cards seen by an agent at the rate of one every two seconds. He scores significantly above the chance level when each of his guesses is checked against the card to be seen next by the agent; it is as if the guesser anticipates the person having the thought. He is then said to display precognitive telepathy.

Here, there is no possibility that the agent transmits information to the percipient, for there is no means by which he could do so, since he is unaware of the symbol until two seconds after the guess has been recorded. The agent could, in fact, be talking freely to the percipient and still be unable to affect his scores.

In the major experiments on precognition, it has always been necessary for there to be an agent who later saw the symbol which the percipient was attempting to guess. Percipient's scores have been above the chance level when the agent was instructed to look at the symbols on the cards during each trial but only at the chance level when he merely touched the backs of the cards. A positive result in the latter instance would have been attributed to precognitive clairvoyance.

What is defined as precognition under these experimental conditions differs to some extent from popular usage of the term, which implies that a person has foreknowledge of something that he himself is going to experience. If precognition were possible, it is indeed reasonable to expect that the percipient would more easily precognize his own thoughts than those of someone else. An experimental situation to test this would require the percipient to see a series of symbols at, say, six-second intervals and to guess each symbol two seconds before seeing it.

Psychokinesis

Psychokinesis differs from the processes already described in that a person is said to influence a physical object by thinking about it. Thus, he causes something to happen in the external world, rather than being influenced himself by an external event. The subjects in psychokinesis experiments, for example, may attempt to influence the fall of a die so that a particular face will land uppermost.

Spontaneous Data

Extrasensory perception and psychokinesis are usually regarded as being well suited to investigation in the laboratory, but not all the phenomena studied in psychical research readily lend themselves to experiment. In the past, considerable attention has been paid to spontaneous events reported from everyday life that seem to permit no normal explanation, and a great deal of attention has been directed to the study of spiritualistic phenomena. In fact, there was greater scientific interest in the phenomena of the séance rooms in the first part of the century than there is today in all of extrasensory perception. At that time, interest was mainly directed to the possibility of communication with the dead, but today many parapsychologists regard mediums simply as persons with highly developed telepathic and clairvoyant abilities. Some parapsychologists would go further and say that the study of spontaneous data and of telepathy, as demonstrated by the mediums, can provide more satisfactory evidence for ESP than can laboratory experiments. It is also a fact that many people claim to have had psychical experiences, and, for most people, personal experience provides more convincing evidence than any number of experimental findings.

3
Examining
the Evidence

Few people have time to examine and test the evidence in parapsychology for themselves. They have to rely on authoritative statements made by investigators and by others who have studied the research. The same is true in any branch of science. A chemist, for example, cannot hope to verify every new claim reported in his field, but he has good reasons for believing that a mistake will be revealed by those specializing in the topic concerned.

How then is an authoritative opinion about the processes postulated by parapsychologists to be obtained? If there were no doubt about the existence of such processes, they would be dealt with as aspects of psychology. However, orthodox psychologists, to judge from what they teach in universities or include in their books, do not regard extrasensory perception as an established process. On the other hand, if a parapsychologist is consulted, he is likely to have no doubts about the existence of ESP.

The Amount of Evidence

Experiments testing for the presence of extrasensory perception are fortunately of such a nature that anyone of reasonable intelligence can understand them and even try them out for himself. Many persons are put off at the start, however, because they have a false impression of the amount and type of evidence that has accumulated. For example, Arthur Koestler wrote in the *Observer* of May 7, 1961:

The card-guessing and dice-throwing experiments repeated over millions of experimental runs with thousands of random experimental subjects—often

whole classes of schoolboys who have no idea what the experiment is about; the more and more refined experimental conditions and methods of statistical breakdown; the increasingly elaborate machinery for mechanical card shuffling, dice-throwing, randomizing, recording, and what-have-you, have turned the study of extrasensory perception into an empirical science as sober, down-to-earth and also too often as dreary as teaching rats to run a maze or slicing up generations of flatworms.[1]

Few parapsychologists who know anything about research in their subject would claim that millions of guesses have been made by thousands of subjects under good experimental conditions or that results claiming conclusive evidence for ESP have been reported from many universities.

The experiments differ markedly in complexity: thus an experiment may be relatively simple, involving, say, four persons who meet one afternoon and record 200 trials at guessing card symbols, or it may be highly complicated. Some of the telepathy experiments have, in fact, consisted of a large number of sittings in which the conditions have been changed from one sitting to another. With this latter type of investigation, it becomes particularly necessary to emphasize three principles that should be considered when assessing a study

1. *Each experiment must be considered on its own merits.* A weakness cannot be excused because it is absent in a second experiment. The first experiment should be ignored and conclusions obtained only from the new experiment.

Professional magicians often rely on the fact that their audience does not practice this kind of assessment. The magician, for example, may demonstrate "thought transference." The essential features of his trick are that a member of the audience takes a card from a pack of playing cards, looks at it, and replaces it. The magician later identifies it. A second member of the audience takes a card. This time, he is allowed to retain it, and the magician again names it. If a member of the audience isolates these essential features of the trick, he may be puzzled as to how it was carried out. He may decide, after the first trick, that the magician is somehow getting sight of the card after it is replaced in the pack. But, on the second occasion, since the performer does not touch the pack after the card is drawn, this possibility would appear to have been eliminated.

Any professional magician is likely to have many variations of a simple trick of this nature. He may, for example, attempt to force the choice of a card, the identity of which is known to him, on each occasion. If he is successful in doing so, the card need not be replaced in the pack. If he is unsuccessful, he has to ask that it be put back so that he can bring it to the top of the pack by sleight of hand and somehow see its face. Few magicians announce in advance exactly what they are going to do.

2. *An experiment that has any defect such that its result may be due to a cause other than ESP cannot provide conclusive proof of ESP.* In parapsychological research, the process being investigated is both hypothetical and, a priori, ex-

tremely unlikely. Any possible known cause of the result is far more likely to be responsible for it than the hypothetical process under consideration.

A possible explanation other than extrasensory perception, provided it involves only well-established processes, should not be rejected on the grounds of its complexity.

For example, in the case of a particular experiment, it may be necessary to decide between two explanations accounting for the scores observed: extrasensory perception, which posits a new process, or a second one that, although complex, is dependent only on known processes. The latter may appear unlikely, but it is *possible*. It must be eliminated before the hypothesis of extrasensory perception can be entertained.

3. *An experiment must be judged on the weakest part of its design.* Inadequacy of control at one point cannot be overcome by extreme control at another.

For example, in the telepathy experiments with George Zirkle as subject, described on page 91, there is a weakness in that reliance must be placed entirely on the accuracy of an experimenter who also acted as agent and who recorded both the symbol she had been thinking about and the guess of the percipient. However stringent the controls of other features of the experiment, they cannot offset this weakness.

The Effects of Error and Trickery

In addition to the above, no factor that could influence the results of an experiment must be overlooked. If there is the slightest possibility that any or all participants in the experiments did anything to influence the result that is not noted in the experimental report, this possibility must be fully considered.

It is necessary to discuss openly possible trickery or cheating by participants to produce a spurious conclusion. If the result could have arisen through a trick, the experiment must be considered unsatisfactory proof of ESP, whether or not it is finally decided that such a trick was, in fact, used. At this point, the concern is with evaluation of the experiment rather than with a decision about whether a particular individual tried to influence the result. As a further step, it may be necessary to establish whether there is any evidence to show that trickery did, in fact, take place.

It may be objected that any experiment can be condemned on the grounds that all of those taking part in it, including the researchers, may be indulging in a trick and that trickery is a well-established process, whereas ESP is not; therefore, no single experiment can be conclusive. This is so. But normally, in science, anyone who suspects an experimental result can repeat the experiment himself and check its conclusions.

Repetition after repetition of an ESP experiment by independent investigators could render the possibility of deception or error extremely unlikely. Thus, if the original result is repeatedly confirmed, the probability of ESP becomes increasingly likely.

Initial Assumptions

Psychical research, in many ways, is like a game, and some of the investigators have emphasized that those taking part in the experiments should treat them as games if they hope to obtain positive results. It may be that conditions required to conduct card-guessing experiments are necessarily somewhat similar to those in which a magician endeavors to demonstrate his powers. The magician has to elaborate the proceedings so that the obvious explanations are ruled out; the psychical researcher, so that normal means of gaining information and of trickery are eliminated. The psychical researcher attempts to remove all loopholes, but the magician has to leave one so that he can perform his trick.

An ESP experiment can be analyzed in much the same way as one tries to discover how the conjurer performs his trick. For example, a girl is sawn in half by a magician. First, she is seen as a complete female figure; later, the legs are seen protruding from one end of a box, the head from the other end. A saw is passed through the region that corresponds with the girl's abdomen. The assumption is that the girl has not, in fact, been sawn in half, since she is intact at the conclusion of the experiment. Thus, no part of the girl was in the space through which the saw passed. Then, either the sawing was an illusion, or she was not in the place through which the saw passed. At a further demonstration, the head and legs protruding from the box are inspected, and the conclusion reached is that they could not be where they are and belong to the same person unless there was a torso in the area through which the saw passed—that is, unless either the head or the legs were dummies. But other observers examine the head and legs and convince us that they are real. Then, the head belongs to the girl, and the legs belong to some other person.

The hypothesis is now formed that two girls are inside the box, so arranged that we see the head of one and the legs of the other and that there is an empty space between them through which the saw can pass. This analysis of the conjuring trick starts with the assumption that what the conjurer claims to do, or appears to have done, is not what he does in reality, since it contradicts too much of what is known about the properties of things.

Thus, in analyzing an experiment that purports to prove ESP, it is wise to adopt initially the assumption that ESP is impossible, just as it is assumed that the conjurer cannot saw the same girl in half twice each evening.

To assume that ESP is impossible is not unreasonable, since there is a great weight of knowledge supporting this point of view, and the main evidence contradicting it is that of the experiment being analyzed. If analysis shows that this assumption is untenable, then the possibility of ESP has to be accepted.

The Statistical Evaluation of an Experiment

It will be found that there are enormous odds against the scores produced in many of the experiments under discussion having arisen by chance. Thus, in Soal's experiments with Mrs. Stewart, discussed on page 157, the odds are quoted as 10^{70} to 1 against chance. If a man bet a penny on a horse at these odds and won, he would have a very difficult task disposing of his fortune. If he gave a million dollars to every man alive—for that matter, if he included every man who has ever lived—he would still have plenty left. After repeating that whole gift a million times every second for a million years, he would not have made the slightest hole in his capital. He would certainly still have a million million times as much money as he had given away.

The great odds against a particular score arising by chance are sometimes quoted as if they indicate that the experiment *proves* the existence of ESP. Thus, in a review of the Soal-Goldney experiment on Basil Shackleton (see pages 000-00). C. D. Broad, Professor of Philosophy at Cambridge University, came to the conclusion that it provided evidence "which is statistically overwhelming for the occurrence not only of telepathy, but of precognition."[2]

Professor Broad appears to have assumed that the result could have been achieved only if the precipient possessed precognitive telepathy. However, if there is even the smallest possibility of some other explanation, the results of the experiment support that as much as they support the hypothesis of precognition. The probability obtained in the experiment is that of the score having arisen by chance. It tells us nothing about the probability of precognitive telepathy. To provide statistically overwhelming evidence for the occurrence of ESP in experiments of this nature requires satisfaction of two conditions: (1) the scores achieved by the subject must be such as are very unlikely to arise by chance, and (2) the experimental conditions must be such that only ESP could account for them.

The first condition is quite simple to assess. The percipient's score is compared with the one expected to arise by chance, and the frequency with which such a score would be expected to arise in a large number of such experiments if the guesses were made purely at random is calculated. Thus, in the case of the Shackleton experiment, it was found that his score would be expected to arise by chance only once in about 10^{35} such experiments.

The second condition causes the difficulties. For any interpretation as to why the experimental result differs significantly from the chance expectation is dependent on what is known about the conditions under which the experiment was carried out. A low probability that a certain result will occur, as noted in the first condition, reveals nothing about the probability that ESP does or does not exist. This is entirely dependent on the second condition. An example will make this clearer.

A magician performs a thought-reading act in which he correctly identifies 50 cards, each drawn from a pack of 52 and then replaced and shuffled. The odds against his guessing these cards by chance are 52^{50} to 1, and this is even more impressive a result than was achieved by Shackleton. The magician is, however, employing a conjuring trick. In this case, the probability of ESP in the second condition is 0, and the total probability of the result being due to ESP is 0.

The weight attached to an experiment's supposed proof of ESP is entirely dependent on how certain one can be that any alternative explanations of the result are completely eliminated. The subject's score and the probability of its arising by chance serve merely to indicate whether an assessment of the experiment should be made at all.

The second condition is the more difficult to assess. The experimental conditions may be examined most meticulously and no flaw found, but there is no certainty that nothing has been missed. The conclusion that an experiment provides statistically overwhelming evidence for the appearance of ESP is misleading if no allowance is made for the possibility of error in the experimental setup. The incidence of trickery, deception, and error in psychical research is such that the probability of their occurrence is certainly far from insignificant. Professor Broad's statement, quoted earlier in this chapter, is based on the assumption that the experiment he is quoting is completely watertight and that there is no possibility of error or trickery.

It could, however, be argued that the probability that ESP exists is insignificantly small and the probability of fraud appreciable. In that case, it could be said that the experiments provide overwhelming evidence for trickery or error. If it can be shown that these conditions could account for the results, a more likely hypothesis has been established.

If, on the other hand, it can be reasonably ascertained that trickery or error have been eliminated through the employment of a completely watertight experimental procedure, then the experiment can provide evidence to support the hypothesis of extrasensory perception. If the result is confirmed by other investigators, ESP eventually will cease to be a hypothesis and will be accepted as fact. If a process really does exist in nature, this fact eventually will silence all objections, since it is as difficult to maintain erroneous criticism as it is to demonstrate the existence of something that is nonexistent. Criticism must be thorough, just as experimental research seeking to establish the facts must be thorough.

Exploratory and Conclusive Methods

Few people are likely to have time themselves to check through all the experiments that have been conducted on ESP. It is, therefore, necessary to make a selection of the data, which must include all those experiments generally agreed to provide the strongest evidence for the presence of ESP. Fortunately, at various times the most prominent workers in this field have surveyed the literature and selected such studies. At the same time, they have rejected experiments that contain weaknesses in design or in which explanations other than ESP can account for the result.

Two of the best known American parapsychologists, Joseph B. Rhine, formerly Director of the Institute for Parapsychology and of the Parapsychology Laboratory at Duke University, and Joseph G. Pratt, also formerly associated with the Laboratory, stressed the fact that not every experiment is designed with the object of establishing the existence of ESP. Thus, in their book, *Parapsychology: Frontier Science of the Mind,* they differentiated between experiments employing an exploratory method and those employing a conclusive method.

Exploratory methods are employed, they say, "on the assumption that final conclusions will require a more cautious type of experiment."[3] According to them, "The chief characteristic of the exploratory stage of scientific inquiry is that in it the explorer is permitted to range widely, venture freely, and look into everything that might be important to his interest without being burdened with too much precautionary concern. It is a more venturesome, a more extravagant phase of investigation. It is always a first stage, of course, but only because of the natural order of investigation. While it is obvious that without this exploratory stage there would be little or nothing for science to verify or establish, it is equally true that with it alone no results would ever be firmly established."[4]

Rhine and Pratt stated four requirements of a conclusive experiment:

1. Sound measurement.
2. Satisfactory experimental safeguards against normal sensory communication.
3. Care in recording. Here they remarked that the responsibility of recording data should be shared between two responsible persons in such a way that no error made by either could go undetected.
4. Precautions against deception on the part of the experimenters themselves.

Proof for the existence of ESP obviously must depend on conclusive experiments, but only a small number of all such experiments are considered to fall into this category, and parapsychologists do not agree which of the experiments should be regarded as conclusive. This was pointed out by J. Fraser Nicol, Research Officer of the American Society for Psychical Research, at an international symposium on extrasensory perception organized by the Ciba Foundation and held at Cambridge University, England, in 1955. (The Ciba Foundation was founded by Ciba Ltd. of Switzerland and is administered independently by a board of British trustees. Among other activities, it organizes international conferences on scientific topics.) After comparing the selection of conclusive experiments provided by different authors, Nicol concluded by saying: "Clearly there is no unity of opinion among leading psychical researchers as to what constitutes valid evidence."[5]

Conclusive Experiments Before 1965

In a section of *Parapsychology: The Evidence for PSI*, Rhine and Pratt named four experiments that, they felt, provided conclusive evidence for ESP. These are:

1. The Pearce-Pratt series.
2. The Pratt-Woodruff series.
3. The Soal-Goldney series.
4. The Soal-Bateman series.

An earlier survey, published in 1940, by five members of the Parapsychology Laboratory at Duke University, isolated the following conclusive experiments after surveying 145 reported up to that time:[6]

1. The Pratt-Woodruff series.
2. The Pearce-Pratt series.
3. An experiment by Lucien Warner.
4. The Turner-Ownbey series.
5. An experiment reported by B. F. Riess.
6. An experiment reported by Murphy and Taves.

A further survey contained in *Modern Experiments in Telepathy*, by Soal and Bateman, published in 1954, lays stress on

1. The Soal-Goldney series.
2. The Soal-Bateman series.

and also mentions without criticism:

3. The Pearce-Pratt series.
4. The Pratt-Woodruff series (mentioned as "fairly good," although no specific feature of the experiment is criticized).
5. A test known as the Martin-Stribic series.

The Riess experiment is dismissed as questionable, and the experiments of Warner and of Murphy and Taves are not mentioned. Soal and Bateman stated that the Turner-Ownbey series result must be accepted or else the two experimenters (Miss Ownbey and Dr. Rhine) were in collusion to deceive.

While it is of the greatest importance that each of the conclusive experiments be included in an assessment of the evidence for ESP, it is also necessary that weak experiments should not be selected for criticism merely with the intention of extending such criticism to the research in general. The following remarks, made by R. A. McConnell, of the Department of Biophysics, University of Pittsburgh, at the Ciba symposium express this view:

A final point about which I want to say something is that, at least in the United States, in my own experience a certain class of critic, who is in a related field and who might be presumed by his colleagues to have some opinion about ESP—I am thinking particularly of certain psychologists—has managed to confuse the thinking of the scientific fraternity as a whole by a very simple procedure. Whenever the question comes up as to what is wrong with the ESP experiments that have been performed, the tactic which has been followed—and I can only conclude it has been followed consciously—is to describe the weaknesses in those experiments which are not the best experiments; to point out all of the things that are wrong with the poor experiments and quietly to ignore the experiments which cannot be explained away.[7]

McConnell did not specify the poor experiments that should be ignored, but in the paper in which the above statement was made, he mentioned only two experiments with approval. These were the Pearce-Pratt series and the Riess study. In *E.S.P. and Personality Patterns* by McConnell and G. R. Schmeidler, Professor of Psychology at City College, New York, published in 1958,[8] there is, however, a chapter, "Evidence that ESP Occurs," in which the following experiments are named:

1. The Pearce-Pratt experiment.
2. The Pratt-Woodruff experiment.
3. The Riess experiment.
4. An experiment carried out by Brugmans, Heymanns, and Weinberg in 1919.
5. The Soal-Goldney experiment.

Thus, for the period up to 1965, a small number of experiments were named in most of the surveys. A full chapter is given in this book to the Pearce-Pratt, the Pratt-Woodruff, and the Soal-Goldney series, since they received unanimous approval. In addition, a chapter is given to the investigation of the two Welsh schoolboys, reported by Soal and Bowden, which was completed after the above surveys were made. Other experiments are included where they are of historical interest or where they illustrate a particular form of experimental error. Some details are also given of experimental work in the Soviet Union, since this work is frequently quoted as providing evidence for ESP.

Experiments After 1965

Since 1965, new experiments have been reported from which it is necessary to select those considered as providing evidence for ESP. In *New Directions in Parapsychology*,[9] edited by John Beloff and published in 1974, three main lines of research are discussed:

1. Experiments using machines to randomize the targets and record the number of hits and misses.
2. Experiments to see whether ESP occurs during sleep.
3. Experiments on precognition in animals.

These same investigations are discussed in detail by John Randall in his *Parapsychology and the Nature of Life*.[10] They are, therefore, included here together with other investigations that have created popular interest. These are the tests on Uri Geller carried out by Russell Targ and Harold Puthoff, as reported in *Nature*,[11] and studies in remote viewing that were mentioned in *Nature* and more fully reported elsewhere.[12]

Other investigations, are included where they have received attention in the popular press or where they illustrate points arising in the discussion.

Notes

1. Arthur Koestler, *The Observer* (London) May 7, 1961, p. 23.
2. C. D. Broad, "Discussion: The Experimental Establishment of Telepathic Precognition," *Philosophy*, 19, 74 (1944): 261
3. J. B. Rhine and J. G. Pratt, *Parapsychology: Frontier Science of the Mind* (Springfield, Ill.: Charles C. Thomas, Publisher, 1957), p. 140.
4. *Ibid*, p. 19.
5. G. E. Wolstenholme and Elaine C. P. Millar, eds., *Extrasensory Perception*, Ciba Foundation Symposium (London: J. & A. Churchill Ltd., 1956), p. 32.
6. J. G. Pratt, J. B. Rhine, Burke M. Smith, Charles E. Stuart, and Joseph A. Greenwood, *Extra-Sensory Perception after Sixty Years* (Boston: Bruce Humphries, Publishers, 1940).
7. Wolstenholme and Millar, eds., *Extrasensory Perception*, p. 51.
8. G. R. Schmeidler and R. A. McConnell, *ESP and Personality Patterns* (New Haven: Yale University Press, 1958) (Reprinted by Greenwood Press, 1973).
9. J. Beloff, ed. "New Directions in Parapsychology," *Elek Science*, London, 1974.
10. J. G. Randall, *Parapsychology and the Nature of Life: A Scientific Appraisal* (Souvenir Press, 1975), p. 82.
11. R. Targ and H. Puthoff, "Information Transmission Under Conditions of Sensory Shielding," *Nature*, 251, 5476 (October 18, 1974): 602-7.
12. *The Journal of Parapsychology*, 35, 2 (June 1971): 92-106.

4

Early Investigations

British Research

Soon after the formation of the Society of Psychical Research, a Committee on Thought Reading was set up, headed by William Barrett, then Professor of Physics in the Royal College of Science for Ireland, together with Edmund Gurney (1847–1888), who devoted his energies to psychical research, and Frederic Myers (1843–1901), an inspector of schools, both formerly fellows of Trinity College, Cambridge. Later in the year, Frank Podmore (1855–1910), a post office official, joined the committee. Henry Sidgwick, in his presidential address to the Society in July 1882, introduced the first report of this committee by saying:

> We must drive the objector into the position of being forced either to admit the phenomena as inexplicable, at least by him, or to accuse the investigators either of lying or cheating or of a blindness or forgetfulness incompatible with any intellectual condition except absolute idiocy.
>
> I am glad to say that this result, in my opinion, has been satisfactorily attained in the investigation of thought reading. Professor Barrett will now bring before you a report which I hope will be only the first of a long series of similar reports which may have reached the same point of conclusiveness.[1]

Sidgwick lived to eat his words, for the investigation described in that report concerned the five young daughters (Mary, Alice, Maud, Kathleen, and Emily) of an English clergyman, the Reverend A. M. Creery. During sitting after sitting, the girls and a young servant, Jane, convinced the investigators of their telepathic abilities. Then, six years later, in 1888, they were caught using a code and admitted to having deceived the researchers.

In the first report of the committee, mention was also made of a G. A. Smith, whose telepathic abilities supposedly were developed to the highest degree.[2] The second and third committee reports contained details of tests carried out on Smith, and it was claimed for nearly twenty years that these tests provided a watertight case for telepathy.

The Smith-Blackburn Experiments

On August 26, 1882, a letter by Douglas Blackburn, editor of *The Brightonian*, appeared in the spiritualist magazine *Light*. This read:

> The way Mr. Smith conducts his experiment is this: He places himself *en rapport* with myself by taking my hands: and a strong concentration of will and mental vision of my part has enabled him to read my thoughts with an accuracy that approaches the miraculous. Not only can he, with slight hesitation, read numbers, words and even whole sentences which I alone have seen, but the sympathy between us has developed to such a degree that he rarely fails to experience the taste of any liquid or solid I choose to imagine. He has named, described, or discovered small articles he has never seen when they have been concealed by me in the most unusual places, and on two occasions, he has successfully described portions of a scene which I either imagined or actually saw.

This letter came to the attention of Myers and Gurney, who forthwith went to Brighton and carried out tests on Smith and Blackburn.

They found that Smith, when blindfolded, could name words that had been shown to Blackburn even when there was no contact between the two men. Smith was also able to reproduce drawings of simple figures shown to Blackburn, provided he touched him. The two subjects then went to London and were investigated in a long series of tests carried out by the Committee on Thought Reading. One of the tests was later vividly described by Blackburn:

> These were the conditions: Smith sat in a chair at the large table. His eyes were padded with wool, and, I think, a pair of folded kid gloves, and bandaged with a thick dark cloth. His ears were filled with one layer of cotton-wool, then pellets of putty. His entire body and the chair on which he sat were enveloped in two very heavy blankets. I remember, when he emerged triumphant, he was wet with perspiration, and the paper on which he had successfully drawn the figure was so moist that it broke during the examination by the delighted observers. Beneath his feet and surrounding his chair were thick, soft rugs, rightly intended to deaden and prevent signals by foot shuffles. Smith being rendered contact proof and perfectly insulated, my part began.
> At the farther side of the room—a very large dining room—Mr. Myers showed me, with every precaution, the drawing that I was to transmit to the

brain beneath the blankets. It was a tangle of heavy black lines, interlaced, some curved, some straight, the sort of thing an infant playing with a pen or pencil might produce, and I am certain absolutely indescribable in words, let alone in a code. I took it, fixed my gaze on it, pacing the room meanwhile and going through the usual process of impressing the figure upon my retina and brain, but always keeping out of touching distance with Smith. These preliminaries occupied perhaps ten or more minutes, for we made a point of never hurrying. I drew and redrew many times openly in the presence of the observers, in order, as I explained and they allowed, to fix it on my brain.[3]

Blackburn went on to describe how he then stood in silence behind Smith's chair while Smith produced an almost line-for-line reproduction of Myer's original drawing.

As a result of their tests, the investigators concluded that they had eliminated the possibility of information reaching Smith through any of the known senses.

Sidgwick suggested a skeptic at the time could have concluded that all of the investigators were liars or idiots. He would more likely, however, have suspected that Smith and Blackburn had been using tricks. In fact, the results of the investigations were of such a nature that this would have been the only reasonable alternative to telepathy.

Not everyone accepted the claims of the Committee on Thought Reading. Sir Horatio Donkin (1845–1927), a physician and a prominent critic, stated in the *Westminster Gazette* of November 26, 1907, that he had been told of two occasions when outside observers were invited to see Smith and Blackburn in action. Once, precautions taken to prevent possible auditory communication put a stop to the thought transference; on the other occasion, precautions against visual communication had a similar effect. Donkin pointed out that no mention was made in the published accounts of the presence of these observers or of the tests they applied and the effects that were observed.

One of the observers, Sir James Crichton-Browne (1886–1938), a neurologist, confirmed these observations in the *Westminster Gazette* of January 29, 1908. He, together with the British scientist, Francis Galton (1822–1911), had been present as an observer at one sitting. After witnessing demonstrations of telepathy by Smith, the two had improved the effectiveness of his blindfold and ear plugs. Further tests showed "not the smallest response on the part of Mr. *S.* to Mr. *B.*'s volitional endeavours. There was no more flashing of images into his mind. His pencil was idle. Thought transference was somehow interrupted."[4]

Notwithstanding these objections, Smith and Blackburn were accepted as authentic by the Society for Psychical Research. Both became members of the group, and Smith acted as Gurney's secretary, assisting him by producing a number of other Brighton youths who gave convincing demonstrations of telepathy after being hypnotized by Smith. For their services to science the youths received financial benefits. After Gurney's suicide in 1888, the experiments were continued by Mrs. Henry Sidgwick, helped by other members of the Society. Successful results were reported until 1892, when Smith left the employment of the Society. Telepathic phenomena ceased with his departure except for one occasion in 1894, when he again helped with an experiment. By 1898, the Society had given up all hope of finding subjects who could display telepathy under hypnosis.

Smith came into the news again on December 5, 1908, when Blackburn revealed in a popular magazine, *John Bull,* that he and Smith had used tricks during the 1882 telepathy investigations. Fuller details were given by Blackburn in the *Daily News* of September 1, 1911, from which the following extract is taken:

> For nearly thirty years the telepathic experiments conducted by Mr. G. A. Smith and myself have been accepted and cited as the basic evidence of the truth of Thought Transference.
>
> Your correspondent "Inquirer" is one of the many who have pointed to them as a conclusive reply to modern sceptics. The weight attached to those experiments was given by their publication in the first volume of the proceedings of the Society for Psychical Research, vouched for by Messrs. F. W. H. Myers, Edmund Gurney, Frank Podmore, and later and inferentially by Professor Henry Sidgwick, Professor Romanes, and others of equal intellectual eminence. They were the first scientifically conducted and attested experiments in Thought Transference, and later were imitated and reproduced by "sensitives" all over the world.
>
> I am the sole survivor of that group of experimentalists, as no harm can be done to anyone, but possible good to the cause of truth, I, with mingled feelings of regret and satisfaction now declare that the whole of those alleged experiments were bogus, and originated in the honest desire of two youths to show how easily men of scientific mind and training could be deceived when seeking for evidence in support of a theory they were wishful to establish.[5]

Blackburn went on to describe how mediums abounded at the end of the nineteenth century and how he had started an exposure campaign. He had then met Smith, and together they had perfected a thought-reading act. One of their performances, after being described in *Light,* had brought them to the notice of the Society for Psychical Research. He explained how they were then approached by Gurney and Myers and "saw in them only a superior type of spiritualistic crank" by whom they were pestered daily. Their first private demonstration was accepted so unhesitatingly, and the lack of reasonable precautions on the part of the investigators was so marked, that Smith and he felt it their duty to show how utterly incompetent these investigators were.

Blackburn concluded by writing:

> In conclusion, I ask thoughtful persons to consider this proposition; if two youths, with a week's preparation, could deceive trained and careful observers like Messrs. Myers, Gurney, Podmore, Sidgwick and Romanes, under the most stringent conditions their ingenuity could devise, what are the chances of succeeding inquirers being more successful against "sensitives" who have had the advantage of more years experience than Smith and I had

weeks? Further, I would emphasize the fact that records of telepathic rapport in almost every instance depend upon the statement of one person, usually strongly predisposed to belief in the occult.[6]

Smith denied all the charges, but Blackburn then provided so much detail of the techniques employed that there was little doubt that tricks had been used. After describing the test in which Smith had been swathed in blankets, Blackburn continued:

> I also drew it, secretly, on a cigarette paper. By this time I was fairly expert at palming, and had no difficulty while pacing the room collecting "rapport," in transferring the cigarette paper to the tube of the brass projector on the pencil I was using. I conveyed to Smith the agreed signal that I was ready by stumbling against the edge of the thick rug near his chair.
>
> Next instant he exclaimed: "I have it." His right hand came from beneath the blanket, and he fumbled about the table, saying, according to arrangement: "Where's my pencil?"
>
> Immediately I placed mine on the table. He took it and a long and anxious pause ensued.
>
> This is what was going on under the blanket. Smith had concealed up in his waistcoat one of those luminous painted slates which in the dense darkness gave sufficient light to show the figure when the almost transparent cigarette paper was laid flat on the slate. He pushed up the bandage from one eye, and copied the figure with extraordinary accuracy.
>
> It occupied over five minutes. During that time I was sitting exhausted with the mental effort quite ten feet away.
>
> Presently Smith threw back the blanket and excitedly pushing back the eye bandage produced the drawing, which was done on a piece of notepaper, and very nearly on the same scale as the original. It was a splendid copy.[7]

If Blackburn had kept his secret, this series of experiments might well have gone down in the history of parapsychology as one of the conclusive investigations providing irrefutable evidence for telepathy, since critics such as Donkin and Crichton-Browne get little publicity and are soon forgotten. As it is, the outcome of the investigations of the Creery sisters (see page 29) and of Smith and Blackburn merely demonstrate the fact, confirmed time after time, that intelligent men can be deceived quite easily when their powers of observation are biased by their underlying beliefs.

Characteristics of Early Experiments

The investigations reported during the first years of the Society for Psychical Research were remarkable for the ease with which subjects produced feats that no investigator today would consider worth investigating. Playing cards selected from a pack were identified with relative ease, and fairly complex drawings having a striking resemblance to those being looked at by some other person were produced under what the investigators invariably claimed were absolutely watertight conditions. By the time Blackburn made his confession, this type of experiment had almost disappeared.

The early experiments in Great Britain had been more in the nature of party games than serious scientific investigations. The energies of the Society for Psychical Research had been directed largely to the study of spontaneous events and phenomena reported from the seance room. But between 1910 and 1930, the experiments became simpler and less ambitious. During this period, the use of *statistical analyses* began, necessitating suitable types of experimental material and a systematic test procedure. In a statistical analysis, the results of a large number of attempts at guessing targets are compared with the scores expected to arise by chance.

Muscular Movements

Although all the investigations supporting ESP carried out before 1930 have been criticized on the ground that experimental conditions were unsatisfactory, they are of considerable interest in revealing the pitfalls that await the researcher. Some of them illustrate the fact, known from the start, that involuntary cues can influence a result and that such cues might be utilized by the percipient without his being aware of their presence.

Many supposedly supernatural phenomena were already known to be due to involuntary muscular movements. In 1852, the English chemist and physicist Michael Faraday (1791–1867), after experimenting on table turning—the phenomenon in which a group of persons sit around a table, touching its surface, resulting in a movement of the table, supposedly without the use of any muscular power—had decided that the table turner exerted pressure on the table without being aware that he was doing so. The French chemist Michel Eugène Chevreul (1786–1889) had demonstrated in 1854 that a pendulum held in the hand of a suggestible subject could be caused to swing owing to his involuntary muscular movements and that the direction and amplitude of the swings could be controlled by suggestions, even when the subject was unaware of receiving them.[8] Later, Barrett and Theodore Besterman, the Research Officer of the Society for Psychical Research, extended this type of investigation and showed that in water divining, the twig moved because of the muscular movements of the diviner.[9]

Such involuntary movements are used as cues by performers to detect hidden objects. They may do this when clasping hands with someone who knows where the object is hidden, thus detecting small muscle movements, or by watching the responses of the audience as they move around in the attempt to locate the object. Such abilities are not confined to human beings. It was found that a horse known as

Clever Hans, which was claimed to make mathematical calculations, was in fact detecting small involuntary movements made by its trainer.[10]

Mental Habits

Another source of error in the early investigations was due to the subjects' preferences for guessing particular symbols and their mental habits in making successive guesses. The manner in which such preferences can give a spurious result is illustrated by early experiments on psychokinesis where the subject tried to make a particular die face, selected by himself, land uppermost (see page 157). The subjects tended to want a 6, and there was also a slight bias on the die, owing to the indentations denoting the spots; this shifted the die's center of gravity, tending to cause a 6 to arise on more than one-sixth of the throws.

Again, a person who thinks he is guessing symbols at random is likely to produce far fewer guesses of some symbols than would arise in a randomly generated sequence—as by tossing a coin. The experiment (described on page 37) carried out by an English electrical engineer and past president of the Society, G. N. M. Tyrrell (1879–1952) demonstrates how such mental habits may influence the result of an ESP test.

Recording Errors

Errors in recording guesses or results may occur in cases where the recorder holds a particular belief or where the data may support his own hypothesis. They may easily arise when there is any ambiguity due to lack of visibility in visual information. These errors are particularly likely to occur when the recorder has to pay attention to more than one factor at a time, which divides his attention, or when he has to see or hear something that is not clearly defined.

The Brugmans Experiment

The result of an experiment carried out in 1919 at the University of Groningen, Holland, by a psychologist, H. J. W. F. Brugmans (1885–1961), who was assisted by two other members of the university psychology department, may have been influenced by factors of this nature.

The subject, a young man named Van Damm, sat at a table with his head and shoulders inside a wooden framework covered with black cloth. He had the back of his head toward the open side of this enclosure, and his right arm extended through an opening so that he could touch any point on a board lying flat on the table in front of him. This board was divided into 48 squares with 8 columns labeled A through H and 6 rows numbered 1 through 6.

A hole had been cut in the ceiling directly above Van Damm. It was covered with two sheets of glass, placed so that there was an air cushion between them. The experimenters, sitting above the glass, looked down through it at the board in front of Van Damm and tried to "will" him to point to a particular square.

Before each trial, slips of paper were drawn from bags. The first slip determined which column the square occupied, the second its row. The subject moved his hand over the board and gave a double tap on it with his forefinger to indicate his choice.

Van Damm obtained 60 successes in 187 trials, and this result had clearly not arisen by chance. Some of the trials were made with the experimenters in the same room as the subject, but although he also succeeded under these conditions, his scores were not as high as when they were in the room above him.

There were three serious weaknesses in this research. First, the experimenter who recorded Van Damm's choice of square was also aware of the correct target; second, he had to observe the choice from a distance and through two thicknesses of glass; third, the men in the room above the subject could provide, quite involuntarily, auditory cues with their feet on the floorboards that would have guided Van Damm as he moved his hand over the board.

Soal, in a most interesting account of his investigations of a stage performer named Marion, found how the most minute cues could be utilized by Marion to find a hidden object, provided a person was present who knew its location. Discussing the experiment on Van Damm, Soal wrote: "We would suggest that this subject may have been a sensitive of Marion's type, and that telepathy may have played no part in the performance."[11]

To eliminate the possibility that the recorder might affect the scores, he should have been kept ignorant of the real target and have been seated beside Van Damm where he could observe the subject's choice accurately. Van Damm should have signified his selection of a square by a completely definite signal.

The greatest difficulty would, however, have been experienced in eliminating any chance that the experimenters who were trying to "will" Van Damm to point to a particular square were inadvertently supplying cues to him. This difficulty could be overcome today by using closed-circuit television to observe the subject.

Some Telepathy Experiments

In another series carried out during the years between 1910 and 1929, Gilbert Murray (1866–1957), Regius Professor of Greek at Oxford University, often demonstrated his own telepathic abilities before a small audience consisting of his daughter and friends. After Murray had left the room, the persons present would write down a "subject," such as a quotation or a description of some incident from literature or current events. Murray would return and state what he thought the subject was. His statement was recorded and compared with the original. Under these conditions, he displayed uncanny knowledge of the subject that had been written down and described during his absence. If Murray's success was due to telepathy, he should have had no difficulty in convincing skeptics by demonstration rather than by discussion and persuasion; but although he referred to these tests in his presidential address to the Society for Psychical Research, and they were reported in the *Proceedings* of the Society, he made no attempt to display his abilities under reasonable test conditions.

In 1927, V. J. Woolley, with the support of Sir Oliver Lodge and the English biologist Julian Huxley, conducted a mass telepathy test in cooperation with the British Broadcasting Corporation. Postcards were sent in by 24,659 listeners, who guessed objects seen by agents in the studio, but no evidence was obtained for telepathy.

An investigation on clairvoyance reported by Miss Ina Jephson in 1929 illustrates the need for strict supervision of the subject in ESP tests.[12] Her subjects were left unsupervised to test themselves in their own homes. They were instructed to take a pack of playing cards, to shuffle it thoroughly, and then to draw one out, keeping it face downwards. They then had to record their guess of which card had been drawn. After that, the subjects were to turn the card over, record it, and then return it to the pack. Each subject made 5 guesses on each of five days. Miss Jephson accumulated 6,000 guesses in this manner and found that her subjects were successful in guessing suit, denomination, and color of the card at well above the rate expected to arise by chance.

This experiment was repeated by her in collaboration with Besterman and Soal.[13] The procedure was changed, however, so that the subjects could not influence the result in any manner. A total of 9,496 guesses was recorded, but the result showed no evidence for extrasensory perception.

An experiment carried out by Tyrrell and reported in 1936 is of considerable interest, since he employed mechanical means for presenting targets and recording errors and successes.[14] Tyrrell constructed a machine consisting of five wooden boxes, each containing an electric lamp, that were placed in front of the subject. At each trial the experimenter pressed a key that lit a lamp in one of the boxes when its lid was raised. The subject, Miss Johnson, raised the lid of the box that she thought contained the lighted lamp. Since the circuit to the lamp was not completed until the lid of the box was raised, it remained unlit until the subject had made her choice; thus, there was no possibility of light leaking from the box and being used as a cue. In this experiment, the subject learned after each trial whether she had secured a hit, since after a success she saw a lamp light.

Tyrrell then introduced a further refinement. The circuits were rearranged by means of a commutator so that when the experimenter pressed the key, he did not know which box constituted the target. The test was now for clairvoyance rather than telepathy.

After long practice sessions with the apparatus, the subject had obtained scores high above chance values. However, when the commutator was introduced, scores dropped to the chance level; but she eventually again obtained above-chance scores.

It was, however, demonstrated by G. W. Fisk, a member of the Society for Psychical Research who took part in the experiments, that anyone could obtain high scores similar to those obtained by Miss Johnson by following a simple procedure. The guesser merely selected one target and continued calling it until he secured a success, after which he selected some other one. Fisk's system worked because the target series was generated by the experimenter. When a person selects targets according to his own whim, he tends to produce not a random series, but one in which repetitions of a particular target are relatively infrequent. This fact may easily be confirmed by the reader writing down the two symbols *H* and *T* at random until he has covered, say two columns of a sheet of paper. The number of times either symbol is followed by the other and also the number of times either symbol is followed by itself should be counted. In a random series a symbol is likely to be followed by itself approximately 50 percent of the time, but most people will display a strong tendency to change the symbol at each trial rather than to produce a repetition. Thus, runs in which the same symbol occurs twice tend to be infrequent, and longer runs of the same symbol are rarer still in comparison with the expected frequencies.

The author conducted a group of tests with student subjects in which they were asked to write a random series of 50 symbols from a choice of the letters *A*, *B*, *C*, *D*, and *E*. It was found that the frequency which which repetitions occurred was low and that runs of the same symbol repeated more than once hardly occurred at all. Some subjects simply wrote the five symbols in some particular order and in the following five entries listed them in a different order, repeating this process throughout their series.

If the experiment used a nonrandom series, it would have been a simple matter for the subject to produce high scores either by deliberately using a system such as Fisk's or by acquiring suitable response habits during the long training series without being aware of the fact. It is in fact possible to improve on Fisk's system. Thus, after obtaining a hit, the probability of success on the following trial is nearer 0.25 than 0.2 if a fresh target is selected. If a further hit is obtained, a target other than the two previous targets may be selected for the following trial. The chances of success on this trial are now improved even further, and this process ensures greater probability of success as the run of successes increases.

In later tests, Tyrrell introduced a mechanical randomizer, and it is of considerable interest to see how it affected the results. Miss Johnson failed to obtain above-chance scores when the randomizer was used directly, but when Tyrrell employed it to prepare lists of random digits and then used these in the experiment to determine which key was to be pressed on each trial, scores were again well above the chance level. The reason for this last result will become apparent if the action of the randomizer is considered in detail.

It consisted of a *stepping switch,* or uniselector, as used in automatic telephone switchboards; this is a rotary switch in which a double-ended arm sweeps through an arc, making contacts at its end with any one of twenty-five positions situated around a half circle. The arm is moved by a ratchet mechanism and an electromagnet. When the electric current flows through the electromagnet, a claw is pulled forward; when it ceases, the arm is pulled to its next position. An interrupter also is operated by the moving claw so that the circuit is broken at the top of its stroke. Thus , the arm of the uniselector moves in a series of steps until the electromagnet is disconnected. Tyrrell wired the first five positions of the switch in order 1, 2, 3, 4, 5. For the remaining sets of five positions, this order was changed. All the 1 positions were then connected together so that if the arm came to rest at any of them, box 1 would be selected. The same was done with each of the other numbered positions. Thus, when current flowed, the arm would move past the contacts and the particular target selected would depend on its position when the current was interrupted. If the uniselector was left running for a reasonable length of time between each trial, a random series would be produced, but if the arm was moving relatively slowly and if the current was applied for only brief intervals, the series produced would by no means be random. For example, if the switch arm was operating at ten contacts per second, and the length of time the current was on to generate each number was less than one-half second, a series would be produced in which there would be a tendency not to repeat any symbol.

Tyrrell went to the effort of producing a list of nearly 8,000 numbers with his randomizer. It is thus unlikely that he had it running for long intervals before recording each number. Even if merely a part of the series was generated by using only short bursts of current, there would still be a nonrandom feature in the sequence that would permit above-chance scores to be obtained.

Soal reported tests for randomness that he had applied to 2,000 numbers generated on Tyrrell's machine. These did not show any evidence of nonrandomness. It is not clear, however, whether the 2,000 numbers supplied to Soal were part of the 8,000 used with Miss Johnson or whether they were specially generated for him.

In spite of the above criticism, Tyrrell's experiment represented a worthwhile attempt to employ some sort of mechanical control of the ESP test. It is remarkable that his work was not followed up more fully at the time.

Coover's Research

The first major experimental research on telepathy to be carried out in an American university was that of John E. Coover, Professor of Psychology at Stanford University, in 1915. It was of particular interest owing to Coover's use of a control series.

The use of a control series is of particular importance in an experiment that may involve a number of known variables as well as possible unknown variables which the investigator can only suspect may be present. In such an experiment, two series of observations—the experimental and the control series—are observed. Conditions under which the two series are studied are identical except for one factor that is present only in the experimental series. Any difference in the result obtained in the two series is then credited to the effect of that one factor, since it constitutes the only difference between them.

Coover realized that there might be factors operating in his experimental conditions of which he was unaware or that were difficult to control; but any such factors would operate in both the experimental and the control series. In his experimental series, the subjects guessed the identities of cards seen by another person. Conditions were similar in the control series, except that no one saw the target cards. Therefore, if telepathy existed, it was a factor that could operate only in the experimental series, and any difference in scores could be attributed to telepathy.

In one of his experiments, the subjects had to guess the identity of a playing card in a pack from which the face cards had been removed, thus leaving ten cards in each suit. Before each run of 40 guesses, a die was thrown to decide whether another person should look at the target card, thereby making telepathy possible and putting that observation into the experimental series, or whether no one should see the card, putting the observation into the control series. Altogether 10,000 guesses were recorded, and it was found that the difference between the mean score of the experimental series and that of the control series was not statistically significant.

Later, critics of Coover pointed out that if the scores in the experimental and control series were lumped together, the combined score was significantly above the chance level. This, of course, proves nothing and is a completely illegitimate procedure, since all control over the experimental conditions brought about by using a control series is then lost. Coover himself considered that auditory cues possibly operated in favor of above-chance scores in both series.[15]

A small number of experimental investigations on telepathy and clairvoyance were carried out in the United States before 1920, but ESP research suddenly made great strides in the United States during the 1930s. This was due to the work of an American, Dr. J. B. Rhine, whose work will be discussed in Part II.

From its founding, the British Society for Psychical Research, apart from examining evidence for thought transference, had actively examined two other types of phenomena. These were accounts of unusual experiences reported as arising in everyday life and events reported as arising in the séance room. It is often claimed that everyday experiences in themselves provide evidence for ESP, and it has also been claimed that mediums obtain knowledge by extrasensory perception. These types of evidence will, therefore, be considered briefly in the following two chapters.

Notes

1. H. Sidgwick, "Presidential Address," *Proceedings of the Society of Psychical Research*, 1, 1 (1882): 12.
2 W. F. Barrett, Edmund Gurney, and F. W. H. Meyers, "First Report on Thought Reading," *Proceedings of the Society for Psychical Research*, 1, 1 (1882): 63
3. *London Daily News,* September 1, 1911.
4. Sir James Crichton-Browne, letter in *Westiminster Gazette,* January 29, 1908.
5. *London Daily News, op cit.*

6. *Ibid.*
7. *Ibid.*
8. M. E. Chevreul, *De la baquette divinatoire, du pendule dit explorateur et des tables tournantes* (Paris: Malet Bachelier, 1854).
9. W. F. Barrett and T. Besterman, *The Divining Rod; an Experimental and Psychological Investigation* (London: Methuen & Co. Ltd., 1926).
10. O. Pfungst, *Clever Hans,* trans. by Carl L. Rehn (New York: Holt, Rinehart & Winston, Inc., 1911).
11. Soal and Bateman, *Modern Experiments in Telepathy,* p. 16.
12. Ina Jephson, "Evidence for Clairvoyance in Card-Guessing," *Proceedings of the Society for Psychical Research,* 37, 109 (1929): 233–68.
13 T. Besterman, S. G. Soal, and Ina Jephson, "Report of a Series of Experiments in Clairvoyance Conducted at a Distance Under Approximately Fraud-Proof Conditions," *Proceedings of the Society for Psychical Research,* 39, 118 (1931): 374–414.
14. G. N. M. Tyrrell, "Further Research in Extra-Sensory Perception," *Proceedings of the Society for Psychical Research,* 44, 148 (1936): 99–166.
15. J. L. Kennedy, "A Methodological Review of Extra-Sensory Perception," *Psychological Bulletin,* 36 (1939): 59–103.

5
Accounts of Strange Experiences

Accounts of unusual experiences that appear to contradict accepted ideas of what human beings can and cannot do are continually being reported in the popular press. It is frequently claimed that these accounts provide proof of telepathy, clairvoyance, precognition, and other processes. Any such story may be examined to decide how closely it checks with what is known to have actually happened and how far it has been elaborated or distorted. If it is decided that the event did take place, it is then necessary to decide how likely or unlikely its occurrence would be in the ordinary run of events. If the happening still appears unusual after such an examination, an explanation may then be sought to account for it.

Anecdotal data tend to be unreliable, since what is reported is dependent on a person's memory and on the observer's interpretation. It is known that various observers may give quite different accounts of what they have seen or heard in the same situation, even when they make their reports at the time of the experience. Also, with the passage of time, accounts may show progressive changes and become increasingly less accurate when checked against the original events.

When the account is that of a single person, it is often impossible to know whether his report relates to an external event or whether he is reporting experiences that had no outside physical cause. Thus, if a man says he saw a pink elephant, it cannot be assumed that a pink elephant actually existed that other observers would have seen and that could have been photographed.

The Apparition Seen by Sir Edmund Hornby

An early case reported by Gurney and Myers was thought at the time to provide irrefutable evidence for the appearance of an apparition. It concerned Sir Edmund Hornby, formerly Chief Judge of the Supreme Consular Court of China and Japan at Shanghai. He had been in the habit of allowing reporters to come to his house in the evening to get his written judgments for the next day's papers. On January 19, 1875, he wrote out these judgments in his study an hour or two after dinner. His report concerning subsequent events, as taken down by Gurney and Myers, was as follows:

I rang for the butler, gave him the envelope, and told him to give it to the reporter who should call for it. I was in bed before twelve. . . . I had gone to sleep, when I was awakened by hearing a tap on the study door, but thinking it might be the butler—looking to see if the fires were safe and the gas turned off—I turned over . . . to sleep again. Before I did so, I heard a tap at my bedroom door. Still thinking it the butler . . . I said "Come in." The door opened, and, to my surprise, in walked Mr. ————. I sat up and said, "You have mistaken the door; but the butler has the judgment, so go and get it." Instead of leaving the room he came to the foot of the bed. I said, "Mr. ————, you forget yourself! Have the goodness to walk out directly. This is rather an abuse of my favor." He looked deadly pale, but was dressed as usual, and sober, and said, "I know I am guilty of an unwarrantable intrusion, but finding that you were not in your study, I have ventured to come here."

I was losing my temper, but something in the man's manner disinclined me to jump out of bed to eject him by force. So I said, simply, "This is too bad, really; pray leave the room at once." Instead of doing so he put his hand on the foot-rail and gently, and as if in pain, sat down on the foot of the bed. I glanced at the clock and saw that it was about twenty minutes past one. I said, "The butler has had the judgment since half-past eleven; go and get it!" He said, "Pray forgive me; if you knew all the circumstances you would. Time presses. Pray give me a précis of your judgment, and I will take a note in my book of it," drawing his reporter's book out of his breast pocket. I said, "I will do nothing of the kind. Go downstairs, find the butler, and don't disturb me—you will wake my wife; otherwise I shall have to put you out." He slightly moved his hand, I said, "Who let you in?" He answered, "No one." "Confound it," I said, "What the devil do you mean? Are you drunk?" He replied quickly, "No, and never shall be again; but I pray your lordship give me your decision, for my time is short." I said, "You don't seem to care about my time, and this is the last time I will ever allow a reporter in my house." He stopped me short, saying, "This is the last time I shall ever see you anywhere."

Well, fearful that this commotion might arouse and frighten my wife, I shortly gave him the gist of my judgment. . . . He seemed to be taking it down in shorthand; it might have taken two or three minutes. When I finished, he rose, thanked me for excusing his intrusion and for the consideration I had always shown him and his colleagues, opened the door, and went away. I looked at the clock; it was on the stroke of half-past one.

[Lady Hornby awoke, thinking she had heard talking; and her husband told her what had happened, and repeated the account when dressing the next morning.]

I went to court a little before ten. The usher came into my room to robe me, when he said, "A sad thing happened last night, sir. Poor ——— was found dead in his room." I said "Bless my soul! Dear me! What did he die of, and when?" "Well, sir, it appeared he went up to his room as usual at ten to work at his papers. His wife went up about twelve to ask him when he would be ready for bed. He said, 'I have only the Judge's judgment to get ready, and then I have finished.' As he did not come, she went up again, about a quarter to one, to his room and peeped in, and thought she saw him writing, but she did not disturb him. At half-past one she again went to him and spoke to him at the door. As he didn't answer she thought he had fallen asleep so she went up to rouse him. To her horror he was dead. On the floor was his notebook, which I have brought away. She sent for the doctor who arrived a little after two, and said he had been dead, he concluded, about an hour. I looked at the note-book. There was the usual heading: "In the Supreme Court, before the Chief Judge: The Chief Judge gave judgment this morning in the case to the following effect'—and then followed a few lines of indecipherable shorthand."

I sent for the magistrate who would act as coroner, and desired him to examine Mr. ———'s wife and servants as to whether Mr. ——— had left his home or could possibly have left it without their knowledge, between eleven and one on the previous night. The result of the inquest showed he died of some form of heart disease, and had not and could not have left the house without the knowledge of at least his wife, if not of the servants. Not wishing to air my "spiritual experience" for the benefit of the press or the public, I kept the matter at the time to myself, only mentioning it to my Puisne Judge and to one or two friends; but when I got home to tiffin I asked my wife to tell me as nearly as she could remember what I had said to her during the night, and I made a brief note of her replies and of the facts.

[Lady Hornby has kindly confirmed the above facts to us, as far as she was cognizant of them.]

As I said then, so I say now—I was not asleep, but wide awake. After a lapse of nine years my memory is quite clear on the subject. I have not the least doubt I saw the man—have not the least doubt that the conversation took place between us.

I may add that I had examined the butler in the morning—who had given me back the MS. in the envelope when I went to the court after breakfast—as to whether he had locked the door as usual, and if anyone could have got in. He said that he had done everything as usual, adding that no one could have got in even if he had not locked the door, as there was no handle outside— which there was not. . . . The coolies said they opened the door as usual that morning—turned the key and undid the chains.[1]

The following November, the *Nineteenth Century* contained a letter from a Mr. Frederick H. Balfour pointing out certain discrepancies between the account and the facts:

1. Mr. ———— was the Rev. Hugh Lang Nivens, editor of the *Shanghai Courier*. He died not at *one* in the morning but between eight or nine A.M. after a good night's rest.
2. There was no Lady Hornby at that time. Sir Edmund's second wife had died two years previously, and he did not marry again till three months *after* the event.
3. No inquest was ever held.
4. The story turns upon the judgment of a certain case to be delivered the next day, January 20, 1875. There is no record of any such judgment.

Before publishing Balfour's letter, the editors of the *Nineteenth Century* had sent it to Judge Hornby, who commented:

My vision must have followed the death (some three months) instead of synchronizing with it. At the same time this hypothesis is quite contrary to the recollection of the facts both in my own mind and in Lady Hornby's mind. . . . If I had not believed, as I still believe, that every word of it [the story] was accurate, and that my memory was to be relied on, I should not have ever told it as a personal experience.[2]

The late John E. Coover, who carried out the controlled experimental test on telepathy (p. 39) and one of the greatest critics of psychical research, in discussing this case wrote:

All these discrepancies are concordant with the results of psychological research on testimony, and are to be attributed to psychological law rather than to either dishonesty or culpable carelessness.

The readiness of metaphysics to rely upon observations of séance phenomena, their insistence that illusion can be avoided, and their quick condemnation of the competence of an observer who is tricked, clearly indicate that they do not understand that error is inevitable. Consequently the psychologist remains incredulous in the face of all the accumulating "evidence."[3]

Gurney and Myers stated when introducing their report that its evidential value depended on the high authority on which it came. But the story illustrates that an eminent judge is no less liable to errors of memory and recall than anyone else.

Some Other Strange Happenings

In 1886, Gurney, Myers, and Podmore published *Phantasms of the Living*. Its two large volumes contained accounts of more than 700 unusual happenings, many of a type to make the flesh creep. The accounts were based on reports received from members of the public about their own unusual experiences. Since that time, thousands more such cases have been collected together by various societies and groups interested in psychical research in the effort to provide conclusive proof of ghosts, apparitions, telepathy, clairvoyance, and precognition. None of the stories investigated has withstood critical examination.

The journals and files of the Society for Psychical Research must contain thousands of these accounts of spontaneous occurrences. In his *The Personality of Man*, written in 1947, G. N. M. Tyrrell gave a few examples drawn from those investigations. He was a firm believer in the supernatural, and it is reasonable to assume that the cases he reports are the best ones he could collect to demonstrate the reality of extrasensory phenomena. But it is necessary only to read them to see how trivial and unsatisfactory they are. Anyone who says, "That may be so but I know of a case far more difficult to explain," should remember that Tyrrell had at his fingertips all the data that could survive any sort of investigation. He reported the first case as

A certain Canon Bourne and his two daughters were out hunting, and the daughters decided to return home with the coachman while their father went on. "As we were turning to go home," say the two Misses Bourne in a joint account, "we distinctly saw my father waving his hat to us and signing us to follow him. He was on the side of a small hill, and there was a dip between him and us. My sister, the coachman and myself all recognised my father and also the horse. The horse looked so dirty and shaken that the coachman remarked he thought there had been a nasty accident. As my father waved his hat I clearly saw the Lincoln and Bennett mark inside, though from the distance we were apart it ought to have been utterly impossible for me to have seen it. . . . Fearing an accident, we hurried down the hill. From the nature of the ground we had to lose sight of my father, but it took us very few seconds to reach the place where we had seen him. When we got there, there was no sign of him anywhere, nor could we see anyone in sight at all. We rode about for some time looking for him but could not see or hear anything of him. We all reached home within a quarter of an hour of each other. My father then told us he had never been in the field, nor near the field in which we thought we saw him, the whole of that day. He had never waved to us and had met with no accident. My father was riding the only white horse that was out that day.[4]

Tyrrell comments on this story:

The cause which set the telepathic machinery in motion in this case is obscure. No accident had happened to Canon Bourne. It more often happens that the vision coincides with some accident or peculiar event happening to the agent. . . . Canon Bourne unconsciously imposed the pattern or theme of his presence in that particular field, with details of horse, etc., on the minds of his two daughters and the coachman.[5]

If the definition of telepathy is to be extended so that it includes cases where the percipient has information that does not accord with any actual happening, it would appear that normal means of verification do not apply. In this case, certain people thought they had had a telepathic communication but, on checking, found that in fact they had not had one. If, on the other hand, an accident had occurred, it would no longer have been a case of telepathy but of normal observation. The feature of the story that appears to require an explanation is why three people simultaneously saw—or thought they saw—a figure on a horse in a distant field. Thus, the explanation is likely to be psychological rather than parapsychological.

To investigate the story fully, it would have been necessary to question the three witnesses independently, but as they had had the opportunity of discussing the matter among themselves, their statements could not be independent. It would appear likely that the witnesses saw something they thought was Canon Bourne although, in fact, it was not Canon Bourne—that is, if his statements about where he had been that day were truthful or if he had had no lapse of memory. They reported that the horse looked dirty, but at a distance they would not recognize dirt as such; they would only infer its presence from the appearance of the horse. They apparently saw a horse that was similar, but not identical, in appearance to Canon Bourne's; they assumed it to be the Canon's and that its changed appearance was due to dirt.

That one of them should see the Lincoln and Bennett mark inside the hat is not unusual. Any psychology student who has worked with a *tachistoscope* encounters many instances of this sort of thing. In the tachistoscope, a drawing is exposed very briefly to a subject so that he sees it for, say 1/50 of a second. He is then asked to draw exactly what he has viewed. Under these conditions, most subjects tend to introduce changes and add details in their reproductions that were lacking in the original. They draw what they think they should have seen based on their identification of the drawing with some known object. In a real life situation, much more striking effects of this nature would appear than in the laboratory. If the statements of the witnesses and of Canon Bourne are reliable, it would appear possible that some other person was present in the field that day whom the sisters mistook for their father. Identification of the father is supported only by the mark inside the hat, which the witness states was too far away for such recognition.

If these people made a false recognition of this nature, particularly if they were emotionally disturbed—as they could have been in this case because of the coachman's remark about an accident—and if they were able to converse together so that each could influence the others by suggestion, it is quite possible that they would feel convinced they had seen Canon Bourne, regardless of the fact that he later told them he was not in the field that day. There is no reason why the witnesses should have been greatly affected by the incident at the time, but no one else in reading about it should suffer any perplexity.

An announcement by the Society for Psychical Research discussed *Phantasms of the Living* in these words: "The conclusion drawn is that the coincidences of the type in question are far too numerous to be accounted for as accidents; and the establishment of some cause for them, beyond chance, is the proof of Telepathy."[6] But stories of this nature, however numerous, cannot provide evidence for ghosts or extrasensory perception unless they are backed by corroborating evidence. Without such evidence, they merely indicate the generality of well-known psychological phenomena. The more of them that are gathered together, the better the chance of finding a really extraordinary coincidence.

The accounts constitute a selected sample from millions of experiences that have arisen in the countries concerned; they are selected because they are unusual and, therefore, one would think, experiences that people would write or talk about. Members of the various societies who have reported these experiences in journals must be aware of the importance of supplying supporting evidence, but, so far, these surveys have failed to provide a single story that is conclusively supported by ample confirmatory data.

Stories purporting to demonstrate supernatural processes are liable to be distorted by the personal characteristics of the witnesses. The following extract from the 1911 confession by Douglas Blackburn, which was discussed earlier, summarizes his impressions after acting as an investigator.

> I am convinced that this propensity to deceive is more general among "persons of character" than is supposed. I have known the wife of a bishop, when faced with a discrepancy in time in a story of death in India and the appearance of the wraith in England, to deliberately amend her circumstantial story by many hours to fit the altered circumstances. This touching-up process in the telepathic stories I have met again and again, and I say, with full regard to the weight of words, that among the hundreds of stories I have investigated I have not met one that had not a weak link which should prevent its being accepted as scientifically established. Coincidences that at first sight appear good cases of telepathic rapport occur to many of us. I have experienced several, but I should hesitate to present them as perfect evidence.
>
> At the risk of giving offence to some, I feel bound to say that in the vast majority of cases that I have investigated the principals are either biased in favour of belief in the supernatural or not persons whom I should regard as accurate observers and capable of estimating the rigid mathematical form of evidence. What one desires to believe requires little corroboration. I shall doubtless raise a storm of protest when I assert that the principal cause of belief in psychical phenomena is the inability of the average man to observe accurately and estimate the value of evidence, plus a bias in favour of the phenomena being real. It is an amazing fact that I have never yet, after hundreds of tests, found a man who could accurately describe ten minutes afterwards a series of simple acts which I performed in his presence. The reports of those trained and conscientious observers, Messrs. Myers and Gurney, contain many absolute inaccuracies. For example, in describing one

of my "experiments," they say emphatically, "In no case did B. touch S., even in the slightest manner." I touched him eight times, that being the only way in which our code was then worked.[7]

Causes of "Inexplicable Happenings"

It is likely that many people have personal experiences that puzzle them and appear inexplicable. In daily life certain types of events may appear strange if a cause cannot be ascribed to them. This inability may arise in a number of ways, some of which are described below.

A common link in two casual sequences

I once was walking along a country road and a tune was running through my head, but I was not whistling or humming it. A boy approached on a bicycle, and as he passed, I heard that he was whistling the tune precisely in time with me. As I walked on puzzling over this occurrence, I passed a house and through the open window heard the radio playing the same tune. I therefore assumed that the boy and I had both started thinking of the tune through having heard it on different radios in houses we had passed. If I had not reached another house after passing the boy, I might have been very puzzled and, if there had been a series of similar experiences, might have started believing in ESP.

Seeming coincidences may often arise in this manner. A common stimulus in the past of two persons may set similar trains of thought going. The cause is no longer apparent when, some time later, one of the persons concerned says something about which the other is thinking.

Another experience of mine may make this clearer. After returning to England from the Duke Parapsychology Laboratory in 1960, I was driving through Manchester with my wife. While in the car, I recalled how I had expected to find laboratories with white-coated researchers turning over packs of Zener cards but had seen little activity of this sort. I also recalled the regular morning meetings at which there was considerable discussion over coffee. I then thought that it would be of interest to know whether more cups of coffee were drunk than runs made with Zener cards. At this point my wife spoke, saying how much she would like some coffee.

In this case, as far as I could see, there was no common stimulus to make my wife and me both start thinking of coffee. However, unless the incident was pure coincidence, it is possible that such a stimulus had been present a few minutes earlier, although no longer apparent at the time. We might have passed a billboard with an advertisement for coffee, or a café, or the aroma of coffee may have been in the air, or a word sounding like coffee might have set going a string of common associations for both of us. It is in fact possible that we had been talking about coffee some time earlier and that I had forgotten about it.

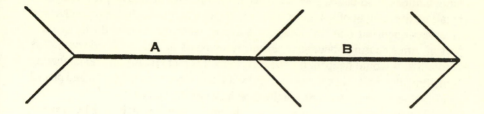

Figure 5-1
Which of the two lines A and B appears to be longer? After deciding, place the edge of a piece of paper against that line and mark off its length. Then compare the length marked off with the length of the line that was judged to be the shorter.

Even if only pure coincidence could be involved, its possibility should not be dismissed. In a world of more than 3 billion people, each person having hundreds of experiences each day, there must, every day, arise numerous coincidences having odds of the order of a million to one against chance expectation.

The elusiveness of memory

Most people are aware of visual illusions. When looking at the drawing in Figure 5.1 most people will say that line *a* looks longer than line *b*. If the lines are measured it will be found that, in fact, *b* is longer than line *a*.

A visual illusion of this nature is puzzling, but its existence cannot be denied, since lines can be measured with a ruler. Illusions of memory are, however, much more intangible, since there is seldom an opportunity to compare our memory of events with what actually happened. When events from the past are recalled, a single fleeting incident that occurred once and was gone is all that can be relied on. In addition, when something happens in everyday life, one is not usually expecting it to happen. It may be necessary to remember something that was quickly over, which at the time no effort was made to remember. The memory of an incident may be vague or startlingly clear, but in both cases there usually is no way of checking its accuracy.

The elusiveness of dreams

Remembering some event from one's waking life of a few years back is a relatively clear-cut process compared with recalling a dream of last night. Many people recount dreams with the greatest of confidence, but since a dream is a private experience, there is no way of checking its factual content. It is not surprising that a large number of so-called psychic experiences involve them. The great danger in recalling the content of a dream is not only the ease with which it may be changed or embellished but that the dating of a dream presents extreme difficulty. If a person, after hearing about some event, remembers having dreamed some days before that it would happen, no one can check this fact. He may be remembering something that really happened, or the dream may have been produced and placed at a suitable position in his past at the time he hears the story.

Most memories of past events can be located at some point in time by virtue of the fact that they arise in a context; there are events before and after them. If this context is lacking, it will be difficult to place the memory in time, and it will lack reality. A dream largely lacks this context, and when it is recalled, there is little to guarantee that it happened last night, some other night, or that it was not primarily generated at the time of recall. Just as perception is affected by memory, recall is affected by contemporary conditions, and when the memory is vague, as when a dream is recalled, the amount of material added to it may be large.

The effects of past experiences

Reactions to a situation are influenced by expectations. If a superstitious man is roaming around a house he believes haunted, he is likely to encounter a ghost at the slightest opportunity. A man who does not believe in ghosts but who has been told that the house is infested with rats is more likely to see rats. A relevant past experience can be recent, or it can be in the remote past of a person. Early events of childhood are particularly likely to affect a person's response in a "psychic" situation. Most children encounter fairy stories, ghost stories, superstitious beliefs, and religious ideas that are more compatible with the world as seen by parapsychology than by science. These ideas all embody principles that form the content of psychic belief.

The adult may have discarded them and no longer believe in ghosts, but the fact that he once believed in them is likely to affect him. He may still get a chill down the spine when reading a good ghost story. Early beliefs would be expected to manifest themselves at times of emotional arousal, stress, fatigue, sickness, and old age. Even the most hide-bound skeptic of the paranormal is likely to find himself having what appears to him irrational thoughts at times.

But most people are not skeptics. They are only too eager to believe anything that will take them further from the harsh world of reality toward the world of superstition. It is not surprising that so many extraordinary experiences are reported or that they bear little critical examination.

The above discussion has considered events in the lives of normal human beings. When allowance is made for abnormal conditions as, for example, those elaborated by D. H. Rawcliffe in his *Psychology of the Occult*,[8] it is even more to be expected that remarkable things should sometimes be reported as having happened. Another explanation for the wide currency of stories of psychic phenomena lies in the fact that newspapers have to attract readers in order to maintain sales. For that reason, their accounts tend to be sensational, and a simple account may be embroidered by both reporters and editors in order to liven it up. Such stories are often presented in a manner calculated to make the reader feel convinced of their authenticity. The distortions may not be intentional on the part of the reporter. He is looking for news and will notice anything of value. He usually has little time to make a thorough investigation and has to rely on what he is told. Those he interviews will be no less eager to impress him than he is eager to impress his readers.

Notes

1. E. Gurney and F. W. H. Meyers, "Visible Apparitions," *Nineteenth Century,* 16 (July 1884): 89–91. Reprinted through permission of *The Twentieth Century.*
2. *Nineteenth Century,* 16 (November 1884): 451.
3. J. E. Coover, "Metaphysics and the Incredulity of Psychologists." In *The Case For and Against Psychic Belief,* edited by Carl Murchison (Worcester, Mass.: Clark University, 1927), p. 261.
4. From G. N. M Tyrrell, *The Personality of Man* (London: Pelican Books, 1947), p. 63. Originally published in *Journal of the Society for Psychical Research,* 6, 103 (1893): 129.
5. *Ibid.*
6. Notice inside back cover, *Proceedings of the Society for Psychical Research,* 6, 17 (1888).
7. D. Blackburn, *London Daily News,* September 1, 1911.
8. D. H. Rawcliffe, *Illusions and Delusions of the Supernatural and the Occult* (New York: Dover, 1959).

6
Spiritualism

Physical Mediums

Spiritualism in its modern form originated in 1847 through the pranks of two young girls, Margaret, aged eight, and Kate, aged six, the daughters of John D. Fox, who lived in an isolated farmhouse in Hydesville, near Rochester, New York. Night after night, when the girls had been put to bed and were assumed to be fast asleep, raps were heard coming from the wall of their bedroom. At this time, Mrs. Leah Fish, an elder sister of the girls, visited Hydesville. She promptly organized a Society of Spiritualists and encouraged people to come to the house to see the children. The affair received considerable newspaper publicity, and Mrs. Fish then took the children to Rochester and arranged meetings at which an audience paid to hear their questions answered from the "spirit world." The girls were later taken to New York and then toured many cities in the United States.

The remainder of the story is best told as it appeared forty years later in a statement by Margaret Fox in the New York *World* of October 21, 1888, part of which is reproduced below.

My sister Kate and I were very young children when this horrible deception began. I was only eight, just a year and a half older than she. We were mischievous children and sought merely to terrify our dear mother, who was a very good woman and easily frightened.

When we went up to bed at night we used to tie an apple on a string and move the string up and down causing the apple to bump on the floor, or we would drop the apple on the floor, making a strange noise every time it would rebound. Mother listened for a time to this. She could not understand it and did not suspect us as being capable of a trick because we were so young.

At last she could stand it no longer and she called the neighbours in and told them about it. It was this that set us to discover a means of making the raps more effectually. I think, when I reflect about it, that it was a most wonderful discovery, a very wonderful thing that children should make such a discovery, and all through a desire to do mischief only.

Our eldest sister was 23 years of age when I was born. She was in Rochester when these tricks first began, but came to Hydesville, the little village in central New York where we were born and lived.

All the neighbours around, as I have said, were called in to witness the manifestations. There were so many people coming to the house that we were not able to make use of the apple trick except when we were in bed and the room was dark.

And this is the way we began. First as a mere trick to frighten mother, and then when so many people came to see us children, we were ourselves frightened and for self-preservation forced to keep it up. No one suspected us of any trick because we were such young children. We were led on by my sister purposely; and by my mother unintentionally. We often heard her say ''Is this a disembodied spirit that has taken possession of my dear children?''

Mrs. Underhill [Mrs. Fish later remarried], my eldest sister, took Katie and me to Rochester. There it was that we discovered a new way to make raps. My sister Katie was the first to observe that by swishing her fingers she could produce certain noises with her knuckles and joints, and that the same effect could be made with her toes. Finding that we could make raps with our feet—first with one foot and then both—we practised until we could do this easily when the room was dark.

In Rochester Mrs. Underhill gave exhibitions. We had crowds coming to see us and she made as much as $100 or $150 a night. She pocketed this. To all questions we answered by raps. We knew when to rap ''yes'' or ''no'' according to certain signs which Mrs. Underhill gave us during the séance.

Katie and I were led around like lambs. We drew immense crowds. We went to New York from Rochester and then all over the United States.[1]

There followed three more pages of confession, in which Margaret described her career as a spiritualist during the ensuing forty years.

During their long career, the Fox sisters had started a cult of spiritualism that swept the United States and rapidly spread to England and Europe. Margaret had appeared at séances for Queen Victoria, and Kate had performed before the Czar of Russia.

The story of the Fox sisters is important in showing how belief in the supernatural can outweigh all rational argument. The source of the raps was questioned almost from the start. E. P. Longworthy, a Rochester physician, investigated them and reported in the New York *Excelsior* on February 2, 1850, that the knockings always came from under the girls' feet or from objects such as doors or tables with which the girls' dresses were in contact. His conclusion was that Margaret and Kate themselves made the noises and that they voluntarily produced them.

John W. Hurn of Rochester, whose articles were published in the New York *Tribune* during January and February 1850, had come to a similar conclusion. In the same year, the Reverend John M. Austin of Auburn wrote to the *Tribune* to state that he had reliable information that the noise could be made by cracking the toe joints without any movement being visible. In December 1850, Reverend D. Potts demonstrated before an audience that he could produce raps in this manner.

By January 2, 1851, Reverend C. Chauncey Burr reported in the New York *Tribune* that he could produce the raps by cracking his toe joints and that he could produce sounds of such volume that they could be heard in every part of a hall large enough to contain a thousand people.

In February 1851, Austin Flint, Charles E. Lee, and C. B. Coventry of Buffalo University reported the results of an investigation they had made of the raps produced by Margaret Fox and her older sister Leah, who it seems was also by now participating in the act. Having studied Margaret's facial expression during the performance, they concluded that the raps were made by voluntary effort. They believed that the sounds were created by dislocation of the bones at the joints of the toes, knees, ankles, or hips; for they had observed that when the girls were placed on a couch with cushions beneath their feet the raps were no longer heard.

On April 17, 1851, Mrs. Culver, a relative by marriage of the sisters, admitted in a signed statement before witnesses that she had assisted Kate by touching her to indicate when the raps should be made. She declared that Kate had shown her how to make raps by snapping her toes and that Margaret had told her that she could produce raps with her knees and ankles when people insisted on seeing her feet and toes.

Professor Page of the Smithsonian Institute reported an investigation he had made in 1853. He concluded that the raps were produced by the girls and that each rap was accompanied by a slight movement. He remarked that he was surprised to notice how the scrutinizing powers of the most astute fail as soon as they entertain the remotest idea of the supernatural.

In June 1857, the Boston *Courier* offered a prize of $500 to any medium who could pass an investigating committee. The Fox sisters were the first to try for the prize. Three Harvard professors were on the committee, whose report was unfavorable to Margaret and Kate. It suggested that the raps were produced by movements of the bones of the feet.

In spite of the criticisms and explanations that had been advanced, and even in spite of the statement by Mrs. Culver, belief in the Fox sisters grew. As the years went by, the sisters started introducing new tricks into their act, and they also took over many devised by other mediums.

The last official investigation of the raps took place in America under the auspices of the Seybert Commission. Henry Seybert (1801–1883), a mineralogist, philanthropist, and a keen believer in spiritualism, had donated a sum of money to the University of Pennsylvania to endow a chair of philosophy, and he had added the condition that the University was to appoint a commission to investigate "all systems of morals, religion, or philosophy which assume to represent the truth and particularly of Modern Spiritualism." The Commission, established in 1884, consisted of members of the faculty of the University.

In a preliminary report published in 1887, it was stated that it had investigated a number of mediums, including Margaret Fox. It reported that raps were heard close to her that could easily have been produced by normal means. Moreover, while the raps were sounding, Professor Furness, the chairman of the Commission, had placed his hand upon one of Margaret's feet and felt pulsations in it. It was also reported that Margaret knew when raps other than her own were produced, no matter how similar they were in sound to hers.

It was not only the uneducated that were impressed by the Fox sisters. The renowned William Crookes, who in 1871 held séances with Kate in London, was so impressed by her performance that he wrote:

> With a full knowledge of the numerous theories which have been started, chiefly in America, to explain these sounds, I have tested them in every way that I could devise, until there has been no escape from the conviction that they were true objective occurrences not produced by trickery or mechanical means.[2]

After their confession, the Fox sisters once more toured theaters together—this time to denounce spiritualism and demonstrate their tricks. They continued touring until 1889, when Kate's drunkenness caused cancellation of their bookings. Kate died in the street near her home in 1892, and Margaret, by this time also an alcoholic, died the following year. The Fox sisters' confession and numerous exposures of mediums at this time had little effect either on the public or on the zeal of the physical researchers.

Remarkably, the Fox sisters are still discussed in the parapsychological literature without mention of their trickery. Thus, a book by Renée Haynes, a Council member of the Society for Psychical Research, after relating how strange knocks were heard in a farmhouse in 1847, continues:

> A cumulative wave of interest in these happenings swept over America and into Europe, generating more phenomena in its course, some genuine, some the work of ingenious persons seizing the opportunity to make money and fame, some genuine at first but eked out by legerdemain as the unknown power to produce them waned.[3]

The account given in the *Encyclopedia Britannica* (1963 edition) is rather similar. A striking feature of both reports is that the reader is given no reason to believe that the Fox sisters were anything but perfectly genuine.

Eusapia Palladino

The year that the Fox sisters made their confession marked the rise to prominence of the greatest medium of all time. Eusapia Palladino was born on January 21,

1854, in Minervino Murge, southern Italy. Uneducated and illiterate, she was employed as a servant at the age of thirteen by a family who indulged in spiritualism. One day she was asked to make up a "circle" at a séance. Surprising manifestations of psychic activity were observed, and Eusapia declared herself to be a medium. In spite of her affiliations with the spirits, she remained very much a woman of this world. "An unlettered peasant, retaining," as one writer put it, "a most primitive morality and of such a decidedly erotic nature that it was said she thought of little else."[4]

After a long apprenticeship in the mediumistic circles of Naples, Eusapia came under the influence of Ercole Chiaja, a keen student of the occult. He was so impressed by her that in 1888 he published an open letter to Cesare Lombroso (1836–1909), the famous Italian criminologist and psychiatrist, inviting him to investigate the phenomena that arose in Eusapia's presence.

Eusapia was introduced to Lombroso in 1888, and, by 1891, she had convinced him of her supernatural powers. This, it should be noted, need not have presented her with as much difficulty as might appear. Lombroso was no hidebound skeptic. In 1882, he had reported the case of a patient who, having lost the power of seeing with her eyes, saw as clearly as before with the aid of the tip of her nose and the lobe of her left ear.[5]

An idea of what went on during one of Eusapia's séances may be gleaned from the detailed report of an investigating committee. Two curtains were hung across the corner of the séance room to form a small triangular space, called the *cabinet*. A small table was placed inside the cabinet, and around and on it reposed a number of objects, including a tambourine, a guitar, a toy trumpet, a flageolet, a toy piano, and a tea bell. Eusapia sat at a light table, the *séance table,* with her back to the cabinet so that the curtains were just behind her chair. The investigators sat at the sides of the séance table.[6]

The scene during the séance, discreetly veiled by the dim light, must have been remarkable. The voluptuous Eusapia sat in the clutch of two very serious gentlemen: "One of us sat on either side of her, holding, or held by, her hand with his foot under her foot, his leg generally pressing against the whole of hers, often with his free hand across her knees, and very frequently with his two feet encircling her foot."[7]

In the dim light, the table in front of her rose from the floor, objects floated from the cabinet, the curtain bulged, sounds were heard from the musical instruments inside the cabinet, and spirit hands touched the investigators. Great thumps were heard. The curtains suddenly blew out over the séance table. Eusapia was in communion with her spirit guide, John King.

In 1892, sittings were held in Milan for the benefit of a committee containing many eminent scientists, including Lombroso and the French physiologist Charles Richet, then Professor of Physiology in the University of Paris. The conclusion, reached with some reserve owing to the unsatisfactory way in which Eusapia's hands were held—the one thing that really mattered—was that none of the phenomena produced in "good light" could have been due to trickery.

A further series of fourteen sittings was held in Warsaw in 1893–1894.

Among twenty-three investigators, ten were convinced that trickery was not used, and three considered that the whole performance was fraudulent. One claimed to have detected, among other tricks, the substitution of hands and feet. He maintained that two persons who thought they were holding the left and right hands of Eusapia were, in fact, both holding one hand.

In the summer of 1895, Eusapia visited Cambridge, England, where she gave twenty-one sittings. Here, suspicions were again aroused, owing to the fact that the conditions imposed on the experimenters were such that fraud would have been difficult to detect had it been present. The investigators were not allowed to feel about in the darkness, and they were forbidden to grab at the hand that floated around, touched them, and played various tricks.

After the Cambridge sittings, Eusapia was classified as a fraudulent medium by the Society for Psychical Research. However, belief died hard. Although her repertoire was such as to invite suspicion, and though she had been detected indulging in trickery, she still had many supporters. During the next few years, many leading European scientists, including Sir Oliver Lodge, visited Eusapia and became convinced of her supernatural powers.

Several further investigations took place, including one series of forty-three sittings under the auspices of the Institute General de Psychologie ("Psychological Institute") of Paris. These experiments extended over three years at a cost of 25,000 francs. They were attended by the great French scientists Pierre and Marie Curie; D'Arsonval, the physicist; Henri Bergson, the philosopher; Richet, the physiologist; and numerous other scientists and savants. The French committee detected many signs of trickery on Eusapia's part, but they were clearly puzzled by some of the phenomena.

In 1908, three members of the Society for Psychical Research, the Hon. Everard Fielding, a barrister, W. W. Baggally, and Hereward Carrington, went to Naples to investigate Eusapia. They obtained the services of Albert Meeson, a stenographer of the American Express Company, and their eleven sittings were reported in considerable detail.[8]

The general arrangement of the curtain and tables at these sittings has already been described. Fielding, Baggally, and Carrington sat at the séance table. The stenographer sat at another table, some distance away and facing Eusapia, where he could witness the whole performance. His job was to record the remarks of the investigators and any visitors who were present.

During the séance there was considerable movement. Eusapia would twist and contort in her chair. The investigators, trying to maintain contact with her feet and hands, would follow her like marionettes. Extraordinary things happened. On one occasion, Baggally even managed to get himself kissed through the curtain, although he decided that there was an element of fraud as the head resembled a closed fist and the sound of the kiss resembled the clicking together of a thumb and finger. Psychic manifestations often followed one another at such a rate that the stenographer must have had difficulty compiling his record as the investigators called out anything they thought should be recorded. Mr. Meeson would write down the initial letter of the investigator's surname against each statement:

R. (A visitor called Ryan). A white object came up by my right eye.

F. I saw it very well from where I am.

B. I saw it.

C. I also.

F. It looked to me like a boiled white cabbage.

R. It seemed to me like an ace of diamonds and about three inches from my right eye.[9]

The investigators were puzzled by what they saw and heard, but it will be seen that the conditions under which Eusapia worked were highly favorable to illusion.

1. The room was in semidarkness so that recognition of objects was difficult and easily affected by other factors, such as suggestion.

2. The investigators were voicing aloud what they saw or experienced, thus tending to influence each other by suggestion.

3. During the séance, the medium was continually moving and, for example, pinching the investigators' hands, thus distracting their attention.

4. The investigators were having to attend to more than one thing at the same time. They had to control the hands and feet of the medium and, concurrently, watch in the dim light for any "psychic manifestations."

5. The séances were held late at night or in the early morning, introducing the element of fatigue. Eusapia always slept until midday as she could not afford to be tired.

6. The investigators had a strong belief in the supernatural, hence they would be emotionally involved.

7. The investigators were men. The subject was a woman. Thus, control of her activities was hampered by the fact that they had to observe the proprieties.

The Naples investigators were convinced that Eusapia was genuine, and her prestige rose considerably. Since that time, many writers have claimed that the conditions of this investigation ruled out the possibility of deception. They have pointed out that Baggally and Carrington were amateur magicians and could have detected fraud had it been present. Looking back on Eusapia's subsequent career, it is only too clear, however, that the important point about an investigator is whether or not he believes in the reality of the phenomena he is investigating. The disbelieving skeptic will approach a study in quite a different frame of mind from the believer.

In 1909 when Eusapia visited the United States, escorted by Carrington, who acted as her manager, the investigators were of quite a different nature. In a fanfare of publicity, Eusapia started giving sittings. The early ones were mainly for the benefit of the press, but at one held on November 19, 1909, a number of scientists were invited to attend, including R. W. Wood, Professor of Physics at Johns

Hopkins; Augustus Trowbridge, Professor of Physics at Princeton; and J. D. Quackenbos, a physician and novelist. Very little of a psychical nature happened at the sittings with scientific observers until, on the night of December 18, 1909, Eusapia was, at last, caught in the act. On this occasion, she was supervised by Hugo Munsterburg, the well-known Harvard psychologist, who showed himself to be a complete realist. His report, from which the following extract is taken, appeared in the *Metropolitan Magazine* for February 1910.

One week before Christmas, at the midnight hour, I sat again at Madame Palladino's favourite left side and a well-known scientist on her right. We had her under strictest supervision. Her left hand grasped my hand, her right hand was held by her right neighbour, her left foot rested on my foot while her right was pressing the foot of her other neighbour. For an hour the regulation performance had gone on. But now we sat in the darkened room in the highest expectancy while Mr. Carrington begged John to touch my arm and then to lift the table in the cabinet behind her and John really came. He touched me distinctly on my hip and then on my arm and at last he pulled my sleeve at the elbow. I plainly felt the thumb and the fingers. It was most uncanny. And, finally, John was to lift the table in the cabinet. We held both her hands, we felt both her feet, and yet the table three feet behind her began to scratch the floor and we expected it to be lifted. But instead there suddenly came a wild, yelling scream. It was such a scream as I have never heard before in my life, not even in Sarah Bernhardt's most thrilling scenes. It was a scream as if a dagger had stabbed Eusapia right through the heart.

What had happened? Neither she nor Mr. Carrington had the slightest idea that a man was lying flat on the floor and had succeeded in slipping noiselessly like a snail below the curtain into the cabinet. I had told him that I expected wires stretched out from her body and he looked out for them. What a surprise when he saw that she had simply freed her foot from her shoe and with an athletic backward movement of the leg was reaching out and fishing with her toes for the guitar and the table in the cabinet! And then lying on the floor he grasped her foot and caught her heel with firm hand, and she responded with the wild scream which indicated that she knew that at last she was trapped and her glory shattered.

Her achievement was splendid. She had lifted her unshod foot to the height of my arm when she touched me under cover of the curtain, without changing in the least the position of her body. When her foot played thumb and fingers the game was also neat throughout. To be sure, I remember before she was to reach out for the table behind her, she suddenly felt need of touching my left hand too, and for that purpose she leaned heavily over the table at which we were sitting. She said that she must do it because her spiritual fluid had become too strong and the touch would relieve her. As a matter of course in leaning forward with the upper half of her body she became able to push her foot further backward and thus to reach the light table, which probably stood a few inches too far. And then came the scream and the doom.[10]

But even that was not enough. Eusapia had clearly been indulging in trickery on this particular occasion, but what about all the things that had happened at other sittings? She was, according to her supporters, only 60 percent fraudulent; she would use a trick if the real thing was not at hand. Anybody could catch her using a trick; the task was to show that she could not produce any unusual phenomena when she was stopped from using tricks. This presented some difficulty, as she and her manager, Hereward Carrington, laid down the conditions under which séances should be held.

In January 1910, a series of six sittings was held at Columbia University. A number of scientists attended, including R. W. Wood, C. L. Dana, a Professor of Psychology at Cornell, and E. B. Wilson, a Professor of Biology at Princeton. The sittings were organized by Dickinson Miller, a Professor of Philosophy at Columbia University.

The séances were held in the Physics Laboratory of Columbia University, and the committee managed to complete the case against her after enlisting the aid of three professional magicians, W. S. Davis, J. L. Kellogg, and J. W. Sargent, together with J. F. Rinn, an amateur magician who spent much of his time hounding mediums. The magicians, who attended the last two sittings, were introduced to Eusapia as professors so that she should suspect nothing. At a séance held on April 17, 1910, Davis and Kellogg sat on either side of Eusapia, controlling her hands and feet. Rinn and a Columbia student, Warren G. Pyne, had hidden themselves under the séance table where they could observe Eusapia's footwork at close range. During this séance, she was left free to do as she pleased, and the magicians showed appropriate surprise at the various phenomena.

At a sitting held a week later, on April 24, 1910, Kellogg and Davis again sat on either side of Eusapia controlling her arms, legs, and feet. On this occasion, it was arranged that conditions should be lax at the start so that Eusapia should have every opportunity to put up a good performance. Levitations and transportations were abundant under these conditions. Then, at a prearranged signal, Kellogg and Davis exerted their control and from then on nothing happened.

A full report was issued in the journal *Science,* with statements by the scientists who had attended. Miller stated that, after her techniques had been observed and controlled, there were no manifestations of psychic phenomena.[11]

Rinn, from his vantage point beneath the table, saw the medium free her left leg by maneuvering her right foot so that her heel rested on Davis' toe and her toe on Kellogg's toe. The following statement which Rinn made was published in *Collier's Weekly* in an article by Joseph Jastrow, Professor of Psychology at the University of Wisconsin, who was present at the séance held on April 24, 1910:

In a few moments, after some ejaculations in Italian from the medium, the table began to wobble from side to side; and a foot came from underneath the dress of the medium and placed the toe underneath the leg of the table on the left side of the medium, and, pressing upward, gave it a little chuck into the air. . . . A short time after the lights were lowered she swung her left foot free from her dress at the back and kicked the curtain of the cabinet quickly, which caused it to bulge out toward the sitters. This was done several times so daringly that under the chairs where I lay it seemed almost impossible that the people above the table could not have observed it.

Later the medium placed her left leg back into the cabinet and pulled out from behind the curtain a small table with certain articles upon it, which was dashed to the floor in front of the cabinet on the left-hand side. It remained there in varying positions and was kicked by the medium a number of times. At one time the medium juggled the table that had been kicked out from behind the curtain on the end of her left toe in a very clever manner, so that it gave the appearance as if the table was floating in the air.[12]

Eusapia had survived many investigating committees, and she might well have survived that at Columbia University, since few people who visit mediums read scientific periodicals such as *Science,* and for every newspaper account Carrington could produce a ready reply. But she now had to contend with magicians, who at that time were at loggerheads with the mediums. The magician earns an honest living entertaining people with tricks. He regards the medium as prostituting his art, for she uses tricks to convince people of her supernatural powers in order to make money. With much publicity, Eusapia was challenged by Rinn to a contest, and she was offered $1,000 if she could perform any trick that the magicians could not duplicate under similar control conditions. A great deal of haggling went on, with much newspaper publicity as to the conditions to be observed. Eusapia would not agree to being encased in a bag nor with being tied with thin thread. Eventually, the conditions appear to have been agreed upon, but Eusapia did not turn up for the contest and later returned to Italy.

One further investigation was reported. Fielding went to Naples in December 1910, and a series of five séances were held. This time, he observed only tricks. If there was any residual element of genuine phenomena present in Eusapia's performance, it made no appearance. Little further was heard of her, and she died on May 16, 1918.

It was at enormous expense of time and money—she was paid 125 dollars per sitting while in the United States—that the secrets of Eusapia Palladino were revealed. Many parapsychologists are still convinced that not all of her act was fraudulent.

Mental Mediums

The stock in trade of the mediums so far discussed was the production of physical phenomena—objects moved, things were seen, and noises were heard. The phenomena produced by these mediums were readily reproducible by stage magicians. Claims about the cause of the effects could be checked by seeing whether they still occurred when the possibility of trickery was removed. The medium's defense against detection lay in the imposition of "rules" and conditions to limit the scope of the investigator. Both the physical medium and the magician decide the order of proceedings. They do not announce in advance exactly what is going to happen next. The magician does not repeat a trick on demand, and the medium decides if, and when, an encore is to be provided.

Three main techniques are used by mental mediums.

1. The medium appears to go into a trance during which her body is said to be taken over by one or more "spirit controls." These are supposed to be the spirits of deceased persons who try to pass on messages from other spirits to the medium's sitters. Their attempts at communication utilize the medium's voice and handwriting, but the controls have their own characteristics and distinguishing features, which are different from those of the medium.

2. The medium acts as if one of the communicators is responsible for her speech and behavior and is in "direct control" of her.

3. The medium produces messages by automatic writing or similar processes while retaining consciousness and apparently being her normal self throughout the proceedings.

In each case, conditions are ill-suited for exact observation. The observer, who may also be the sitter, has to note, or remember, not only what the medium says but also what is said to the medium and any other responses that may be made e.g. nodding the head. This is clearly an impossible task. The observer is likely to report those utterances that attract his attention. He cannot expect to record every sound made in the séance room. What he hears will, in addition, be dependent on what he expects to hear. Other responses that may provide information to the medium are likely to be missed altogether. Anyone reporting on the performance of a stage performer who finds hidden objects by using audience reactions is at the same disadvantage. He is unlikely to become aware of the cues utilized by the performer even if they are pointed out to him.

Mrs. Piper

Perhaps the most closely studied of all mental mediums was the American, Mrs. Leonore Piper. She first came to the notice of the distinguished American psychologist William James in 1886, and he introduced her to Richard Hodgson, the Secretary of the American Society for Psychical Research. These two men studied and reported on her trances from 1886 to 1892. In 1889, she visited England to be studied by the British Society for Psychical Research, which appointed for the purpose a committee headed by Sir Oliver Lodge. Reports on the period from 1892 to 1897 were made by Hodgson and Professor Romaine Newbold (1865–1926) Professor of Philosophy at the University of Pennsylvania. James Hyslop, (1854–1920), Professor of Logic and Ethics at Columbia University, reported on her trance activities from 1897 to 1905.

Mrs. Piper was regarded by her investigators as being of reasonable intelligence, education, and integrity. In 1884, she paid visits to a "psychic healer," a person who claims to cure disease through the intervention of spirits, for medical advice. During her second visit, she went into a trance herself and soon became able to do this at will. During her trance state, she seemed to assume other personalities and speak to or write on matters of which she was ignorant after she regained her normal state.[13]

Soon a regular "control" appeared; this purported to be the spirit of a French Physician named Phinuit. Phinuit turned out to know little French and even less medicine. He explained the former fact by claiming that in life he had lived so long in an English community in Marseilles that he had forgotten his native tongue. Of more likely significance is that Mrs. Piper had only learned a little French at school. Phinuit could give little information regarding his life on earth, which is not surprising as inquiries in France yielded no record of his birth, life, or death. On the other hand, he was adept at fishing for information and often contradicted himself. Also, he often displayed signs of temporary deafness when posed with a difficult question. Much of his "communication" was garbled, incomplete, or merely gibberish; but of more concern to the investigators was the fact that he was unable to demonstrate, even to the investigators' satisfaction, that he was in contact with the spirits of deceased people.

Mrs. Piper was able, however, to impress many people, including William James, of her supernatural powers. Since most of the same people were impressed by the Creery sisters and Eusapia Palladino, they are hardly likely to have made suitable investigators.

Mrs. Leonard

Mrs. Gladys Osborne Leonard baffled psychical researchers for forty years. Although she was a professional medium, she claimed to have entered the field only to bring comfort to those bereaved during World War I. Thus, her usual opening for new sitters was the presentation of messages from the spirits of young men who had recently died. These men were almost always described as soldiers, always officers. Mrs. Leonard's control was an Indian girl called "Feda." She was described as a gay, lovable child with an impish sense of humor. Feda had pet names for her regular sitters, and she seems to have elicited warm affection from many of the investigators. Thus, the English writers Radclyffe Hall and Lady Una Troubridge end the introduction to their major report with acknowledgments, not to Mrs. Leonard, but to Feda.

"Our thanks are due to Feda for the full and accurate records which we have been able to obtain. She has always shown the greatest solicitude on this point, repeating slowly and carefully, more than once, anything intricate that appeared to her to be of evidential value. . . . [She] has been known to rebuke the communicator, saying "Don't speak so quickly, Mrs. Twonnie" [or "Mrs. Una," as the case may be] hasn't got that down yet . . . a very real mutual liking has grown up between ourselves and Feda."[14]

Feda showed an awareness of the need for clear evidence lacking in many investigators of the psychic. She would urge her spirit communicators to provide verifiable facts. But her pronouncements were seldom impressive to anyone without a belief in spiritualism. It has been claimed, however, that she provided proof, if not for a spirit world, at least for Mrs. Leonard's remarkable powers of extrasensory perception.

The veracity of Mrs. Leonard's claims was accepted as being especially established by Feda's communications with the late Raymond Lodge and "A.V.B." Raymond Lodge was the young officer son of Sir Oliver Lodge and A.V.B. was an old friend of Radclyffe Hall. It is of interest to see how these identifications were established at the first sittings. The description Feda gave of Raymond was as follows:

Is a young man, rather above the medium height; rather well-built, not thick-set or heavy, but well-built, he holds himself up well. He has not been over long. His hair is between colours. He is not easy to be described, because he is not building himself up too solid as some do. He has greyish eyes; hair brown, short at the sides; a fine shaped head; eyebrows also brown, not much arched; nice shaped nose, fairly straight broader at the nostrils a little; a nice shaped mouth a good sized mouth it is, but it does not look large because he holds the lips nicely together, chin not heavy, face oval."[15]

A check by Mrs. W. H. Salter, a Research Officer of the British Society for Psychical Research, of the descriptions of fourteen young men given by Feda at first sittings reveals this as her stock description of any departed male.[16] In all cases in which height is mentioned, the young man is described as being tall or "above medium height." Nine of these were also described as "well-built." In the twelve cases where the color of the hair is given, it is brown. It is always cut or "cutted short at the sides." The fourteen times that the color of the eyebrows is given, it is brown; eleven sets of eyebrows are "a little arched." Twelve times the shape of the nose is described as "straight or almost straight," while eleven noses are further described as having "rounded tips" or as being "broader at the nostrils." Six mouths have a "nice shape."

As a matter of interest, about half of the sitters found the descriptions given them to be fairly close to that of some relative or friend killed in the war. Feda had evidently developed a model of the average young British officer as remembered by the average mother: a young man, tall and well-built with brown hair cut short at the sides, a straight nose broadening at the tip, and slightly arched brown eyebrows. A few other variations appear; faces are either oval or between round and oval, hair is always brushed back and often sticks up at the top. Eyes are either blue-gray or gray.

One regular feature of Feda's officer-communicator is that he often spoke of group photographs. This was a fairly safe bet, as it must be exceptional for a British officer to avoid regimental and mess photographs. But Sir Oliver Lodge was very impressed when "Raymond" mentioned such a portrait, which only subsequently turned up at the Lodge's home.

When Radclyffe Hall first visited Mrs. Leonard, it was as an investigator. But Feda, doubtless taking it for granted that she was one of the run-of-the-mill bereaved relatives, immediately produced the spirit of a young soldier. Radclyffe Hall disclaimed any romantic affiliations with army officers, and Feda then adopted her second line of approach—an elderly lady. The description of this lady, whose initials were A.V.B., was eventually elicited as:

> F(eda): The lady is of medium height has rather a good figure but is inclined to be fat, Feda thinks: she has a straight nose, a well shaped face, but the face is inclined to lose its outline a little. The eyebrows are slightly arched, her hair is not done fashionably.
>
> R. H.: Is it worn in the neck?
>
> F.: No it's done on the crown of her head . . .[17]

Of Feda's ten descriptions of women that Mrs. Slater reported, eight are called elderly or past middle age. In the nine cases where height is mentioned, eight ladies are of "medium height," while three are specified as having a "good figure." All five references to noses describe them as "straight," and three faces are mentioned as "losing their outline." Three sets of eyebrows are "slightly arched." Of eight hair styles referred to, six are "on the crown of the head."

The psychologist and critic of psychical research, Joseph Jastrow, pointed out that perception is dependent on two components forming the extremes of a continuum. These he called the *sensorial* and *memorial* components. The sensorial component is dependent on information available to the individual through his senses; the memorial component is dependent on the past experience of the individual and learning. Normal perception is dependent on both components and falls between the two extremes of the continuum.

Jastrow pointed out that when the sensorial component predominates completely, we may experience a visual illusion. We may know that two lines are of equal length (see page 51), but the sensorial component overrides this, and we still perceive them as being different. When the memorial component is present in the absence of the sensorial component, the delusion or hallucination arises. Objects are seen based on past experience in the absence of any real object being present in the field of view. A pink elephant—or a ghost—is perceived.

The conditions of the séance room favor Jastrow's memorial component. The sensorial component is reduced by employing dim illumination. The memorial component is enhanced through suggestion imparted by the medium or the sitters themselves. With the mental medium, the sensorial component is reduced by making the messages he transmits garbled, ambiguous, and difficult to interpret exactly. The sitter is in the situation of a person being given what is called a *projection* test by a psychologist. Vague, ambiguous, or meaningless material that can be interpreted in various ways is presented to the subject, thus providing full scope for the memorial component. Conclusions about the subject are then drawn from the manner in which he responds.

A physical act, such as levitating a table, requires premeditation on the part of the medium. But a mental medium may genuinely believe that he is in communication with the dead. The position is summed up in a letter written by Mrs. Piper to the New York *Herald* on October 20, 1901. In it she denied that she was a spiritualist or had ever experienced any proof of spirit return. She then asked herself why she had remained so long with the Society for Psychical Research and replied, "Because of my desire to learn if I were possessed or obsessed."[18]

The trance medium, if she is not merely shamming, is a person who finds herself experiencing fits or states of changed consciousness. These occur involuntarily, but at some stage she finds it possible to elicit one at will. While in one of these states, she is no longer able to function normally. She hears imaginary voices and may have visual and kinesthetic delusions. Some other person seems to take over her body and her mind. Her voice speaks through her vocal chords, expressing thoughts and experiences of which she has no knowledge. She may write or communicate in some manner characteristic of her control. She is, in fact, suffering from dissociation. Conscious awareness of everyday events may still exist during such a state, but, even so, the ability to think and communicate is changed. When herself again, she may sometimes display a retrograde amnesia, that is, a loss of memory for the events that took place during the fit. There is little doubt that, if she complained that she was unhappy about this state of affairs or if she presumed that the person who took over from her was the representative of some political or religious organization, a psychiatrist would diagnose mental illness.

If mediums such as Mrs. Piper and Mrs. Leonard utilized cues provided by their sitters, this could have been established by systematically removing such cues. Since each of these ladies retained her abilities for more than twenty years, they would have made admirable subjects for ESP research.

Today, recording devices may be employed, but, when evidence was collected on the great mediums, reliance had to be placed on notes taken at the time. In 1960, the British Broadcasting Corporation televised a sitting between Douglas Johnson, a professional medium, and a stranger he met for the first time in front of the television cameras. Dr. Donald West, a psychiatrist who was Assistant Director of Research at the Cambridge University Institute of Criminology and a former Research Officer of the British Society for Psychical Research, was present. He commented: "The medium scored some striking hits and many viewers, including the present writer, were impressed by his success."[19]

The program was recorded and re-broadcast later with a critical commentary by Christopher Scott, a psychologist and leading critic of parapsychology research. West later commented that it then became apparent to him that almost everything the medium said could have been deduced from changes in facial expression and tone of voice induced in the sitter by the medium's leading questions.

Many persons attributed to the medium statements that appeared to be in remarkable accordance with the facts as later revealed by the sitter at the end of the first program. But when the sitting was seen for the second time, it was found that statements attributed to the medium were never uttered. Thus it was decided that the medium had scored a hit in saying that the sitter's mother had died of cancer of the stomach. The audio record revealed that cancer of the stomach had, at no time, been mentioned by the sitter or by the medium during the interview. Without the availability of the complete audio-visual record, the medium's performance would have been greatly overrated by most people who watched the program.

A revealing account of the manner in which a present-day reputed psychic, Peter Hurkos, gains information and elicits responses from an unknown person is given by Ronald A. Schartz in an article "Sleight of Tongue." He concludes his article:

> The eagerness with which people latch on to the fanciful idea of extrasensory perception to explain the apparent accuracy of the utterance, rather than to the recognition of their own complicity, is the really intriguing aspect of the demonstration. Perhaps recognition of one's own contribution is just too lackluster an explanation to be given much credence. Our persistent delight with fanciful explanations suggests that skilled practitioners of sleight of tongue will enjoy a bright and prosperous future.[20]

Notes

1. Margaret Fox, *New York World*, October 21, 1888.
2. William Crookes, *Researches in the Phenomena of Spiritualism* (London: Burns & Oates, 1874), p. 88.
3. Renée Haynes, *The Hidden Springs* (New York: Devlin-Adair , 1961), p. 223. First published in England by Hollis & Carter, 1961. Copyright 1961 by Renée Haynes.
4. E. J. Dingwall, *Very Peculiar People* (London: Rider, 1950), p. 190
5. Herbert Thurston, *The Physical Phenomena of Spiritualism* (London: Burns & Oates, 1936), p. 336.
6. E. Fielding, W. W. Baggally, and H. Carrington, "Report of a Series of Sittings with Eusapia Palladino," *Proceedings of the Society for Psychical Research*, 23, 59 (1909).
7. *Ibid*, p. 328.
8. *Ibid*.
9. *Ibid*, p. 359
10. H. Munsterburg, "Report on a Sitting with Eusapia Palladino," *Metropolitan Magazine*, February, 1910.
11. D. S. Miller "Report of an Investigation of the Phenomena Connected with Eusapia Palladino," *Science*, 77 (1910).
12. J. Jastrow, "Unmasking of Palladino," *Collier's Weekly*, 45 (May 14, 1910): 21–22.

13. J. F. Rinn, *Searchlight on Psychical Research* (London: Rider, 1954).
14. Radclyffe Hall and U. V. Troubridge, "On a Series of Sittings with Mrs. Osborne Leonard," *Proceedings of the Society for Psychical Research,* 30, 78 (1919): 346–47.
15. Oliver Lodge, *Raymond or Life and Death* (London: Methuen, 1916), p. 125.
16. W. H. Slater, "A Further Report on Sittings with Mrs. Leonard," *Proceedings of the Society for Psychical Research,* 32, 82 (1921), 74–85.
17. Hall and Troubridge, "Sittings with Mrs. Osborne Leonard," p. 348.
18. Leonore Piper, *New York Herald,* October 20, 1901.
19. D. J. West, *Psychical Research Today* (London: Penguin, 1962), p. 101.
20. Ronald A. Schwartz, "Sleight of Tongue," *The Skeptical Inquirer,* 3, 1 (1978), 47–53.

7
Summary to Part One

The first forty years of psychical research produced nothing that could be regarded as scientific evidence for supernatural processes. It was, in the main, a history of fraud, imposture, and crass stupidity.

Dr. Trevor H. Hall who has written the most revealing and systematic accounts of the events and personalities during the early days of psychical research in Britain, is also a leading expert on conjuring and has been a Vice President of the Magic Circle for twenty years. In his book *The Strange Case of Edmund Gurney*[1] where much information is given on the investigations of the Society for Psychical Research's Committee on Thought Transference, he writes:

> The sensible reader looking back on these events of long ago, may well wonder how men like Myers, Barrett and Gurney could possibly have been taken in for a moment by such nonsense as the "phenomena" of the Creery girls. The answer is, I fancy, three fold. First, the leaders of the S.P.R. seem to have been rendered credulous to a degree almost impossible to understand by their overwhelming desire to believe in the marvels about which they wrote with such enthusiasm in the Proceedings of the Society. Second, they seem to have been entirely ignorant of the elementary principles of conjuring. Third, they held the curious idea that any story, however improbable, told by a person of unblemished character such as a clergyman, a judge, a man of academic standing or a member of one of the professions, must necessarily be factual and could be accepted and published virtually without examination.

Extraordinary blunders made particularly by more eminent members of the Society became evident in almost every investigation they undertook. Sidgwick,

Crookes, Lodge, Myers, and Gurney were each involved in fiascos revealed by later confessions.

Even today much of that history has still to be written. It was only in 1962, for example, that Trevor Hall made public his detailed study of one of the most prominent investigators of that time, Sir William Crookes, in which he revealed that Crookes and Florence Cook, a young medium whom he was investigating, were both accomplices and lovers.[2]

But evidence from that period, including evidence provided by Florence Cook during her séances with Crookes, is to this day put forward as providing proof of supernatural processes. A recent book, *Natural and Supernatural—A History of the Paranormal* by Brian Inglis, is a case in point.[3] It was first brought to the attention of the public in a prepublication review by leading journalist Bernard Levin in the London *Times* of January 10, 1978. Levin had been so impressed after thumbing through the manuscript that he felt impelled to inform his readers of what was in store for them. He wrote:

> It is simply not possible for any fully sane person to deny that there have been a vast, an unaccountable, number of supernatural happenings that *cannot* be rejected as the products of fake, hallucination, chance, misunderstanding or the effects of powers and senses already known to be possessed by human beings."[4]

In the ensuing correspondence, Professor D. F. Lawden, a mathematician at the University of Aston in Birmingham, commented on "members of the scientific establishment [who] . . . refuse to acknowledge as facts a certain class of phenomena, since these run counter to prevailing theories." Lawden rubbed this well in for the benefit of anyone likely to disagree with him. He continued, "This is the well established Galileo syndrome; so called because Galileo was plagued by idiots who denounced his Copernican ideas but refused to look through his telescope at the moons of Jupiter for fear that actual contemplation of the evidence might weaken their resolve to place the earth at the centre of the universe. The moons have now been displaced by psychic phenomena but the idiots are still with us."

Inglis's book was a history of psychical research up to World War I, which is the same period as is covered in Part 1 of this book. He devoted two chapters to Eusapia Palladino, but made no mention of Simon Newcomb.

Newcomb, besides being the leading astronomer of his day, was a skeptical but interested observer of psychical research. He became the first President of the American Society for Psychical Research after its foundation in 1884. Newcomb certainly did not refuse to look through his telescope at the "class of phenomena" referred to by Lawden, and what he observed was reported under the title "Modern Occultism" in the *Nineteenth Century* magazine in 1909.[5] There he wrote that two years of experiment study and reading had confirmed his ideas on the subject reached after a half century of occasional study, coupled with reading the best he could find in support of occultism. He concluded: "Nothing has been brought out by the researchers of the Psychical Society and its able collaborators except what we should expect to find in the ordinary course of nature.'' It was after Newcomb's death in 1909 that Eusapia Palladino was exposed as fradulent during her visit to the U.S.A. and that Blackburn's confession received publicity in the *Daily News* in 1911.

If Brian Inglis was looking through his telescope, he appears to have cast a blind eye at the report in *Science,*[6] in which Eusapia was finally exposed. He makes no mention of the report in his ''mountain of evidence searchingly examined and scrupulously evaluated'' (Bernard Levin, in the *Times*). But both Inglis and Levin had presumably read about the report on Eusapia and about Blackburn's confession, since each of them reviewed my earlier book.

The first forty years of psychical research provided experiences that should have been of the utmost value to anyone capable of learning from past mistakes. But events tend to repeat themselves. After the exposure of Eusapia Palladino, it might be thought that more care would have been taken in the event of a new physical medium arising with a similar type of repertoire. But the exposure by no means marked the end of scientific interest in séance-room phenomena. Other mediums became headline news, and then in May 1923, the most famous of all American mediums first came before the public eye.

Margery Crandon

Margery was the wife of L. R. G. Crandon, a distinguished Boston surgeon who was present at all her séances and who, many of the investigators believed, was responsible for much of what went on.

Her performance was in some ways similar to that of Eusapia Palladino, but she had many new tricks in her repertoire. During a séance, she went into a trancelike state during which ''Walter,'' purportedly her deceased brother and her master of ceremonies, manifested himself. Walter's voice emanated from Margery's mouth, and sometimes his hand would be seen. He had a great sense of humor, although some of his utterances were calculated to make any nice girl blush.

Margery operated under conditions very much in her favor compared with those enjoyed by Eusapia Palladino. Her séances usually took place in complete darkness relieved only by a flash of red light provided by an apparatus fixed up by Crandon and operated when Walter gave the signal. Also, investigators had to agree to rigid conditions laid down by the Crandons before they were allowed to take part in a séance.

Margery was also much better able to win the sympathy of her investigators than was Eusapia. She was young, witty, and attractive. Even in a photograph, in which a considerable quantity of what look like jellied eels have deposited themselves on her right ear, it is clear that her physical charms far surpassed those of the rather stout Eusapia.

Margery, like Eusapia, was studied by several groups of investigators. The first research was carried out by four Harvard psychologists, William McDougall,

A. A. Roback, Gardner Murphy, and Harry Helson. They were not favorably impressed, but a report was not issued at the time.

The second investigation was made by a committee appointed by the *Scientific American,* which had offered $5,000 to anyone who could exhibit genuine psychic phenomena. The great American magician Harry Houdini was a member of the committee, but he was ignored until some eighty sittings had been held and Margery was about to get the prize. He was eventually asked to participate at a séance held on July 23, 1924. After he had detected trickery, the committee withheld the prize, although one of its members, J. M. Bird, an associate editor of *Scientific American,* appears to have been convinced that Margery was at least 40 percent genuine.

One of Margery's tricks was described by Houdini as follows:

> During the second intermission "Walter" asked for an illuminated plaque to be placed on the lid of the box which held the bell and Bird went to get it. This left the right hand and foot of the medium free. Bird had difficulty in finding the plaque and while he was searching "Walter" suddenly called for "control."
>
> Mrs. Crandon placed her right hand in mine and gave me to understand that I had both her hands. Bird was requested to stand in the doorway, but without any warning, before he could obey, the cabinet was thrown over backwards violently. *The medium then gave me her right foot also, saying:*
> "You have now both hands and both feet."
> Then "Walter" called out:
> "The megaphone is in the air. Have Houdini tell me where to throw it."
> "Towards me," I replied, and in an instant it fell at my feet. The way she did these tricks is as follows: when Bird left the room it freed her right foot and hand. With her right hand she tilted the corner of the cabinet enough to get her free foot under it, then picking up the megaphone she placed it on her head, dunce-cap fashion. Then she threw the cabinet over with her right foot. As she did so I distinctly felt her body give and sway as though she had made a vigorous lunge. As soon as this was done "Walter" called for "Better control" and she gave me her right foot. Then she simply jerked her head, causing the megaphone to fall at my feet. Of course with the megaphone on her head it was easy and simple for her to ask me or anyone else to hold both of her feet and also her hands, and still she could snap the megaphone off her head in any direction requested. This was the *"slickest"* ruse I have ever detected, and it has converted all skeptics.[7]

Houdini's exposure did not convince those who believed in the supernatural. In 1925, Margery was investigated by Dr. E. J. Dingwall of the British Society for Psychical Research. He showed that most of the phenomena could have been produced by trickery on the part of Margery and her husband, but he was puzzled by some of the phenomena.

Toward the end of Dingwall's investigation, Hudson Hoagland, a young

Harvard psychologist later to become well known in experimental psychology, became interested in the affair. Subsequently, a committee was formed consisting of Hoagland and four instructors from the University. A number of senior members of the University also attended some sittings and associated themselves with the findings.

In November 1925, Hoagland published an article in the *Atlantic Monthly* in which more than twenty separate items of evidence were produced to support the fact that Margery was a trickster. Although the Harvard committee had pronounced Margery fraudulent, the American Society for Psychical Research was not satisfied and wanted a further investigation.

Another committee was formed consisting of R. W. Wood, who had been on the committee investigating Eusapia Palladino; a skeptical psychologist, Knight Dunlap, of the Johns Hopkins faculty; and G. McComas, Associate Professor of Psychology at Princeton. The Crandons terminated the proceedings after the fourth sitting with this committee when the following episode took place.

> Wood very cautiously *touched* and finally *pinched* the end of the "ectoplasm" that issued from Margery's mouth, without any sign of detection on her part. The significant point here is that a medium always insists that even *touching* the ectoplasm is sure to result in her illness or possible death. Wood states that it felt like a steel knitting needle covered with one or two layers of soft leather. As Wood, at the conclusion of the séance, solemnly dictated this stunt into the record, Margery shrieked and pretended to faint, and *that* was the end of the committee's séances with *her*. A full report of the committee's findings was sent to the American Society for Psychical Research, but the Society never saw fit to publish it.[8]

In 1929, Margery gave three séances in London in the rooms of the Society for Psychical Research. By this time, an important part of her act consisted of fingerprints that Walter impressed on a lump of wax. It was found that some of the fingerprints were Margery's, although her hands were supposed to have been controlled throughout the séances, other fingerprints belonged to no one present—except perhaps Walter.

The main supporter of Margery, apart from her husband, had been J. M. Bird. He had been fired from the *Scientific American* after their investigation and had become Research Officer of the American Society for Psychical Research of New York. Another staunch supporter was a member of the Boston Society for Psychical Research, E. E. Dudley. It was Dudley who eventually made the discovery that gave the *coup de grace* to Margery.

In March 1932, Dudley found that fingerprints left behind by Walter were those of Margery's dentist, who had attended many of her séances prior to 1925. It was also found that prints left behind by Walter in London were those of the dentist. The New York Society for Psychical Research refused to publish Dudley's findings, but they were eventually published by its rival, the Boston Society for Psychical Research. Walter Franklin Prince, the principal Research Officer of the

Boston Society, declared that the Margery case would come to be considered the most ingenious, persistent, and fantastic complex of fraud in the history of psychic research, but that was forty-five years ago.

She continued to give séances until 1938, when her husband died, after which she lost her powers. She died on November 1, 1941, at her home in Boston.

It may well be asked why it is necessary to explore in so much detail these ridiculous episodes in the history of psychical research. But it should be realized that, at the time, such things were taken very seriously by completely sane men. At great expense of time and energy, many eminent men provided evidence of the background of trickery that was responsible for the alleged psychic phenomena. Such efforts should not be required in a rational community but it is evident that, even in the twentieth century, superstition is far from dead.

Commenting on Professor Miller's report on the exposure of Eusapia Palladino, an editorial in the *New York Times* of May 10, 1910, concluded with the words: "But no one can read his trenchant analysis of her repeated and long continued conquests without feeling that the men of science have been her willing dupes and her abettors in a sort of conspiracy to mystify society."[9]

That sentence contained some truth. Both Eusapia Palladino and Margery Crandon were investigated by committee after committee, but it is significant that on all those occasions when professional magicians were present, the mediums were completely exposed. Neither Eusapia nor Margery could fool the magicians because they knew all the tricks and how to combat them.

If another Eusapia or Margery were to arise tomorrow, how would she succeed? The answer is quite clear. If she could avoid the attention of investigating committees, she would find public credulity no less than it was in 1889 or 1924. The present spate of television programs dealing with the supernatural indicates how popular allegedly true accounts of supernatural happenings are and how strong must be people's underlying beliefs.

Today, there are Eusapias and Margerys by the thousand, but they are more concerned with making money than with convincing investigating committees of their abilities. Man will pay for what he needs. He pays heavily for quack medical remedies, since health is an invaluable commodity. He will also pay heavily a spiritualist who claims to be able to contact a departed relative, for this is a service that no one else claims to provide.

Notes

1. Trevor H. Hall, *The Strange Case of Edmund Gurney* (London: Duckworth, 1964). See also John L. Campbell and Trevor H. Hall, "Strange Things." The story of Fr. Allan Mcdonald, Ada Goodrich Freer, and the Society for Psychical Research's Enquiry into Highland Second Sight (London: Routledge & Kegan Paul, 1968).
2. Trevor H. Hall. *The Spiritualists: The Story of Florence Cook and William Crooks.* (London: Duckworth, 1962).

3. Brian Inglis, *Natural and Supernatural—A History of the Paranormal* (London: Hodder and Stoughton, 1977).
4. Bernard Levin, *London Times,* January 10, 1978.
5. Simon Newcomb, "Modern Occultism," *Nineteenth Century Magazine,* (January 1909), 126–99
6. D. S. Miller, "Report of and Investigation of the Phenomena Connected with Eusapia Palladino," *Science,* 77 (1910), 776–80.
7. W. B. Gibson and Morris N. Young, eds. *Houdini on Magic* (New York: Dover, 1953), pp. 141–42. Copyright 1953 by Dover Publications, Inc. Reprinted through permission of the publisher.
8. W. B. Seabrook, *Doctor Wood: Modern Wizard of the Laboratory* (New York: Harcort Brace, 1941), p. 215.
9. Editorial, *New York Times,* May 10, 1910.

PART TWO

8
Salad Days at Duke University

In 1920, William McDougall (1871–1938), the well-known British psychologist, was appointed to the chair of psychology at Harvard University. McDougall at that time was president of the British Society for Psychical Research, having become interested in the subject while a student at Cambridge. He found a history of psychical research at Harvard, for ten years earlier, the German psychologist, Hugo Munsterburg—McDougall's predecessor in the chair at Harvard—had exposed the great Italian medium Eusapia Palladino, and an experiment on telepathy had been carried out there in 1916 by L. T. Troland, a professor of psychology in the department.

Psychical research flourished at Harvard during the 1920s. McDougall found funds for the work lying idle and quickly put them to use. Experiments on telepathy were conducted by the psychologists Gardner Murphy and G. H. Esterbrooks, and before long McDougall, together with most of the staff of his department and several senior members of the university, was involved in the investigation of "Margery."

While at Harvard, McDougall was contacted by a young Chicago botanist, Joseph Banks Rhine. Rhine and his wife Louisa had become interested in psychical research, partly through hearing a lecture on spiritualism given by the English author and physician Sir Arthur Conan Doyle (1859–1930). Rhine began a correspondence with McDougall, and in 1926 he joined the Harvard psychology department as a research assistant. When McDougall joined the faculty of Duke University in 1927, Rhine went with him.

Figure 8-1
ESP Cards (formerly called Zener Cards

Rhine's first publication on telepathy appeared in 1929 and concerned a telepathic horse named Lady.[1] In view of the considerable doubts about this experiment and the fact that Rhine admitted that the owner of the horse had later resorted to using signals, there is little point in considering it in detail.

In 1934, he published *Extra-Sensory Perception*,[2] in which he gave details of research at Duke University and claimed to have found overwhelming evidence for the existence of extrasensory perception. Further research followed, and in 1940 the Duke Parapsychology Laboratory was formed with Rhine as its director.

Early Exploratory Tests

The first part of the research described in *Extra-Sensory Perception* consisted of exploratory tests made under comparatively loose conditions in which the aim was to discover subjects who would be used in later research.

Some of the major tests carried out during this exploratory period (1930–32) are detailed below:

1. In the summer of 1930, children at a summer recreational school were asked to guess a number (0–9) seen by the experimenter. Approximately a thousand trials were made in this manner, but not a single child was discovered whose performance warranted any further investigation.

2. In the fall, Rhine in collaboration with a colleague in the psychology department, K. E. Zener, carried out clairvoyance experiments on students in class. Tests were made using three types of material: numbers (0–9), letters of the alphabet, and Zener cards. The latter, so named because they had been chosen by Zener, consisted of five different symbols: a circle, a rectangle, a plus sign, wavy lines, and a star. In a total of 1,600 trials, the scores were close to the chance expectation, and after the experiment Zener became too burdened with other work and dropped out of the research.

3. In the winter of 1931–32, Rhine obtained what he called his first really convincing result. A clairvoyance test using Zener cards on twenty-four subjects yielded an overall score of 207 hits in 800 trials. As there were five different symbols, the score expected to arise by chance was 160 hits, and the odds were greater than a million to one against a score of 207. Twelve of the twenty-four subjects obtained an average of five hits or more in twenty-five trials, while the other twelve subjects scored below chance. Of the latter group, Rhine said that none of them "developed," and few were tried again. But as, on the average, fewer than fourteen trials were made with each of these low-scoring subjects, it is difficult to see how they were given much chance to develop. A surprising feature of these tests was, in fact, the small number of trials some of the subjects made. During each trial the subject might look at the back of the card and pick it up before making his guess; but this would hardly have taken more than about five seconds for each guess. Even so, several subjects recorded only fifty or fewer trials, and the twelve low-scoring subjects averaged less than fourteen trials—about one and a half minutes work each.

4. Two further experiments yielding significantly high scores were carried out at this time by Dr. Rhine's assistants, but in neither case were the exact conditions of the experiments stated. Charles E. Stuart tested nine subjects and J. G. Pratt, fifteen. In each case, the over-all score for the group had high odds against arising by chance. From the meager details given, it would appear that the experimenter sat at a table with the subject and handed him a pack of Zener cards. The subject took each card in turn, holding it face downward, and made his guess, which was recorded by the experimenter. The guesses were, on some occasions, checked for hits after a run of five and on the other occasions after a run of twenty-five trials had been completed.

These "early and minor tests," Rhine stated, were published so that the reader might see the whole of the group's work in its infancy. They included 23,550 trials, and the overall score achieved had odds greater than a billion to one against arising by chance. But, as Rhine commented, "Some of the weaknesses of these beginnings one only has to read here to avoid."

A feature of the early tests was the fact that, among a large number of subjects who were tested at this time, only two—A. J. Linzmayer and Stuart, both undergraduate students—later showed themselves capable of obtaining consistently high scores. The experiments gave results that were statistically significant because the groups of subjects scored slightly above the chance level over a large number of trials.

In 1930 and early 1931, progress was slow, and subjects with ESP seemed hard to find; but later in 1931 there were dramatic changes, and by the end of 1932 almost everyone tested among the graduate psychology students at Duke was found to have some ability. Thus, Rhine stated in *Extra-Sensory Perception* that, of the fourteen graduate students in psychology present in the previous two years, six showed ESP ability that was statistically significant, another had been reported to have done work that was appreciably significant, and the remaining seven students had not to his knowledge been tested.

Tests on High-Scoring Subjects

The second part of Rhine's research consisted of investigations carried out on eight high-scoring subjects. Each of them in a relatively short time displayed remarkable powers of ESP, and his final assessment of the combined score of his subjects gave odds greater than 10^{1000} to 1 against chance occurrence.

Various types of tests were used, but they had a common characteristic: the subject guessed one of five different symbols, which were either depicted on cards or were thought of by some other person. The cards were in packs of 25, containing 5 of each of the different symbols. When a subject guesses the order of such a pack, provided he is not told whether he is correct or not after each trial, an average score of five hits per run of twenty-five is expected to arise by chance. A subject's score will vary in different runs of 25 trials; thus, in 100 runs, several scores of 9, one or two 10's and, with luck a 12 would probably arise. A score of 13 would not be extraordinary (odds are about 6 to 1 against getting a score of 13 in 100 runs), but a 14 would be unlikely. A score of exactly 5 hits would be expected to arise on about 40 occasions.

Rhine's high-scoring subjects would often average 8 or 9 hits over a large number of runs. Thus, the most outstanding subject, Hubert E. Pearce, a student for the Methodist ministry in the School of Religion at Duke, averaged 8 hits per run over 690 runs, constituting a total of 17,250 trials. This performance would not seem remarkable unless an observer were well acquainted with the probabilities of the different-sized scores arising by chance. But, in fact, if a person could average even 5.3 hits per 25 trials over 690 runs, there would be odds greater than 1 million to 1 against this result arising by chance, although the subject would only be averaging 1 extra hit in each 76 guesses.

The experimental techniques employed by Rhine were:

1. BT (*Basic Technique,* later referred to as the "Before Touching" technique). The pack was shuffled, cut, and placed face downward on the table. The subject attempted to guess the first card, which was then removed and placed in a separate pile. He then attempted to guess the second card, and the process continued until he had guessed at the identity of each of the twenty-five cards in the pack. On some occasions, the subject himself took the card from the pack, held it face downward, attempted to guess it, and then placed it in a second pile.

2 DT (*Down Through*). The pack was shuffled, cut, and placed face downward on the table. The subject attempted to guess the cards one by one, from the top, without disturbing the pack.

3. PT (Pure Telepathy). Here no cards or records of the targets were used; the aim was to study telepathy as distinct from clairvoyance. Thus, a second person, the agent, had to think of a symbol; but it was argued that if a pack of cards was used, the subject might obtain above-chance scores by clairvoyance. And so, the agent thought of a symbol that did not exist as a card in a pack or as an entry on a list. He thought of five of the ESP symbols in a particular order, and the subject called aloud his guesses. The agent made a record of each of the subject's calls and checked them for correctness as he recorded them.

In *Extra-Sensory Perception*, Rhine commented that success or failure depended very much on the conditions under which the tests were made, and he listed the following suggestions to those who might care to repeat his experiments.

1. The subject should have an active interest in the tests and be fairly free from strong bias or doubt. These would, of course, hinder effort and limit attention. An open-minded, experimental attitude is all that is required. Positive belief is naturally favorable but not necessary.

2. The preliminary tests should be entered into very informally, without much serious discussion as to techniques, or explanations or precautions. The more ado over techniques, the more inhibition is likely; and the more there is of explanations, the more likely is introspection to interfere. Playful informality is most favorable.

3. If possible to do so honestly, it is helpful to give encouragement for any little success but no extravagant praise is desirable, even over striking results. The point is that encouragement is helpful, apparently, but only if it does not lead to self-consciousness. If it does, it is quite ruinous. Many subjects begin well, become excited or self-conscious, and then do poorly.

4. Some begin more easily with PT [Pure Telepathy] and some with PC [Pure Clairvoyance]. It depends upon personality, I think, but I cannot explain it except to link sociability with PT preference. However, both conditions should be tried, following the subject's preference in the beginning.

5. It is highly important to let the subject have his own way, without restraint, at first. Later, he can be persuaded to allow changes, after he has gained confidence and discovered his way to ESP functioning. Even then it is better for him to have his way as far as experimental conditions can allow. It is a poor science that dictates conditions to Nature. It is a better one that follows up with its well-adapted controls and conditions.

6. It is wise not to express doubts or regrets. Discouragement seems to damage the delicate function of ESP. Here again no doubt personalities differ. One subject, I know, has worked in the face of doubt expressed; but she is exceptional in this.

7. Above all, one must not, like several investigators, stop with only 25 or 50 or even 100 trials per subject. Most of my good subjects did not do very well in the first 100. With few exceptions, the first 50 to 100 trials give the worst scores. With all my major subjects this is true. Several different occasions or sittings, too should be allowed, for there is with most subjects an adjustment phase at first that may take some time.

8. It is best at first to have the subject alone with the agent in PT and in PC to leave him alone entirely. If not, he may be inhibited from the start; but, once he has a start, he can gradually work back to other conditions. When he has observers present, the experimenter should do all he can to put the subject at ease.

9. Simple cards with 5 suits seem best as a compromise of several features of concern: easy calculation, easy recall, easy discrimination of images, etc.

10. Short runs are desirable, say 5 at a time, with a checkup after each 5. Then it is best to go casually and quietly on without too much discussion of results.

11. It is advisable not to bore or tire the subject. When he wants to stop, or even before he expressly wishes to, it is better to stop work.

12. It is best to try good friends for PT at first—or couples, single or married, who feel certain they have thought-transference; and, above all, to try those people who say they have had "psychic" experiences or whose ancestors conspicuously have had.

These are suggestions, not rules, for we do not yet know enough of the subject to lay down rules. They will help toward success, without endangering conclusions. One can always tighten up on conditions before drawing conclusions later. But any investigator must first of all get his phenomena to occur—or exhaust the reasonable possibilities in trying to.[3]

Linzmayer, the first of the high-scoring subjects, had been noticed as promising in the early 1930 tests. When tested again in 1931, he first produced a score of only 4 hits in 20 trials, which is exactly that of chance expectation. In the next series, made on May 21, 1931, he was far more successful achieving 25 hits in 45 trials with 9 of these hits on successive cards. However, the conditions in this test could hardly be considered stringent. Rhine took a card from a shuffled pack. After first looking at it, he held it face downward under his hand and tried to visualize the symbol. He did this rather than thinking of its name so that, as he put it, the "involuntary whispering ghost need not haunt us."

Ten days later, Linzmayer was given a further 535 trials, making a total of 600. Of these, 360 were made under conditions in which the experimenter knew the symbol being guessed (described as undifferentiated ESP, Telepathy and Clairvoyance); and 240 trials were made in which the symbol was unknown to anyone (described as Pure Clairvoyance Condition). In the overall 600 trials,

Linzmayer got 238 successes, and there are odds well over 10 million to 1 against this result arising by chance.

The conditions under which the tests were carried out are nowhere described in detail. The following report is, however, given of one test in which Linzmayer produced his most remarkable feat. Linzmayer and Rhine were seated in Rhine's car with the engine running. Linzmayer was leaning back so that he looked at only the roof of the car, and there were no mirrors or shiny surfaces to assist him in seeing the cards. Rhine held the pack out of sight, face down, and shuffled it several times during the series. He drew the card with his right hand, keeping it concealed as he leaned forward; then he tilted it a little, glanced at it, and laid it on a large record book resting on Linzmayer's knees. About 2 seconds after it was laid on the book, Linzmayer made his guess aloud. Rhine then said whether Linzmayer had been right or wrong and laid the card on the appropriate pile. The hits were counted and recorded "at the end of the 15 calls, here, and then at the end of each five calls after." On this occasion, Linzmayer was successful in 21 out of 25 trials. He also obtained 15 consecutive hits, the odds being 30 billion to 1 against the chance achievement of such a feat.

Linzmayer obtained significantly above-chance results with each of the three experimental techniques given on page 88, but he was unsuccessful when tested with the cards at a distance from him. Eventually, his results started declining until, at the finish, he was unable to score above chance.

Charles E. Stuart, the second of the high-scoring subjects, was an assistant in the psychology department. He was successful both as a subject and an experimenter with the BT technique, but this was in part due to the fact that in most of his observations he used himself as subject. He was unsuccessful when tested with the DT and PT techniques.

Following a successful result in one of the early exploratory experiments, Stuart started making ESP tests in the autumn of 1931. In a total of 7,500 unwitnessed trials carried out on himself under conditions that are not stated, he obtained 1,815 hits as compared with the expected number of 1,500. There are enormous odds against this result arising by chance.

Hubert E. Pearce, the divinity student, was by far the most versatile of all the high-scoring subjects and produced high above-chance scores when tested with each of the three techniques. He was successful with the BT and DT techniques only when seated at a table with the cards, but he succeeded in making high scores with the PT technique when at a distance of 8 to 30 feet from the agent. His most impressive result was in an experiment, later known as the Pearce-Pratt experiment (see Chapter 10), being conducted during the writing of *Extra-Sensory Perception*. Here, he obtained high scores in sitting after sitting when he was situated more than 100 yards from the cards.

The results for the remaining five high-scoring subjects were presented as a group in *Extra-Sensory Perception*. These subjects were all psychologists: George Zirkle and Sarah Ownbey being graduate assistants, while May Frances Turner, June Bailey, and T. Coleman Cooper were students in the psychology department.

George Zirkle was unsuccessful with the BT and DT techniques, but when tested with the PT technique, he averaged 11 hits per 25 trials over 3,400 trials. On several occasions he obtained 22 hits in 25 trials, and on one occasion he got an unbroken run of 26 successes. Zirkle was also able to obtain high scores when at distances of up to 10 feet from the agent when PT was used.

Miss Ownbey resembled Stuart in that she was successful both as an investigator and as a subject. Like Stuart, she really succeeded as a subject only when tested by herself. She carried out the first ESP test at Duke University in which the cards were at a considerable distance from the subject.

Miss Turner, the subject in the above long-distance test, Coleman Cooper, and Miss Bailey were all successful when using BT and PT, but obtained only moderate success with the DT technique.

The combined data from these last five subjects gave an average score of 8.4 hits in each run of 25 over a total of 26,950 trials. The odds against such a result arising by chance are astronomical.

Weaknesses in the Experimental Techniques

BT has the obvious danger that the subject may recognize the cards by marks on their backs or sides; in addition, if he handles them, he may recognize a particular card by its feel.

In 1937, when ESP cards were first supplied to the public, it was shown that they could be read quite easily from their backs and sides (see pages 100–101). It is thus of considerable significance that subjects could obtain above-chance scores with the basic technique only when seated close to the cards, and that as soon as they were moved away, their scores dropped to the chance level.

A second difficulty that arises with this technique is that the cards may tend to cut at a particular symbol. It was mentioned in *Extra-Sensory Perception* that some of the early cards were found to be unsatisfactory because one of the symbols was printed on a slightly larger card than the others. Such a pack would tend to cut so that the larger one would fall toward the bottom and one of the four remaining symbols toward the top of the pack. During the shuffling, cards of a particular size might also tend to come together, so that it would be possible to obtain extra hits in other positions than at the top and bottom of the pack.

With BT, the subject's score was checked, on some occasions, at the end of 25 guesses (BT25), on other occasions after 5(BT5). It is significant that in BT25, the hits tended to arise in the first five and last five cards of the pack. Details are not given of the scores on the first and last cards, but they were clearly very high, since in 60 runs of the BT25 type, Pearce got 52 of his last calls correct.

Experiments with Pearce using BT took the following form: Pearce shuffled the pack, since he claimed it gave more real contact, and the observer cut it. Pearce would then pick up the cards and remove the top one, keeping the pack and the removed card face down on the table. The observer would record the call after either 5 or 25 calls—the two conditions being used about equally. The cards would be turned over and checked against the calls recorded in the book. The subject was asked to help in the checking by laying them off. For the next run, another pack of cards would be used.

When the BT5 technique was employed, correct scores followed a cyclical effect, being the highest for positions 2, 7, 12, 17, and 22; second highest for positions 1, 6, 11, 16, and 21; and relatively low for the remaining positions. Since, after each 5 guesses, the cards were sometimes replaced in the pack, which was shuffled and cut before the next 5 were recorded, this effect could have arisen because particular symbols tended to be brought to the top and bottom of the pack.

The down-through technique suffers from the same drawbacks as the BT25 procedure, and again it is significant that when it was employed, the subject scored most of his hits on the first and last 5 cards. Details are not given of the scoring rate at each position in the pack, but it is recorded that in 40 of Pearce's DT runs, he correctly called 33 last cards. It also appears that the DT procedure was partially originated by Pearce himself.[4]

The salient question in connection with both the basic and down-through techniques is what would happen if the cards were no longer visible to the subject? In one experiment, Pearce was tested at three distances: across a table, at 8 to 12 feet from the cards, and at 28 to 30 feet from the cards. Using both the BT and DT techniques, the scores were significantly above chance when Pearce was close to the cards, and with both techniques, scores dropped when he was at any distance from them.

The pure-telepathy technique is by far the most unsatisfactory of the three. Anyone who tries to carry out the duties of the experimenter will find them extremely difficult and tiring to perform. The possibility that errors will arise is large under these conditions, and there is no check on them if they are made.

The procedure adopted was for the experimenter to think of 5 Zener symbols in any order he liked, and then concentrate his attention on each one as its turn came while the subject made his guess. The experimenter, after signaling the subject with a key that he was to say his guess, noted down the guess and whether it was correct. After the first five targets had been guessed, another 5 would be preselected in some order, usually different from the first, and the process continued.

Under these conditions, high scores would be expected to arise owing to the manner, already discussed, in which people behave when they think they are generating a random series.

Also, each run of five trials tends to contain all 5 of the symbols arranged in a fresh order each time. Under these conditions, the subject's chances of obtaining high scores are greatly increased. In such cases there are 120 possible arrangements of the 5 different symbols, and the subject would expect to achieve 5 hits once in each 120 attempts, whereas in a true random distribution, the number of arrangements of the 5 symbols is 3,125 (5^5). If the experimenter tended to include all 5 symbols in each run, and the subject tended to avoid repeating his calls, the mean score would be augmented considerably.

George Zirkle, who was able to obtain high scores only when using the PT technique and only when tested by Miss Ownbey—who later became his wife—averaged 10.7 hits per 25 guesses in 5,025 trials. An extraordinary feature of these experiments was that at no time during the 5,025 trials did anyone appear to consider the possibility that the targets generated by Miss Ownbey could be influenced by her hearing Zirkle's calls, or even that she might make mistakes in her recording. A check could easily have been made. Miss Ownbey could have been provided with a list of symbols arranged in random order, and one of the faculty members could have recorded Zirkle's calls. The purely academic point whether Zirkle was displaying telepathy or clairvoyance could have been forgotten for the time being, and, in any case, Zirkle had already shown that he was unable to obtain above-chance results when tested for clairvoyance.

Looking at the results of the experiments and bearing in mind the pitfalls of the techniques employed, several features cannot but strike the critic.

It was reported that placing the subject away from the cards removed high scores, except when the PT technique was used. Since the obvious weakness of BT and DT lies in the possibility of the subject receiving sensory cues from the cards, it is to be expected that subjects would be unable to maintain high scores in the event of their using such cues when placed at any distance from the cards.

In the case of PT, distance would not affect the calling habits of the experimenter. The subject and agent could be a hundred yards apart, with a telephone link for the agent to hear the subject's call, and this would not remove the inherent weakness of the experimental technique.

Rhine commented after studying the results:

> These bring out the point of the difference between PT and BT results with distance, and their similarity at close range, suggesting that while PT can clearly be done at such distances, it may be that BT may not. It is still more strongly suggested that DT may be limited to close range.[5]

This observation fits precisely with what would be expected if the subjects utilized sensory cues with the BT and DT techniques. With the DT technique, these cues would be weakest, since only the sides of the cards, other than the top card, are visible to the percipient.

A Long Distance Experiment

While BT and DT experiments with the subject at a distance from the cards showed no evidence for ESP, one other test was reported in which the result was of quite a different nature. This was a series of runs in which Miss Turner was situated 250 miles from the cards at Lake Junaluska, North Carolina, while the experimenter, Miss Ownbey, was at the Parapsychology Laboratory in Durham.

Each day, Miss Turner was to record 25 guesses at prescribed times and to send a record of her guesses directly to Rhine. The agent was likewise to send a record of her targets each day directly to Rhine. There were 3 series of tests. In the first, 8 runs of 25 trials each were completed. The first 3 made on June 30, July 5, and July 7, 1933, resulted in scores of 19 out of 25, 16 out of 25, and 16 out of 25; the probability that these scores arose by chance is fantastically remote. Rhine states in *Extra-Sensory Perception* that it was then discovered that Miss Turner's record had not gone directly to him as planned, but that it had been transmitted through Miss Ownbey. Twelve days later, tests were resumed and further runs were made on July 19, 20, 21, 22, and 24. On these days, both records were sent directly to Rhine, but the scores were not now significantly above the chance level.

Further tests, at a distance of 300 miles, were made on August 22, 24, 29, and 31, but again the scores did not differ significantly from chance expectation.

In spite of the lapse in the experimental conditions during the first three days and the remarkable scores that emerged, Rhine did not suspect either lady of duplicity. He commented that the subject's recordings were unmistakably in Miss Turner's handwriting and in ink with no evident changes. He then came to the conclusion that the young ladies had not been deceiving him. However, it should be noted that if Miss Ownbey had wished to deceive Rhine, she would merely have written out her record of the target series after seeing Miss Turner's guesses.

General Observations on the Experiments

The scores obtained by each of the high-scoring subjects were such that no one could deny that some factor other than chance was involved. Rhine discussed five alternative hypotheses to ESP: chance, fraud, incompetence, unconscious sensory perception, and rational inference, and came to the conclusion that he had eliminated the possibility of each of them and that ESP stood without a serious opposing hypothesis. Even a superficial examination makes it difficult, however, to understand why the alternative hypotheses should have been so summarily dismissed.

It is clear that there can be little dispute about the inapplicability of the hypothesis that the high scores were the result of chance. Some criticisms have been made of Rhine's statistical treatment, but the result is undisputed. The method he employed was suitable for randomly distributed targets; that is, those that would arise if the card was returned to the pack after each guess and, after shuffling, a fresh card was selected as the next target. But since the packs of cards Rhine used contained exactly five of each symbol, a *closed pack,* the distribution of targets was not random. The use of a closed pack would not, however, affect the conclusions very much. Whether the odds of Pearce's result are 10^{100} to 1 or merely 10^{90} to 1 against chance is quite irrelevant.

The question of statistical analysis does arise when the results obtained from experiments where PT was employed are considered. Here, the subject guessed at five symbols arranged in a particular order, after which he was presented with five more targets consisting of a new order of symbols. If the experimenter merely produced the symbols in different orders for each run, the subject's chances of high scores would be considerably increased when compared with the possibility of high scores when guessing a randomly generated series of symbols.

The most remarkable feature of Rhine's discussion of the fraud hypothesis was that he made no mention of the first three runs in the Turner-Ownbey experiment. Whether or not he thought that there had been any tampering with the records, this case was highly relevant and should have been discussed.

Rhine considered two possibilities: fraud on the part of the subjects who tested themselves, and fraud both by subjects and experimenters. In the case of subjects who tested themselves, there was no check other than a comparison of scores obtained when they were alone with those made when witnesses were present. In most cases, the results agreed, but there was an exception in the case of Miss Ownbey, who tested herself using the down-through technique. She obtained most of her hits in the middle of the run, whereas all the other subjects who had been witnessed obtained most of theirs at the start and end of the run when this technique was used. Also, Miss Ownbey, who averaged 8.4 hits when unwitnessed, was unable to obtain a result that was statistically above the chance level when an observer was present.

When Rhine discussed the competence of the researchers and observers, he concluded that the experimental conditions had been steadily tightened up and pointed out that no adequate loophole had been discovered. His final conclusion was that the hypothesis of incompetence would find "few adherents and no justification"; but the critic cannot but be struck with the numerous occasions when a simple test on the part of an investigator would have saved a great deal of argument after the event.

It is possible that the Pearce-Pratt experiment was intended to satisfy some of these criticisms, but that does not make it any easier to understand how the investigators could have gone on for week after week blindly trusting a rather weak experimental design. When, for example, it was found that Pearce could not obtain above-chance scores with the down-through procedure when more than a yard away from the cards, why was he not tested at close range, completely screened from the cards until he had recorded all his guesses? If this was tried, no details are given. Pearce was tested with the cards *held behind a screen,* but in these tests, it transpires that Pearce himself held the cards in this position and handled each card as he guessed it.

The manner in which normal sensory cues may be employed by subjects has already been touched on. Whether such cues are used unconsciously or consciously does not affect the argument very much. Rhine raised the point that Pearce did not usually look at the pack before he called his guess, although it seems that he occasionally glanced absent-mindedly at the pack. Rhine also mentioned that Pearce's favorite posture was with eyes closed, sometimes with his hand on his eyes or forehead. It should be noted that if anyone wished to look at the backs of the cards without making this too obvious, he could do so by half-shutting his eyes or by screening them with his hands. A person with half-closed eyes can be facing away from the cards with his eyes turned to them, and an observer would not necessarily be aware of the fact. A photograph of Rhine testing Pearce with the down-through technique shows that Pearce had every opportunity to study the top card and the sides of others in the pack.

Rhine also discussed unconscious whispering cues, and seemed to consider that to have a fan going or to be in a car with the motor running was sufficient safeguard against them.

The last hypothesis, that of rational inference, arises, for example, with the BT5 technique. Since the subject sees the targets after each five trials, he is in a position after the first 20 calls to know exactly which symbols are left in the pack. He will not know the order in which they will arise, but except in the case where exactly 4 of each symbol have come up in the first 20 cards, he is in a position to obtain extra hits. Thus if the wavy-lined symbol has arisen only 3 times in the first 20 calls, the subject has merely to call it for each of the last 5, and he is bound to obtain 2 hits. Rhine himself pointed out that the subjects obtained high scores in the last 5 trials when the BT5 technique was used. He also discussed rational inference in relation to PT, but the essential points were completely missed. It can easily be demonstrated that, by employing rational inference, it is possible for a subject to obtain extremely high scores in this type of experiment.

In view of the conditions under which most of the results reported in *Extra-Sensory Perception* were obtained, it is difficult to see how the experiments can be considered as other than exploratory The final study with Pearce at a distance from the cards was, however, of quite a different order from those previously carried out. In these tests, since he was a hundred yards or more from the cards, sensory cues were eliminated, and from the other details of the experimental conditions, it appeared that Pearce was at last having to perform under reasonably strict conditions. The Pearce-Pratt series, has remained to this day one of the few ESP experiments that the majority of parapsychologists agree to call conclusive; it will be considered in detail in Chapter 10.

Notes

1. J. B. Rhine, "An Investigation of a Mind Reading Horse," *Journal of Abnormal and Social Psychology*, 23 (1929).
2. J. B. Rhine, *Extra-Sensory Perception* (Boston: Bruce Humphries, 1964). Reprinted by permission of Faber & Faber Ltd., and J. B. Rhine. Page numbers that follow refer to the edition published in England (London: Faber & Faber).
3. *Ibid*, p. 229.
4. *Ibid*, p. 83.
5. *Ibid*, pp. 113–14.

9
The Years of Controversy 1934–1940

The publication of *Extra-Sensory Perception* aroused enormous interest among the general public, and ESP became a household word; but at the same time, the book was criticized severely. It was natural that the main onslaught should come from psychologists and that some of those reading about the experiments should wish to see whether they could get the same results for themselves. Since, according to Rhine, one in five of the population could display ESP, a confirmatory test must have seemed a relatively simple matter to arrange.

Attempts at Repeating the Duke Experiments

The first attempt to reproduce the results was reported in 1936 by W. S. Cox of the psychology department at Princeton University. Prospective subjects were told about the work at Duke, emphasis being put on the positive nature of the scores obtained there, with the aim of putting the subjects in a favorable frame of mind for the experiment. Cox noted that the majority of his subjects displayed a belief in extrasensory perception and that many of those who were skeptical about it eventually did not participate.

A total of 132 subjects produced 25,064 trials in which they attempted to guess the suits of playing cards; but there was no evidence for ESP. The data were then examined to see whether any persons displayed an aptitude for ESP. Cox's conclusion was:

It is evident from the above results and computations that there is no evidence of extrasensory perception either in the "average man" of the group investigated or in any particular individual of that group. The discrepancy between these results and those obtained by Rhine is due either to uncontrollable factors in experimental procedure or to the difference in the subjects.[1]

Other psychologists attempted to confirm Rhine's findings. E. T. Adams of Colgate University reported the results of 30,000 trials in which 30 subjects were individually tested;[2] J. C. Crumbaugh of Southern Methodist University tested over 100 subjects and recorded a total of 75,600 trials;[3] Raymond Willoughby of Brown University tested 9 subjects and recorded 41,250 trials;[4] and C. P. and J. H. Heinlein of Johns Hopkins amassed 127,500 trials.[5] The results obtained at Duke University were not confirmed in any of these investigations. On the contrary, it was found that subjects could not score significantly above the chance level when sensory cues were excluded.

Attempts to repeat the experiments were also made in England by Britain's best known parapsychologist, Dr. S. G. Soal.[6] Between 1934 and 1939, after testing 160 persons for telepathy or clairvoyance and recording 128,350 guesses, Soal obtained a score that was at the chance level, and only one of his subjects, Mrs. Gloria Stewart, produced a result that was in any way out of the ordinary. Her score had odds greater than 100 to 1 against chance occurrence, but as 160 persons had been tested, it was to be expected that at least one of them would produce such a score.

Further reports appeared in which Rhine's results were not confirmed, but on the other hand, several investigations were reported in which the subjects had no difficulty in displaying ESP. It is significant, however, that of the 36 experimental reports supporting the existence of ESP published in the period 1934–40, only 5 were later assessed by members of the Duke Parapsychology Laboratory as being controlled sufficiently rigorously to provide conclusive evidence.

Criticism of the ESP Cards

In 1936, ESP cards were put on sale to the general public in the United States. On the package was printed "ESP Cards for testing Extra-Sensory Perception, developed in Parapsychological Laboratory at Duke University, patent applied for by J. B. Rhine." It was soon noted by the psychologists R. H. Thouless, B. F. Skinner, and L. D. Wolfe, among others, that under certain lighting conditions the symbols on the faces of the cards could be seen by examining their backs. One prominent critic, J. L. Kennedy of Stanford, included a photograph to illustrate this point in an article he published in 1938.[7]

In a note published in the May 1938 *Journal* of the Society for Psychical Research, C. V. C. Herbert, who was then Research Officer of the Society, reported an investigation he had made of the cards.[8] He noted that they were of two types: the first consisted of playing-card blanks on which the symbols were impressed by means of rubber stamps or stencils; the second type was professionally manufactured. It seems that, some two years before, two packs of the first type had been sent to Thouless as examples of the actual cards used in the tests at Duke University. He found that with one pack it was possible to detect the symbol on a card's face by scrutinizing its back when it was held so that light was reflected from it. With the light from a window, 9 out of a pack of 25 cards were identified in this way, and with a 60-watt lamp hanging from the ceiling, 14 cards were so identified.

The second type was that made available to the American public. When these were held at a certain angle, it was found that the symbol on almost every card could be read easily from its back. It was further found that the pattern on the backs extended to the edges, so that the identities of some cards could be detected when the sides of the pack were inspected. Thus, four of the cards marked with a circle were identified by the white mark on their sides where the cutting machine had sliced through a particular part of the pattern printed on the back.

Replying to Herbert, Rhine commented that the cards used in the earlier years were cut from heavy, opaque stock and carefully inspected. He also stated that no conclusions about extrasensory perception were published unless supplementary tests had been made in which sensory contact with the backs of the cards was eliminated. But homemade cards cut from heavy stock are all the more likely to be recognizable from their sides, and it is difficult to see, after reading the account in *Extra-Sensory Perception,* how it can be said that sensory contact was eliminated. Screening cards with the hand, for example, hardly eliminates the possibility of sensory contact, since the back of the card that is to follow the one being held is visible.

The experiments in which subjects, after obtaining high scores when seated at a table with the cards in front of them, were moved away from the cards, merely demonstrated the manner in which ESP scores dropped to the chance level as soon as it was made difficult for the subject to utilize sensory cues. It is possible that the supplementary tests to which Rhine referred were of the pure-telepathy type, in which cards were not used, and the tests on Pearce at distances of 100 and 250 yards. These excluded the possibility of the subject directly using cues from the cards, but it must be confirmed whether they were satisfactory in other respects. In the early experiments with Pearce, his scores certainly dropped in a remarkably consistent manner as soon as he could not see or feel the cards.

J. L. Kennedy's Review of ESP Experiments

In 1939, Kennedy reviewed in detail the experimental work on extrasensory perception carried out up to 1938.[9] He started by listing and discussing the known sources of experimental error. These were:

1. Minimal and Subliminal sensory cues.

      a. Kinesthetic and Tactual cues
      b. Visual cues
      c. Auditory cues

2. "Mental Habits" and preferences.

3. Recording errors.

In a separate section he discussed the statistical methods used and the effects of selection of data on the experimental results.

Kennedy concluded his review by isolating those experiments in which the experimental conditions eliminated the possibility of all the above forms of error. He was left with three "inexplicable" experiments, about which he wrote: "Eventual explanation of these results appears to the present writer to rest on an entirely different basis than the foregoing ESP data."[10]

The first of these three experiments was an investigation by Lucien Warner, a research fellow, assisted by Mildred Raible, a psychologist, both at Duke University.[11] The subject was in a ground floor room, and two experimenters were in a locked room on the first floor in an opposite wing of the same house. One of the experimenters selected the target at each trial by drawing a card from a pack that was shuffled after each trial. The subject signaled the experimenters when the next target was to be selected by pressing a key that operated a light in the experimenters' room. Only 250 trials were recorded, and the average score was 9.3 hits per 25 trials.

Kennedy noted two aspects of this experiment. First, the recording was not completely independent, since the flash of light in the experimenters' room could be varied in duration by the subject and thus provide a possible cue. Second, there were five different symbols in the target series, but the experimental record showed that two of these arose more frequently than the other three. A test showed that the observed distribution would be expected to arise by chance in one out of fifty such experiments. In view of this fact, the method by which the targets were selected was suspect. For example, if after the pack was shuffled, it had been cut before each card was drawn, a bias could easily have manifested itself if there were variations in sizes of the cards bearing the different symbols. The report did not give full details of the parts played by the two experimenters, but it would appear that further tests could have been made with little difficulty, since 250 trials would take about two hours. Even so, further results were not reported, and the subject who displayed these remarkable powers of clairvoyance sank into anonymity.

The second experiment Kennedy isolated was reported in 1937 by B. F. Riess, Professor of Psychology at Hunter College, New York.[12] His subject lived about a quarter of a mile from Riess's home, and the experiment was conducted between the two houses. Starting at 9 P.M., Riess exposed cards at one minute intervals from a freshly shuffled pack lying on his desk, and the subject recorded her guesses at the same times in her home. Two packs of 25 cards were exposed each day in this manner. The very high scores obtained startled even the parapsychologists. Thus, the score in 25 trials gradually built up over successive days until over 20 hits were being obtained, and scores were consistently high day after day. The hits per pack for the last ten days were 17, 18, 19, 20, 20, 20, 19, 20, 21, and 21. Altogether, 53 runs were completed, yielding the most remarkable scoring ever observed in an ESP experiment. Then, after a break in the testing, further runs were made, and the scores dropped to the chance level. The next 10 runs yielded 2, 4, 7, 12, 7, 5, 4, 3, 5, and 4 hits per pack. Even so, the odds against the overall score arising by chance have been assessed at greater than 10^{700} to 1. Since Kennedy made his review, further information about this experiment has become available. It appears that after Riess had been openly skeptical about ESP in discussion with his psychology classes, one of his students volunteered to produce a friend with high ESP. This friend turned out to be a young woman who had the reputation of being an amateur psychic, and it was she who had acted as the subject for the experiment. After it was over, she refused to take part in further tests under more strict conditions.

Riess kept his records of the card order in the drawer of a desk that was left unlocked during the day, and he did not receive the record of the subject's calls until the day after the session. A servant employed in Riess's home was known to the students, and the records were easily accessible to anyone in the house. Also, it seems that, at times, a period of a week or longer elapsed before the two lists were compared. Riess himself has written: "In view of the many uncontrolled factors, the data as presented are to be thought of as suggestive only."[13] Thus, this experiment cannot now be considered as in any way inexplicable.

The third inexplicable experiment noted by Kennedy was the Pearce-Pratt series, but here Kennedy was not satisfied with the information given about the method of checking the scores. At that time, very meager details of the experiment had, in fact, been revealed, and it was not until 1954 that a complete account was published.

Kennedy commented on Rhine's suggestions for experimenters as follows:

Attitudes of expectancy of good scores, playful informality and positive suggestibility in the subject seem best to help the unnoticed or unconscious use of sensory cues. But it is these conditions at work in the experimenter or recorder which seem to be most important in attempting to understand the production of ESP. It should be noted further that the encouragement of playful informality by the experimenter involves the condition of split attention which is a favorable if not an absolutely necessary condition for unconscious error production.[14]

Kennedy suggested that the following controls should be present in ESP experiments:

1. Distance or shielding sufficient to eliminate sensory cues.
2. Calls and cards should be recorded by two different persons and checked by comparing the two records.

3. To produce a random distribution of targets, a tested method should be used.

4. A limit to the number of trials should be established before the experiment begins, and comparisons of records might well be postponed until after the end of the experiment.

5. To assure objectivity, there should be no possibility of fraud on the part of the subject. This might involve testing high-scoring subjects in several different laboratories.

In classifying experiments as inexplicable, Kennedy had not excluded the possibility of fraud: he merely implied that the experiments were not explicable in terms of the sources of error he had discussed in his article and that fraud was the only remaining explanation other than ESP.

The ESP Symposium of the American Psychological Association

In September 1938, during its annual meeting at Columbus, Ohio, the American Psychological Association held a symposium on the methods of ESP research. Various criticisms raised in the past were discussed, and the experimental methods in use at that time at Duke University were considered. According to Soal and Bateman,[15] Professor Chester Kellogg, one of the most outspoken critics of ESP, told Rhine that if he went on with the methods he was then using, he would get no more extrasensory perception.

After the meeting, a committee was set up under the chairmanship of S. B. Sells, a psychologist at Columbia University, to review and criticize reports of ESP experiments. A group of eminent psychologists formed the committee, including Lillian Dick, J. J. Gibson, E. R. Hilgard, J. L. Kennedy, and R. R. Willoughby.

Appraisal of ESP Experiments by Members of the Parapsychology Laboratory

In 1940, the Duke parapsychologists published their own appraisal of ESP research in *Extra-Sensory Perception after Sixty Years*.

The expressed aim of the authors was to survey the published reports and to assess them in terms of the criticisms that had been raised. Over the years, thirty-five counter-hypotheses to ESP had been put forward to account for the scores obtained in the tests. The authors stated that the final step was to determine whether there was a remainder of evidence—an inexplicable portion of the summarized results of the ESP research—that could not be met by all the hypotheses combined.

Each of the experiments reported since 1882 was first considered in relation to each of the thirty-five counter-hypotheses. Those that survived this examination were then listed, and it was pointed out how each of the counter-hypotheses could be shown to be inapplicable. A total of 145 experiments carried out between 1882 and 1939 were assessed, of which the first two were the investigations of the Creery sisters and of Smith and Blackburn discussed in Chapter 4.

Only six experiments survived after being checked against the counter-hypotheses, and these were then arranged in order of merit. Kennedy had, with reservations, included only one Duke experiment among the three he considered to be inexplicable. The Duke critics included three of their own experiments among their selected six. These three were: the Pratt-Woodruff experiment (considered first in quality), which had not been published at the time Kennedy made his review (see Chapter 11); the Pearce-Pratt experiment (considered third best; see Chapter 10); the Rhine-Ownbey series (considered fourth best; see pages 105-108).

The other three experiments were the Warner experiment (second on the list); the Riess experiment (fifth on the list; see pages 102-103); and in last place, an experiment reported by Ernest Taves and Gardner Murphy, psychologists at Columbia University. This last experiment did not yield an above-chance score and will not, therefore, be discussed any further.

The Turner-Ownbey Series

The presence of the Rhine-Ownbey series no doubt evoked some surprise in parapsychological circles, since no one had heard of it before. It is described in *Extra-Sensory Perception after Sixty Years* as follows:

> A fourth series meeting successfully all the requirements made by the combined counter-hypotheses is the following long-distance test on pure telepathy reported by Rhine and conducted by him in conjunction with Miss Ownbey (Mrs. George Zirkle) as co-experimenter. The shorter of the three distances that obtained in the three series was 165 miles. A total of 650 trials was reported in 1934 (238) under these conditions, with independent records turned over to (mailed or personally delivered to) Rhine by Miss Ownbey and the subject (Miss Turner or Mr. Zirkle).[16]

In Appendix 20, in which the scores for each session are given, it is stated only that the "Agent and Percipient mailed the records to Rhine."

From examination of the scores and dates on which the tests were made, it seems that the Rhine-Ownbey series consisted of the Turner-Ownbey series combined with a similar long-distance test in which George Zirkle acted as the percipient and Miss Ownbey as the experimenter. The tests on Zirkle consisted of 13 runs made during August and September of 1933 with a distance of 165 miles between the percipient and the cards, but the score achieved by Zirkle was not significantly above the chance level.

It will be remembered that the first three runs of the Turner-Ownbey series were sent to Miss Ownbey before being given to Rhine. The score of both percipients (Turner and Zirkle) combined in 650 trials was 177 hits as compared to the chance expectation of 130 hits; the odds are about 1 million to 1 against this result arising by chance. If, however, the scores obtained in the first three days of the Turner-Ownbey series are omitted, it is found that in 23 runs a total of 126 hits was obtained, compared to the chance-expectation score of 115 hits. Here the odds are 3 to 1, and it is unnecessary to invoke ESP to account for these scores. Thus, the result of the Rhine-Ownbey series is entirely dependent on the scores achieved during the first three days of the Turner-Ownbey series, when the conditions certainly did not eliminate the possibility that Miss Ownbey influenced the result of the experiment.

It is therefore of considerable interest to see how the authors of *Extra-Sensory Perception after Sixty Years* managed to cope, when discussing the experiments, with three of the counter-hypotheses. Remarkably, no hint was given in the discussion of the unfortunate lapse in the conditions during the first three days of the experiment, although it would appear to be difficult to provide a full discussion of the counter-hypotheses without mentioning that lapse.

The reply to counter-hypotheses 21, "the data must have been tampered with by the subjects, assistants, or other persons," was:

> The short series which make up this work are the only ones of their kind and are sufficiently unique to be easily remembered by both E's [experimenters]. They were summarized in record books and all data reported by one E, both to the other E and to the subject. The presence of two E's, together with the independent records, and the easy recall of such unique tests, is sufficient guarantee against these hypotheses.[17]

The two experimenters referred to are Rhine and Ownbey; the subject was either Turner or Zirkle. It is agreed that Rhine had no evidence that Miss Ownbey tampered with the records, but some mention might have been made of the fact that she could have done so, and that the experimental result was not inconsistent with her having done so.

The reply to counter-hypothesis 27, "the results are due to loose conditions and poor observation by the experimenter," ran:

> Distance excludes a multitude of conceivable experimental weaknesses in telepathic tests. The only criticisms on this work bear on the questions (a) of its *p*-value, the probability of the result arising by chance, and (b) of possible pattern and preference similarity. Both are met by the data of Table 13, p. 127, giving back-check and cross-check averages on this work.[18]

The reply to counter-hypothesis 30, "general untrustworthiness (moral or psychopathic) of the experimenters explains the results," was:

If over-enthusiasm or dishonesty are back of these results, *it is difficult to account for the striking decline in scoring level.* The main extra-chance results occurred during the first few days of the series . . . and the rest of the scores were but little above chance. *There was no change of instructions that might account for the decline:* only a shortening of the inter-trial interval from 5 to 3 minutes. *Any act of bad faith would of necessity have involved the collusion of one E with the other or with the S*[subject]. While an instance of this character is yet to be encountered in academic research, its possibility cannot, of course, be flatly denied. But again, to take the collusion hypothesis seriously throws the burden upon the group of confirmatory E's as a whole, and the mutual support of these must supply the answer needed.

That is to say, Ownbey and Turner, or Ownbey and Rhine, might be regarded as conspirators to deceive the world regarding ESP much more easily than could the combination of Ownbey and Rhine, Pratt and Woodruff, Warner and Raible, and Pratt and Rhine (to speak only of the above mentioned names). The notion of such wholesale conspiracy would be to most students more fantastic than the ESP hypothesis.[19]

These comments contain three statements, which I have put within quotation marks, each of which is misleading.

1. "It is difficult to account for the striking decline in scoring level." If the readers of *Extra-Sensory Perception after Sixty Years* had been informed that the records were not sent directly to Rhine during the first three high-scoring sessions and that they were sent directly to him after this, there would have been no difficulty accounting for the decline.

2. "There was no change of instructions that might account for the decline." But there was a change in the *procedure* after the third day that coincided with the sudden decline in the score.

3. "Any act of bad faith would of necessity have involved the collusion of one E with the other or with the S." This statement would be true if the original instructions had been followed, but in view of what happened during the first 3 sessions, it is not true. Miss Ownbey could have intercepted the mail and completed her record after seeing Miss Turner's record.

Subsequent published accounts of the Turner-Ownbey series make no mention of the unfortunate lapse during the first three runs. Thus, in *Parapsychology: Frontier Science of the Mind* by Rhine and Pratt, published in 1957, the series is described with reference to *Extra-Sensory Perception after Sixty Years,* rather than to *Extra-Sensory Perception,* which did note the one important point about the experiment.

In 1975, John L. Randall, in his *Parapsychology and the Nature of Life—A Scientific Appraisal,*[20] referred to the Turner-Ownbey experiment as follows:

"The most staggering result of all was an average of 10.1 hits per run obtained over a distance of 250 miles in July 1933." Randall raised one criticism of the experiment i.e. that Miss Ownbey may not have produced a random series (which is hardly very relevant) and dismissed it. He then concluded "It therefore seems reasonable to accept the Ownbey work as evidence for the operation of ESP over large distances."[21]

He made no mention of the lapse in the experimental conditions or of the fact that above chance results were only obtained for the first three runs of the series and fell to the chance level immediately the experimental conditions were made more foolproof. Randall presumably knew of this criticism since he had read my earlier book and included it in his list of references. A further feature of Randall's account is that he refers to the "staggering 10.1 hits per run achieved by the percipient," but in fact she achieved an average of 17 hits per run, for those first three runs. This is one of the most remarkable performances in the history of ESP research.

The August before the ESP symposium of the 1938 meeting of the American Psychological Association, an experiment had been carried out as part of the requirements for a higher degree by J. L. Woodruff, then an undergraduate student in the psychology department at Duke. In this experiment, a significant above-chance score had been obtained by a group of 42 subjects. The experiment as it stood could not be considered other than exploratory, and it would certainly not have impressed the critics who were present at the Psychological Association meeting. In October 1938, immediately after the meeting, a further experiment based on Woodruff's work was started. It was called Series B, and Pratt participated as second experimenter, with much more effective control conditions in force. Both for parapsychologists and their critics, the Pratt-Woodruff experiment has been regarded as the best of the card guessing investigations producing evidence for ESP carried out in the United States. The other investigation, as has been noted, regarded as conclusive by members of the Parapsychology Laboratory, is the Pearce-Pratt experiment.

These are both of quite a different order from the earlier tests carried out at Duke University, and they will be discussed in detail in the next two chapters.

Notes

1. W. S. Cox, "An Experiment in ESP," *Journal of Experimental Psychology*, 12, 4 (1936): 437.
2. E. T. Adams, "A Summary of Some Negative Experiments," *Journal of Parapsychology*, 2, 3 (1938): 232–36.
3. J. C. Crumbaugh, "An Experimental Study of Extra-Sensory Perception," (Master's Thesis, Southern Methodist University, 1938).
4. R. R. Willoughby, "Further Card-Guessing Experiments," *Journal of General Psychology*, 18 (1938): 3–13.
5. C. P. Heinlein and J. H. Heinlein, "Critique of the Premises and Statistical Methodology of Parapsychology," *Journal of Psychology*, 5 (1938): 135–48.

6. Soal and Bateman, *Modern Experiments in Telepathy*, pp. 135–48.
7. J. L. Kennedy, "The Visual Cues from the Backs of ESP Cards," *Journal of Psychology*, 6 (1938): 149–53.
8. C. V. C. Herbert, "Experiments in Extra-Sensory Perception: 1.A. Notes on Types of Zener Cards," *Journal of the Society for Psychical Research*, 30, 545 (1938): 215–18.
9. J. L. Kennedy, *Psychological Bulletin* (1938).
10. *Ibid*, p 94.
11. L. Warner, "A Test Case," *Journal of Parapsychology*, 1, 4 (1937): 234–38.
12. B. F. Reiss, "A Case of High Scores in Card Guessing at a Distance," *Journal of Parapsychology*, 1, 4 (1937): 260–63.
13. *Ibid*, p. 263.
14. J. L. Kennedy, *Psychological Bulletin* (1939): p. 91.
15. Soal and Bateman, *Modern Experiments in Telepathy*, p. 49.
16. Pratt, et al., *Extra-Sensory Perception after Sixty Years*, p. 163.
17. *Ibid*, p. 165.
18. *Ibid*.
19. *Ibid*, pp. 165, 166.
20. J. L. Randall, *Parapsychology and the Nature of Life: A Scientific Appraisal* (Souvenir Press, 1975).
21. *Ibid*, p. 82.

10
The Pearce-Pratt Experiment

Hubert E. Pearce had been acting as a subject in ESP experiments for more than a year before he took part in the Pearce-Pratt experiment, or Campus Distance Series as it is also known, which was started in August 1933 and completed in March 1934. Rhine has stated that the aim of the experiment was to set up experimental conditions strict enough to exclude all factors, other than ESP, that could produce above-chance scores. The experiment has been described in several articles and books, but the most complete account was provided in a 1954 article in the *Journal of Parapsychology*.[1] The description given here is based on this account of the experiment.

It was basically a clairvoyance test, in which Pearce guessed at cards in a pack controlled by Pratt, then a graduate student in the psychology department, while he was situated in another building on the campus.

The Procedure

The two men met in Pratt's room on the top floor of what is now the social sciences building on the west campus of Duke University. (At the time of the experiments this was the physics building, and the psychology department used a few rooms in it.) Both men synchronized their watches and fixed a time at which the test would start. Pearce then went across the quadrangle to the library, where he sat in a cubicle in the stacks at a distance of about 100 yards from Pratt, who from his window could see Pearce cross the quadrangle and enter the library.

The Targets

Pratt sat down at a table, took a pack of ESP cards, and, after shuffling and cutting it, placed it face downward on the right side of the table. At the time fixed for the experiment to start, he took the top card and placed it, still face down, on a book in the center of the table. At the end of a minute this card was transferred to the left side of the table, and the second card in the pack was placed on the book. In this manner, each card was placed on the book at its appointed time and then transferred to a pile on the left side of the table. After a run of twenty-five cards, an interval of five minutes elapsed, and then the same procedure was followed with a second pack. Pratt did not see the faces of the cards until the end of the sitting when he turned them up to record their order. He then made a duplicate of his record, sealed it in an envelope, and later delivered it to Rhine.

The Percipient

In his cubicle in the library, Pearce recorded his guess as to the identity of each card lying on the book. After recording 50 guesses, he made a duplicate copy of his record sheet and sealed it in an envelope that was later delivered to Rhine. The two sealed records were usually delivered personally to Rhine before Pratt and Pearce compared their lists and scored the number of successes.

The Experimental Conditions

The above procedure was followed at each of 37 sittings held between August 1933 and March 1934. The sittings were divided into four subseries: Subseries *A* consisted of 6 sittings, carried out under the above conditions; subseries *B* was composed of 22 sittings at which Pratt carried out his part of the proceedings in a room in the medical building, which would have put him about 250 yards away from Pearce; subseries *C* consisted of 6 sittings with the same conditions as subseries *A*; in subseries *D*, there were 3 sittings with the same conditions as subseries *A*, except that Rhine was with Pratt in the room in the social sciences building.

The Results

The scores at successive sittings obtained in each subseries are shown in Table 10–1.

Something other than chance obviously was operating in each of the four subseries. The odds against the over-all result arising by chance are greater than 10^{22} to 1, and the result of each subseries is statistically significant.

Table 10-1
Scores in each run of the Pearce-Pratt experiment

Sitting	Subseries A (100 yards)	Subseries B (250 yards)	Subseries C (100 yards)	Subseries D (100 yards)
1	3	1, 4	9, 8	12, 3
2	8, 5	4, 4	4, 9	10, 11
3	9, 10	7, 6	11, 9	10, 10
4	12, 11	5, 0	5, 4	
5	11, 12	6, 3	9, 11	
6	13, 13, 12	11, 9	2, 7	
7		0, 6		
8		8, 6		
9		9, 4		
10		10, 6		
11		11, 9		
12		5, 12		
13		7, 7		
14		12, 10		
15		6, 3		
16		10, 10		
17		6, 12		
18		2, 6		
19		12, 12		
20		4, 4		
21		3, 0		
22		13, 10		
Total trials	300	1,100	300	150
Total hits	119	295	88	56
Average score per run of 25 trials (hits)	9.9	6.7	7.3	9.3

Elimination of Alternative Hypotheses

When discussing the experiment in 1954 in the *Journal of Parapsychology,* Rhine and Pratt stated that the only alternative to an explanation in terms of ESP would involve collusion among all three participants.

It is difficult to see how either Rhine or Pratt, unaided, could have cheated to bring about the result obtained in all four subseries; but, owing to the fact that Pearce was not supervised during the experiment, there are a number of ways in which he could have cheated to attain high scores.

Pratt saw Pearce disappear into the library; then, some time later, after the sitting was over, he met him and checked his scores. He had no confirmation, other than Pearce's word for it—if he ever asked him—that Pearce had stayed in the library. He could quite easily have walked back to where Pratt was conducting his part of the experiment. In view of this, the possibility that Pearce obtained knowledge of the targets must be carefully considered.

It would not have been necessary to obtain sight of the cards at every sitting, since the scores given in Table 10–1 were only higher than chance at some of the sittings. Ten or more hits would be expected to arise by chance once in each 52 runs. If such a score is considered high, it will be seen that one was not obtained at sittings 1 and 2 in series A. In subseries B, only 9 of the 22 sittings produced high scores; in subseries C, high scores were obtained only at sittings 3 and 5; and only in subseries D were high scores obtained at each of the 3 sittings. The distribution of scores shows a distinct bimodal characteristic—that is, having two maxima: one between values of 4 and 6, the other between values of 9 and 12—as if the cause of high scores was in operation on some occasions and not on others. At approximately half of the sittings, the scores reveal no evidence of either ESP or cheating. Thus, if Pearce left the library, he need only have gained sight of the cards while Pratt was recording them on those occasions when it was safe to do so.

An important point to note is that the experiment was conducted according to a strict timetable. If Pearce had chosen to cheat, he knew to the second—from the time he was supposed to start his recording to the time when he was supposed to make his last guess—what Pratt was doing. He knew that he had 55 minutes during which Pratt would be fully occupied and that at the end of that time Pratt would be busy making first a list of the order of the cards in the two packs and then a duplicate of his record. Provided it was possible to see into Pratt's room, Pearce could have left the library and observed Pratt, gaining sight of the cards when they were turned up for recording at the end of the sitting or, if they could be identified from their backs, he could have inspected them while they were isolated on the book in front of Pratt. Clearly, it is essential to know something about the two rooms in which Pratt carried out his part of the proceedings and about the way in which he turned up the cards when recording their order.

From Pratt and Rhine's statement, the reader might assume that they had carefully considered every conceivable explanation other than a trick involving all three participants in the experiment. He may assume, since no description was given of the rooms in which the tests were carried out, that they were quite adequate for their purpose and that no one could possibly have seen into them. If he takes anything of the sort for granted, he may be led sadly astray. A first principle when assessing an experiment should be: never assume anything that is not stated in the experimental report.

The Rooms Used for the Experiment

When I was at Duke University in 1960, Pratt showed me the rooms he used during the experiment. While doing so, he mentioned that, since 1934, structural alterations had been made to both rooms. We first visited Pratt's old room, 314, in the social sciences building. I located the position of the table as shown in Figure 10–1. Pratt then pointed out that the wall beside the table had been further back in 1933. After its original position had been located, it was apparent that the room in its original state contained a large clear-glass window that would have permitted

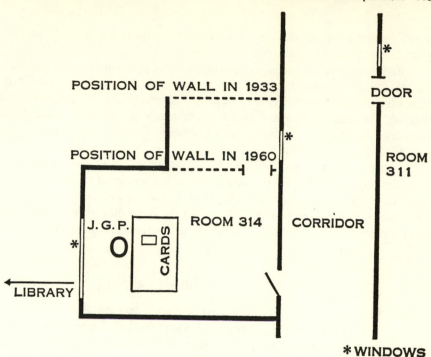

Figure 10-1
Plan, not to scale, of the rooms in the social sciences building,
Duke University

anyone in the corridor to see into the room at the time of the experiment. I judged the window to be about 2 feet square and to be about 5 feet 10 inches from the floor at its bottom edge. Anyone looking through this window from the corridor would have had a clear view of Pratt seated at his desk and of the cards he was handling.

There were similar windows leading into the offices on the other side of the corridor as well as clear-glass windows above the doors of all the rooms. Later, I went into a room on the opposite side of the corridor, 311, and found that the line of vision when looking through the transom above the door was through the window into Pratt's room and down onto his desk. It was impossible to be certain of this point since the wall in its new position hindered my view. However, there was a good possibility that Pearce could have returned to the social sciences building, locked himself in Room 311, and then observed Pratt with comparative safety by standing on a chair or table and looking through the transom above the door.

The room in the medical building had been changed drastically since 1934, and it was now used for making X-rays. There was a transom above the door and a window, but both of these were of ripple glass, and it is doubtful whether the cards could have been identified through them. In this room there was, however, a trap door in the ceiling, measuring about 4 feet by 1½ feet and situated immediately over the position occupied by the table at which Pratt sat during the experiment. Its cover had a large hole that looked as if it had been made recently. There was also a small metal plate on the trap door that could have covered another hole, and this plate looked as if it had been there a long time.

The room was on the top classroom floor of the building, and the main staircase went up another flight to a large attic, which extended over the floor beneath it. At the time of my visit, the attic was used for storage purposes, but I was told that most of the contents had been put there well after 1934. It would thus have been possible for an intruder to have positioned himself above the trap door to see the cards on Pratt's table.

I went to the architect's office of the university and asked to see plans of the rooms as they were in 1933. I also asked for details of structural alterations that had been made to the rooms, together with the dates on which they had been made, and the persons who had asked for them. These details were to be forwarded to me, but I never received them. I wrote again requesting them, but had no reply.

Further Details of the Procedure

The day after we had seen the rooms, I asked Pratt to demonstrate to me the exact procedure he used during the experiment. I was particularly interested to see how he turned up the cards to record them, whether he shuffled the packs after use, and how he left them on the table.

From his demonstration it was clear that anyone looking into the room would have obtained a clear view of the faces of the cards when they were being listed. Each was turned on its back while an entry was made on the record sheet. Pratt did not shuffle the packs after noting down their order, and after recording the first pack he moved it to the top left corner of the table. He told me that he did not lock his door during the sitting or after it was over and that he made his record on notebook paper. I also learned that the room across the corridor from the one Pratt had been in was used by students at the time of the experiment.

Pratt gave every assistance. He himself pointed out the structural alterations made to the rooms. He also emphasized, quite reasonably, that he was forced to depend on his memory of events that had taken place twenty-six years ago.

The Possibility of Viewing the Cards

Later, I asked W. Saleh, a member of the research staff at Duke, to run through a pack of ESP cards while I sat in an office further down the corridor. He was to record the cards on a sheet of paper at the end of the run using a procedure similar to that used by Pratt during the experiments with Pearce and to keep his door closed and locked. I slipped back to Saleh's room and saw the cards by standing on a chair and looking through the crack at the top of the door. I had a clear view of them and obtained 22 hits in 25 attempts. Saleh's desk was about 16 feet from the door, and he had no suspicion of what I had done until I told him.

In a second test, I asked him to record the cards in a room in which I had left a sheet of blotting paper on the desk to take an impression of what he wrote. I then read off the identities of the cards from the impressions of his writing on the blotting paper. But by this time Saleh was tired of having his leg pulled. He had carefully written out a second list, using the blotting paper for it, so that I was given false information. It was clear, however, from these tests that knowledge of the cards could have been obtained by the use of either method, provided other factors in the situation did not eliminate the possibility.

General Features of the Experiment

Now that information has become available about the conditions in which the experiment was carried out, it is clear that it was far from foolproof, and the result could have been brought about in a variety of ways. The conditions were remarkably loose compared to those imposed on Smith and Blackburn, and it is difficult to understand how the experiment came to be designed in such a manner that any would-be trickster could fake his scores with comparative ease. It is thus of particular interest to know to what extent Pearce participated in the design.

In *New Frontiers of the Mind*, Rhine states that after Pearce had been relatively unsuccessful in earlier distance tests, the formality and fixed routine of experimental conditions were loosened, and Pearce was allowed to suggest changes himself. "He could say 'Let's try some D. T.' or 'Let me go over to the next room awhile. . . .' This broke the monotony and very probably contributed to his doing successful scoring."[2]

In the Pearce-Pratt experiment the distance of 100 yards was fixed from the start, although it was, "possibly, suggested by Pearce." Whether Pearce made other suggestions is not mentioned. It would be of interest to know, for example, who selected the rooms used for the experiment.

The experiment contained some 37 sittings in all. For sitting after sitting, Pratt sat in his room slowly turning over packs of cards and recording them at the end of each day's runs. Pearce, after having failed miserably in earlier experiments as soon as he was moved more than a yard from the cards, was now suddenly obtaining very high scores at 100 yards or more. One would expect that anyone in Pratt's position would have examined the room carefully and taken elaborate precautions to insure that no one could see into it. At least he might have covered the windows leading to the corridor. Also, the cards should have been shuffled after they were recorded, and the door of the room might well have been locked during and after the tests. These experiments were not a first-year exercise. They were intended to provide conclusive proof of ESP and to shake the very foundations of science. If Pratt had some misgivings, there is no evidence that he ever expressed them. He took no precautions to ensure that Pearce stayed in the library or to prevent the cards being visible to anyone looking into his room.

Again, Rhine might well have been wary of trickery, for neither he nor Pratt were novices in psychical research. Both of them were fully aware of the long history of trickery in that area.

Counter-Criticisms

I criticized the experimental conditions under which the Pearce-Pratt experiment was conducted in the *Journal of Parapsychology;*[3] Rhine and Pratt made a joint reply in the same number of the journal. Their answer was that the subseries D experiment, in which Rhine was with Pratt while it was conducted, eliminated the possibility of Pearce cheating:

> In this series J. B. R., who had remained in the background previously, came into the test room with J. G. P. and sat through a series of six runs through the test pack (150 trials) for the purpose of scrutinising the entire procedure from that point of vantage, to ensure that it was faithfully executed. He, like J. G. P., *could see the subject from the window as the latter entered the library* (and, of course, could see him exit as well). He was in the experimental room at the end of each session to receive the independent records from both J. G. P. and H. E. P. immediately on the arrival of the latter at the close of the session. Thus the subject was obviously allowed no opportunity to enter the room alone and copy the order of the cards or the impressions left on the record pad. Even with the somewhat imaginative supposition that H. E. P. had a collaborator, there was no time for the latter, even if he had (unnoticed by J. B. R.) observed the card-turning and recording by J. G. P., to have communicated the knowledge of card order thus gained to H. E. P. as he arrived in the building for the check-up. H. E. P. had to have his duplicate record in his own handwriting, with one copy sealed in an envelope, ready to hand to J. B. R. on entering the room. J. G. P. had to do the recording of the last run of each session after the test was over and H. E. P. was already on his way to the test room. Yet these final runs of the session were, in themselves, independently significant statistically.[4]

However, what is important here is not whether Rhine could have seen Pearce leave the library if he had been watching for him, but whether he did actually see him leave at the termination of the experiment each day. Did Rhine stand by the window watching for Pearce to leave the library? If so, how did he know that Pratt was not busy faking his record? Rhine was with Pratt to see that he did not cheat, for it was assumed that a trick was possible only if both Pearce and Pratt were in collaboration, and Pratt need only have made about five false entries for each run to create scores such as those obtained by Pearce.

Rhine could not have been watching the window leading into the corridor to see that no one was looking in and at the same time have been looking through the window on the opposite wall to see Pearce leave the library. In fact, according to the experimental report, he was watching Pratt record the cards.

That Rhine saw Pearce leave the library, or the fact that he could have seen him had he been watching for him, now appears to be a most important control feature of the experiment. But even if Rhine or Pratt had watched to see Pearce leave the library—and there is no mention in any of the reports that this was done—it would have been a simple matter for Pearce to have deceived the experimenters. He could have returned to the library without being seen. He could have left a few gaps in his record and noted them as they were turned up. He could then have completed his list after entering the social sciences building. Only ten entries, each a simple symbol, were required. The envelope addressed to Rhine could already have been prepared by Pearce while he was in the library.

It might be expected that Pearce would arrive at Pratt's room before the listing was completed, since he had merely to make copies of his record, whereas Pratt had to write down the order of the cards and then make a duplicate copy. What did Pearce do? Did he tap on the door and wait until he was called in? Did he peep through the window to see whether Pratt had finished? How long after the last run did Pearce make an appearance? Were his records checked to see that they were all in his own handwriting? He wrote down a list of symbols, not words or letters, and it would be difficult for even a handwriting expert to detect forgery.

The Facts of the Experiment

Up to this point, criticism of the experiment has been based on the account published in the *Journal of Parapsychology* in 1954 and on my viewing of the room used at Duke by Pratt. (I never saw the room used by Pearce; Pratt was unable to remember where it was located.) The 1954 version of the experiment has been used because it is by far the most complete, but when it is checked with the other descriptions provided from time to time since 1934, it is clear that it may have little resemblance to what actually took place.

The experiment was first mentioned, while in progress, in *Extra-Sensory Perception* (1934). Brief accounts were later given in the *Journal of Abnormal and Social Psychology* (1936),[5] the *Journal of Parapsychology* (1937),[6] *New Frontiers of the Mind* (1938),[7] *Extra-Sensory Perception after Sixty Years* (1940),[8] *The Reach of the Mind* (1948),[9] and *New World of the Mind* (1954).[10] Pratt has given further details in a recent book, *Parapsychology: An Insider's View of ESP* (1964).

Close examination of these sources indicates that while it is likely that some sort of long-distance test was carried out on Pearce in 1933–34, the reports of the experiment may have changed with the passage of years. Completely contradictory statements appear in these various sources on the procedure adopted by Pratt, the recording of the targets, the number of sittings, and the actual scores obtained. For example, in *New World of the Mind,* the procedure adopted by Pratt when he moved the cards from a pile on the right of his desk, via the book, to a pile on his left is completely reversed. Also, there is doubt whether the experiment as reported constituted only a part of a larger series of tests.

The duplicate records made by both Pearce and Pratt were an essential control feature of the experiments. It is, therefore, surprising to find no mention of them in the four accounts of the experiment published before 1940.

The duplicates are first mentioned in *Extra-Sensory Perception after Sixty Years,* where the various counter-hypotheses to ESP were being considered. After

1940, however, the duplicate records are mentioned in each of the four additional published accounts of the experiment.

In *New Frontiers of the Mind,* it is stated that there was to be no discussion between Pearce and Pratt until the records had been delivered to Rhine in sealed envelopes. In *New World of the Mind* the revised statement is that Pratt sealed his copy of the record in an envelope for delivery to Rhine before he met Pearce and that Pearce placed his copy in a sealed envelope before checking his duplicate with Pratt. The version in the *Journal of Parapsychology* is that the two sealed envelopes were delivered personally to Rhine "most of the time" before Pratt and Pearce had compared their records.

The *Journal of Parapsychology* article discusses the recording of targets as follows: "Over in his room J. G. P. recorded the card order for the two packs used in the test as soon as the second run was finished." *New Frontiers of the Mind* contains a similar statement. When replying to my criticisms of their experiment, Rhine and Pratt appeared to be implying that the recording of the targets in the first pack was made before the second run was started. "J. G. P. had to do the recording of the last run of each session after the test was over and H. E. P. was already on his way to the test room." In case there was any doubt as to the precise implication of these words, Pratt later clarified the matter in his book *Parapsychology: An Insider's View of ESP,* in which he stated:

> When all the cards had taken their turn on the book, I made a record of the twenty-five cards in the order in which they had been used. As a rule, we went through this procedure again on the same day after taking a recess of five minutes to allow time for me to make the record and shuffle and cut the cards for the next run.

This new account of the procedure with the cards would invalidate a criticism I raised: that the two packs used in the experiment could have been inspected after the tests were over while Pratt was delivering his sealed record to Rhine, but it is strange that Pratt should only remember this revised procedure thirty years after the experiments were completed.

Extra-Sensory Perception states that when the cards were moved 250 yards from the percipient, there was a low-scoring adjustment period at first.

But in *New Frontiers of the Mind,* it is stated that after increasing the distance to 250 yards in subseries B, there was no falling off in the score at the first sitting and that Pearce obtained scores of 12 and 10 in the two runs. Scores for the next 5 days are given as follows: second day, exactly chance; third day, two 10's; fourth day, a 2 and a 6; fifth day, a 5 and a 12; sixth day, a 7 and a 5. Similar scores are given in *Extra-Sensory Perception after Sixty Years,* but these are different from those given in the *Journal of Parapsychology* and reproduced in Table 10–1. Yet in *The Reach of the Mind,* we read: "For a time Pearce did as well at 250 yards as at 100; then something went wrong. . . ." Moreover, the scores published in the *Journal of Abnormal and Social Psychology* disagree with those in the *Journal of Parapsychology.* They give total hits for the four subseries as: A, 179; B, 288; C,

86; D, 56. The individual scores quoted are also in a different order for subseries B and C from those given in the *Journal of Parapsychology*.

In *Frontiers of the Mind,* it is said that in six runs made on three successive days, Pearce five times made a score of 4 hits and that he scored 1 hit in the other run. This cannot be reconciled with the data given in the *Journal of Parapsychology*. According to the figures published in the *Journal of Abnormal Psychology,* there were 8 runs, the scores were obtained over four successive days and were 12, 4; 4, 1; 4, 4; 4, 7.

The *Journal of Parapsychology* article states that subseries D consisted of 6 runs, and the dates are given as March 12 and 13; but the scores for subseries D are given as 12, 3; 10, 11; and 10, 10; we are told also that the division between days or sessions is marked by the use of semicolons. Thus, it appears that two of the three sessions must have taken place on one of the two days. But in *New Frontiers of the Mind,* Rhine says that he witnessed a three-day series. Thus, either the dates in the table or Rhine's memory are at fault. Rhine has remarked about subseries D: "As a matter of fact, it is not easily overlooked and would be, for most readers, quite obviously, the climax series in the paper."[11] As this subseries was the only part of the experiment in which Rhine actively participated, he might well be particularly aware of it. But in *New Frontiers of the Mind,* published three years after the experiment, Rhine completely forgot the subseries, saying that, after the tests in the medical building, "Pratt moved back to the Physics building for another 300 trials." According to this account, "The next step involved a distance of two miles, and things went wrong from the start. The room arranged for the tests was not open when it should have been and for several days there was frustration in the physical details of the experiment. After things were finally straightened out, there was no appreciable success." In *New Frontiers of the Mind,* further tests are also mentioned in which Pearce went in a car to different places in the country and recorded calls, but it appears that he was not hopeful, and there was no success. By 1954, however, the tests at a two-mile distance had been forgotten. The *Journal of Parapsychology* article, after reporting subseries A, B, C and D comprising 74 runs, states: "The 74 runs represent all the ESP tests made with H. E. P. during this experiment under the conditions of working with the subject and target cards in different buildings done at the Duke Laboratory at the time."[12]

It is stated by Rhine that, shortly after the experiment was concluded, Pearce received a letter one morning that distressed him greatly. This incident was claimed to have been responsible for his loss of ESP. In fact, the last sitting of the Pearce-Pratt experiment appears to have been the last occasion on which Pearce displayed any supposed ESP ability although he was later tested on several occasions.

Further Counter-Criticisms

My account of the Pearce-Pratt experiment given above has been criticized on the grounds that my plan of the positions of the rooms in the former physics building was inaccurate. The criticisms were contained in a review by Ian Stevenson, M.D., a leading expert on reincarnation, that appeared in the *Journal of the American Society for Psychical Research*.[13]

While I was at Duke University in 1960, I drew only a rough plan of the room positions in the physics building, as I was expecting to receive more detailed plans from the Architect's office. It is remarkable that Stevenson, who it appears visited the laboratories, and obtained a plan has not revealed what mistake I made.

The diagram in Figure 10–1 contains one error, which does not in fact alter the argument in any way. This can be remedied by crossing out the lettering "Room 311" and writing it about 1½" higher up.

It should be noted that my impression, when examining the rooms, was that it was possible to view the cards from one of the rooms on the other side of the corridor by looking at an oblique angle across the corridor. But I wrote that it was "impossible to be certain." In fact, the simplest way of obtaining sight of the cards would have been from the corridor. Stevenson writes that no one could have spent "hours on a chair or on tiptoe" without drawing attention to himself. But the time at which the cards were to be recorded was known exactly—the two men had synchronized their watches (p. 111). The total time for recording the 25 cards in a pack would be about 30 seconds. The top floor of the physics building was at that time very little used except by the psychology department, which had a few rooms in it. The experiments were carried out at times agreed between Pearce and Pratt but which were unlikely to have been known to others except Rhine. If Pearce had wanted to use a trick, he would have arranged times when other students were not likely to be in the corridor.

Summary

The Pearce-Pratt experiment cannot be regarded as supplying evidence to support the existence of extrasensory perception for the following reasons:

1. The various reports of the experiment contain conflicting statements, so that it is difficult to ascertain the precise facts.

2. Essential features of the experimental situation were not reported. Readers of the reports have been led to assume that the experimental conditions were foolproof and that every possibility of trickery had been considered and guarded against, when this was not so.

3. A number of aspects of the experimental design enabled the result of the experiment to be brought about by a trick. These features were: the subject was left unobserved; the rooms used by Pratt were not screened to make it impossible for anyone to see into them; Pratt recorded the targets at the end of each sitting in such a manner as to expose their faces to anyone looking into the room.

A further unsatisfactory feature lies in the fact that a statement has not been made by the central figure, Hubert Pearce. The experimenters state that trickery was impossible, but what would Pearce have said? Perhaps one day he will give us his own account of the experiment.

Notes

1. J. B. Rhine and J. G. Pratt, "A Review of the Pearce-Pratt Distance Series of ESP Tests," *Journal of Parapsychology*, 18, 3 (1954): 165–77.
2. J. B. Rhine, *New Frontiers of the Mind* (London: Faber & Faber, 1938), p. 222. Reprinted by permission of Faber & Faber Ltd., and Holt, Rinehart and Winston, Inc.
3. C. E. M. Hansel, "A Critical Analysis of the Pearce-Pratt Experiment," *Journal of Parapsychology*, 25, 2 (1961): 87–91.
4. J. B. Rhine and J. G. Pratt, "A Reply to the Hansel Critique of the Pearce-Pratt Series," *Journal of Parapsychology*, 25, 2 (1961): 93, 94.
5. J. B. Rhine, "Some Selected Experiments in Extra-Sensory Perception," *Journal of Abnormal and Social Psychology*, 31 (1936): 216–28.
6. J. B. Rhine, "The effect of distance in ESP tests," *Journal of Parapsychology*, 1 (1937): 172–84.
7. Rhine, *New Frontiers of the Mind*, p. 226.
8. J. B. Rhine, *Reach of the Mind* (London: Faber & Faber, 1948).
9. J. B. Rhine, *New World of the Mind* (New York: Sloane, 1953).
10. J. G. Pratt, *Parapsychology: An Insider's View of ESP* (London: W. H. Allen, 1964), p. 49. Reprinted by permission of W. H. Allen & Co., and Doubleday and Company, Inc.
11. Rhine, *New Frontiers of the Mind*, p. 226.
12. Rhine and Pratt, "A Review of the Pearce-Pratt Distance Series," p. 165.
13. Ian Stevenson, *Journal of the American Society for Psychical Research*.

11

The Pratt-Woodruff Experiment

The Pratt-Woodruff experiment was carried out at Duke University between October 1, 1938, and February 28, 1939. It was originally intended as a test to determine the effects of the size of stimulus symbols on clairvoyance, but owing to the results obtained, the care taken in the experimental design, the precision of its execution, and the careful account of the procedure contained in the report,[1] it has remained as the classic ESP experiment. Rhine and Pratt, when discussing conclusive test methods some fifteen years later, commented: "Those who wish to acquire a reading acquaintance with the highest standards of controlled psi testing may, for example, consult the Pratt and Woodruff report."[2] Rhine made even stronger claims: "The experiment was designed for the express purpose of meeting all the criticisms that came up in the years of controversy. In the entire history of Psychology no experiment has ever been carried out with such elaborate controls against all possible error."[3]

The Persons Taking Part

Three persons were present at each sitting: a main experimenter, J. L. Woodruff; a second experimenter, J. G. Pratt; and a subject. Pratt's task was to ensure that the experiment was carried out efficiently and that all the controls were observed; he will therefore be referred to as the "observer." In addition, one of the laboratory secretaries was responsible for seeing that all the score sheets, which were serially numbered in advance, were completed and included in the final analysis so that all tests would be contained in the final result and that only the predetermined number of runs would be made.

The Experimental Procedure

The experimenter and the subject sat at opposite ends of a table. Between them, across the width of the table, was a screen 18 inches in height and 24 inches in breadth. This screen had a gap 2 inches high and 20 inches across along its bottom edge so that five blank cards placed on the table beneath it were visible to both the subject and the experimenter. A smaller, sloping screen attached to the main one on the experimenter's side permitted the experimenter to see the five blank cards, but ensured that the subject could not gain sight of the experimenter or of a pack of ESP cards that he was handling.

On the subject's side of the screen, five "key cards," each bearing one of the five different ESP symbols, were hung on pegs above the gap at the bottom of the screen. Each card was then directly above one of the blank cards lying on the table. Before each run of 25 trials, the observer took the key cards from the pegs and handed them to the subject who changed their order and replaced them.

The experimenter, on the other side of the screen, could not see their positions on the pegs, and only the five blank cards were visible to him. He shuffled and cut a pack of ESP cards and then gave the signal to start. Thereupon the subject attempted to guess the top card in the pack. He indicated his guess by pointing with a pencil to the blank card beneath the key card with the appropriate symbol. The experimenter, seeing the end of the pencil through the gap at the bottom of the screen, laid down the top card from the pack, face downward, opposite the blank card the pencil pointed to. The subject made 24 more guesses in the same manner, and the experimenter put the cards in five piles in accordance with the positions indicated by the pencil. At the end of the run of 25 trials, with the screen still in position, the experimenter made a record of the cards in each of the piles on one of the serially numbered forms. At the same time, the observer recorded the order of the key cards, the subject's name, and the date of the sitting on a form bearing the same serial number as that used by the experimenter. When these two records were completed, they were clipped together and put through a slot into a locked box. The observer was careful to ensure that his record was not seen by the experimenter until the latter had recorded the five piles of cards.

The screen was then laid on its side. The cards in each pile were compared with the key cards, and the observer placed the hits together, next to the key card. The number of hits was counted and checked by the three persons present. It was then recorded by both the experimenter and by the observer in their personal notebooks. Thus, the scores as later determined from the serially numbered forms could be checked with these two other records.

Before the start of the next run, the screen was placed back in position. The key cards were "rearranged on the pegs," and the observer returned to his seat about 6 feet behind the subject and slightly to his right. The experimenter shuffled and cut his pack. He then gave the signal to begin the next run.

On the average, each run of 25 trials, including scoring, took two minutes. The experiment included 2,400 runs of which 2,000 were conducted in the above manner (called the STM procedure). In the remaining 400 runs, a modification was introduced: before each run the key cards were removed from the screen by the observer and replaced by him in different positions with their faces toward the screen (BSTM procedure).

The Results

The 32 subjects who took part in this experiment obtained a total of 12,489 hits in 60,000 trials. This constituted an excess of 489 hits over the score expected to arise by chance. The mean-scoring rate for the group was, however, only 5.204 hits per run as compared with the chance expectation of 5.0 hits per run. Thus, only 1 extra hit need have arisen in each 100 trials to account for the scores. Even so, the odds against the observed result arising by chance are greater than a million to 1, and this provides an example of the way in which a mean score, only slightly above the chance-scoring rate, can assume enormous significance provided it is based on a sufficient number of trials. Such a result must be treated with caution, since even the slightest laxity in the experimental conditions or the presence of weak sensory cues can make itself manifest.

Closer examination of the results of this experiment shows, however, that the explanation is unlikely to be in terms of such forms of error. The subjects varied considerably in their performance, but one subject in particular achieved scores at some sittings that, merely by inspection, can be seen to involve much more than chance. Even though the high scores of this subject, designated P.M. in the report, arose mainly in three out of eight sittings, her over-all score of 947 hits in 4,050 trials had odds greater than 20 million to 1 against arising by chance. Four other subjects also obtained scores having odds greater than 20 to 1 against their arising by chance. Thus, there are clear indications that something other than guesswork or experimental error was involved in this experiment and also that its effects were by no means negligible in the case of at least one subject.

Analysis of the Experimental Conditions

If the experimenter had carried out his duties efficiently, it would have been extremely difficult for the subject to have achieved high scores in the absence of ESP. The following criticism of D. H. Rawcliffe should, however, be noted:

When we hear that the screened touch-matching technique involves the personal handling of a face-down pack of cards by the experimenter who is sitting only a couple of feet away from the percipient, the claim to have imposed the strictest experimental controls must raise a smile.

The only value of a screen between the percipient and the experimenter is that it probably prevents direct visual cues from reaching the percipient. If, in the absence of a screen, the possibility of direct visual cues reaching the *percipient* is admitted, then plainly the same possibility exists in regard to the experimenter; for he can not only see the backs of the cards but he can also touch the backs of the cards and probably the faces as well. Any information he may get from the cards, perhaps subconsciously, may be readily transmitted by unconscious articulation or *endophasic enneuoris,* by an auditory code of ideomotor movements, by intonations and variations in breathing, or by involuntary reactions to any tentative movements of the percipient's pointer over the exposed "key cards."[4]

While it has been established that individuals are capable of responding to minute auditory, visual, and tactile stimuli as mentioned by Rawcliffe, it is unlikely that the result of the Pratt-Woodruff experiment could have arisen in this way. The time taken to make the 25 guesses during each run was about 20 seconds. The experimenter was watching the fast-moving pointer and sorting the cards into five piles. It would have been difficult for him at the same time to have looked at the backs of the cards unless he was bent on identifying them. In that case, he could quite easily have turned them over and looked at their faces. It is difficult to understand why the experimenter and the subject should have been placed in such close proximity, particularly after Pearce's results at more than 100 yards, but if the experimenter carried out his duties efficiently, it is unlikely that high scores could have arisen either through the unconscious utilization of cues or by deliberate cheating on the part of the subject. If, on the other hand, the experimenter had any knowledge of the positions, or likely positions, of the key cards, and wished to influence the result of the experiment, he was clearly in a position to do so. He was completely screened from the other persons present and had ample opportunity, either while distributing the cards or while recording them, to change the positions and numbers of the cards in the five piles.

While at the Parapsychology Laboratory in October 1960, I inspected the apparatus used in the experiments and found that, when acting in the role of experimenter, it was quite a simple matter for me to detect the positions at which cards were being replaced on the pegs on the other side of the screen before the start of a run. I obtained the assistance of Michael Sanders, who at that time was a research fellow in the Parapsychology Laboratory, and asked him to remove the cards from the pegs in order from left to right and then to replace them in different positions. Having noted the symbol occupying the left-hand position among the key cards while the screen was turned on its side at the end of the previous run, I was able to detect the position in which it was replaced. Thus, in the role of the experimenter, I would have been able to place cards in a position where they would secure extra hits during the following run.

If the experimenter had wished to influence the results of the experiment in this manner, he could have adopted the following procedure.

When the screen was turned on its side during the scoring at the end of a run, he could have noted the symbol occupying position 1 (or position 5) in the row of key cards. After the screen was placed back in position, and when the key cards were removed from the pegs by the observer, he could have noted the order in which they were removed. When the subject changed their order and replaced them, he could assume that the last card replaced would be the one that occupied position 1 or 5 in the last run, depending on whether they had been removed from the pegs from left to right or from right to left. If, on the other hand, the positions of the key cards were changed by moving them about on the pegs, he could keep track of a particular card during this process, getting to know the position of one key card. He would allocate the cards to one of the piles during the run and then, after turning up the cards to record them at the end of the run, he would move cards bearing the appropriate symbol into the position where they would result in hits.

A trick of this type would cause a high score to arise frequently on a key-card symbol that had occupied one of the outside positions (1 and 5) during the *previous* run. The effects of such a procedure would also manifest themselves with the best possibility of being detected in the records of the highest-scoring subject (P.M.). The following preliminary analysis was, therefore, carried out to check whether this was so.

All runs made by the high-scoring subject yielding a score of 8 hits or more were considered. The symbol that secured the maximum number of hits in each run was noted. Where two or more symbols secured an equally high number of hits, that run was rejected for the purpose of the analysis. Having identified the symbol that secured the maximum number of hits in a run, its position was checked among the key cards in the previous run.

It was found that in 22 runs considered, the high-scoring symbol had occupied either position 1 or 5 among the key cards in the previous run in 17 cases. Most of the cases in which high scores involving preceding positions 1 or 5 did not arise were in the last two sittings. These were the two sittings in which the BTSM procedure was used and in which the key cards had their faces to the screen. When considering the first six sittings, in which the STM procedure was employed, it was found that in only one case out of eighteen had the high-scoring symbol occupied a position *other* than 1 or 5. Thus, it was clear that something had happened during the experiment to cause hits to arise in this remarkable manner.

The analysis was then extended to include all runs in which more than 5 hits were obtained. The result is shown in Table 11–1.

The number of hits arising on a particular symbol should be independent of the position of that symbol in the key cards in the previous run. Thus, the highest score should arise on a symbol previously occupying positions 1 or 5, 40 percent of the time, and it should arise on symbols previously occupying positions 2, 3, or 4, 60 percent of the time.

However, of the 55 cases considered in Table 11–1, there are 39 in which the high-scoring symbol occupied positions 1 or 5 in the previous key-card order, and 16 where it had occupied positions 2, 3, or 4 during the previous run. The

Table 11-1
Positions that high-scoring symbols occupied
in the row of key cards used for the previous run

(S = Star,   R = Rectangle,   P = Plus,   W = Waves,   C = Circle)

Subject P.M.

Date and type of sitting	Run	Score on run	Highest scoring symbol	Position of symbol in previous run
Nov. 21, 1938	3	6	S	1
STM	5	6	P	1
	6	6	R	5
	12	10	W	5
	14	8	S	5
Nov. 28, 1938	2	7	P	5
STM	3	8	W	5
	4	6	C	5
	5	6	R	5
	6	6	C	2
	8	9	C	3
	9	9	S	5
	10	9	W	5
	11	7	W	1
	12	11	R	5
	14	11	P	1
	15	6	P	2
Dec. 12, 1938	6	10	S	5
STM	7	7	R	5
	8	11	W	5
	10	6	C	5
	12	10	C	5
	15	8	R	5
Jan. 9, 1939	2	6	C	5
STM	3	7	P	1
	6	10	C	1
	8	7	C	4
	12	6	S	1
	18	6	C	1
	19	10	W	1
	20	7	C	5
	22	9	R	1
Jan. 31, 1939	3	10	W	5
STM	4	6	C	3
	5	7	S	5
	7	8	P	1
	11	7	S	1
	13	6	W	3
	15	6	R	1

Table 11-1 (continued)

Date and type of sitting	Run	Score on run	Highest scoring symbol	Position of symbol in previous run
Feb. 3, 1939 STM	2	6	C	1
	7	6	P	2
	10	7	W	1
	15	7	R	1
Feb. 10, 1939 BSTM	2	7	S	4
	15	7	P	2
	16	9	S	2
	17	7	R	3
	22	8	R	3
	24	7	S	5
	27	10	S	4
Feb. 17, 1939 BSTM	8	8	R	2
	9	6	C	2
	11	12	P	1
	16	7	C	5
	25	7	W	4

contingency table of Table 11–2 is obtained. A statistical test indicates that the numbers of cases observed in the two categories would be expected to arise by chance in only 1 in 100,000 similar experiments.

The high-scoring subject obtained 946 hits in 4,050 trials. Table 11–3 shows the number of *hits* arising on symbols that, in the previous run, occupied positions 1 and 5 among the key cards compared with the number of hits on symbols that occupied the remaining positions. The first run cannot be included in this analysis; therefore, it relates only to the remaining 4,025 trials in which 941 hits were scored.

Thus it will be seen from Table 11–3 that the above-chance scores are accounted for entirely in terms of hits made on symbols that occupied positions 1 or 5 in the previous run. The odds on the scores achieved on symbols that occupied positions 2, 3, and 4 in the previous run are nearly even, whereas the odds on the scores achieved for positions 1 and 5 are greater than 100 billion to 1.

The Randomization of Key-Card Order

It would have been impossible for such a trick as described above to have been carried out by the experimenter if the observer had thoroughly shuffled the key cards before they were replaced on the pegs. There is no mention of the cards having been shuffled in the experimental report, but when I was at the Parapsychology Laboratory, Pratt told me that he remembered shuffling them. However, a study of the key-card order of many runs of the second highest-scoring subject (D.A.) shows little evidence of shuffling. At the first sitting, comprising 14

Table 11-2
Positions occupied, during previous run,
by symbols securing maximum number of hits in present run

Position that highest-scoring symbol occupied in previous run	Cases observed	Cases expected
1 or 5	39	22
2, 3, or 4	16	33
Totals	55	55

runs, the order of the key cards remained unchanged for the last 7 runs. At the second sitting, comprising 18 runs, the order of the key cards remained unchanged from one run to the next on six occasions. On three occasions the order of the cards was simply reversed; another time, two cards were interchanged and then put back to their original positions on the following run. These effects are confined to the first two sittings in which the STM procedure was used. In the third sitting, using the BSTM procedure, the order of cards appears to have been randomized effectively.

Unless the cards were systematically shuffled after every run, a trick could have been employed, and the experimental report makes it clear that the investigators had not seriously considered the necessity of such shuffling. It is stated that Woodruff shuffled the pack of cards that he used, but the word "shuffle" is at no time used with reference to the key cards.

The Remaining High-Scoring Subjects

Five of the 32 subjects obtained scores significantly above the chance level, at odds greater than 20 to 1. The number of cases in which the high-scoring symbol occupied each of the five positions in the key-card order for these subjects, when the STM procedure was used, is shown in Table 11-4.

The total expected frequency is 25.2 for each position, and the observed values have odds greater than 1 million to 1 against arising by chance. When only subjects C. C., D. A., D. L., and H. G. are considered, their result is also significant, having odds greater than 100 to 1 against arising by chance.

As has been stated, in the last subseries of the experiment the BSTM procedure was used; that is, the observer removed the key cards from the screen and replaced them in different positions with their backs toward the subject. It will be seen from Table 11–1 that the scores under these conditions dropped markedly for the high-scoring subject P.M. and that there was no indication that hits were being obtained on symbols that had occupied one of the end positions in the

Table 11-3
Analysis of scores arising on symbols that occupied positions 1 and 5 on previous runs compared with scores arising on symbols that occupied positions 2, 3, and 4

Subject P.M.

Position of symbol in previous run	Trials	Hits obtained	Hits expected to arise by chance	Odds against score arising by chance
1 and 5	1,670	453	336.6	greater than 10^{11} to 1
2, 3, and 4	2,355	488	471.0	less than 2 to 1

previous run. The overall score for all subjects under BSTM conditions was, however, above chance, and the scoring rate was about the same as under the STM conditions with odds of 20 to 1 against arising by chance. When the results of all subjects are analyzed to show the positions occupied in the previous run by the high-scoring symbols, the figures shown in Table 11–5 are obtained. The distribution here is by no means random, although positions 5 and 4 are mainly involved, rather than 1 and 5 as was found with the STM procedure.

The BSTM series started after the STM series was completed, and a different technique was employed to change the positions of the key cards, since they were handled only by the observer. If a trick, as described above, was employed in the BSTM series, a modification of the procedure by which extra hits were obtained was necessary. If, for example, the observer had a tendency to exchange cards in pairs on the pegs, a new technique could have been employed.

Table 11-4
Positions occupied during previous run by high-scoring symbols

STM procedure

Previous position of symbol	CC	DA	DL	HG	PM	Totals
1	13	2	2	13	16	46
2	3	1	4	5	3	16
3	6	2	2	5	3	16
4	3	0	3	6	1	13
5	5	0	5	3	20	33
Totals	30	5	16	32	43	126

Table 11-5
Previous positions of high-scoring symbols

BSTM condition   14 subjects

Position	Observed number of cases	Expected number of cases
1	8	14
2	14	14
3	5	14
4	22	14
5	21	14

Testing the Method of Obtaining High Scores

After returning to Manchester, I made some tests with the help of two colleagues to ascertain the conditions under which it was possible for a person acting in the role of the experimenter to keep track of the position of a key card. A screen with a gap at the bottom and a second, smaller screen were arranged on a table in a manner closely resembling that of the original experiment. Five ESP cards were hung on pegs above the gap.

J. P. Anderson, a senior technician in the department, acted in the role of the subject of the original experiments. He was asked to replace the cards in random order on the screen after they were handed to him by the observer (myself). E. J. Dearnaley, lecturer in psychology, acted in the role of experimenter. Prior to each test, Dearnaley saw the previous order of the key cards. I then removed them and handed them to the subject, who was asked to replace them on the pegs at whatever positions he liked, and the experimenter was asked to indicate the position of any card.

The experimenter was tested under the following four conditions:

1. I removed the cards from the pegs in order from left to right, and Dearnaley attempted to identify the position of the first card replaced.

2. The cards were removed as above, but Dearnaley attempted to identify the last card replaced.

3. I removed the cards from left to right or right to left at my own discretion, without Dearnaley knowing which order was being used.

4. I removed the cards in random order from the screen.

The results of the four tests were as given in Table 11–6.

A fifth test was then made in which condition 4 was used, and Dearnaley was asked to distribute cards from a pack as in the original experiment. He was informed that we would turn up the cards to record the symbols in each pile before

Table 11-6
Number of cards successfully identified
under four different experimental conditions

Subject E.J.D.

Test	Attempts	Cards successfully identified
1	10	8
2	10	9
3	10	9
4	10	9

the screen was lowered, and that he was to move cards to secure extra hits. Dearnaley was asked to write a report giving his observations on the tests and this is reproduced below:

Report Made By Mr. Dearnaley

Four methods were used to determine the position of a symbol:

1. I noted the symbol of the end key card on the left of Mr. Hansel and by watching the shadow cast by his hand saw that he picked up this card first. I assumed that Mr. Anderson would replace the same card first. By watching the shadow of Mr. Anderson's hand, and listening to the noise he made when placing the cards on their hooks, I was able to tell whether each card was placed to the left of the first one he replaced. I counted the number of placings to the left and right and was able to deduce the position of the known card.

2. I noted the symbol of the end card on the right of Mr. Hansel and, using the same cue as before, saw that he picked up this card last. I assumed that Mr. Anderson would replace it last. By listening, and watching the shadow of Mr. Anderson's hand, I counted the sequence in which each card was replaced to the left or right of the one before it. This count was not used to check my assessment of the position of the last card. This was more difficult than the first method, and I was less confident of success.

3. I noted the symbols of the two end key cards and using the same cues as before noticed which was picked up first. I memorized this symbol and assumed that it would be replaced first. Its position was then determined by the first method. This was easier than the second technique but not as simple as the first.

4. I noted the symbol of the end key card on the left of Mr. Hansel. By listening to the noise made in picking up each card, I counted the number of

cards removed until I saw by the shadow that the card I knew had been taken. I assumed that the cards would be replaced in the same order. By this time I had learned the relationship between the shadows and the positions of the cards so that I knew immediately in which position each card was hung. By counting the cards as they were replaced, I determined the position of the card I knew.

5. The position of the symbol determined by any of these methods was remembered during the 25 trials. The speed with which Mr. Anderson pointed to the positions during each trial was so rapid that I was fully occupied in laying the cards down in the places indicated. As this made a noise that might be heard by Mr. Anderson, they had to be put in their proper places. At the end of the run I first turned up the cards in the position for which I knew the correct symbol and then leisurely turned up the other cards. Whenever I found a symbol for the position I knew, it was exchanged with a card incorrectly placed in that position.

Counter-Criticisms Raised by Pratt and Woodruff

When replying to my criticism[5] of their experiment in the *Journal of Parapsychology*, Pratt and Woodruff objected that I selected the data used in my analysis.[6] They stated that out of P. M.'s series of 4,050 trials I selected a relationship that depended upon only 55 observations. The data given in Table 11–1 included 55 runs, which were isolated from a total of 162 made by this subject in which an above-chance score was obtained; it was selected in this manner to save time and to give reasonably high sensitivity.

Pratt and Woodruff provided an alternative form of analysis in which the effect I had pointed out was confirmed. It should be noted that their own analysis also involved selection of data. They took all runs in which a score of more than 5 hits was obtained. They then counted the number of hits and misses secured by each symbol in relation to its position among the key cards during the previous trial. This form of analysis also involves selection, however, and is rendered relatively insensitive because attention is confined to those runs in which an above-chance score is obtained. If all runs are included, it becomes much more sensitive than my original analysis. Thus, the data given in Table 11–3, which was not included in my report published in the *Journal of Parapsychology*, shows how marked the effects become when account is taken of all the observations.

The second point raised by Pratt and Woodruff was the assertion that the effect present with P. M. was absent in the other high-scoring subjects. This is not so. It is only absent when the relatively insensitive analysis that they used is applied to the data. When the data for subjects C. C., D. A., D. L., and H. G. are taken together (see Table 11–4), the effect is certainly present, and in the case of subject D. A., his results given in Table 11–7, show an effect similar to that of the high-scoring subject P. M.

If the results of the three other high-scoring subjects were analyzed in a similar manner, it is likely that they would show the same effect.

Table 11-7
Analysis of scores on symbols that occupied positions 1 and 5 on previous runs compared with scores arising on symbols that occupied positions 2, 3, and 4

Subject D.A.

Position of symbol in previous run	Trials	Hits obtained	Hits expected to arise by chance	Probability of result arising by chance
1 and 5	491	126	98.2	0.002
2, 3, and 4	734	162	146.8	0.200

Three alternative explanations were put forward by Pratt and Woodruff to account for the effects present in the scores of P. M. They wrote:

1. Actually, one can offer a consistent and reasonable ESP hypothesis, as follows: For the subject P. M., the run began, in the psychological sense, when she rearranged and placed the target cards. The ESP task being a difficult one, she dealt with it by a "narrowing of attention" procedure. For her the task became one of attempting to identify only *some* of the cards in the deck: those with the particular symbols which had become salient because of their prominent end positions in the preceding run.

2. There may be an alternative ESP interpretation, such as a differential rate of scoring on the five symbols, coupled with some habitual tendency in the placement of the symbols on the pegs.

3. Finally, as stated above, this may be a selected, meaningless, statistical effect, for statistical oddities are a dime a dozen. To take one seriously it is necessary to confirm it. The data of other subjects in our series fail to support this oddity, whereas they do support the significant scoring level of the experiment. Therefore the Hansel effect is still unconfirmed and unexplained, and it certainly could not explain the Pratt-Woodruff result.

Their first explanation is difficult to consider seriously. First, it assumes ESP; moreover, it describes a new salience effect that arises in more than one subject. It is difficult to see how the second explanation works. While at the Parapsychology Laboratory, I did investigate P. M.'s results to see whether they could be accounted for in terms of the tendency of the subject to assign more cards to one pile than another, coupled with a tendency to replace key cards in particular positions. There was no evidence that any such effects could account for the result. If this second explanation is to be taken seriously, it must be described more clearly, and further data should be provided from the record sheets.

The third explanation can hold no water whatsoever. The effect in P. M.'s data is so definite that it emerges with any analysis that is applied. The fact that it is not present with all the other subjects is quite immaterial. If any of the subjects did shuffle the key cards before replacing them a trick would not have been possible. If, in an experiment of this type, just one of the subjects did not perform this operation, the effects should then only appear in the records of that one subject. If some subjects omitted shuffling the cards on a small number of occasions before replacing them, the over-all score for the experiment could easily give a result that was statistically significant without the result for any single subject displaying any evidence that a trick had been used.

Pratt and Woodruff assert that the lack of randomness in the key-card arrangements for the subject D.A. may have arisen because he decided to try out the effect of putting the key cards in a particular order for a certain number of runs.

It should, however, be noted that there is evidence in the record of the key-card arrangements of other subjects to indicate that the cards were not shuffled between runs. Thus, when the position of the symbol occupying each position among the key cards is tabulated against the position of that symbol in the previous run, a high degree of nonrandomness appears in the case of the subject P. M. The odds against her arrangements arising by chance are greater than 100,000 to 1.

Pratt and Woodruff also claimed in their reply in the *Journal of Parapsychology,* that my suggestion of the manner in which one of the experimenters might have brought about the observed result arose after I had searched through the records of the highest scoring subject (P. M.) until I came across something that I could interpret as evidence of fraud. This, in fact, was not the case.

Having worked out what seemed to me the only possible way in which the result could have been brought about in the absence of ESP, it came as a considerable surprise to find such clear-cut evidence for it in the records of the highest scoring subject.

Pratt and Woodruff also asserted that the effect was only present in the case of one subject (P.M. in the report) and was absent in the case of other high-scoring subjects. For this reason I showed that it was also present in the case of subject D.A. (see Table 11-7) when taking into account *all* the trials made by that subject under the STM condition. The effect was also present when taking the four high-scoring subjects—other than P. M.—together (see Table 11-4). In this case, I had taken into account only those runs in which a score of 8 or more was obtained. The particular statistical analysis employed is unlikely to have affected the findings very much, but it was not possible to answer criticisms raised by Pratt and Woodruff owing to the nonavailability of the record sheets. (These were in my possession for only a fortnight while at Duke University and had to be returned after I refused to sign a form that would have made publication of my findings dependent on the consent of the Laboratory.)

Dr. Ramakrishna Rao, of the Parapsychology Laboratory, in a book *Experimental Parapsychology* published in 1966, disposed of my criticisms of the experiment more succinctly, writing: "This is, of course, the disgraceful argument of the dogmatic goat and has no merit as scientific criticism."[7]

Further Evidence Provided by Scott and Medhurst

Christopher Scott and R. G. Medhurst, thinking that confirmation of the effect on high-scoring subjects other than P. M. was of paramount importance, obtained the record sheets from the Parapsychology Laboratory. They carried out an analysis of the results for these subjects, which showed the effect to have odds of one in a hundred of arising by chance. This finding was reported in the *Journal of Parapsychology* in 1974.[8]

It should be noted that if a trick was employed, it was entirely at the discretion of the trickster whether he employed it with one subject or with a number of subjects. The evidence from the records supports the conclusion that a trick was employed with more than one subject.

Medhurst and Scott suggested that such a trick might not have been consciously employed. They suggest that the experimenter might have been able to identify the cards from their backs owing to the fact that the cards had been used many times over and that he might "occasionally misplace one unconsciously into the pile where he knew it ought to go."

But, to do this, he would have had to learn where "it ought to go," and, in addition, he would have had to learn to identify cards from their backs. He would hardly do this through continued use of the cards, since he merely placed them into piles without learning their identities until they were turned up at the end of the experiment. In any case, an alternative explanation of this type implies that the result of the experiment cannot be accepted as providing evidence for ESP.

Conclusion

Whether or not a trick was employed in the Pratt-Woodruff experiment is a secondary matter. Since above-chance scores in the experiment could have arisen through the use of a trick, it cannot be considered as providing conclusive evidence for ESP. There is no reason why the experiment should not be conducted again under conditions similar to those originally employed but with additional precautions to eliminate the possibility of a trick being used. It is remarkable that, in spite of the great claims that have been made for this experiment and its relative simplicity, it was not repeated at the Parapsychology Laboratory itself.

Notes

1. J. G. Pratt and J. L. Woodruff, "Size of Stimulus Symbols in Extra-Sensory Perception," *Journal of Parapsychology*, 32, 2 (1939): 121–58.
2. Rhine and Pratt, *Parapsychology*, p. 39.
3. J. B. Rhine, *New World of the Mind* (London: Faber & Faber, 1954), p. 55. Copyright 1953 by J. B. Rhine. Reprinted by permission of Faber & Faber Ltd., William Sloane Associates, and J. B. Rhine.

4. D. W. Rawcliffe, *Illusions and Delusions of the Supernatural and the Occult* (New York: Dover, 1959), p. 388. Reprinted through permission of the publisher.
5. C. E. M. Hansel, "A Critical Analysis of the Pratt-Woodruff Experiment," *Journal of Parapsychology*, 25 (June 1961): 99–114.
6. J. G. Pratt and J. L. Woodruff, "Refutation of Hansel's Allegation Concerning the Pratt-Woodruff Series," *Journal of Parapsychology*, 25, 2 (1961): 123.
7. R. K. Rao, *Experimental Parapsychology. A Review and Interpretation* (Springfield Thames, 1966), p. 18.
8. R. G. Medhurst and Christopher Scott, "A Re-Examination of C. E. M. Hansel's Criticism of the Pratt-Woodruff Experiment," *Journal of Parapsychology*, 38 (1974) 163–84.

12

The Soal-Goldney Experiment

In Britain, Dr. S. G. Soal of Queen Mary College, London University, dominated research on ESP much as Rhine did in the United States. Soal first became interested in psychical research through meeting Mrs. Blanche Cooper, a well-known medium, in 1922. He took part in Woolley's 1927 radio tests of telepathy as one of the agents, and, in 1929, with Theodore Besterman, he repeated Ina Jephson's tests of clairvoyance. In neither of these early tests was any evidence found for ESP.

During the thirties, when Soal was carrying out extensive tests to check the claims made by Rhine, his attitude was skeptical, and he was extremely critical of Rhine and his experimental conditions. At that time, Soal's investigations revealed no evidence to support Rhine's claims, and only one of his subjects obtained above-chance scores regarded as significant. He stated that, until the autumn of 1939, he believed that it was practically impossible to find persons, at any rate in England, who could demonstrate extrasensory perception by guessing cards.

However, in November, 1939, according to Soal, it was suggested to him that he should re-examine the record sheets of his unsuccessful ESP tests to see whether any of the subjects were scoring, not on the target card but on the card one ahead or one behind in the target series. After doing this, he found that his most promising subject in the early tests, Mrs. G. Stewart, displayed significantly above-chance scores, both for the target one ahead and for the target one behind. He also claimed that, after checking the score sheets of the remaining subjects, a second subject, Basil Shackleton, a professional photographer, displayed similar high scores.

Mrs. Stewart had been introduced to Soal in 1936, and in that same year Shackleton had first called to see him at the offices of the Society for Psychical Research in London. Shackleton had read an account of Soal's investigations in a Sunday newspaper, and he declared that he had come, not to be tested, but to demonstrate telepathy. J. Alred, a barber by profession and an old friend of Soal's, happened to be present when Shackleton called, and he acted as agent. Shackleton did not succeed, at the time, in convincing Soal of his ability to guess the card being seen by some other person. The high displacement scores that Soal alleges he found three years later were the first indications of any striking effects in Shackleton's score sheets.

The Soal-Goldney Experiment

In 1941, with the collaboration of a council member of the Society for Psychical Research, Mrs. K. M Goldney, Soal started a new investigation to test the telepathic abilities of Shackleton. The investigators aimed at designing a completely foolproof test, and the Soal-Goldney experiment of forty sittings, held during the London blitz between January 1941 and April 1943, was to become the most extensive and best known of all experiments on extrasensory perception carried out in Britain.[1]

The Procedure

One basic procedure was used throughout the experiment, but it was not always enforced in full, and changes were introduced at some of the sittings. The first thirty-eight sittings were held at Shackleton's studio on Shaftesbury Avenue; the remaining two in the rooms of the Society for Psychical Research.

Shackleton guessed the identity of cards bearing drawings of animals seen by only one other person, the agent, situated in an adjoining room. The door between the two rooms was slightly ajar so that Shackleton could hear an experimenter (EA) in the other room call out when he was to record his guess, but he was seated in a position where he could not see the agent.

The Agent

The agent and EA sat at opposite sides of a table. A screen, 31 by 26 inches with an aperture 3 inches square in its center, was placed across the table and screened the agent from EA. Resting on the table, on the agent's side of the screen, was a rectangular box, about 16 inches wide by 10 inches high by 10 inches deep, with its open side toward him. Before each run of 50 guesses, five key cards, each bearing a different symbol, were shuffled by the agent or by an observer and placed face downward in a row in the box so that while they could be seen by the agent, they were screened from the view of other persons in the room. The key cards bore on their faces pictures of five animals: an elephant, E, a giraffe, G, a lion, L, a pelican, P, and a zebra, Z. The agent was instructed to lift one of the key cards, look at the symbol on its face, and then replace it during each trial.

The experimenter indicated to the agent which key card he was to look at by holding up a card bearing one of the numbers 1 to 5, so that it could be seen by the agent through the hole in the screen. Thus, if the number 3 appeared at the hole in the screen, the agent raised the key card occupying the position third from the left among the five cards that lay in the box before him, and after looking at the symbol on its face, he replaced it face downward in the box. EA also called out the serial number of each trial so that it could be heard by Shackleton in the adjoining room, thus indicating when he was to record his guess.

The number that EA displayed to the agent at the hole in the screen during each trial was decided by consulting a record sheet, which was composed of two columns of 25 entries each. Each column had two sections, A and G. Before each sitting, Soal entered one of the numbers 1 to 5 in random order 50 times in the A sections of the columns on a number of record sheets. These sheets were then kept under lock and key until brought to the sitting in a suitcase that was never out of his sight. At the start of each sitting, Soal produced these sheets of prepared random numbers, which were then serially numbered 1 to 50 to show the order in which they were to be used by EA. The same number of blank record sheets were serially numbered. These were to be used by the percipient, Shackleton, who recorded his guesses in pencil in section G of the columns. Shackleton's guesses were not of the number of the key card but of the letter identifying the symbol shown.

The Percipient

After hearing the serial number of the trial, Shackleton wrote down the initial letter of the animal which he guessed was depicted on the card being seen by the agent. He was watched throughout by a second experimenter, EP, to ensure that he wrote his guesses on the correct lines of the sheet.

Recording the Order of the Key Cards

After each run of 50 trials, the five key cards in the box in front of the agent were turned up by EA who was watched by the agent and by any observers present. The code showing which number each symbol occupied was then entered on the sheet of prepared random numbers that had been used by EA during the run. Before the next run, the key cards were shuffled and replaced by the agent or observer. Eight or more sheets of 50 guesses were completed in this manner at a sitting.

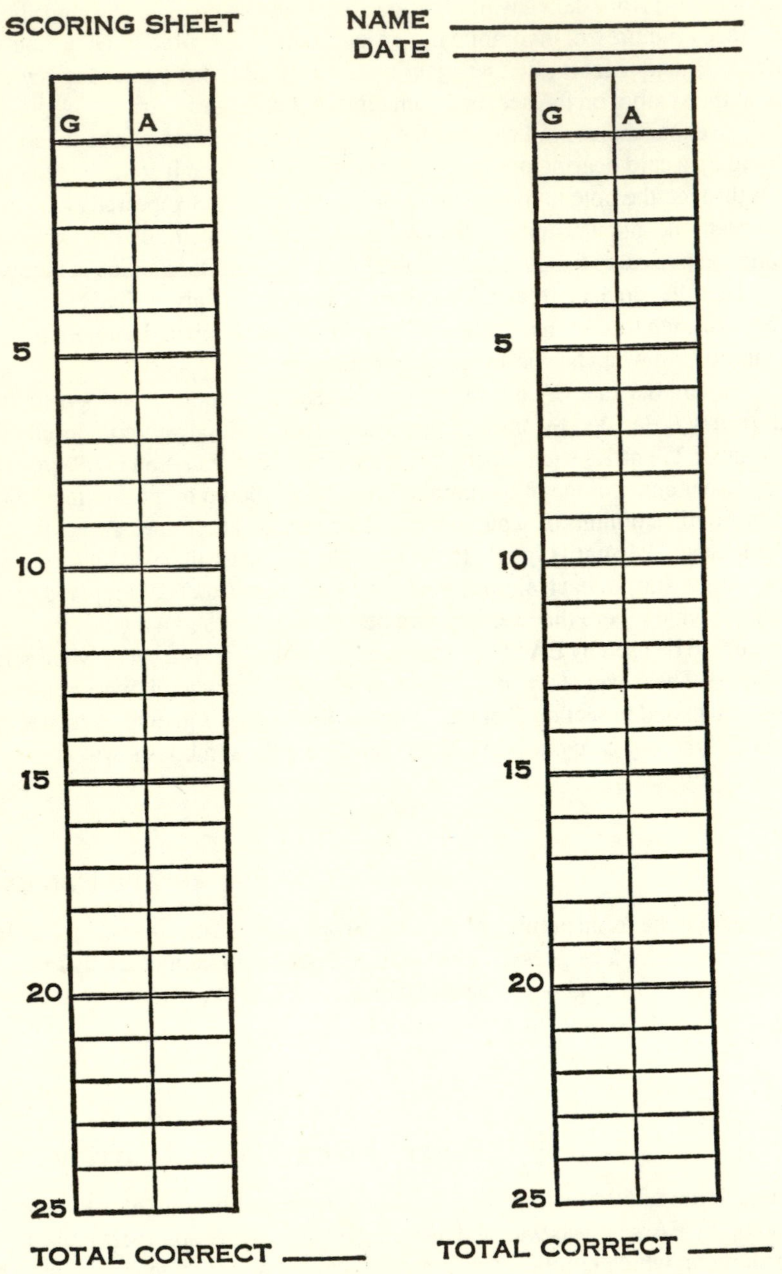

SCORING SHEET   NAME _____
                  DATE _____

Figure 12-1
Type of record sheet used in Soal-Goldney experiment

Scoring

At the end of each sitting, the two sets of record sheets were brought together in the presence of the experimenters and any observers present. The letters written down by the percipient on his record sheets were converted into numbers according to the positions that the key cards had occupied during the run and entered in the G column of the sheet of prepared random numbers used by EA.

The percipient's guesses were checked against the targets for straight, 0, hits and for $+1$, $+2$, -1, and -2 hits. $+2$ hits signified that the percipient's guess at, say, trial 4 agreed with the target that arose at trial 6, that is, 2 trials ahead. A duplicate set of records was then placed in a stamped envelope and posted, in sight of three persons, to C. D. Broad, Professor of Philosophy at Trinity College, Cambridge.

The main modifications to the basic design used at some of the sittings can be classified as follows:

1. *Experiments with counters*. In some experiments, instead of using sheets of prepared random numbers to decide which key card the agent should look at, EA drew a counter from a bowl containing equal numbers of five different-colored counters. Each color denoted a position of one of the key cards. Soal, who acted as recorder, sat near the agent, where he could see the counters as they were displayed at the hole in the screen. After mentally converting the color into the appropriate number, he recorded it in the blank column of the record sheet. These records were later checked with Shackleton's guesses, using the same procedure as when prepared random numbers were employed to decide the targets. To carry out the above procedure, considerable skill is required, particularly when the calls are being made at a rapid rate.

2. *Clairvoyance experiments*. At some sittings, runs of 50 guesses were recorded under clairvoyance conditions. In these runs, the agent did not see the faces of the key cards either before or during the run; he merely touched the backs of the cards in accordance with the numbers that appeared at the hole in the screen.

3. *Prepared random numbers compiled independently*. At three of the sittings, to avoid any possibility that Soal was in collusion with either the percipient or agent, the sheets of prepared random numbers were prepared by someone other than Soal.

4. *Outside observers*. At some sittings, observers were present. They included C. E. M. Joad, a well-known philosopher, and C. A. Mace, Professor of Psychology, both at Birkbeck College, London University; H. Habberley Price of New College, Oxford University; and Sir Ernest Bennet, a Member of Parliament.

Findings of the Shackleton Experiment

Shackleton obtained high above-chance scores with three agents. In 3,789 of the +1 type trials with one agent, Miss Rita Elliott, in which prepared lists of random numbers were used, he scored 1,101 hits compared with the chance-expectation score of 776 hits. The odds against such a score arising by chance are greater than 10^{35} to 1.

In the 1,578 +1 trials with this agent, in which the random series was obtained by drawing counters from a bowl at the normal rate, Shackleton obtained 439 hits compared with a chance expectation of 321. This gives odds against chance occurence of 10^{11} to 1.

In experiments using counters at the rapid rate of guessing, Shackleton scored at the chance level on +1 targets but greatly exceeded the chance score on +2 targets. That is to say, he now scored on the card that the agent would be looking at two trials after he was recording his guess. In 794 trials at the rapid rate, with Miss Elliott as agent, Shackleton obtained hits on 236 +2 targets, compared with the chance-expectation score of 159. The odds against this score arising by chance are more than 100 million to 1.

The clairvoyance experiments in which the agent did not look at the letter cards gave scores that did not differ significantly from those to be expected by chance. Cross-checks were also made by comparing the targets intended for the second 25 guesses on each sheet with the guesses made for the first 25 targets, and the targets intended for the first 25 guesses with the guesses of the second 25 targets. These cross-checks in no case showed significant deviations from chance scores, thus showing that the results were not due to characteristics of the number series or the manner in which the percipient made his guesses

Shackleton was also highly successful during nine sittings in which Aldred acted as agent. With Aldred, he scored at above-chance levels both on the +1 and the −1 targets at the normal rate and on both the +2 and the −2 targets at the rapid rate. Thus, in 720 trials at the normal rate he obtained 203 hits on +1 targets and, at the same time, 207 hits on −1 targets. The odds against this result arising by chance are greater than 10^{11} to 1. At the rapid rate, his scores on +2 and −2 targets were equally impressive. With this agent, Shackleton scored significantly below chance on 0 targets.

Significantly above-chance results were also obtained at two sittings in which Mrs. G. Albert acted as agent, and at sitting 5, at which Mrs. Goldney acted as agent. She was not, however, very much impressed by her own abilities as a transmitter and did not act as agent again until sitting 12, two months later. On that occasion, over three runs, scores were low, and Mrs. Goldney never acted as agent again.

Shackleton's rate of scoring with the successful agents was such that his result at most of the individual sittings had extremely large odds against arising by chance. He was, however, unsuccessful with ten other agents.

After the experiments were over, Shackleton's powers waned. He emigrated to South Africa and was tested there for extrasensory perception, but he displayed no ability to obtain high scores. In 1961, he returned to England, but further tests again revealed no evidence for his precognitive abilities.

Evaluations of the Experiment

In an extensive review of the experiment, Broad wrote:

> There was already a considerable mass of quite good experimental evidence for telepathy, e.g. in the work of Dr. Rhine and his colleagues at Duke University, but Dr. Soal's results are outstanding. The precautions taken to prevent deliberate fraud or the unwitting conveyance of information by normal means are described in great detail, and seen to be absolutely water-tight.[2]

G. Evelyn Hutchinson, Professor of Biology at Yale University, wrote concerning the experiments: "they appear to be the most carefully conducted investigations of the kind ever to have been made," and that "Soal's work was conducted with every precaution that it was possible to devise."[3] Rhine spoke of the experiment with approval, and compared it favorably with the best of the Duke experiments.

> A research can be so carried out that no errors can be made to favor any theory or mislead anyone. All such safeguards should be included in the design of the experiment. As already demonstrated, in the Pearce-Pratt and the Pratt-Woodruff series the experiment was so set up that these precautions were included. Similar provisions were made against error in the Soal and Goldney experiments.[4]

The public has to take statements such as those made by Broad, Hutchinson, and Rhine on trust. However, it is reasonable to ask whether all thirty-five alternative hypotheses to ESP discussed by Rhine and his colleagues in 1940 were adequately eliminated in the Soal-Goldney experiment, whether the precautions against fraud were absolutely water-tight, and whether the Soal-Goldney experiment, in fact, was conducted with every precaution that it was possible to devise as was claimed by the investigators.

By 1939, Soal had shown himself to be a careful and critical investigator. Unlike Rhine he had no overwhelming faith in the reliability of his fellows, and from the start it was stressed in the Soal-Goldney report that the investigators were aware of the necessity of adequate safeguards against trickery on the part of any participant. In their report, Soal and Goldney stated that they had given much thought and discussion to the question of making the conditions of the experiment "proof, so far as was humanly possible, against even the possibility of fraud, on the part of percipient and experimenters alike.'' To decide whether the experiment supports the hypothesis of precognition, a critical examination must ensure that Soal and Goldney were successful in accomplishing their aim. In the event of some alternative explanation being found, the experiments cannot be regarded as providing *conclusive* evidence for precognition. They could then just as well be said to provide conclusive evidence for this alternative explanation.

Sensory Cues

Any possibility of Shackleton's score having arisen through sensory leakage appears to have been eliminated by the fact that he scored on the symbol not yet seen by the agent and, in the experiments with counters, not yet decided by a process of random selection.

During the first eight sittings, however, Shackleton called "right" immediately after he had recorded his guess. He was thus in a position to transmit information of what he had written back to the agent and others present. Thus, if Shackleton called "right" in a certain manner, such as by imposing a particular emphasis or delay, after he had written down one symbol, or even if the manner in which he said "right" was affected involuntarily by the symbol he had just written down, the agent could have been given information to enable him to move the appropriate key card for the following trial so that it occupied the position designated by the number card displayed by EA, thus securing a +1 hit. This possibility, however, was present after the eighth sitting on only one occasion.

It should also be noted that the speed at which EA had to manipulate the cards was such that he would almost certainly have had to look ahead to the next symbol on his list at the time he was displaying his number card at the hole in the screen. EA was thus in a position, consciously or unconsciously, to transmit information concerning the number series when he called out the serial number of the trial. The fact that the order of the key cards was unknown to EA ensured, however, that he could not provide cues relating to the target, but merely to the number shown at the hole in the screen.

A Trick on the Part of Agent and Percipient

It is clear that the percipient could not have brought about his high scores by means of a trick unless he was aided by either the agent or EA.[5] In considering the possibility of Shackleton having been aided by the agent, it becomes quite clear that above-chance results could have been obtained and that this possibility was not eliminated in the experimental design. I suggested one such system to Dr. Soal when he visited Cambridge University in 1949.

The percipient memorizes a series of five symbols, say, *P, G, L, Z, E*, that he will write down on lines, say, 5, 10, 15, 20, and 25 of his record sheet when listing his guesses. The agent memorizes the same information. During the experiment, whatever random number comes up at trial 5, the agent places card *P* into the position designated by the number that appears at the hole in the screen. The percipient thus scores a hit on trial 5. On the tenth trial, the agent attempts to place card *G* in the position designated by the random number that appears at the hole in the screen. He may not always be able to do so as the same random number may arise as at trial 6. If the percipient and agent have memorized five different symbols, they can expect to obtain, on the average, 3.36 hits in the 5 trials by means of this trick. In the remaining 45 trials, they should obtain an average of 9 hits, thus giving a total of 12.36 hits in 50 trials. Higher scores can be obtained by memorizing more symbols, but the trick then becomes difficult to implement. In order to produce precognitive +1 hits in the above example, the percipient writes down his guesses one trial ahead, that is, on lines 4, 9, 14 and so on.

There has been considerable discussion over the possibility of such a trick having been used, and during it Soal has pointed out that it is impossible to account for the high scores achieved at some sittings by its application. In addition, it is difficult to believe that the percipient and agent would go to the effort of memorizing long lists of symbols and their positions on the score sheets for week after week. The fact that such a trick could have been employed constitutes, however, a weakness in the experiment, and it is difficult to see how Soal and Goldney could claim that their design completely eliminated the possibility of fraud.

The Criticisms of George R. Price

In 1955, George R. Price, a research associate in the Department of Medicine at the University of Minnesota, in a brilliant analysis of ESP research dealt with the problems of trickery in considerable detail. One statement that must have impressed parapsychologists and their critics alike was:

> Surprisingly, it is not only believers who are reluctant to imagine fraud, but virtually all skeptics as well will prefer almost any other type of explanation. It would be tedious for me to cite statistics to show that "the knavery and folly of men" are indeed "common phenomena," for everyone is aware of this—in an intellectual way. But when we try to imagine knavery and folly in connection with a particular individual, we encounter a surprising emotional blockage, and the possibility seems unreasonable. And thus we find skeptics searching for every other conceivable sort of explanation. While the one explanation that is simplest and most in accord with everyday experience is dismissed as inconceivable.[6]

Price pointed out that if Soal himself had wished to cheat and had got others to collaborate with him, he could have faked high scores in a number of ways. He then described six methods that could, he thought, have been employed. In the following quotation Price is assuming that he is taking the part that Soal had in the experiment and that he is bent on trickery.

(1) The percipient and the agent are in the trick. The agent arranges the code as previously directed by me, and the percipient writes down a memorized sequence or takes a list from a drawer if no outsider is watching him. (This would be preferred procedure in most experiments except when an outsider determined the order of the code cards. It would succeed with outsiders as EA and EP.)

(2) The percipient and the agent (or the EA or an observer) are "in the trick." The code-card order is determined by an outsider. The agent (or the EA or an observer) notes this order, classifies it into 1 of 6 groups, and signals the group number to the percipient before or after the run. Only 2.6 bits of information are needed to designate a choice of 1 out of 6. For example, the agent glances at the backs of the cards and then says "Ready," "All ready," "Yes, I'm ready," "Yes ready"—and so forth. The percipient then takes from a drawer the designated guess sheet, which is already filled out in his hand-writing. (If the agent is an outsider, the EA or an observer can note the card order when it is recorded at the end of the run and signal it in the conversation then.)

(3) the percipient and the agent are "in the trick." The agent notes the card order and signals it (6.9 bits for the 120 possible permutations) before the start of the run. The percipient has memorized a number sequence, and he uses the card order to encipher each number mentally. (This can work with outsiders watching both the agent and the percipient and shuffling the code cards; or if the agent is an outsider, the signaling can be done by an observer who shuffles the cards.)

Next consider some of the procedures that could be used even when the number sequence was not known to me in advance:

(4) The percipient and the agent are "in the trick." They have copied or memorized the same lists of letter symbols. During the run the agent records (concealed by the box) the numbers corresponding (precognitively) to the letters that he knows the percipient is guessing, and at the end he rearranges the code cards to give the desired degree of success. For example, with a record like that shown in Figure 12-1 [a contingency chart compiled by the agent showing the number of times each symbol arose in each position], the agent could see that card arrangement *LEGZP* will yield a large number of hits. (This procedure would be particularly useful when the EA was an outsider.)

(5) The percipient and the EA are "in the trick." The EA learns the order of the code cards and signals information to the percipient during the run. The percipient has memorized a random sequence of letter symbols. The EA, in calling out the serial numbers, slightly alters his voice or timing a few times during each run (5 times per 50 trials to give 14 hits). Ordinarily the percipient is to guess at random, but at each signal he writes down the next

letter on the memorized sequence. (I would use this method particularly in experiments when an outsider who wore glasses served as agent. Then the preferred experimental arrangement would be that in which the cards are turned face up for 30 seconds, the screen aperture would be located as it was in the Stewart sittings, and the lighting would be so arranged that EA could see the cards by reflection in the agent's glasses.)

(6) The percipient plus the EA, the recorder, or the agent are "in the trick." In runs where the number sequence is generated by counters, I would have the EA draw counters of the needed color at particular points, or the recorder could keep false records of counters drawn. And in some experiments, procedures 1, 4, or 5 could be used. . . .

The procedures that could give the highest degrees of success, and that thus would be chosen when I wanted simultaneous "−1" and "+1," or "−2" and "+2" successes, are procedures 1 and 3. Any of the others would be more than adequate for scores of 12.68 hits per run of 50, or 13.77 hits in 48 trials. For long-distance experiments, procedures 1 and 4 would work. Or I could employ procedure 2 by telephoning the percipient after the sitting to tell him which lists to mail in.[7]

Price pointed out that many other procedures were possible, but the six chosen for description were selected as examples of what could be done by simple means. He concluded:

> . . . thus it should be clear that Soal's work was *not* conducted with every precaution that it was possible to devise. The work would have been enormously more nearly fraud-proof if Soal, instead of employing his highly complex arrangements, had simply had many different agents send directly from lists prepared by outsiders and given directly to the agent at the start of each run.[8]

Some time after Price's criticism of the experimental conditions, it was revealed that Mrs. Albert, one of the three agents with whom Shackleton obtained above-chance results, had stated after one sitting that when glancing through the hole in the screen, she had seen Soal, while acting as EA, altering figures on the score sheet.[9] Whether Soal was in fact altering figures or merely tidying them up is immaterial. But, looking back at the records of the experiment, it is clear that this incident had a considerable effect on the duties allocated to the experimenters during subsequent sittings. The allegations were made after sitting 16 held on May 25, 1941, and from the detailed list of sittings in the Soal-Goldney report, it is found that until sitting 16, Soal had acted as EA on all occasions when prepared random numbers were used to decide the targets. After that sitting, he never again acted as EA but, at all sittings where prepared random numbers were used, he took the role of EP. (There was one sitting at which Soal was not present, but then the regular agent was also absent, and Shackleton scored at only the chance level.)

It would appear then, that the conditions of the Soal-Goldney experiment were such that Soal could have cheated, if he had wished to do so, in the following ways.

1. *Sittings 1-14 in which prepared random numbers determined the targets.* The percipient and, preferably but not necessarily, the agent would need to have been in the trick. At these sittings, Soal acted as EA, and he brought to the experiment the sheets of prepared random numbers and the blank record sheets to be used by the percipient. Soal could then have used Price's method 1. To avoid a great deal of memorization, however, at sittings 3, 7, and 8, when high scores were obtained with an EP present, the sheets handed to the percipient could have contained faint marks—for example, dots made in pencil—in three or four of the positions in each column. Thus, a dot in the top left corner of the space in which Shackleton was to record his guess would indicate that on that trial the letter *P* should be written down. Other positions of the dot would be used as a code for the remaining four letters. Shackleton, who recorded his guesses in pencil, could have written over the earlier marks when recording his guesses, thus ensuring that they would not be detected if anyone inspected the record sheets at the conclusion of the tests.

The agent would have been instructed to move the key cards to predetermined positions for each run, or, if the agent was not in the trick, Soal could have misrecorded the order of the key cards.

Alternatively, Soal could have entered the order of the key cards on some sheet of random numbers other than that later checked with the percipient's guesses. It would, for example, have been possible to have available a sheet of random numbers with gaps at suitable positions. The key-card order would be transferred to this sheet, behind the screen, and suitable entries made in the gaps. This trick would have been easy to manage since Soal kept all the records used before and during the experiment in a suitcase that never left his possession.

2. *Sittings 15 and 16.* Here, with a new agent not in the trick, Soal could have ensured that the key cards were recorded in a predetermined order on the score sheet at the end of the run. If he had had any difficulty doing this, he could have altered the code when hidden behind the screen, or he could have entered the code on some sheet of random numbers other than that subsequently checked with the percipient's guesses.

3. *Sittings in which counters were drawn from a bowl.* At these sittings, Soal always acted as recorder. He could have handed the percipient serially numbered record sheets to be used by him during the experiment and marked in pencil as described in 1. Then he could have had a set of marked and serially numbered sheets, similar to those used by the agent, to be used by him as recorder. He could then have misrecorded so that the percipient obtained extra hits. Soal could have arranged that the agent should put the key cards in some prearranged code. Alternatively, since he sat where he could see the cards under

the box in front of the agent, he could have carried out such a trick without the agent's help.

It would have been difficult to implement this trick if an observer were present to note the recording of the numbers, but according to the chronicle of the experiments, such an observer was present at only two of the sittings in which counters were used with a regular agent. The first of these, sitting 17, followed six sittings, 7, 8, 9, 10, 11, 13, at which counters had been employed, and at each of these high scores had been observed throughout. At sitting 14, counters were used and above-chance scores were not obtained, but at this sitting, the regular agent was absent. Thus, at all the sittings previous to this one in which counters were used with the regular agents, high scores had been obtained.

At sitting 17, H. H. Price, Professor of Logic at Oxford University, was present as observer. He sat with Shackleton for the first three runs in which counters were used, and the scores continued to be high. For the next four runs he sat where he could observe EA, the recorder, and the agent. Scores now dropped to the chance level. It should be remarked that these four runs were, for the first and last time, made with counters at a "slow rate" (that is, five seconds per trial).

At the next sitting, 18, Dr. H. G. Baynes, a member of the Society for Psychical Research, was present as observer. He sat with Shackleton for runs 1–4 and during the last two runs, 5 and 6, he sat behind the agent "so as to check her selection of the cards as well as record the counters shown by (EA)." At this sitting, scores were at the chance level throughout.

At sitting 29, the next and last at which counters were used with a regular agent, an observer was not present, but scores were at the chance level throughout. No further experiments were carried out with counters, except at sittings 30 and 35 when a regular agent was not present and scores were at the chance level. Thus, following six sittings at which high above-chance scores were consistently obtained when counters decided the targets, high scores were still obtained for the first four runs at the seventh such sitting. Then, as soon as an observer watched Soal recording the targets, scores dropped to the chance level. They remained there for two more sittings, and thereafter counters were no longer used to determine the target order—except at two sittings when the regular agent was not present and at which scores were at the chance level.

4. *Sittings 17–40 at which prepared random numbers were used*. Here, Soal always acted as EP, but in all but three sittings he was in charge of the prepared sheets of random numbers until the sitting began. When he had charge of these sheets, he could have ensured that Shackleton's records were serially numbered to agree with those used by EA. The agent would have been responsible for getting the key cards into prearranged positions for each sheet. The percipient's sheet could have been marked as in 1, or Soal, who sat with the percipient, could have told him what to write down at appropriate positions in the run.

5. *Sittings where sheets of prepared random numbers were compiled by outsiders*. For three of the sittings, 27, 28, and 34 at which the sheets of random

numbers were prepared by someone other than Soal and sent directly to Goldney or to Mrs. Wooland, who acted as EA, the following method could have been employed.

At sittings 27 and 34, Soal was alone with Shackleton, and he could have looked through the partly open door to see the numbers displayed at the hole in the screen. He could then have told Shackleton what to write down. The agent, who would need to have been in the trick, would have arranged the key cards in a predetermined order.

For sitting 28, C. A. Mace brought to the meeting sheets of prepared random numbers that had been prepared for him by C. U. Blascheck, of Clare College, Cambridge. He handed these sheets to EA (Goldney) one by one as required, and they were not seen by either Shackleton or Soal until after the sitting. During runs 1 and 3, Mace was in the room with Shackleton and Soal, and during the remaining runs he was with the agent.

This sitting is of special interest, since the conditions were far more stringent than at any other. Here, an outside observer had been in charge of the sheets of prepared random numbers, and he had watched the percipient and then the agent during runs when high scores were recorded. Thus, it would have been difficult during those two runs for Soal to have looked through the partly open door to observe the number cards. During this experiment, however, the normal procedure was changed, as noted in the chronicle of the report.

> At B. S.'s own request, an innovation was made in the method of recording guesses. B. S. and "EP" sat facing each other on opposite sides of the table. In front of "P" were five cards bearing pictures of the five animals. When "P" heard the serial number of the call, he spoke his guesses in a low tone, and S. G. S. recorded the initial letter of the animal's name in the appropriate cell of the G column.[10]

Thus, at this sitting, the first at which cheating was impossible except by using the substitution method, the conditions were changed so that the agent heard Shackleton's calls.

The substitution method was thereby made possible without any effort of memory on the part of percipient and agent.

The only one of the tricks discussed above that might have presented any difficulty is the one in which EP was required to look through the partly open door and observe the number EA showed at the hole in the screen. But closer examination of the experimental report indicates that this trick need only have been used at sitting 34.

In the original report, the chronicle was reproduced for only three of the sittings, 8, 28, and 39, but it was stated that duplicated copies of the complete chronicle of the experiments could be obtained from the Society for Psychical Research. In that copy, which was obtained by me in September 1960, the accounts given for sittings 8 and 39 agree with those published in the Soal-Goldney report, but the chronicle for sitting 28 is different. The note about the new method of recording Shackleton's guesses is not present. It is merely reported that he spoke in a low tone. For the previous sitting a similar statement is also made, as well as for sittings 26, 25, and 24.

For sitting 23, at which Joad was present, it is stated that Shackleton sometimes registered his guesses by touching one of the cards in front of him and sometimes by saying the initial letter of the card. This is the first sitting at which there is any mention of Shackleton speaking his guesses aloud.

Thus it appears that Shackleton started verbalizing his guesses at sitting 23, and the substitution method of cheating could have been used at sitting 28 without involving the agent in any feat of memory.

At sitting 34, only Shackleton, Soal, Goldney, and the two successful agents were present. The rapid-rate type of test was used, and Goldney acted as EA. Another innovation was introduced at this sitting. The screen in front of the agent was removed and the five number cards were laid in a row on top of the box containing the key cards. Goldney consulted the list of prepared random numbers and then pointed to a key card at each trial. Since she was fully occupied and had her back to the door between the two rooms, it would have been relatively safe for anyone to look through the aperture left by the partly closed door, opening it a little if required so as to see the number cards pointed at by EA. Alternatively, the agent could have given a signal by moving his feet, according to a code. Such signals could not have been detected by Goldney, but they could have been observed by anyone in the other room standing at the door.

Using tricks such as those described above, it would have been possible for Soal, provided he had the assistance of three other persons—Basil Shackleton, Rita Elliott and J. Aldred—to have faked the result of the Soal-Goldney experiment. Thus, the experiment did not conform with the aim of its designers in that it did not eliminate the possibility of fraud.

If a team of independent investigators had been invited to test Shackleton and one of his successful agents first under conditions similar to those of the original experiment and then under conditions in which further safeguards were introduced, much tedious discussion might have been avoided.

It is impossible now to check on the methods of trickery that have been suggested as possible. If the records were marked in any way, it could not be detected, since the original sheets are no longer available. When visiting the Society for Psychical Research in 1956 to inspect the records, I saw only the duplicate copies. In correspondence, Soal informed me on January 26, 1956, that the original copies had been lost, having been left on a train in 1946. This loss was subsequently reported in the March 1956 issue of the *Journal of the Society for Psychical Research*.

The loss of the records in 1946 is difficult to reconcile with a 1954 statement in *Modern Experiments in Telepathy*. There, when answering criticisms raised by the American psychologist B. F. Skinner, Soal stated: "Separate records were kept of card lists prepared before the experiment and of Shackleton's own guesses recorded by himself and these independent records could be rechecked at any future time."[11]

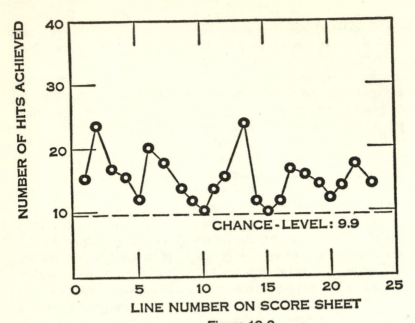

Figure 12-2
Periodicity of effect present in the scores on successive line numbers
in the rapid-rate experiments

Interestingly, Soal seems to have concluded that lists of prepared random numbers might be used by the investigators themselves to bring about fraudulent results. Some fifteen years after the Soal-Goldney experiment was over, when he carried out a series of experiments on two Welsh schoolboys, he stated: "We have eschewed the use of lists of random numbers prepared before the experiment, because, unless the most tedious precautions are taken, such lists definitely lend themselves to fraudulent manipulation by the regular experimenters."[12]

It would be valuable to know what tedious precautions were taken in the Soal-Goldney experiment. During most of the tests made on Shackleton, Soal alone was in charge of the lists from start to finish, and he was the one person whose presence was always necessary if Shackleton was to obtain a high score.

When Shackleton's hits are examined in relation to their place on the record sheet—which was ruled so that there was a double line after every fifth blank, a single line for the others (Figure 12-1)—it is found in the case of the rapid rate experiments that there is a marked periodicity effect (Figure 12-2). The odds are greater than 100 to 1 against the distribution of hits. Thus, it appears that the subject's ability to score hits was in some way dependent on the position of his guess on the score sheet. It is difficult to explain the periodicity of the scores on the basis of any supposed precognitive ability, but it is quite consistent with the hypothesis that the subject was making prearranged "guesses" at predetermined positions on the form or with the hypothesis that the forms had been marked in some way to signify positions at which particular guesses had to be made.

When this effect was reported by me in *Nature* in 1960[13], Soal replied by pointing out that what had been brought to light was a most interesting "segmental salience" effect that had previously escaped notice. *Salience effects* had been reported by Rhine in *Extra-Sensory Perception*. There he used this term to describe variations in the scoring rate at different positions in the run. The usual salience effect was a tendency to obtain hits on the first and last five targets in the run, but another salience effect resembled the periodicity in scores present in Soal's data. This "salience" effect was present in the results of the BT5 experiments, in which the subject's calls were checked with the targets after each five trials.

In a test carried out by me, students were asked to select at random and mark with a pencil dot four or five positions in each column of a form similar to Figure 12-1. It was found that the overall distribution was not random and that some of the students tended to prefer certain positions and to avoid others within the block of five positions contained between the double lines on the form. They displayed segmental salience effects similar to those observed by Rhine and present in Shackleton's records for the rapid-rate tests.

The Tests on Mrs. Stewart

In 1945, Soal started further tests on Mrs. Gloria Stewart, his other successful subject in the early experiments. A total of 130 experiments were carried out, 120 of which took place at her house.

The experimental conditions basically were similar to those of the Soal-Goldney experiment. Two rooms were used; the agent was in one and the percipient in the other, and the door between the rooms was left ajar. The screen and the box containing the key cards were employed, but the aperture in the screen was raised from 13 inches to 18 inches from the bottom of the screen. The system of synchronizing calls was changed. In the new experiments, Mrs. Stewart called "right" after each guess, whereupon EA displayed the next number at the hole in the screen.

Although the tests were similar in many ways to those on Shackleton, the control conditions were not as stringent. *Modern Experiments in Telepathy,* by Soal in collaboration with F. Bateman, a civil servant and former pupil of Dr. Soal's, stated:

> The primary object of the new experiments was something quite different from a mere demonstration of the existence of telepathy; it was rather to find out something about it. . . . We have not, therefore, in these new experiments concentrated on ultra-rigorous precautions against fraud on the part of the *experimenters,* for, after all, if the experimenters (academic people) are not to be trusted, there is no point whatever in their doing experiments.[14]

The Results

Mrs. Stewart's overall scores were no less impressive than Shackleton's. In a total of 37,100 trials, she obtained 9,410 straight hits. This represents, 1,990 more hits than would be expected to arise by chance. The odds against such a result are greater than 10^{70} to 1. She also scored slightly, but significantly, below chance on both $+1$ and -1 targets.

The results of Mrs. Stewart's tests were similar in some ways to those of Shackleton, but in other respects they were markedly dissimilar. Her scoring rate was 25.4 hits out of each 100 guesses, which is identical to Shackleton's scoring rate on $+1$ targets when prepared random numbers were used. Both subjects were only successful with certain agents, but whereas Shackleton was successful with only three agents among twelve with whom he was tested, Mrs. Stewart had some degree of success with fifteen out of thirty agents.

In the 1936 experiments, both Shackleton and Mrs. Stewart had made displacement hits, on $+1$ or -1 targets, but in the later experiments, Shackleton continued to give $+1$ hits with one agent and also produced -1 hits with another. Mrs. Stewart, however, scored a slight deficiency of hits on $+1$ and -1 targets and only obtained above-chance scores on straight hits.

The main types of experiment with Mrs. Stewart can be summarized as follows:

1. Experiments in which the duties of the agent were the same as in the Soal-Goldney experiment and also those in which the agent did not lift and look at the key cards while the percipient was making her guesses, but in which he had seen the positions of the key cards under the box for a predetermined length of time before the run started.

Experiments in which the percipient had to choose between two letters instead of five when making her guess.

Experiments in which two or three agents took part, each agent having in front of him a different arrangement of the five letter cards.

Experiments in which the percipient had to guess the identity of playing cards.

In all the above types, Soal acted as EA, and he supplied the lists of prepared random numbers used in the tests. No precautions were taken to guard against a trick similar to the second possible trick in the Shackleton runs (see p. 152).

2. Long-distance tests in which Soal did not act as EA or compile the lists of prepared random numbers. There were two of these. In the first, between London and Cambridge, I acted as EA and compiled the sheets of prepared random numbers; but during these tests, comprising 8 sittings, at each of which 200 trials were made, Mrs. Stewart displayed no telepathic abilities.

The second of the long-distance tests was between London and Antwerp. In this case, the sheets of prepared random numbers were prepared by outsiders, but they were handed over to Soal before the experiments. The main weakness in these tests was the fact that Mrs. Stewart's answer sheets were sent directly to Soal, and no precautions were taken to ensure that he could not determine the outcome of the experiment.

3. In split-agent experiments, two agents took part, one touching the backs of five blank cards as the numbers appeared at the hole in the screen, the other shuffling the five key cards, looking at them for a predetermined length of time before the guessing started, and then taking no further part in the experiment. During these tests, Soal always acted as EA, and he could have brought about high scores using the second type of trickery discussed in reference to the Shackleton tests.

4. In an experiment carried out on June 18, 1946, L. A. Rozelaar, Senior Lecturer in French at Queen Mary College, acted as agent. For sheets 2, 4, 6, and 8, the 5 cards were used inside the box in the customary fashion, but for sheets 1, 3, 5, and 7, blank cards were substituted for the key cards. Rozelaar was asked to keep in his head an arrangement of the five letters that was easy to memorize, and no record of any sort was made of this order until the end of the run. At each trial, Rozelaar touched the blank card corresponding to the arrangement he had decided on. At the end of the run the order of the five symbols as memorized by Rozelaar was revealed to Soal, who recorded it on the sheet of prepared random numbers. In this experiment, the same type of trick again could have been employed.

Soal in collaboration with Mrs. Stewart could have brought about high scores without the help of any agent, since he either producd the lists of random numbers or had control of the score sheets on occasions when the tests were prepared by an outsider.

Secondary Effects

In previous discussions of the Stewart series, considerable space has been given to what are called the secondary effects. These are the low scores observed on +1 and −1 targets and a tendency on Mrs. Stewart's part to score below chance on the first members of pairs of the same symbol in the target series and even lower on first members of longer runs of the same symbol. Any detailed analysis is useless unless it can be assumed that the sheets of prepared random numbers were in fact reasonably random.

It has since been revealed, however, that the random numbers used with Mrs. Stewart had a high degree of nonrandomness. Thus, if a run of three targets is taken at any position in a true random-number series, one expects to get a pattern of the type *ABA* (where *A* is any symbol and *B* some other one) about 16 percent of the time. J. Fraser Nicol, the Research Officer for the American Society for Psychical Research, has pointed out that a deficiency in patterns of the type *ABA* was described as "very significant" by Soal and Pratt when they checked the target series used in the Stewart tests. In *Modern Experiments in Telepathy* it is called "a certain deficiency." Nicol pointed out that the expression "very significant" might be taken as meaning odds of 100 to 1 or 1,000 to 1, but that the actual odds were of the order of 10^{200} to 1. These are greater by a factor of 10^{130} than the significance of Soal's overall result with Mrs. Stewart. This implies that if one generated true sets of random numbers and compared each set with Mrs. Stewart's guesses, by the time one obtained a set having *ABA* characteristics similar to those actually observed in Soal's prepared list of numbers, one would expect to have obtained a similar score to that obtained by Mrs. Stewart on 10^{130} occasions.

Nicol also stated, "The percentage deficiency of *ABA*'s *below* chance was, according to my understanding, almost the same as Mrs. Stewart's score *above* chance."[15]

Further Information About the Soal-Goldney Experiments

Further information about Mrs. Albert's allegations that she had seen Dr. Soal altering figures on the record sheets (see p. 151) was revealed in 1971 in an article by R. G. Medhurst.[16]

He pointed out that the published details of the charge of fraud made by Mrs. Albert were incomplete. Three documents relating to the fraud episode were held by Mrs. Goldney, Soal's co-experimenter at the sitting in question, and in one of these, which had not been published, Mrs. Albert stated that she had seen Soal altering Figures 1 to 4 or 5, not once but four or five times.

Checking Allegations of Fraud

Medhurst first showed that there was an excess of hits on target numbers 4, 5 at the sitting in question (number 16) having odds of 70 to 1 against chance occurrence. He then investigated the random numbers employed.

It will be recalled that during the experiment, sheets containing fifty prepared random numbers (1–5) were used for each run of fifty targets. The identity of the target was then dependent on the animal card occupying the particular position (1–5) among the five animal cards under the box, in front of the agent, indicated by the random number.

At the end of each run of fifty targets the order of the five animal cards was recorded on the sheet of random numbers. At the sitting in question, after the first four runs the checkup was made. The letters signifying Shackleton's guesses were converted into the relevant numbers according to the code for the animal cards and entered in the "guess" column of the record of prepared random numbers that had been employed during the run. Medhurst concluded that the alterations must have been made on the list of numbers identifying the target sequence during the checkup and probably after the second half of the sitting.

Table 12-1
Targets remaining on the score sheets
and hits for each target number.

Sitting 16 and all relevant sittings (no. 8, 16 and first 3 sheets of 17)

Target number	Sitting 16		Sittings 8, 16 and first 3 sheets of 17	
	Targets on score sheet	Hits on score sheet	Targets on score sheet	Hits on score sheet
1	59	20	142	46
2	78	20	156	38
3	77	19	167	40
4	64	33	158	79
5	58	26	143	62
Totals	336	118	766	265

Medhurst also reported that a computer search revealed that the lists of random numbers had not been prepared in the manner stated by Soal and Goldney in their report.

The Method of Fraud

In 1974 Christopher Scott and P. Haskell gave details of further findings.[17] They calculated that if target 1's were changed into 4's and 5's in order to score hits, this would lead to (1) a deficiency of 1's among the targets; (2) an excess of 4's and 5's among the targets; (3) a deficiency in the number of cases where a guess 4 or 5 arose against a target 1 and (4) an excess of hits on 4's and 5's. The data at sitting 16, when Mrs. Albert had made her allegation, did not conform completely with these predictions. In particular the deficiency of 1's could not account for the overall score.

They then examined an alternative procedure, which was that an excess of 1's had initially been placed in the list of prepared random numbers together with a deficiency of 4's and 5's. The data should then display effects (1) to (4) above and they also predicted two further effects: (5) A high scoring rate on "4's" and "5's" together with an above chance score on 1's (since a 1 would only be changed to a 4 or 5 if it was a miss); (6) no tendency for the number of cases where Shackleton called 1 against a target 1, to exceed cases where he called 2 or 3 against a target "1." This would arise, since when a 1 arose in the target sequence it might be altered to "4" or "5" when the subject had called 4 or 5, but if he had called 1, 2, or 3, it would not be altered.

All six effects were found to be present, both in the sitting where Mrs. Albert had made her allegations of fraud and also in two other sittings (see Table 12-1) at which two different agents took part. These included sittings in which the list of targets was written down by Dr. Soal when he was watching the colored token that appeared at the hole in the screen. Scott and Haskell showed that all the observations including the significant ESP score could be accounted for in terms of their proposed procedure by producing an example to fit the data.

They assumed the numbers of targets originally present at sitting 16 to be 1, 100; 2, 78; 3, 77; 4, 43; 5, 38 (the values for 1, 4, and 5 being arbitrarily selected to give a good fit when 41 targets 1 were changed into 21 4's and 20 5's.

It is perhaps more satisfactory to ask, if 1's were converted to 4's and 5's, what is the most likely number of changes to have been made and what numbers of the different target numbers would have been present originally?

Let the numbers of targets (1–5) in the record sheets be T_1, T_2, T_3, T_4, T_5 and the scores observed on these targets be S_1, S_2, S_3, S_4, S_5. Let n be the number of target 1's converted to 4's or 5's. Then before changes were made from 1's into 4's and 5's there were $T_1 + n$ target 1's. The expected chance score on these is

$$\frac{T_1 + n}{5}$$

Before changes were made, there were $(T_4 + T_5) - n$, targets 4 and 5. The expected chance score on these is

$$\frac{(T_4 + T_5) - n}{5}$$

In addition, n hits will arise through the conversions of 1's to 4's and 5's giving an overall expected score on targets 4 and 5 of

$$\frac{(T_4 + T_5) - n}{5} + n$$

To calculate n (the number of 1's that when changed into 4's and 5's best fit the data), an equation may first be obtained to give the squares of the deviations of the calculated scores from the observed scores for targets 1 and for targets 4 and 5 combined. Call this value D, and let T_{45} be the numbers of targets 4 and 5 combined; S_{45} be the score on targets 4 and 5 combined. Then:

$$D = \left(\frac{T_1 + n}{5} - S_1\right)^2 + \left(\frac{T_{45} + 4n}{5} - S_{45}\right)^2$$

This gives:

$$D = \frac{1}{25}\,(T_1^2 + ST_1n + n^2 - 10S_1T_1 - 10S_1n + 25S_1^2 + T_{45}^2 + 8T_{45} + 16n^2 - 10S_4T_{45} - 40S_{45})$$

Table 12-2
Observed and calculated scores on targets 1 and targets 4 and 5
for sittings 16, and sittings 16, 8, and 17 combined

	Sitting 16		Sitting 16, 8, and part of sitting 17	
	Observed	Calculated	Observed	Calculated
Hits on target 1	20	20.42	46	48.45
Hits on targets 4 and 5	59	58.89	141	140.39

Differentiating and equating to zero gives the value for n, making D a minimum and giving the best fit.

$$n = \frac{40S_{45} - 8T_{45} + 10S_1 - 2T_1}{34}$$

Taking the values from Table 12-1, the value for n at sitting 16 is 43.12 (or 43 to the nearest whole number) and for all sittings combined 100.24. The observed and expected scores for targets 1 and targets 4 and 5 combined are then as shown in Table 12-2.

Confirmation of Fraud

The calculated values will be seen to agree closely with those observed at the sittings. Since sitting 16 consisted of 7 sheets, each containing two columns of 25 guesses, it was only necessary to change a 1 into a 4 or 5 about three times in each column to bring about the observed scores.

After noting the fit of the data to their six principles, Scott and Haskell asked the question, ". . . can these findings be attributed to the capricious behaviour of ESP?" They pointed out that such an hypothesis faces several difficulties: (1) The observed anomalies appear in terms of *digit* symbols whereas the ESP task was defined in terms of *letter* symbols, the code linking the two being changed after each 50 guesses. (2) The anomalies are present in consistent form at three different sittings and with two different agents. (3) The effects are entirely those that Mrs. Albert's observations would lead one to expect, and they arise at the sitting in which she reported it.

Shackleton's guesses were converted into numbers—according to the position of the letter he called among the key cards—and these numbers were written in the "guess" column of the sheet of prepared random numbers employed for the run.

The effects noted by Scott and Haskell were not present in the letters written down by Shackleton; i.e., there was no tendency for high scores to arise on particular letters. It was only present in relation to the numbers—changed each 50 guesses—into which the subject's guesses were converted. The effects were, therefore, not related to Shackleton's guesses or to particular animal cards, but to the numbers allotted to the animal cards.

The effects would be expected to arise if Shackleton tended to score above chance only on the target numbers occupying particular positions under the box in front of the agent, but it would then be difficult to explain why there is a precise relationship between the score on targets 1 and on targets 4 and 5 combined. Thus, Scott and Haskell could have put forward a seventh principle of the form

$$ S_{45} = \frac{T_{45} + 20S_1 - 4T_1}{5} $$

There was a considerable dispute about the truth of the allegations made by Mrs. Albert. It is remarkable, however, that this keen-eyed lady made a specific observation—i.e., that 1's had been changed to 4's and 5's—and that if what she claimed to have seen did take place, it would have led to precisely those features in the record sheets that are in fact present. Mrs. Albert's observations led to testable hypotheses about the record sheets and these were confirmed.

The Markwick Findings

Further dramatic evidence that irregularities had arisen in the conduct of the experiments was provided by Betty Markwick in 1978.[18] Following up Medhurst's investigation of the prepared random numbers, she confirmed his findings that Soal had not followed the stated procedures. But also she discovered some remarkable properties present in the target numbers which clearly indicated that they had been tampered with.

First, she found two sequences of nineteen digits from two different sittings that matched. A further case was then found, involving the same two sittings where a run of twenty-four digits was involved. In other cases, two series matched when one of them was taken in reverse order. Eventually, following a computer search, it was found that there were frequent cases of matchings of this nature, many of which were not exact, but in which one of the series had extra interpolated digits. These interpolated digits almost invariably secured hits.

One such case is shown below where an boldface number denotes a hit.

Sitting 24 Sheet (1a)	**5** 1 **4** 3 2 5 3 **2** 5 4 3 **2** 5 **1** 1 4 2 3 2 1 5 4
Sitting 25 Sheet (1a)	5 1 4 3 **1** 2 5 3 2 **2** 5 4 3 2 5 1 **3** 1 4 2 3 **2** 1 5 4

Markwick observed that, in one run of sitting 23, five single extra digits were present at five-digit intervals, and each of the five extra digits secured a hit. Overall, three out of four of the extra digits secured hits. When the targets corresponding to the extra digits were omitted, scores were at chance level.

Miss Markwick concluded that Soal might have left gaps when preparing the target lists (in ink) and then have penciled in 1's for future manipulation. This, it will be noted, is not inconsistent with Scott and Haskell's finding or with the finding reported on p. 156 that hits tended to arise at particular positions on the score sheets at some of the sittings.

Miss Markwick interpreted these features as showing that there had been manipulation of the score sheets. She concluded that all the experiments reported by Soal had thereby been discredited.

Thus, when making sheets of prepared random numbers, particular locations would be filled with 1's in order to obtain extra hits when these were later changed. The remaining spaces would then be filled with "random numbers" taken from old sheets. This would confirm Scott and Haskell's findings that extra 1's were placed on the sheets before these were changed to secure hits. Soal was only in a position to perform this type of trick during sittings 1 to 16. For the remaining sittings, 17 to 40, he did not act as EA, and if the record of the experiments is exact, would have been in no position to change the record sheets.

Markwick's data shows repeated runs with interpolated hits at the first seven sittings and then at sittings 12 and 16 (where Mrs. Albert made her allegations). After that they are present again in sittings 21–26, 29 and 36. At these sittings Mrs. Goldney was EA and had charge of the sheets of random numbers, while Soal was in the room with Shackleton. It is significant, however, as stated earlier, that at sitting 20 Shackleton called aloud his guesses so that they could be heard by Soal. This would have permitted the agent to change the positions of the key cards to suitable positions in accordance with the agreed positions on the score sheet. Shackleton need not have been in the trick, since Soal was recording the guesses and could have done this on a marked sheet.

Experiments with counters drawn from a bowl would, however, have required either that Goldney was in league with Soal or that Shackleton wrote down guesses at predetermined positions. Since, in the later experiments, other persons than Mrs. Goldney acted as EA—Mr. L. A. Rozelaar (sitting 38), Mr. R. G. Medhurst (sitting 39), and Dr. D. J. West (sitting 40)—it is more likely (on the basis stressed by critics of my earlier suggestion of fraud) that only Shackleton and the two agents, Rita Elliott (later Mrs. Soal) and J. Aldred, were in the trick with Soal.

Thus, my conclusions drawn in 1965 (p. 152) are consistent with Scott and Haskell's findings and also with those of Markwick. They also can account for the above chance scores observed in all the experiments.

Conclusions

Looking back at the Shackleton experiments, it is clear that a great deal of time could have been saved, had the original experimental report been accurate and complete. Soal did not work by himself as experimenter, but had a collaborator, Mrs. K. M. Goldney, and a most important feature of the experiments stressed in the report was the presence of observers who were there to ensure that nothing untoward took place. But on the one occasion when an observer reported witnessing a trick, this was not mentioned in the report nor in the chronicle of the experiments. It was only subsequently reported following some pressure exerted by R. G. Medhurst.

Furthermore, since Soal was able to make changes on the sheets throughout the experiments, it is established by Markwick's findings that any attempt made to control his activities must have been ineffective. It is also clear that unless the accounts of the experiments are completely inaccurate, persons in addition to Soal must have assisted in the deception at most of the sittings.

The long history of events following the Soal-Goldney experiment indicates that, even in cases where a second experimenter or observers are present, they have little effect on a determined trickster. It is likely that if Soal had not been careless in filling in the random numbers around his interpolated digits, or if he had been more careful in changing digits, the Soal-Goldney experiment would still be claimed as providing conclusive evidence for precognitive telepathy. It is seen that its meticulous experimental design was an illusion. It tended to be too complicated in design, and insufficient attention was paid to the really important point—the targets that were being guessed. While independent observers were invited to attend the experiments, they at no time had control of the arrangements, and as a check on the experimental conditions, they were useless. If above-chance scores had been obtained when all the regular investigators were absent, or if a critical observer had been left free to change the experimental conditions imposing his own safeguards, a positive result would have been vastly more impressive.

During the course of the experiments on Basil Shackleton and Mrs. Stewart, the experimental conditions rather than being tightened up became more lax. In Soal's next series of tests some six years later, this relaxation in test conditions is even more evident. As experimental conditions in the United States have been tightened up, so have the results become less impressive, until high scores have disappeared. In Britain, Soal started by testing 160 persons and producing no evidence for ESP. Thereafter, as the rigidity of his conditions relaxed, the evidence became more abundant and the results more impressive. Neither Mrs. Stewart nor Shackleton ever got twenty successes in twenty-five attempts. Such scores were, however, commonplace to Soal's next subject, a telepathic Welsh schoolboy.

Notes

1. S. G. Soal and K. M. Goldney, "Experiments in Precognitive Telepathy," *Proceedings of the Society for Psychical Research,* 47 (1943): 21–150.
2. C. D. Broad, *Philosophy* (1944): 261.
3. G. E. Hutchinson, "Marginalia," *American Scientist,* 26 (˜948): 291.

4. Rhine, *New World of the Mind*, p. 59.
5. C. E. M. Hansel, "A Critical Review of the Experiments with Mr. Basil Shackleton and Mrs. Gloria Stewart, *Proceedings of the Society for Psychical Research*, 53 (1960): 1-42. (This number includes a reply by Dr. Soal.)
6. G. R. Price, "Science and the Supernatural," *Science*, 122 (1955): 362.
7. *Ibid.*
8. *Ibid.*
9. S. G. Soal and K. M. Goldney, "The Shackleton Report," *Journal of the Society for Psychical Research*, 40 (1960): 378. Dr. Soal's answer to Mrs. Albert's statement is to be noted in the same article.
10. Soal and Goldney, *Proceedings of the Society for Psychical Research* (1943): 128.
11. Soal and Bateman, *Modern Experiments in Telepathy*, pp. 346, 347.
12. S. G. Soal and H. T. Bowden, *The Mind Readers* (London: Faber & Faber, 1959), p. 192.
13. C. E. M. Hansel, "Experimental Evidence for Extra-Sensory Perception," *Nature*, 184 (1959): 1515–16. Reply by Dr. Soal and counter-responses in: *Nature*, 185 (1960): 950–51; *Nature*, 187 (1960): 171–72.
14. Soal and Bateman, *Modern Experiments in Telepathy*, p. 203.
15. J. F. Nicol, "The Statistical Controversy in Quantitative Research," *International Journal of Parapsychology*, 1, 1 (1959): 56.
16. R. G. Medhurst, "The Origin of the 'Prepared Random Numbers' Used in the Shackleton Experiments," *Journal of the Society for Psychical Research*, 46 (1971): 44–55.
17. C. Scott and P. Haskell, "Fresh Light on the Shackleton Experiments," *Proceedings of the Society for Psychical Research*, 56 (1974): 43–72; also C. Scott and P. Haskell, "Normal Explanation of the Soal-Goldney Experiments in Extra Sensory Preception," *Nature*, 245 (1974): 52–54.
18. Betty Markwick, "The Soal-Goldney Experiments with Basil Shackleton: New Evidence of Data Manipulation," *Proceedings of the Society for Psychical Research*, 56 (1978): 250–80.

13
The Telepathic Welsh Schoolboys

Since 1923, Soal had been in the habit of taking climbing holidays in the Snowdon area of North Wales, where he stayed each year with a couple named Jones. The Joneses and their three sons, Tom, Richard, and Will, lived in a small cottage near the village of Capel Curig. In 1936, Soal tested the telepathic abilities of the boys but found no signs of ESP.

Apparently, in 1955, Soal had an idea that unsophisticated children in rural communities might be telepathic and went to Wales to test Richard's son Glyn, and Will's son Ieuan. In *The Mind Readers,* he described how, over a period of two years, these thirteen-year-old schoolboys displayed extraordinary telepathic powers and earned large financial rewards for doing so under a variety of experimental conditions.

Before the book was published, considerable doubts were voiced in parapsychological circles over the experiment's merits. The Parapsychology Foundation of New York, which had helped finance the research, insisted that a note be included saying that it did not necessarily endorse the methods, findings, or conclusions of the authors. Rhine, who had been asked by Soal to comment on the page proofs, was enthusiastic about the research but called it "exploratory."

After the book was published, however, it received highly favorable reviews in leading British newspapers, including *The Times* and *The Observer;* the only unfavorable review—written by myself—appeared in the *Manchester Guardian.* It also received the longest and most enthusiastic review ever given an ESP experiment in a psychological periodical, the *Journal of Statistical Psychology.* In that review, Sir Cyril Burt, who at the time was editor of the journal, declared,

"Finally, it must, I think, be owned by every impartial reader that, alike for their success and for the care with which they have been conducted, the experiments here recorded are unrivalled in the whole corpus of psychical research."[1]

It would take a great deal of space to consider in detail the long series of tests. In *The Mind Readers* the experiments are split into ten main groups. Six groups contain experiments carried out in the homes of the Jones boys, while the remaining four consist of tests conducted during their visits to London. Since the conditions under which the experiments were conducted in Wales were far from ideal, it is those carried out during the London visits that are of principal interest. In the discussion that follows, therefore, only brief details will be given of the work in Wales leading up to each London visit.

The Early Experiments

In the initial tests carried out in Wales in August 1955, the boys sat at either end of a 4¼ foot table, with a large suitcase placed across the table between them to act as a screen. Soal sat with one of the boys, the agent, and after shuffling a pack of cards he showed them to him, one at a time, taking care that he himself could not see the faces. He or the agent then tapped once on an ash tray as a signal to the other boy to call aloud his guess. Soal recorded the guesses and after each 25 trials the order of the cards in the pack was recorded in a second column. The targets consisted of pictures of five animals, depicted in different colors: a lion (indian red), a giraffe (pale brown), a penguin (dark blue), an elephant (gray), and a zebra (darker gray). Each card also bore the initial letter of the animal (*L, G, P, E,* or *Z*), and these letters were used for recording purposes.

At first, results were disappointing, and no evidence for telepathy was forthcoming; but on August 10, 1955, Glyn, acting as percipient, obtained a high score when his sister Rowena was agent. Then, at the next sitting, on August 12, with Ieuan acting as agent, Glyn secured the highly significant score of 59 hits out of 200 guesses as against a chance expectation of 40.

After this encouraging result, Soal decided to introduce an incentive system. The approximate odds against a score of 9 or more hits arising by chance in a run of 25 are 20 to 1; 10 or more, 60 to 1; 11 or more, 180 to 1; 12 or more, 650 to 1. Soal offered a shilling (a shilling was worth 14 cents in American currency) for every score of 9 out of 25 guesses; 2 shillings for a score of 10; 4 shillings for a score of 11; and so on, the reward increasing in geometrical progression. At this rate of remuneration, the boys would have earned between them 6,553 pounds, 12 shillings (the pound was worth $2.80) for about 2 minutes work on each of the 2 occasions when they scored 25 hits out of a run of 25, and Soal would have parted with about 80,000 pounds before the experiments were over. As it was, he owed the boys 15 pounds, 13 shillings each by the end of his first visit. The scale of rewards was thereafter changed to an arithmetical series, starting with sixpence (half a shilling) for a score of 9, a shilling for a score of 10, one and sixpence for a score of 11, and so on. It was, however, argued that a score of 18 was so remotely improbable that it was worth a pound, that 19 was worth 30 shillings, 20 worth 2 pounds, and so on. Thus, a score of 25 would earn the boys 4 pounds, 10 shillings apiece. In spite of this reduction in the rewards, the boys must have earned about 200 pounds each in prize money during the next two years.

The early experiments, during which the boys were seated at opposite ends of a table, can clearly prove very little, since they could have communicated by means of kicks or by touch under the table. This possibility seems to have occurred to Soal after the event, because it is later stated that the boys were too far apart to make contact with their feet and that, "For a boy of thirteen Glyn had short legs."[2] Anyone who cares to carry out an experiment will find that most thirteen year old children can touch feet with ease under such a table, and Glyn must have had remarkably short legs if he was not able to make contact with Ieuan, who is described as being tall. It may be objected that Soal could have arranged for the boys to sit back from the table, but there is no mention of such an instruction; in fact, Soal stated that when he glanced behind the screen, which he did at intervals, Glyn was sitting close to the table.

At one of these early sittings, an observer was present who might have been in a position to observe the boys' feet under the table. But the observer, Mrs. Goldney, was seated at the side of the table alongside Soal, who was displaying the cards to Ieuan. At this sitting, H. T. Bowden, a schoolmaster who was recording Glyn's guesses, sat at a second table. Any chance he had of seeing any possible contact under the table was removed by the fact that he was seated with his back to Mrs. Goldney and, even if he had turned his head, his view was completely blocked. In a further test, Bowden sat closer to Glyn, who indicated his guess by pointing at a row of specimen cards. In the last case, even if he could have seen under the table, Bowden would have been occupied watching which card Glyn pointed at and then recording Glyn's guess.

At a sitting held on September 25, 1955, without giving the boys any warning, Soal moved Glyn from his position at the opposite end of the table from Ieuan and positioned him fifteen feet away at a table in another room, but in line with Ieuan through a doorway. Glyn now obtained 159 hits in 325 guesses, as compared to the chance-expectation score of 65. Mrs. Goldney, who was present, paid special attention to Ieuan, watching his face and lips and listening for any signs of a code. No one appears to have paid any attention to Ieuan's leg movements, and these would have been visible to Glyn. In fact, the experimenters seem to have disposed themselves to the best advantage to the boys had they wished to signal by means of foot movements. Soal was behind the screen, seated at the table with Ieuan, so that he could not see the boys' legs. Mrs. Goldney was concentrating on Ieuan's face and lips. Bowden sat at a small table opposite Glyn and recorded his guesses. It might appear difficult for Glyn to have seen Ieuan's legs since Bowden was sitting opposite him blocking his view, but this difficulty had somehow resolved itself, for the table at which Glyn and Bowden sat had been rotated 90 degrees so that Glyn by looking sideways could get an uninterrupted view of the other boy's legs.

A few days later, Bateman arrived to assist with an experiment. He appears to

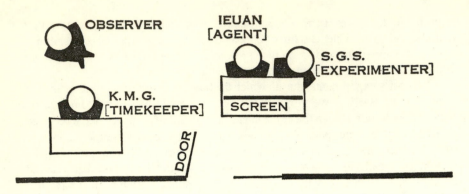

Figure 13-1
Arrangement of tables (above and below) at first London visit

have realized the possibility of visual cues being used, and after four runs in which high scores were observed with the boys seated at the table, he moved Glyn to the position fifteen feet from Ieuan and shut the door between the two boys. Scores now dropped and were not significantly above the chance level. Soal observed that it was hard to draw any conclusions as to the cause of the decline in scores and that the boys were becoming tired.

The First London Visit

On October 10, 1955, the Jones boys had their first test under anything approximating reasonable experimental conditions when they were taken to London to be tested in the rooms of the Society for Psychical Research. The boys were seated 24 feet or more apart in different rooms in line with and facing each other through a doorway (see Figure 13–1). Ieuan, acting as agent, sat at a table with a screen across it and index boxes piled under it, forming a screen to hide his legs. Neither boy, according to the account, could see any part of the other.

At the first sitting, Glyn made high scores in the first three runs of 25 guesses and scored at the chance level during the next three runs after he was moved just out of alignment with Ieuan through the open doorway. During subsequent tests, it was found that on occasions when the boys were out of alignment with one another or when the door was shut, scores were always at the chance level. As Soal wrote,

"It soon became very probable that Glyn (or Ieuan) was suffering from a psychological inhibition with regard to closed doors and shifting out of alignment."

During this first London visit, high scores were observed at the second, third, and fourth sittings, including scores of 18 out of 25 achieved twice

The most likely cause of these high scores was a signal that could only be used when the boys were in alignment through the open doorway. In this position, removal of the screen above Ieuan's table and of the index boxes below the table would have left him in full view of Glyn. It is likely that signals could have been passed by Ieuan moving his knee or foot so that it became visible to Glyn. The edge of the table at which Ieuan was seated was in direct line with Glyn through the open doorway. If Ieuan had wished to signal, he could have done so by moving his toe or knee until it became visible to Glyn outside the edge of the screen formed by the pile of index boxes. Ieuan heard Glyn's calls and would have known when the movement he made was sufficient for it to be detected.

When answering this criticism after it was put forward in the *New Scientist*,[3] Soal doubted whether Ieuan could have edged himself to the end of the table; but if a tall thirteen-year-old boy is seated together with an experimenter at one side of a small table, he will have to be careful to *avoid* extending some part of his body outside the line of the edge of the table.

A further point raised by Soal was that the agent would have been seen by Thouless, who was an observer in the experiment and who stood close to Glyn. But Thouless' letter reads:

If your records show that when I attended the session in London the body of Ieuan was completely screened from Glyn, I have no doubt that this was the case. I thought that I's legs were visible to Glyn and that you would not regard that experiment as being done under completely rigid conditions.[4]

Such a trick might be difficult to implement by the agent owing to the fact that he would not know when he was being observed closely by someone standing in the same room as the percipient. He would know when he was being observed by a person standing beside him, but the screen across the agent's table blocked his view of anything that was happening in front of him. Under these conditions, however, the percipient would know when there was any danger of the agent being detected, and he could then stop the signals by calling his guess as soon as he heard the bell for the start of the trial. Obviously there would be no point in the agent signaling if the percipient had already made his guess. On occasions, when the boys were scoring at the chance level, the percipient was, in fact, calling in this manner:

After he heard the single tinkle of the bell Glyn would normally wait a few seconds before making his call, but it was noticed that when he was bored and scoring badly his method changed and he would call out a letter in a drawling tone *immediately* the bell was rung. At such times he did not trouble to conceal his boredom.[5]

Further Tests in Wales

After arriving back in Wales, the boys were tested on Guy Fawkes Day, November 5, 1955, in their old position, seated fifteen feet apart, and in line through a doorway. It seems to have occurred to someone that Ieuan's legs might be a vital factor, for a rug was hung over the end of the table at which he was seated to screen his legs from Glyn's gaze. Telepathy was now absent. Then the experimenters noticed that Ieuan was coughing at fairly regular intervals. Later Mrs. Goldney noticed that Ieuan creaked his chair on three occasions when the lion card was shown to him and that Glyn got his guesses right. She then observed Ieuan sniffing when the penguin was shown. The boys admitted the attempt to cheat in this manner. Thus, it was possible that after having the means of visual signals blocked, the boys resorted to auditory signals, but without much success. After being caught cheating, the boys were given a good scolding and Glyn's father, Richard, suggested that the experiments should be carried out in his cottage so that he could supervise the proceedings.

Further tests were held in Richard's cottage in the afternoon. For the first four runs, the boys were again seated fifteen feet apart and obtained impressive scores. Then the door between them was shut, and the high scores were maintained. It was reported that there was a "tremendous" and "terrific" noise of exploding fireworks from the street outside, but this does not seem to have inhibited the Jones boys. It may, however, have made it difficult for the experimenters to stop them from using audible signals. It is puzzling that these sittings were the first and last time that the boys were able to communicate through a closed door. Oddly, on this quiet country road miles from anywhere in an isolated part of Wales the sounds of all hell were let loose. Agreed Guy Fawkes Day is one on which fireworks are set off, but it is usual to confine the celebrations to after dark.

By evening the inhabitants of Capel Curig appeared to have consumed their stock of explosives, and at sittings held after 5:30 no further noises were reported. Professor C. W. K. Mundle from the Department of Philosophy, Bangor University, and Mrs. Mundle had arrived, and they saw Glyn obtain high scores—10, 9, 9, and 11 hits over 4 runs of 25 trials. During these runs, Ieuans's father, Will Jones, acted as a joint agent with his son and rang a bell once as a signal to Glyn to make his guess. The door between the two boys was either left just ajar or closed. Will Jones was in a position to communicate information by varying the manner in which he rang the bell. A slight emphasis or delay, for example, could have signified a particular symbol, and only five such signals need have been given in each run of 25 trials to account for the high scores. When Mundle took over the job of ringing the bell, the scores dropped to chance level. Ieuan was by now falling asleep, and the tests were terminated.

During further tests the following morning, when Mrs. Goldney had the job of ringing the bell, scores remained at the chance level. The boys complained that they could not make good scores while she was around, and she felt compelled to stay away from the experiments until the following August.

A month later, the boys were tested in adjoining hotel rooms, but they produced no evidence for telepathy in that setting. The boys complained that it was a strange place and said that they could not make any better scores there. Everyone went to Glyn's cottage for a further batch of experiments, and it was again noticed that the boys were augmenting any ESP ability they had with coughs, creaks, and stamps. The boys were not told that they had been detected and went off to the cinema with Bowden. When they got back, they were given further tests, and it was found that they had managed to change the code during the recess. This was a relatively simple matter, since they spoke Welsh and none of the investigators could understand that language. Referring to the cheating episode, Mundle wrote, "I think this episode adds to rather than detracts from, the authenticity of the report."[6] Soal said, "We were perfectly aware that boys of the calibre of Glyn and Ieuan could never hope to deceive us for more than a few minutes."[7]

Up to this point in the investigations, the boys had failed to obtain high scores under certain, well-defined experimental conditions, but the investigators do not appear to have asked themselves why this was the case. Many times, after a successful run, a change in the conditions that eliminated a possible source of trickery caused their scores to drop. Thus:

1. They obtained high scores under clairvoyance conditions when seated at a table with a rather inadequate screen consisting of a suitcase and a firescreen. They failed as soon as the screen was covered with a cloth.

2. They obtained high scores when in alignment through a doorway, but failed to score when out of alignment.

3. They obtained high scores when Ieuan was seated at a table with his legs visible to Glyn. They failed to score when Ieuan's legs were screened by a rug and when the door was shut.

4. They obtained high scores while Will Jones, who was sounding a bell to signify the start of each trial, was seated where he could see the target cards, but their scores dropped to the chance level after he was relieved of this post.

The Rehabilitation Period

After having been caught cheating on the last occasion, the boys were left in disgrace for four months. When experiments were resumed, the first batch of sittings, held between April 6–13, was referred to as the rehabilitation period. Bowden was away at this time, and his place was taken by Bateman. During the four months' rest, the experimenters appear to have reconsidered their experimental arrangements, and the Jones boys had been given a good opportunity to improve their techniques.

The first test after resumption was made with the boys seated at a table with a cardboard screen between them. Tom Jones, the boys' uncle, was asked to sit near

Ieuan to listen for sniffs and coughs, to watch his mouth, and to be on the lookout for foot movements. Over six runs, the boys averaged 8.9 hits per run. It is difficult, however, to see how Tom Jones was able to watch Ieuan's feet and mouth at the same time without the boy being perfectly aware of where the danger to any trick lay.

When Glyn was moved eight feet away from Ieuan, whose legs were screened by a tablecloth draped over the end of the table, the scores rose to 30 hits in 50 trials. Then, when Glyn sat with his back to Ieuan ten feet away from him, high scores were still obtained. Thus, the Jones boys were now displaying a definite improvement in their performance.

At a sitting held on April 7, without warning the boys were tested with fresh cards bearing symbols that they had not seen before. They were now seated across a table from one another with a screen between them. Their score on the first run was 10 hits out of 25, and in the following three runs they obtained 8, 14, and 15 hits. They were then moved 16 feet apart, and the tablecloth was hung over the end of Ieuan's table. The scores continued to be high—14, 12, 10, and 7. From the result of this experiment, it was argued that the boys could not have been using a code of any sort, as the change of cards would render a code useless. But it would have been a simple matter for the boys to have established a code in the first trial. Both knew that new cards were being used and knew the symbols to be guessed. At the start of the first trial Ieuan could have kicked Glyn. Glyn would immediately call, say, "Policeman" and the code would be established. Other signals could be added. A score of 21 out of 25 is possible in the first run with new cards if this system is carried to its limit. Alternatively, since these new cards were colored, the old code could have been transferred to cards of the same color in the new set. During sittings held between April 9–12, 1956, the boys showed signs of succeeding under conditions that previously had beaten them. On April 9, Glyn and Bateman sat at a table in one room, and Ieuan and Soal sat at a table in another. The door between the rooms was open and the boys were in alignment with each other. The tablecloth was draped over the end of Ieuan's table to hide his legs from Glyn. Under these conditions, high scores were obtained. On April 10, under similar conditions, "ESP was not functioning." But on April 11, under similar conditions, high scores again were obtained. After the tenth run a more efficient screen, consisting of a blanket, was suspended to hide from Glyn the whole table at which Ieuan was seated. The boys were again successful if the door was left open. They obtained a high score when Soal showed the cards to Ieuan as well as when this duty was taken over by Richard Jones.

On the following day, similar results were obtained, and then in two runs, 13 and 14, Soal investigated the possibility that Ieuan might be making sounds by asking him to place both hands over his mouth. Soal sat where he could observe Ieuan at close range. The scores during these two runs dropped to the chance level. In the following three runs, Ieuan was allowed to remove his hands from his mouth. The scores remained low. This test did not appear to increase any suspicions Soal might have had that auditory cues were being provided by Ieuan and does not appear to have been repeated.

The scores for successive runs during sittings held on April 11 and 12, 1956, are of particular interest since one feature was systematically varied. A curtain consisting of a blanket screened the boys throughout, but a door between them was shut in some runs and open in others.

After these tests, Soal came to the conclusion that a possible explanation for the drop in scores when the door was shut was that Glyn had developed a "psychological inhibition" for closed doors. He corresponded with Thouless, who said that he had experienced the same difficulty with one of his subjects and that he had been unable to overcome the inhibition.

When the boys were tested on their home ground, there were innumerable possible means by which above-chance scores might have been brought about. The results of the tests carried out during the rehabilitation period do, however, suggest that auditory cues might, for the first time, have been successfully used. The most likely source of such cues would be sounds made with the mouth, but the possibility also exists that Ieuan could have operated some device while he sat with folded arms. In such a position he could easily have operated a whistle blown by means of a bulb, and if he had been doing this, it is not surprising that scores should drop as soon as he had to sit with both hands over his mouth.

After these experiments, it was decided to shift the scene of operations to the field behind the house, and most of the tests carried out with the boys in Wales from then on were conducted outside. The next two sittings are of special interest as they constituted a dress rehearsal for the second London visit. Glyn and Ieuan sat from 50 to 60 feet apart with a screen between them consisting of a curtain pegged to a clothes line.

Soal and Richard Jones acted as experimenters. During these runs other members of the Jones family were indoors, and we know nothing of their activities. As the first floor of the house was well situated for observation of the test area, it was possible for Ieuan to have given signals with his legs or feet below the table at which he was seated, signals that could have been visible to someone in the house. Information could then have been passed on to Glyn in a variety of ways. However, as the boys had already shown their ability to obtain high scores when separated by a curtain, it is also possible that Ieuan could communicate directly with Glyn using a means that was not affected by its presence.

The Second London Visit

The second visit to London took place on May 19–22, 1956. Soal intended to conduct the experiments on the playing field of St. Paul's School, but since it was not available on the first day, the tests were carried out in Birkbeck College, London University. These experiments at Birkbeck are mainly of interest because it was stated that three scientists were present as observers. Soal, Bowden, and Richard Jones acted as experimenters. The first ten runs did not yield above-chance scores, but during the next two runs, the observers left the laboratory, and scores rose to 10 and 11. One of the scientists returned, and scores dropped to 8 hits on each of the next two runs. When the other observers returned, a score of 5 hits was observed. Soal now assumed the boys had a "psychological inhibition" for scientists.

On the following day, May 20, the first two sittings were held on the playing field, and a third was held there on May 21. Until the ninth run of the third sitting, telepathy lay dormant, but before this run experimental conditions were drastically changed, and thereafter the boys obtained high scores on every run. Since the experimental conditions of the first two sittings were similar to those of the first eight runs of the third sitting, only this last sitting will be described.

Soal, Bowden, Richard Jones, Gareth Jones (Glyn's brother), G. W. Fisk, and a number of visitors were present. Only one of the visitors, A. T. Moakes, the Senior Mathematics Master of the school was present, however, during the latter part of the third sitting when high scores were observed.

The boys were seated at tables 50 feet or more apart. A canvas screen, 6 feet high and 14 feet wide was between them; Ieuan sat close behind this screen at a table with Bowden, who handled the cards, while Glyn sat at a table out in the field with Soal. Fisk acted as signaler and stood at the end of the canvas screen where he could see the card being displayed but could not see the symbol on its face, and where he could be seen by Glyn (Figure 13–2). During runs 1 and 2, Fisk held up his hand to indicate to Glyn when he was to record his guess. For runs 3 and 4 he shouted "next," and for runs 5, 6, 7, and 8, he waved a white handkerchief. Under these conditions, the boys were unable to obtain above-chance scores. It should be noted that visual signals could not be passed from one boy to the other past the large canvas screen. Auditory signals made by mouth would have been virtually impossible at such long range with observers present. If Fisk had been an accomplice, no doubt a method of relaying signals could have been devised, but he was in

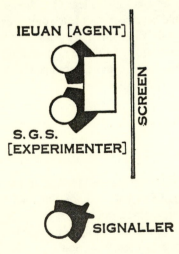

Figure 13-2
Arrangement of tables and screen with which scores were at chance level

a position from which it would have been very difficult to see any movements on the part of Ieuan, since he was standing some distance to the side of the table at which the boy was seated, and Soal was at the same table in such a position that he blocked Fisk's view of Ieuan.

After run 8, Glyn and Ieuan exchanged places but not roles. Glyn was now seated with Soal directly behind the screen, and Ieuan was at a table with Bowden 69 feet away from Glyn. At this point in the proceedings, Gareth Jones took over the job of signaler, and he stood in front of the screen so that, while he was separated from Glyn by the screen, he was only about 9 feet from him (Figure 13–3). Gareth called out "Guess number one," "Guess number two," and so on, in a loud voice. Fisk now acted as observer and at the same time took some photographs. He watched Ieuan for a time, then he watched Gareth, and at the end of run 16 he departed. Moakes was also present, but his exact duties and where-abouts are not specified.

Before run 19, the table at which Ieuan was seated was moved farther back so that Ieuan was 99 feet from Glyn. The scores for runs 9–22 were as follows:

RUN	9	10	11	12	13	14	15	16	17	18	19	20	21	22
SCORE	9	8	6	6	8	11	9	8	13	11	10	12	14	12

As soon as the new experimental conditions had been introduced, the boys scored above chance and during runs 17–22, when Fisk was no longer present, the scores rose even higher.

There is good reason to believe from the result and description of the first London visit that the boys were able to communicate by means of signals given by movements or positionings of Ieuan's feet or legs. In the present experiments, Ieuan could not have signaled directly to Glyn, but when he was moved from behind the screen after run 8, hits immediately rose above the chance level. Ieuan

H. T. B.
[EXPERIMENTER]

GLYN
[PERCIPIENT]

Figure 13-2 (continued)

was now visible to both Gareth and Richard Jones, and his feet and legs were fully exposed. The elder Joneses were in a position to observe foot movements and to pass on signals to Glyn. Gareth was in an ideal position, as he was standing just in front of the screen behind which Glyn was making his guesses and also was acting as signaler. The other signalers had merely called "next," but Gareth said, "Guess number one," "Guess number two," and so on. A slight accentuation of any word or syllable, or a slight delay, could have been a cue for Glyn, and as Gareth had a strong Welsh accent, such a trick would have been difficult for the other five to detect. Emphasis on either the first, second, or third words would have been sufficient to enable three kinds of signals to be passed, giving a score of 20 hits out of 25.

It is strange that after the eighth run not only was Ieuan put out in the field where he would be visible to other members of the family, but also that Gareth took over the duties of the signaler. What is even more remarkable is the fact that no one present thought of getting someone else for that role, or of changing the method of signaling. There is ample evidence that the experimenters were well aware of the possibility of information being communicated to the percipient through the manner in which a person called for the next trial. In earlier experiments, a bell or ash tray had been used with the aim of removing this possibility. To an observer such as Moakes, the mathematics master, it might appear difficult to see how inflections of the voice could be used to transmit information, but Soal was an authority on the subject. In spite of this, Gareth Jones was left to signal the next trial by calling out, and, moreover, he used a longish phrase with which he had every opportunity to use a code.

Soal discussed the possibility that Gareth might have relayed information by voice-inflection cues after observing Ieuan's foot movements and came to the conclusion that to have made scores of 12, 13, and 14 the same movements would have had to have been made many times. In fact, scores of 12, 13, and 14 were made only after Fisk left, when the sole outside observer was a schoolmaster quite unused to this type of situation, and his position during the runs in question is not

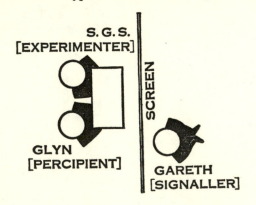

Figure 13-3
Arrangement of tables and screen with which high scores were obtained

certain. If he were on Glyn's side of the screen, he would have been unable to see Ieuan. To obtain an average score of 12 hits per run would require a signal on 8 or 9 of the cards in each run of 25. Only two different types of signal had to be used. Soal commented that any regular system of movements that was obvious to Gareth standing 60 feet away would be still more obvious to Fisk or Bowden at a distance of only 2 feet; but Bowden was certainly in no position to detect leg movements, since he was seated at a table close to Ieuan and busy displaying the cards to him. So far as Fisk was concerned, it would have been difficult for him to detect movements or postures unless he knew precisely what to watch for and was paying continuous attention. In his statement, Fisk reported that he was partially occupied taking photographs. Ieuan could see when he was being observed and could quite easily have stopped giving signals when in danger of being detected. The signal used could have been extremely slight. For example, for three different signals to be transmitted, the left foot could remain on the ground and the knee could be moved slightly to the right, remain in the vertical position, or be moved to the left. The vertical position would denote one of three cards, say E, G, or L; the knee to the left would denote P and to the right Z. If the gaps between the knee and the table leg were observed, a movement of 1 inch would be detectable at 60 feet. It is most unlikely that anyone not looking along the same line of view and not knowing the precise signal would detect anything. An alternative method that would be very difficult to detect would be for the agent to make some slight movement at a certain time interval after the signaler indicated the next guess, intervals of one, two, three, and four seconds could each denote a card and the absence of a signal would then denote the fifth one. It would be difficult to be totally accurate using such a method, but such accuracy was neither required nor achieved.

When outsiders act as observers, it is interesting to know what they expect to see if the agent is cheating. Do they expect to see a series of five different movements? If so, they are likely to notice nothing. The agent's signal may be any natural movement likely to arise over an interval of time. It may be one of several movements, or a very slow motion of, say, the knee towards the table leg. If this is

IEUAN
[AGENT]

H. T. B.
[EXPERIMENTER]

Figure 13-3 (continued)

practiced until it is only just detectable to someone watching for it and aware that it may take place, it is unlikely to be detected by anyone who knows nothing of it and who is having to watch for anything that may occur. Also, the agent can always stop signaling if he sees he is watched, and he need give only small signals in the hope that some of them may convey information to raise the score above the chance level.

The Third Series of Experiments in Wales

In the next series of experiments carried out two months after their second London visit, the boys started producing very high scores, and on two occasions they got 25 hits in 25 attempts. The first experiments were carried out in the field at the back of Richard Jones's house. The boys obtained high scores both when Richard was present and when he was absent. Glyn was behind a screen so that he could see only the experimenter who noted his guesses; the distance between the boys was 80 feet or more. When Richard was present, he stood where he could not see Glyn, but he was able to see the agent.

As high scores were obtained in the absence of other members of the Jones family, it would have been necessary either for Ieuan to produce a signal that could be detected by Glyn or for an intermediary in the house or near the test area to relay signals. He could have done this by watching the agent and receiving a cue from him, as described earlier.

In one experiment the boys were asked to perform in bathing trunks. Glyn said, before they started, that he was not going to try, and the score was only 11 hits out of 50 tries. The next day, the boys, fully clothed, obtained a high score with visitors present. At this sitting Ieuan turned out his pockets. On the following day the boys performed in bathing trunks, and the agent was closely examined to see that he had no apparatus concealed on his person. It would appear that if the search of Ieuan was adequate, as no doubt it was, any signals reaching Glyn must have been given by an intermediary. It is not stated whether other members of the family were present in the field at the final experiment when Ieuan was searched, but if all the family were absent from the test area, it would have been quite possible for anyone concealed at an upstairs window to have observed the agent and give signals. In fact, the safest way for an intermediary to operate is at a distance and screened from others.

An experiment conducted in a schoolroom in the village at this time was similar in many respects to those carried out on St. Paul's playing field during the second London visit. Tests were made under two conditions: either the percipient was behind a screen at one end of the room and the agent was seated 40 feet away in the open room, or the percipient was behind the screen and the agent was out in the room. Soal's brother, C. W. Soal, acted as signaler. Significantly above-chance scores were obtained under the first condition but not the second. Again, high scores were only obtained when the agent was visible to some other member of the family. In this case, however, if Richard Jones was screened from Glyn as the report implies, he could only have relayed signals by auditory means. But as Richard did not speak during the experiment, he could not have provided voice-inflection cues.

The important point to note about the experiments after the rehabilitation period, including those carried out in the open air, is that when the boys were on their home ground, high scores were obtained without any other member of the family taking part in the experiments; but, when they were away from home, as in the tests on St. Paul's playing field and in the schoolroom, high scores were obtained only in the presence of a member of the family who was in a position to see some part of the agent.

The outdoors experiments in Wales can prove very little as no attention was paid to the activities of members of the Jones family inside the house. In some of the tests, however, Glyn appears to have been relatively effectively screened, and if this was so, it is unlikely that visual signals could have been employed. Taking into account the fact that the boys had shown their ability to obtain high scores when separated by a blanket, an auditory cue would appear to be the only possible simple means of communication that could account for their improved performance. Earlier, the boys had been caught attempting to use auditory signals; it is possible that they had now perfected a more satisfactory method of comunication using sounds and that, on at least some occasions, they were assisted by a third person, who relayed signals after observing movements made by Ieuan.

A Possible Source of Trickery

After reading *The Mind Readers*, I carried out some tests on two Welsh school-girls, aged eight and nine years, using an Acme "silent" dog whistle. I had purchased this in Cambridge in 1948 when I had considered its possible use in a fake demonstration of telepathy. The whistle was about three inches long, but the operative portion was only about one inch in length. After removing the super-fluous parts of the whistle, it was attached by means of a length of rubber tubing to a bulb. It could then be suspended down one trouser leg and blown by the bulb which was kept in the trouser pocket.

In one demonstration I was standing between the agent and percipient who were fifty feet apart in the open air. The percipient was behind a screen and watched throughout by an observer. I arranged with the agent that on each trial I would sound pips on the whistle until she signaled me to stop by making a small movement of her foot when she had heard the requisite number of pips according to a prearranged code. The percipient also heard the whistle, and knowing the code, was able to state the identity of the card. After about fifteen minutes' instruction and practice, my percipient was able to score 16 hits out of 25 attempts during her first run in the presence of witnesses. The agent and percipient were watched throughout and signed statements were obtained saying that no sounds or movements were observed. The girls were successful both when I stood between them and when I was relaying signals from an upstairs window of a house near the test area.

In further tests using other children and carried out indoors, the agent and percipient were in different rooms with a doorway between them, and a blanket was hung over the doorway. I was in the room with the agent and gave signals according to a prearranged code. The percipient, a nine-year-old Welsh school-boy, obtained 23 successes in 25 attempts. This percipient also obtained high scores when I both acted as agent and operated the whistle. The tests were observed by the boy's father, who detected no signs of trickery and had no idea of how the trick was carried out.

It was found that the whistle could be detected over considerable distances by young people while it was quite inaudible to elderly people standing a few feet away, even when they were listening for it. Since the average age of the investigators in the experiments on the Jones boys was nearer seventy than forty, such a technique could quite easily have been employed without fear of detection.

It is possible to improve on results obtained with the dog whistle by using a Galton whistle, which may be obtained from firms who supply apparatus for school laboratories. This whistle is formed from a tube of very small bore, tuned by a plunger. It can produce notes with frequencies extending through and well above the audible range. After removing the extraneous parts of this whistle, one is left with a small tube, about 1/16 inch in diameter and ½ inch long, which can be blown by means of the bulb from an eyedropper. Such a whistle can be adjusted so that it is completely inaudible to adults but audible to children over considerable distances. I found that my nine-year-old daughter could detect it at 150 feet in the open air, and a larger bulb extended the range to 500 feet. If a small reflector from a pocket torch was fitted to the apparatus, the range was further increased, and the whistle was then more directional. The nine-year-old child could detect the whistle quite easily through a closed door or in almost any room of a house when the doors were open. Thus, her performance was much more striking than that of the Jones boys. It is possible, however, that the boys communicated by making sounds with the mouth, such as by whistling through the teeth in many of the short-range tests.

The Third London Visit

After the sittings held in the summer of 1956, the boys made their third trip to London. The experiments during this visit are of particular interest because Soal was not present and Jack Salvin, a professional magician, took charge of the proceedings. Salvin, at the time Chairman of the Occult Committee of the Magic Circle, was said to be skeptical of ESP, although he was a member of the British Society for Psychical Research. The sittings were held in the rooms of the Society, and Salvin was allowed to arrange the experiments in his own way. He supervised six sittings. In the first three of these, the boys obtained high scores. In the remaining sittings, they failed completely. This is of interest because *The Mind Readers* states, "Until the end of the third sitting the boys did not know who Mr. Salvin was or why he was there."[8]

The boys sat in the two rooms of the library of the Society for Psychical Research, more or less as in the first London visit. On this occasion, however, the only screen was a large, white blanket suspended from a line whose ends were fixed to bookcases. Glyn sat at a table behind this blanket with Bowden who recorded his guesses. At each of the successful sittings, the fathers of the two boys were present, but little is said about their precise whereabouts. The scores obtained at these three sittings are given below. Two unsuccessful runs are omitted. In one of these, clairvoyance conditions were used; in the second, Glyn and Ieuan had exchanged roles.

Sitting 1

RUN	1	2	3	4	5	6	7	8
SCORE	4	8	15	10	17	7	14	11

Sitting 2

RUN	1	2	3	4	5	7
SCORE	17	3	14	16	11	15

Sitting 3

RUN	1	2	4	5
SCORE	21	20	18	19

It will be seen that after the first two runs scores were high except in run 6 of the first sitting, and run 2 of sitting 2. These last 2 runs are the only ones in which Glyn and Bowden were not alone behind the screen. Salvin is reported to have gone behind the screen with Glyn during the first half of run 6, sitting 1, and to have sat beside Glyn throughout the second run of the second sitting. On that occasion, Glyn is reported to have made his guesses very rapidly.

After the first sitting, Salvin wrote in his statement: "I am completely satisfied, after making all the observations I desired and having permission to do what I wished, that no code or trickery took place, either on the part of the boys or on the part of anybody else (including the fathers of the two boys); and, in fact, that code or trickery in the experimental conditions I witnessed was impossible."[9] Similar statements were made by Salvin after the other two successful sittings.

It is difficult to place much reliance on Salvin's report, since it is unlikely that he could have heard the whistle even if it was sounded a foot from his ear. He had established the fact that high scores ceased when he went behind the curtain with Glyn, but this did not raise his suspicions. One elementary precaution he might have taken would have been to have asked the boys' fathers to leave the room.

More than two years later, on March 21, 1959, Salvin supervised a sitting at which Mr. and Mrs. Christopher Scott took over the roles of the Jones boys.[10] Salvin took complete charge, and under similar conditions to those employed by Glyn, Mrs. Scott obtained equally high scores. Mr. Scott, in Ieuan's role, had signaled to his wife by means of a Galton whistle. Salvin stated that he was baffled and immensely impressed.

The next day, a demonstration was given to Alec Reeves, an acoustics expert who had been present at two of the sittings of the third London visit and who had been sure no auditory or visual signals could have been used.

In fact, almost any boys could communicate with one another, using a Galton whistle or a dog whistle in complete safety when supervised by most adults over fifty years of age. At the time he made his tests, Salvin was nearer eighty than fifty.

It should be borne in mind that the Jones boys lived in a part of Wales where almost every child would have seen sheep dogs controlled by a whistle. They are likely to have attended a sheep dog trial, where the dogs appear to be controlled by some invisible influence. Their parents would also have known that as one grows older the whistle becomes increasingly difficult to hear. As Francis Galton commented when he first described his whistle, "there is a saying in Dorset that men over forty cannot hear the Bat's cry."[11]

The third London visit was the last real test for the Jones boys. Back in Wales, high scores were observed under a variety of conditions, all pitifully inadequate, until April 1957. After that month, no further experiments were reported and, it is understood, the boys' powers suddenly disappeared.

It is of interest to note that two books have been published since the conclusion of the experiment, each of which was written by a member of the Society for Psychical Research who attended some of the sittings on the Jones boys, and in neither case is any reference made to the experiment.[12]

At the present time, little is heard of the experiment, but it is also apparent that little has been learned from it. What it should have revealed is (1) that it is not possible to carry out experiments, reminiscent of the early days of the Society for Psychical Research, where subjects are tested in their own habitat, (2) that well-known academic persons who attend experiments and voice their opinions about them are as good as useless unless they adopt a critical attitude towards the experiments. Thus Burt's comment on the experiment, "finally, it must, I think, be owned by every impartial reader that, alike for their success and for the care with which they have been conducted, the experiments here recorded are unrivaled in the whole corpus of psychical research," is valueless.

A further feature that emerges is that the most important attribute required in an observer at these experiments is skepticism about the possibility of ESP rather than any expertise in trickery. Salvin was a member of the Magic Circle where he was regarded as an expert on fake telepathy, but he was completely taken in by a simple trick that he had not previously encountered.

Perhaps the most fitting judgment on the experiments was expressed by Soal: "What the investigation does demonstrate is the all-powerful influence of an intense motivation (in this case the love of money) in maintaining scores at a high level over a period of years."[13]

Notes

1. Sir Cyril Burt, "Experiments on Telepathy in Children," *British Journal of Statistical Psychology,* 12, 1 (1959): 721.
2. Soal and Bowden, *The Mind Readers,* p. 48.
3. *Ibid,* p. 26.
4. *Ibid,* p. 282.
5. *Ibid,* p. 61.
6. *Ibid,* p. 281.
7. *Ibid,* p. 81.
8. *Ibid,* p. 177.
9. *Ibid,* p. 178.
10. Christopher Scott and K. M. Goldney, "The Jones Boys and the Ultrasonic Whistle," *Journal of the Society for Psychical Research,* 40, 703 (1960): 249–260.
11. Francis Galton, *Inquiries into Human Faculty* (London: J. M. Dent, 1907), p. 235.
12. D. J. West, *Psychical Research Today* (London: Penguin, 1962); and R. H. Thouless, *Experimental Psychical Research* (London: Penguin, 1963).
13. Soal and Bowden, *The Mind Readers,* p. 235.

NOTES

14

Psychokinesis

Early Investigations

The first attempt to test whether a person's thoughts could influence the movement of a physical object was made by the great English scientist Michael Faraday (1791–1867) in 1853. At that time, the American mediums had arrived in Britain and a cult of table turning was sweeping the country. Faraday, who had become involved in a controversy over spiritualism at the Royal Society, thought it likely that the tables were moved through the application of a force transmitted by the hands of those touching them rather than by any psychic influence. This, he decided, could be established experimentally.

Faraday found that there was no need to have a group of people sitting round the table; a single person could cause the table to move. Also, he observed that the table's motion was not necessarily circular but might be in a straight line. He then glued together four or five pieces of cardboard, one over the other, with pellets of a soft cement consisting of wax and turpentine. The bottom piece was attached to a sheet of sandpaper that was resting on the table. The edges of the cardboard overlapped one another slightly and a pencil line was drawn on their undersurface to indicate the positions of the cards before the test. The upper cardboard was larger than the rest, so that it covered the remaining sheets. The cement was strong enough to offer considerable resistance to mechanical motion and also to hold the cards in any new position they acquired. However, it was weak enough to give way slowly to a continued force. The table turner placed his hands on the upper card and results were awaited. Faraday found that when the table, hands, and cards all moved to the left together, the displacement of the cardboard sheets, as compared to the line showing their original position showed that the hands of the table turner moved farther than the table. His hands had pushed the upper card to the left, and the under cards and the table had followed and had been dragged by it.

Faraday's subjects were all successful table turners who believed in their own abilities. Thinking that they moved the table as a result of a "quasi-involuntary" motion, Faraday next carried out tests in which the turner could become aware, by watching an indicator, when he was exerting any pressure. Under these conditions the table did not move. Faraday wrote:

> No form of experiment or mode of observation that I could devise gave me the slightest indication of any peculiar natural force. No attraction or repulsions, or signs of tangential power,—nor anything which could be referred to other than the mere mechanical pressure exerted inadvertently by the turner.[1]

Faraday had been investigating what is today called psychokinesis. A later investigation to determine the effects of thought on a physical system was carried out by Sir William Crookes using a delicate chemical balance, which, if there were powers of psychokinesis, might, he thought, be caused to move. He was, however, unsuccessful in moving the balance, and it is a remarkable fact that this rather obvious way of testing for psychokinesis has been ignored by later investigators.

At the turn of the century, a physical medium named Eusapia Palladino (see pages 58–64) claimed to be able to move a balance, or at least to get her spirit guide, "John King," to move it for her. She was tested by a committee in Paris that included the French physicist and codiscoverer of radium, Marie Curie (1867–1934), but it appears that on this occasion Eusapia was assisting "John King" by the use of a fine thread held between her hands. When suitable precautions were taken to screen the balance, it no longer moved.

The Experiments at Duke University

The topic of psychokinesis was almost forgotten until Rhine began his investigations of it in 1934. He was interested in finding out whether subjects could influence the fall of dice by wishing for a particular outcome. The early tests carried out at Duke University were conducted under informal experimental conditions. Subjects were often tested in private homes or in dormitories. Some investigators used themselves as subjects, and the experiments were hardly more than exploratory.

The results of some nineteen investigations carried out between 1934 and 1942 do not appear to have been very convincing at the time, since no mention was made of them in published reports of Rhine's work until after 1942. He has said that it was the discovery, in 1942, of a secondary effect in the old score sheets that convinced him of the reality of psychokinesis. Looking back at the records of the early experiments, he found that subjects tended to score higher in the first runs of a session than in the later ones and higher in early trials than in the later trials. He said: "The significance of these hit distribution data, found long after the tests had been made, was so great that we were at last fully convinced that the PK [psychokinesis] effect was a real one."[2]

In *Reach of the Mind,* published in 1949, Rhine reported the discovery of several new characteristics of psychokinesis. Subjects were more successful if they tried to influence many dice at the same time—the more the better; the distance of the subject from the dice did not affect the scores; metal dice produced above-chance scores whereas wooden ones did not; dice made of lead gave higher scores than those made of aluminum; rounding the corners of the dice so that they would roll more easily did not affect the scores. It is significant that techniques had developed to such an extent by 1949 that these detailed characteristics of psychokinesis could be determined, whereas in the first eight years of research (1934–1942) the scores had been insufficient even to provide a convincing case for its existence.

J. Fraser Nicol, at a symposium held by the Ciba Foundation in 1955, criticized these claims:

> On the strength of dice throwing said to have been performed at Duke University, it is recorded elsewhere that the psychokinetic force is more effective on heavy metal dice than on wooden ones; and also, from the same source, that the shape of the dice—sharp corners, rounded corners, or extremely rounded corners—makes no difference to the power of the human psychic force. Neither of these strange claims can be validated in any of the published reports on psychokinesis. It is mainly on the basis of these and similar unverifiable assertions that the author concludes that "the finding that *mass, number, and form* [of dice] *are not determining conditions of PK tests,* takes its place, then, alongside the discovery that time and space were not limiting factors in ESP."
>
> Only a few of these rash pronouncements have been quoted in the above paragraphs. Many others could be cited. One wonders what the more objective but friendly type of scientist must think when he is confronted with such highly adorned claims. He might, one surmises, rather easily turn away from psychical research, moved by the uncomfortable realization that a subject in which scientific method and the need for careful reporting are so casually pushed out of the way, is not a field of study in which he would care to indulge.[3]

The experiments on psychokinesis carried out since 1934 have been assessed in an extensive review made by the American psychologist Edward Girden of Brooklyn College. He divided the investigations into four categories:

1. The early dice tests carried out between 1934 and 1937 and mostly published in the *Journal of Parapsychology* between 1943 and 1946.
2. Later dice tests in which more care was paid to experimental design.
3. Tests in which objects other than dice were used.
4. Tests in which subjects attempted to produce lateral displacement of an object.[4]

Early Dice Tests

The main objections raised by Girden to the early dice tests were:

1. They were "largely free-wheeling and off the cuff." Variations of test conditions were a common occurrence.

2. When subjects attempted to obtain a particular face upper-most, they tended to attempt to throw a 6, and the dice were not tested for bias.

3. Little or no attention was paid to accuracy of recording.

4. Adequate control tests were lacking. Thus, if the proportion of, say, 6's arising in 960 trials when the subject had attempted to obtain them had been compared with the number of 6's arising in an equal number of trials when the subject had made no effort to obtain them, any bias on the dice could have been allowed for. Trials of the two types could have been alternated or targets could have been decided by a series of random numbers (1–6).

Only one of the early experiments employed a control series. This was carried out by Frick, a graduate student at the Parapsychology Laboratory in 1937. He tested himself when throwing dice from a cup under two conditions: (a) when wishing to throw 6's; (b) when wishing part of the time to throw 1's and part of the time *not* to throw 6's. When condition *a* operated, he obtained a positive deviation of 582 hits for the 6 face out of 52,128 trials, and under condition *b*, 576 hits for the 6 face out of 52,128 trials. Thus, the experiment provided no evidence for psychokinesis but clear evidence for bias of the dice, since the dice tended to fall with the 6 face uppermost whether it was being wished for or not. If the control series had been omitted, it could have been claimed that the experiment provided evidence for psychokinesis comparable to that provided by similar experiments reported at that time.

Frick's negative results indicated, according to Rhine and psychologist Betty Humphrey, then a research fellow in the Parapsychology Laboratory, that there was "no place in Frick's personal philosophy to accommodate the PK hypothesis. . . . It appears that Frick must have, as it were, completely deceived himself in the conduct of series B. He was not well unified in his motivational elements."[5]

Girden remarked:

On a number of interesting considerations, it is self evident that the most elementary requirement necessitated the equal representation of all six dice faces as targets in some randomised order and the tabulation of all dice faces in all trials. There is no need to make use of higher mathematics to conclude that biased dice could account for the obtained results.[6]

He also commented in his review that nineteen early reports from the Duke Laboratory were characterized by the presence of only one negative result, whereas two other experiments carried out at that time in other laboratories each gave negative results.

The first of these experiments, reported by Nicol and W. Carington, a well-known English parapsychologist, in England, was far better in design than any of the American tests. All throws of the dice were recorded and all faces were used as targets in systematic fashion. No evidence was obtained for psychokinesis, and detailed examination showed that decline effects were not present.[7] The second study, carried out by C. B. Nash of the Biophysics Department at St. Joseph's College, Philadelphia, in 1944, in which all 6 die faces were used as targets equal numbers of times, also provided no evidence for psychokinesis.[8]

Since the majority of the early Duke experiments were conducted in the investigators' homes or in dormitories by students, business people, and interested amateurs without professional supervision, the observed decline effects might well have arisen because of the way in which the tests were carried out. As such effects had not been envisaged at the time of the experiments, it is unlikely that any precautions were taken to guard against them. Similar decline effects were reported in the early experiments on clairvoyance carried out by Miss Jephson (see page 37). When her experiment was repeated, the result indicated that her original result was not due to extrasensory perception but to the fact that the subjects were not supervised. Whatever brought about high scores in her experiment also, presumably, produced the decline effect.

If a number of reports are collected together from people who have been left much to their own devices, such decline effects may be expected. Thus, for example, if an investigator tests a number of persons before finding one who gives high scores, and then goes on testing him, we should expect, in the absence of psychokinesis, the subject's record to show a decline effect across the record sheet. His scores would be high at the start, that being the reason he had been selected as a subject, but they would be unlikely to remain high. Also, if the number of runs in a test is not specified at the start, similar effects may be expected to arise. The initially successful subject may become discouraged and terminate the tests, after a run in which he has made a low score, but if he has made a number of hits in the last few trials of the run, he may feel encouraged to attempt a further run.

It is remarkable that the decline effects, when they were first noted, did not throw doubt on the experiments but were interpreted as providing convincing evidence for psychokinesis.

Later Dice Tests

These include investigations carried out after the development of the decline hypothesis. Following criticism of the earlier work, more attention was paid to experimental design and to effects such as bias on the dice. In some cases, all throws were recorded rather than only successes.

Among thirty of these later investigations listed by Girden, thirteen supported the psychokinesis hypothesis. The remainder did not produce a significant above-chance score, and in only one case was there a decline effect.

The conditions for a conclusive test for psychokinesis as stated by Rhine and Pratt in their book *Parapsychology* are: (1) a two-experimenter plan; (2) randomization of targets or systematic variation of the targets with all faces of the dice acting as target equal numbers of times; (3) independent recording of targets, hits and misses.

On these criteria, none of the thirteen tests giving positive evidence for psychokinesis can be regarded as conclusive, whereas several of the remaining seventeen investigations that failed to provide such evidence do satisfy the requirements.

Experiments Using Objects Other Than Dice

Experiments using disks, coins, and other objects have been reported by four investigators. The first of the tests, reported by Elizabeth McMahon, a zoologist working at the Parapsychology Laboratory, was on children and college students; plastic disks were used, and the subjects wished for a particular face to fall uppermost. A decline effect was present, but the score in both cases was not significantly above chance.[9]

Thouless, who made the second of these investigations, used coins thrown ten at a time off a ruler, and came to the conclusion, "It is obvious that the result is not of any value as independent evidence for PK."[10]

A third investigation, in which a subject tested himself by throwing a penny onto a rug for 100 trials per session over 10 sessions and also by throwing a die 216 times, was reported by Dorothy Pope, managing editor of the *Journal of Parapsychology*, with the comment that these attempts "offer suggestive data on the comparative success of dice and discs in PK experiments."[11] The odds against the combined score arising by chance were about 90 to 1.

The fourth and most extensive of these investigations was made by S. R. Binski, a government official, while working for his Ph.D. degree.[12] In one series, 117 subjects threw 100 coins at a time until altogether 153,000 coins had been thrown. In a second series, 123 subjects attempted to guess the winning number of roulette wheel spins. Neither series yielded evidence for PK.

Further tests were made by Binski with another subject whose scores, it was claimed, were highly significant. However, Girden has pointed out that these tests had no pre-experimental plan and involved no set number of runs. Gardner Murphy, when criticizing Girden's report in the *International Journal of Parapsychology*, pointed out that Binski's subject, using a coin, obtained 548 successes out of 1,000 attempts. Such a result is not very unusual—the odds are about 3 to 1—if one takes into account the fact that Binski had tested 240 subjects. It should also be noted that the 1,000 attempts represented only 10 throws of 100 coins. In such tests, where a large number of dice, for example, are thrown together, the greatest care must be taken with the randomization of the targets, otherwise the observations cannot be said to apply to independent events, and the statistical analysis may yield a misleading result.

Lateral Displacement

The best known of the experiments in which subjects attempted to produce the lateral displacement of objects by wishing it have been carried out by H. Forwald, of the Swiss Federal Institute of Technology at Zurich.[13] He not only claims that subjects have been able to obtain lateral displacement of objects, but also that he has been able to measure the psychokinetic force by observing the distance a cube slides sideways along a surface when dropped onto it from a height. His calculations are based on the assumption that if the object moved laterally a greater distance than the height from which it was dropped, then a psychokinetic force was present. For his work he was given the $1,000 McDougall Award, which is presented each year by the Duke Parapsychology Laboratory for outstanding research. Two objections have been raised concerning Forwald's research. The late C. C. L. Gregory, formerly Professor of Astronomy at London University, criticized the assumptions underlying Forwald's calculation of a psychic force in *Psychic News*, after having attempted without success to air his criticism in the *Journal of Parapsychology*. He pointed out:

> If anyone cares to perform the experiment of successively pushing wooden blocks from a child's building set over the edge of a low table on to a linoleum floor, he can easily satisfy himself that the cubes will scatter in a random manner equally in any direction up to a distance even greater than the height of the fall. *The reason for this scatter is not a sideways force, psychic or otherwise*, it is determined by the horizontal distance between the cube's centre of mass and the point of contact on striking the floor.
>
> Unless this distance happens to be zero, an impulsive couple will be imparted to the wooden block causing it to leap in a contrary direction to that of the point of contact with respect to the point below the centre of the cube. The sideways distance of the jump, roll or slide, will also depend on the friction, as Mr. Forwald found.[14]

The second objection was raised by J. Fraser Nicol. Forwald acted mainly as his own subject, and Nicol remarks:

> At what state in the difficult history of psychical research it became permissible for sensitives to report their own results and expect them to be accepted as serious evidence in psychical research, I do not know.[15]

As Girden has pointed out, Forwald's 1954 work began some nine years after publication of *Extrasensory Perception after Sixty Years*, and yet by the standards of that book, all his data would be unacceptable.

In seventeen reports on placement wishing, a result favoring the existence of a psychokinetic force was obtained in four. Only two investigations other than Forwald's report positive findings. The first of these, conducted by W. E. Cox, a businessman and amateur magician associated with the Parapsychology Laboratory, gave a significant below-chance score, but the researcher recognized that the experiment involved unwitnessed observation and recording.[16]

The remaining investigation, that of Miss Elsie Knowles, lecturer in applied statistics at Birmingham University in England, suffered from the weakness that the experimenter and her brother constituted the only two subjects.[17] Miss Knowles acted as recorder for her brother and also for herself at two of the three sessions.

Psychokinesis in Everyday Life

A more general objection against claims for the existence of psychokinesis is that, if it were a real process, its effects might be expected to manifest themselves in many situations in everyday life. Thus, the American science author Martin Gardner writes:

> Another disturbing question comes to mind. For decades Chicagoans have played the "26 game" in their bars and cabarets. The dice are shaken from a cup, the player betting a certain number will show up at least 26 times in 13 rolls. Obviously the tired and bored dice-girl, who tallies each roll, doesn't care one way or another. Obviously the player is doing his damndest to roll the number. How does it happen that these tally sheets, year after year, show precisely the percentage of house take allowed by the laws of chance? One would expect PK to operate strongly under such conditions.[18]

It is also only natural that experts such as the American authority on dice, John Scarne, should be astounded by the claims for psychokinesis.

A further objection to the claims that such a force exists is the fact that, if PK really operates, a statistical analysis of repeated throws of dice should be unnecessary. As Gardner says, "There is an obvious and suggestive analogy between para-psychology's preoccupation with purely statistical evidence, with all its murky aspects, and the preoccupation of mediums with phenomena that for some odd reason take place only in darkness."[19]

This has always been the main objection to the claims for psychokinesis. If such a factor exists, its effects should be detectable by means of a sensitive instrument, such as a chemical balance. Parapsychologists have always found it difficult to reply to this objection and have not published details of research aimed at obtaining a direct measure of psychokinesis.

During a lecture given at Manchester University in 1950, Rhine was asked whether psychokinesis could not be measured directly with a sensitive balance. He replied that it was a good suggestion and that they might get around to trying it sometime. After sixteen years of research and after the same question must have been asked countless times, such a reply was hardly satisfactory. The plain fact is that if a direct measurement is made of the psychokinetic force by any known means, it is found to be zero.

Why do these processes investigated by parapsychologists never manifest themselves directly? Why do they only manifest themselves under experimental conditions that are extremely conducive to error? But a further question arises Why does any prediction made on the basis of the data turn out to be useless? If Forwald can measure lateral displacement indirectly after an extensive statistical analysis, why cannot such a displacement be measured directly? A force applied over a period of time would more likely manifest itself to an increased extent; one hundred "willers" would produce more push than a single one. A simple demonstration in which the effects of the psychokinetic force could be observed directly would be far more convincing than any number of experiments where the result can only be expressed after a statistical analysis or where psychokinesis is claimed to exist owing to the presence of a *post hoc* secondary effect in the data.

It is significant that, in the past fifteen years, individuals have claimed to have abilities rather like those of the physical mediums in the nineteenth century. In many cases these could be classified as involving psychokinesis. Thus, the ability to move the needle of a magnetometer, to stop a watch, or to bend a fork involve the imposition of a physical force of one kind or another. But in spite of the availability of such people, no clear cut demonstration of psychokinesis has been produced to date.

Notes

1. Michael Faraday, "Experimental Investigation of Table-Moving," *The Athenaeum* (July 1853): 801–3.
2. Rhine, *New World of the Mind*, p. 37.
3. J. F. Nicol, "Some Difficulties in the Way of Scientific Recognition of Extrasensory Perception." In *Extrasensory Perception*, edited by Wolstenholme and Millar, p. 36.
4. E. Girden, "A Review of Psychokinesis," *Psychological Bulletin*, 59 (1962): 353–88.
5. J. B. Rhine and Betty M. Humphrey, "The PK Effect with Sixty Dice per Throw," *Journal of Parapsychology*, 9, 3 (1945): 215.
6. Girden, *Psychological Bulletin*, p. 361.
7. J. F. Nicol and W. Carington, "Some Experiments in Willed Die-Throwing," *Proceedings of the Society for Psychical Research*, 48, 173 (1946): 164–75.

8. C.B.Nash,"PK Tests of a Large Population," *Journal of Parapsychology*, 8, 4 (1944): 304–10.
9. Elizabeth McMahon, "A PK Experiment under Light and Dark Conditions," *Journal of Parapsychology*, 9, 4 (1945): 249–63.
10. R. H. Thouless, "Some Experiments on PK Effects in Coin Spinning," *Journal of Parapsychology*, 9, 3 (1945): 169–75.
11. Dorothy Pope, "Bailey's Comparison of a Coin and a Die in PK Tests," *Journal of Parapsychology*, 10, 3 (1946): 213–15.
12. S. R. Binski, "Report on Two Exploratory PK Series," *Journal of Parapsychology*, 21, 4 (1957): 284–95.
13. H. Forwald, "A Continuation of the Experiments on Placement PK," *Journal of Parapsychology*, 16, 4 (1952): 273–83.
14. C. C. L. Gregory, letter in *Psychic News*, May 9, 1959.
15. J. F. Nicol, "The Design of Experiments in Psychokinesis," *Journal of The Society for Psychical Research*, 37, 681 (1954): 355.
16. W. E. Cox, "The Effect of PK on the Placement of Falling Objects," *Journal of Parapsychology*, 15, 1 (1951): 40–48.
17. Elsie A. G. Knowles, "Report of an Experiment Concerning the Influence of Mind over Matter," *Journal of Parapsychology*, 13, 3 (1949): 186–96.
18. Martin Gardner, *Fads and Fallacies in the Name of Science* (New York: Dover 1957), p. 307. Copyright 1952, 1957, by Martin Gardner. Reprinted through permission of the publisher.
19. *Ibid*, p. 353.

15
Group Experiments

Before 1934, investigators at Duke University had no difficulty finding subjects who could consistently obtain high scores in ESP tests. But such subjects became increasingly scarce as experimental designs were made more rigorous. Then following the discussions at the meeting of the American Psychological Association in 1938 and publication of Kennedy's criticisms in 1939, high-scoring subjects became extinct. Since 1939, not a single subject has appeared who can consistently obtain high scores guessing ESP cards.

Humphrey's Experiment

After 1940, many of the experiments on ESP carried out in the United States relied on a new technique introduced by Betty Humphrey at the Duke Parapsychology Laboratory. She first used it to test the relationship between ESP ability and personality characteristics.[1] In her experiment ninety-six subjects were first classified by means of a test into "compressive" and "expansive" types. After this, the subjects were given a test for clairvoyance, and the mean ESP score of the compressives was compared with that of the expansives. It was found that the expansives scored significantly higher on the test, the odds being greater than 300,000 to 1 against the difference in scores arising by chance. The overall score for the ninety-six subjects was, however, not significantly above the chance level, nor was the score of any one subject significantly above chance.

The personality test used in the experiments required the subjects to draw anything they pleased on a blank sheet of paper. Subjects who filled the area of the paper with a bold drawing were classified as expansives, while those who used only a part of the paper were classified as compressives. Thus, while ignoring any assumptions that related the manner in which a person draws to other personality characteristics, Miss Humphrey's experiment seemed to indicate that people who fill a sheet of paper when drawing on it tend to obtain high scores in ESP tests and that people who make small drawings covering only a part of the paper tend to obtain low scores. A further remarkable result reported by Humphrey was that when telepathy tests were used instead of clairvoyance tests, the result was reversed: compressives got high scores and expansives low ones.

J. Fraser Nicol and Betty Humphrey (now Mrs. Nicol) carried out two further experiments of the same type. The first of these gave scores that tended in the same direction but were not statistically significant.[2] The second has not been published, but Nicol informed me in correspondence that the result was "pure nullity" and that the whole affair needs to be reexamined. Dr. D. J. West of the Society for Psychical Research also repeated this experiment and found no difference in the scores of the groups and no signs of ESP.[3]

Sheep and Goats

Since 1940, several investigators have divided their subjects into two groups, but they have used different criteria from those of Humphrey. In most of the research the results have the same general characteristics as in Humphrey's experiment.

The most extensive of these tests were those conducted by Dr. Gertrude R. Schmeidler of the City College of New York.[4] She divided her subjects into sheep and goats, a sheep being a person who believed in ESP and a goat being one who did not. She then found that sheep scored above chance and goats below chance. Again, the overall score did not differ significantly from the chance level, and again repetition of the test by other investigators did not confirm the original result.[5]

Experiments in the Classroom

A similar technique was employed in a number of experiments carried out in classrooms with the aim of seeing whether pupils who had good feelings toward the teacher displayed ESP. Margaret Anderson of the Biophysics Department at the University of Pittsburgh, and Rhea White, a research fellow in the Parapsychology Laboratory, employed a questionnaire to determine childrens' attitudes toward the teacher and the teacher's attitude to the children.[6]

The children were then given a clairvoyance test, and it was claimed that where there was mutual good feeling between teacher and pupil, the scores tended to be above the chance level, where there was lack of good feeling scores were below it. Repetitions of these experiments by other investigators have again failed to confirm the original result, and a repetition by White herself also failed to achieve any confirmation.[7]

Target Missing

A peculiar feature present in the results of the group experiments is that above-and below-chance scores obtained by the subgroups balance out so that the overall score is at the chance level. In the event of any weak ability being present in a population which is more evident in certain types of individual, say men, than in others, say, women, there would be a point in confining the sample to men, as scores from the women would lower the average value obtained. The group experiments do not, however, show less ability in one subgroup than the other—or even complete lack of any ability. They show *negative* ESP ability, i.e., the subjects, when attempting to identify targets, tend to identify them wrongly. It is as if when they are attempting to identify a target something makes them miss it.

In order to obtain scores consistently below the chance level, the subject has to receive information just as he does to obtain above-chance scores. But equal amounts of information will not produce equal numbers of hits and misses. Let a subject obtain information sufficient to enable him to obtain H hits in 100 attempts. He will then obtain H hits through receiving this information and on the remaining cards $(100 - H)$ he will score at the chance level. His score denoted by S_H is then equal to $H + (100 - H)/5 = 20 + .8H$.

If, using the same amount of information, the subject is to avoid securing hits, he can achieve this on H cards but will score at the chance level on the remainder. His score denoted by S_M is then equal to $(100 - H)/5 = 20 - .2H$.

Thus if ESP were being employed by equal-sized subgroups, the overall score would not be expected to be at the chance level.

It may be objected that ESP does not operate in this manner to cause low scores. But whatever its way of operating, it is remarkable that scores should invariably balance between subgroups so as to give an overall score at the chance level.

Precautions Necessary in Group Experiments

Provided adequate precautions are taken in its design and execution, the group experiment has several advantages over one testing a single subject. A high-scoring subject may lose his ability, making it impossible to verify the original result by further tests; but in the group experiment, subjects selected at random from the population should give the same average score as other similar-sized groups within the limits indicated by statistical theory. None of the subjects need by himself display any significant signs of ESP. Anyone can repeat such an experiment by drawing a group of subjects from the same population.

The type of group experiment in which two subgroups are compared does, however, introduce further hazards into the experimental situation. There are two potential sources of error that need to be carefully guarded against. It is necessary to take as stringent safeguards against spurious high scores as in experiments with single subjects, but extra precautions are necessary to ensure that the experimenter himself cannot unwittingly influence the result. (In the earlier types of experiments, the main aim was to keep the subjects from getting any information about the targets; in the new group experiments, it is, in addition, necessary to ensure that the scoring of the tests and the classification into groups are completely independent and exact.) In a split-group experiment, the lack of confirmation of a result in which one subgroup has scored above chance and the other subgroup below chance while there is an overall result at the chance level at once points to some form of error in allocating individuals to their groups. Ideally, the groups should be decided and the result made public before the ESP tests are carried out, so that there can be no possibility of the original classifications being changed after the scores of the ESP tests become known.

It is also necessary that the nature of the test and the number of trials to be given to each subject be standardized before any tests are made. It would be quite easy to obtain a spurious result when dividing people into believers and disbelievers in ESP if the number of trials to be given to each subject was not decided from the start. The skeptical goat might otherwise carry on with run after run until he had proved his point by getting a total score below the chance expectation. In this way, he would influence the outcome of the experiment. If some goats, after obtaining high scores, decided that they did believe in ESP after all, and change their classification, this again would result in a lowered score for the goats and a higher one for the sheep.

In the card-guessing experiments carried out by Rhine and Soal, the aim was to design the experiment so that above-chance scores could not be attributed to anything other than ESP. Emphasis was placed on the accurate recording of targets and guesses, the isolation of the subject from normal sensory contact with the targets, and accurate checking of the guesses against the targets. In a group experiment, at least as much emphasis must be paid to maintaining the groupings into which subjects are placed before the testing starts. Whereas in the early card guessing tests, emphasis was placed on controlling the activities of the subject, in the group experiments it is of even greater importance to control the investigator.

The group experiment, if its results can be trusted, provides the ideal way of giving repeatable results. Its failure to do so implies that lack of efficient control of the investigators is the determining factor.

Notes

1. Betty M. Humphrey, "Success in ESP as Related to Form of Response Drawings 1. Clairvoyance Experiments," *Journal of Parapsychology*, 10, 2 (1954): 78–106.

2. J. F. Nicol and Betty M. Humphrey, "The Exploration of ESP and Human Personality," *Journal of the American Society for Psychical Research,* 48, 4 (1953): 133–78.

3. D. J. West "ESP Performance and the Expansion-Compression Rating," *Journal of the Society for Psychical Research,* 36, 660 (1950): 295–308.

4. G. R. Schmeidler, "Separating the Sheep from the Goats," *Journal of the American Society for Psychical Research,* 39, 1 (1945): 47–50.

5. W. R. Smith, E. F. Dagle, M. D. Hill, and J. Mott-Smith, "Testing for Extrasensory Perception with a Machine, *Data Sciences Laboratory Project 4610,* AFCRL-63-141, May, 1963; and S. D. Kahn, "Studies in Extrasensory Perception," *Proceedings of the American Society for Psychical Research,* 25 (October 1952): 1–48.

6. M. Anderson and R. White, "Teacher-Pupil Attitudes and Clairvoyance Test Results," *Journal of Parapsychology,* 20, 3 (1956): 141–57.

7. M. E. Rilling, Clare Pettijohn, and John Q. Adams, "A Two-Experimenter Investigation of Teacher Pupil Attitudes," *Journal of Parapsychology,* 25, 4 (1961): 257–59; and R. White and J. Angstatd, "A Resume of Research into Teacher-Pupil Attitudes," *Journal of the American Society for Psychical Research,* 55 (October 1961): 142–47.

16

Research Behind
the Iron Curtain

Soviet research on ESP was started during the 1920s at Leningrad University by the physiologist V. M. Bechterev, who is noted for his pioneer work on the conditioned reflex. Early experiments, in which Bechterev collaborated with an animal trainer, V. L. Dourov, to investigate the effects of mental suggestion from a distance on a group of performing dogs, were mentioned by Rhine in *Extra-Sensory Perception*.

Later in the 1920s, considerable publicity was given to the theories of an Italian physicist, Ferdinando Cazzamali, that telepathic communication was dependent on a type of electromagnetic radiation, "brain waves," a centimeter in wavelength. In 1932, the Institute for Brain Research at Leningrad received an assignment to start experiments with the aim of finding a physical basis for telepathy. This research was put in the hands of L. L. Vasiliev, one of Bechterev's pupils, who became Professor of Physiology at the University of Leningrad. Between 1932 and 1938, the experiments carried out by Vasiliev included tests in which an attempt was made to influence a person by telepathy while he was screened inside a metal chamber.

After 1938, no mention was made of telepathy in the Russian press until 1959, when Vasiliev published a popular book, *Mysterious Phenomena of the Human Psyche*, in which one chapter was devoted to the topic.

At the end of 1959, an article appeared in the French journal *Constellation*, entitled "La Transmission de pensee—arme de guerre," ("Thought Transmission—Weapon of War") describing experiments said to have taken place on the American submarine Nautilus. This was followed by a similar article in February

1960 in *Science et Vie* (*Science and Life*) entitled "Du Nautilus" ("About the Nautilus"). Copies of the articles were sent to Vasiliev, who decided that the experiments showed it was possible to communicate by telepathy through sea water and the metal side of a submarine. He concluded that his own experiments, in which the percipients had been screened inside a metal box, were confirmed by the American tests. He commented later that such stories must be treated with caution, since authoritative sources in Washington disclaimed any such experiments; at the same time, he pointed out that the Parapsychology Laboratory at Duke University had received a financial grant from the United States Office of Naval Research in 1952 for experiments on ESP.

Vasiliev seems to have taken the French reports seriously, for he later stated, "This totally unexpected confirmation of our twenty-five year old experiments compelled me to make them known to a wide circle of scientific workers."[1] A symposium was then organized at Leningrad University in 1960, after which a special laboratory was set up for the study of telepathic phenomena under Vasiliev's direction.

Vasiliev's *Experiments in Mental Suggestion* was published in 1962, and an English translation was made available in 1963.[2] In this book, Vasiliev describes the experiments he carried out in the 1930s that, in his opinion, prove conclusively that human subjects can be put into a state of hypnotic sleep and wakened by an agent situated in another room.

Vasiliev's investigations are reported in four sections with the following four chapter headings: "Visual Images," "Mental Suggestions of Sleeping and Awakening," "Critical Evaluation and Improved Method," "Experiments in Mental Suggestion at Long Distances."

The main experiments in the first category consist of telepathy tests in which the subject had to guess whether an agent was seeing a black or a white disk at each trial. A simple randomizer utilizing black and white disks mounted back to back on a vertical rod rotating in a socket was used to select the targets. The disks were rotated before each trial and came to rest with one of the two colors facing the agent; the percipient then had to guess which was being seen.

Slightly above-chance scores were obtained both when the subject was in a metal-screened chamber and when he was unscreened. Under both conditions the overall scores of groups of subjects were above chance and statistically significant. The experimental conditions were unsatisfactory, however, since the targets and subject calls were recorded by the one experimenter.

Vasiliev himself seems to have been dissatisfied with the tests, for at the end of the chapter describing them, he wrote: "In order to substantiate our preliminary conclusions we were thus forced to employ another method of mental suggestion—one which yields far more significantly positive results; this turned out to be the procedure of putting to sleep, and awakening, by means of mental suggestion."[3]

Vasiliev's second type of test was one in which an agent attempted to induce sleep or waking in a subject positioned at a distance or screened in a metal chamber. The subjects used in these tests had taken part in conventional hypnosis tests and could be put to sleep or awakened by the agent with ease when telepathy was not involved. In most of the experiments, the subject and agent were situated in different rooms. In some tests the subject was placed in a Faraday Cage, a metal-screened box that largely excludes electromagnetic radiation. In other tests, the agent was placed inside a lead chamber sealed with mercury. The subject held a small rubber bulb and was told to press it rhythmically. This bulb was connected by tubing to a pen which was thus moved through changes in pressure, and a record of the oscillations was made on a drum rotating at a constant speed. When the subject went to sleep, these oscillations ceased; they resumed when he woke up and proceeded to press the bulb again.

At a time unknown to the subject, the agent would move a switch that marked a second tracing on the rotating drum, and he would then attempt to induce sleep. Sometimes, after the subject had fallen asleep, the agent would move the switch again, making another mark on the second tracing and then attempt to wake the subject. The times between suggestion and the subject's falling asleep and between suggestion and waking up could then be determined from the record.

Since, however, a control group was not employed, this data can reveal nothing about the part played by the agent. To assess this effect it would, at the least, be necessary to know the length of time elapsing between mental suggestion and the subject's going to sleep or waking up and the time taken for the subject to fall asleep or wake up in the absence of any mental suggestion.

Vasiliev seems to have been aware of these objections, since in the next group of experiments, described under the heading "Critical Evaluation and Improved Method," he employed a control series in which mental suggestion was withheld. It is the experiments in this section that provide Vasiliev's main evidence for the possibility of mental suggestion at a distance.

In the new tests the subject was left alone in a room and requested to press a bulb rhythmically. The agent went to another room where he started the rotating drum and operated the black-and-white disk-randomizing apparatus. If the black disk showed, he immediately started trying to induce sleep (experimental series) until the oscillations of the pen tracing stopped, showing that the subject was asleep. If the white disk showed, he made no effort to induce sleep (control series). The agent is also reported to have noted with a stopwatch the time elapsed between the start of the test and the subject's falling asleep.

A total of fifty-three tests of this nature were carried out, using four different subjects. The results for each subject are not given, but the pooled results gave twenty-seven observations in the control series (without suggestion), having a mean time of 17.7 minutes (standard error 0.54 minutes), and twenty-six observations in the experimental series, having a mean time of 6.8 minutes (standard error of 0.54 minutes). Standard error is a measurement of dispersion and, in the case of the control series above, signifies that if a large number of similar experiments were made, and the mean time was calculated for each experiment, we should expect 68 percent of the experiments to produce a mean falling between $17.7 \pm .54$ minutes, i.e. between 17.16 and 18.24 minutes. The difference between the two means was significant with odds greater than 3,000 to 1 against arising by chance.

It should be noted that not much reliance can be placed on this final calculation, since each of the subjects fell asleep in the control situation when the agent
did not try to induce it. If there were large individual differences in the times at
which the different subjects tended to fall asleep, as appears to be the case from
other data, a misleading result might easily be obtained unless each subject was
tested an equal number of times in each condition.

The data given by Vasiliev in Table 12 of his book are unlikely to give one
much confidence in the accuracy of the time measurements. Times were recorded
both on the tracings and with a stop watch, and the fifty-three observations in this
table are, with one exception, to the nearest five seconds. However, among the
observations, twenty-two of them are to a whole minute, whereas the expectation
would be that only about four would be of this type.

Taking Vasiliev's result as it stands, however, and accepting the difference in
mean time between the control and experimental series, it is still doubtful whether
this experiment can provide conclusive evidence for the possibility of suggestion
at a distance.

It will be noted that Vasiliev's control series was necessary, since the subjects
ultimately tended to go to sleep without any suggestion being given. His method of
allocating tests between the experimental and control series by means of a randomizer is excellent, provided his rotation apparatus produced a random series.

The main weakness of the experiment lies in the manner in which readings
were taken. It has long been known that it is essential in ESP tests that records of
targets and of subjects' calls be maintained by independent observers. Thus, when
a subject is guessing cards, the real order must be recorded by an experimenter who
is unaware of the subject's calls, and the subject's calls must be recorded by
someone who is unaware of the targets. Counting the number of hits with cards is a
relatively simple operation, however, compared to deciding the exact point in time
at which a wavy line on a drum comes to rest. In certain cases, there may be no
doubt, but others are likely to arise in which there will be ambiguous features in the
record. The decision as to the exact time at which the subject has gone to sleep
must be made by someone who is unaware of whether he is dealing with a test
falling into the experimental or control series and, having made his decision, he
must stand by it.

In Vasiliev's test, the agent was in the room with the recording apparatus; he
also used a stopwatch to determine the length of time elapsing before the subject
went to sleep. To provide reasonable test conditions without completely automat-
ing the recording procedure, it would be necessary for the recording apparatus to
be in a separate room with an experimenter who was completely unaware of the
nature of the test to record the exact time at which the subject had gone to sleep.
The agent would be informed by a signal from a randomizer whether or not he was
to try to induce sleep, and this information would have to be kept secret from any
other person until the test was complete and the time at which the subject went to
sleep had been decided. It would also be essential to predetermine the exact
number of tests to be carried out so that there could be no possibility of selection of
data.

Vasiliev made little attempt to control the human factor in his experiments, although a long history of research on hypnosis, with which he was familiar, shows the errors that can arise when such control is omitted. Also, insufficient information is given in Vasiliev's book about the precise conditions under which his experiments were carried out. It would be of interest to know, for example, the exact order in which the tests were made; what information was given to the subject after a sitting in relation to what had transpired at that sitting; and whether the tracings were inspected by assessors who were without knowledge of the nature of the test.

The Soviet research reported by Vasiliev is similar in many ways to work carried out elsewhere in the 1930s; it is on much the same level of sophistication as the early work at Duke University. The chief weakness lies in the lack of precautions against errors in recording and against the experimenter being affected by what he knows about the experiment. With modern apparatus and techniques, it would be a simple matter to repeat the experiments and to obtain more conclusive information.

Notes

1. L. L. Vasiliev, *Experiments in Mental Suggestion,* trans. not given (Church Crookham, Hants., England: Institute of Mental Images, 1963).
2. Originally published in Russian as *Suggestions at a Distance* (Moscow: Gospolitis, The State Publishing Company, 1962).
3. Vasiliev, *Experiments in Mental Suggestion,* p. 74.

17
Summary to Part Two

The majority of ESP experiments carried out between 1915 and 1965 required subjects to guess the identities of cards depicting one of five different symbols. It is a simple matter to test whether a person is capable or not of utilizing sensory information to identify a stimulus. If a person had the ability to identify symbols in the absence of any sensory information, there should have been no difficulty demonstrating this to the satisfaction of anyone having any doubts on the matter. But after fifty years of card guessing no such demonstration of ESP has been forthcoming.

The Repeatable Experiment

The failure to confirm the results of the early Duke research, and the criticisms that were made of the experimental methods employed, resulted in attempts being made to improve the rigor of the experiments and to devise the "conclusive experiment" in which subjects would achieve above-chance scores under foolproof conditions. A number of experiments were declared to be foolproof, but each of these failed both to stand up to criticism or to yield a repeatable result. The difficulty was not so much the inability to confirm the result but the fact that the contrary result was obtained. Rather than equal the scores obtained in the original experiment, subjects failed to obtain above-chance scores at all. In the absence of the repeatable demonstration, the critic is asked to accept the one-off demonstration. He has to accept the investigator's claim to have eliminated the possibility of anything other than ESP being responsible for the result of the experiment. He has to rely completely on the capability and integrity of the investigator. He is, furthermore, asked to accept the result obtained in the original experiment despite the fact that the result is not confirmed in further experiments.

The critic is informed of numerous experiments in which subjects have obtained high above-chance scores and told that each of these provides confirmation of the findings of the others. But this is not the same thing at all as replication of an experiment. Error, trickery, and ineptitude may each result in high above-chance scores. It would, thus, be remarkable if they were not at times responsible for above-chance scores. Even the Michelson-Morley experiment on the velocity of light relative to the direction of the earth's motion gave a contrary result on some occasions.

But there is a difference between an experiment that almost invariably gives the original result and one that gives a result on some occasions and a contrary result on most others. It is clear also that there is little point repeating an experiment in which the experimental design is suspect unless the original design is modified. The mere repetition of a weak experiment can only confirm its inadequacy. Repetitions of an experiment should be possible by critics who modify points in the procedure if they think it necessary.

A further point arises when discussing confirmation of results. Some experimental results should be obtained by anyone who can set up the original experimental arrangements, but others depend on the availability of a high-scoring subject. When Shackleton obtained high scores in precognitive telepathy, he could have been sent to a completely independent laboratory for testing and confirmation. A high-scoring subject such as Hubert Pearce might have been sent to some of the critics around at that time who were busy trying to confirm Rhine's results in psychology laboratories in different parts of America. This was never done and, as subsequent events suggest, would not have been successful had it been done, since high-scoring subjects invariably lost their ESP abilities altogether immediately after the experimental report describing their feats was published. Confirmation of the results with a high-scoring subject by independent investigators employing their own techniques can also establish that high scores are not dependent on a particular experimental procedure being employed. This is particularly important in the case of a subject who has stipulated the conditions under which he was tested in the original experiment.

Facts Emerging from the Experiments

While many of the claims made for the experiments must be disputed, a number of generally agreed facts have been established:

1. Subjects obtained scores in some card-guessing experiments that were not due to chance.

2. Some of those taking part in experiments brought about high above-chance scores by cheating.

3. The ability of a subject to obtain high scores was dependent on the experimental design and procedure employed.

4. Some experimenters obtained evidence for ESP from their experiments; others, in similar experimental conditions, always failed to do so.

5. In the United States the experimental designs employed tended to become more rigorous after the exploratory tests carried out at Duke University in the thirties.

6. There was lack of agreement among the investigators about the phenomenon being investigated.

This last fact may be amplified.

Telepathy and Clairvoyance

In the United States, Rhine discovered that ESP was as easily demonstrated under clairvoyance as under telepathy conditions. It was unnecessary to have an agent view the cards, thereby making the experiments simpler in design and reducing the danger of sensory leakage between the percipient and agent. In Britain, attempts were made by Soal to obtain evidence for clairvoyance with each of his high-scoring telepathy subjects, but without any success at all.

High-Scoring Subjects

In the thirties Rhine decided that ESP was present to some extent in about a fifth of the population. He had no difficulty in finding five high-scoring subjects whose performance was such that any skeptic should have been silenced on the spot by seeing one of these subjects at work. These subjects disappeared when the experimental conditions were tightened up. In the Turner-Ownbey series, the high-scoring subject lost her powers half way through the experiment at a point corresponding precisely with the introduction of safeguards against trickery. High-scoring subjects became extinct in the United States during the fifties. At the same time as they disappeared in the U.S.A. they made an appearance in Britain. But by 1960 they were impossible to find in Britain also and they have never reappeared.

Effect of Distance on ESP

The investigators produced conflicting findings on the effect of the distance between the percipient and the agent or the object that he was seeking to identify.

In America, subjects had little difficulty displaying ESP at a distance. In Britain, subjects displayed marked individual differences. Ieuan Jones's telepathic emanations were blocked by a single door, although he could transmit satisfactorily to his cousin Glyn over a few hundred yards. Mrs. Stewart's agents were able to penetrate the outer suburbs of London and Antwerp.

Two significant changes arose between 1940 and 1960. These were the introduction of the group-type experiment and the use of machines to randomize targets and record the score of the subject. The group experiments afforded a means of providing a repeatable experiment in the absence of high-scoring subjects, provided ESP was present to some extent in part of the population as claimed by Rhine. Thus, in the case of high-scoring subjects, it might be assumed that these were present in very small numbers and that for some reason they were confined to Durham, North Carolina. Anyone testing a large number of subjects in New York might, thus, miss finding one. But if ESP ability was generally distributed in the population and present to a measurable extent in a fifth of the population in Durham, it would be unlikely in any random sample of a hundred individuals that none would be included in New York. However, the extraordinary new characteristic of ESP that emerged implied that any random sample of the population would be expected to score at the chance level in spite of the fact that it contained individuals with ESP ability. The underlying hypothesis is easily testable by testing the same sample twice and determining the degree of correlation between the two sets of measurements. But this does not appear to have been done.

The gradual introduction of automated means of testing was the most important development. It provided a tool for use by the investigators, but it was also to require intelligent use and no less emphasis on rigorous experimental design than in the past. In 1965 I suggested that experiments carried out by the U.S. Air Force using a machine provided an acceptable model for future research.

These investigations marked the end of card guessing and are discussed in Part Three.

PART THREE

18
Testing ESP
with a Machine

By 1965, card guessing was almost a thing of the past, and the repeatable experiment had failed to materialize. In that year, J. B. Rhine retired from the Parapsychology Laboratory, and in the same year Duke University withdrew its support. A new organization, The Institute for the Study of Man, was set up by Rhine outside the campus.

Since 1965, new developments have arisen in ESP research, the most important of which is the use of machines and automated procedures.

Automatic Recording

Although it is a simple matter to randomize targets, present them to a subject, and record his successes and failures, it is remarkable that few attempts were made to use machines until recent times. Tyrrell's machine (see p. 37) employed automatic randomization, presentation of targets, comparison of guess and target, and registration of hits and trials made. When all these features were operating, so that the testing was completely automatic and the targets were decided by the randomizer, subjects' results were consistently at the chance level. As soon as any human element was present, e.g., when Tyrrell compiled random numbers with his randomizer and then used these in an experiment without further use of the machine, the subject obtained above-chance scores.

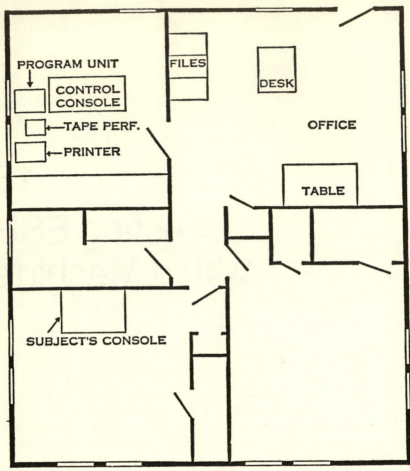

Figure 18-1
Layout of rooms used with VERITAC

VERITAC

The first full-scale investigation using automation was conducted at the United States Air Force Laboratories in 1963.[1]

The investigators, William R. Smith, Everett F. Dagle, Margaret D. Hill, and John Mott-Smith, approached their research with the idea that it was a waste of time to conduct further experiments merely to demonstrate the occurrence of ESP and that it was more important to discover how ESP worked. The apparatus they used was called VERITAC. It automatically generated random targets, registered the subjects' guesses, compared them with the targets, and registered scores. There were two consoles in different rooms: the subject's console, at which he sat and indicated his guess at each trial by pressing a button, and a control console on which the targets were generated (Figure 18-1).

The targets, consisting of the digits 0-9, were created by means of a random-number generator. The number selected by the generator at each trial appeared on an indicator tube on the control console. The subject's console contained two electromechanical counters that indicated to him the number of trials he had made and his number of successes. In addition, a light flashed on the console each time he secured a hit. Thus, the subject had partial knowledge of the result after each trial. Provision was made for the automatic recording of the targets, the number selected by the subject, and the time at which each trial was made. In addition, the total numbers of trials and hits were recorded. A record was also maintained to show the response time of the subject at each trial.

The rooms in which the consoles were situated were separated by a third room, and the doors between the rooms were kept closed during tests. VERITAC was checked for operational effectiveness, and several pilot studies were run to ensure that the apparatus was reliable in operation. The numbers generated by the randomizer were checked and found to meet rigorous statistical criteria for randomness.

Each subject had been given an indirect probing interview which classified him as a sheep or a goat. The thirty-seven subjects each then completed 5 runs of 100 trials for each of three types of experiment:

1. *Clairvoyance*. At each trial the subject depressed the button representing the digit he thought had been selected, and it was indicated but not seen by anyone on the control console in the other room.

2. *Precognition*. Here the subject had to select the number he thought would be generated on the next trial. He started and stopped the random-number generator, and the numbers so generated were presented on the control console but were not shown to the subject or to anyone else.

3. *General extrasensory perception (GESP)*. The subject indicated the number he thought had been selected. The target was shown on the control console in the other room where it was seen by one of the experimenters.

The group of thirty-seven subjects completed a total of 55,500 trials.

It was found that neither the group as a whole nor any member of it displayed any evidence of ESP. The difference in scores between the sheep and the goats was also not significant.

The apparatus used in these tests was carefully designed and could be standardized and used by parapsychologists for testing extrasensory perception.

A feature of VERITAC was that the subject was informed of the correct result after each guess. In most of the earlier card-guessing experiments, the subject completed at least twenty-five trials before learning how he had scored, and he had no means of knowing whether he had made a hit or a miss at each trial. If ESP is possible and exists to a small extent in most subjects, as some parapsychologists claim, performance would only be expected to improve if subjects are given the chance to learn from knowledge of results in previous trials. The conventional methods of testing would, in fact, be expected to impair future performance.

With VERITAC subjects can be given long practice sessions so that if any ESP ability is present it would be expected to become strengthened. Thus, it can be employed as both a testing and a training machine. It could also be modified to provide a reward or punishment in the form of mild electric shock, after each attempt according to the outcome, converting it into an "instrumental conditioning" machine, where reward or punishment is contingent on the subject's response.

The Experiments of Helmut Schmidt

In his 1975 review of ESP research, John Randall[2] commented that in 1969 "an extraordinarily brilliant piece of work was being performed in the U.S.A. which was to lift parapsychology out of the doldrums and raise it to a position of respectability never before achieved." According to Randall, this research confronted the critics with the most powerful challenge they had had to face so far, and parapsychology "was now about to enter the space age." Randall was referring to experiments carried out by Helmut Schmidt, a physicist at the Boeing Research Laboratories, employing a machine for randomization of targets and checking of scores.

Randall quoted a statement made in my earlier book about VERITAC in which I wrote that "an acceptable model for research has been made available by the investigators at the United States Air Force Research Laboratories." He then claimed that Schmidt's machine "satisfies all the requirements laid down by Hansel." This is certainly not the case. A machine may be well-designed, foolproof, and accurate, but "an acceptable model for research" consists of more than a piece of apparatus. The words "model for research" were based on the report published by the VERITAC team in which they wrote: "A design of a scientifically rigorous experiment in ESP is presented as an acceptable model for work in this field." While automatic generation of targets and scoring are desirable in an ESP experiment, the design and conduct of the experiment are of paramount importance. The use of a machine—however foolproof—does not permit the experimenter to drop other experimental safeguards.

It is necessary to examine in detail the apparatus and the experimental procedures employed by Schmidt to see whether they can be considered to be as adequate as those employed by the VERITAC investigators.

The Research of Helmut Schmidt

In 1969, Dr. Helmut Schmidt published details of research carried out at the Boeing Research Laboratories,[3] in which he claimed that subjects, when tested on a machine, were able to predict a target before its identity had been established by a process of random selection. His results were, thus, contrary to those obtained with VERITAC. Schmidt had constructed a machine for use in the experiments that generated a random sequence of four targets and gave automatic recording of the number of hits and trials. The subject attempted to predict which of the four targets would arise after he had pressed a button.

The targets consisted of four lamps (blue, green, orange, and red). The subject signified his selection of a particular lamp by pressing one of four buttons. Before each trial, the lamps were unlit. After the subject had pressed a button indicating his guess, the correct lamp lit up so that he became aware of whether he had predicted correctly or not.

Randomness was achieved in the following manner. An oscillator generated pulses at the rate of a million a second. These operated a two-bit counter and decoder giving four outputs that ran in a repeating (A B C D A B C D A B . . .) sequence. After the subject had pressed a button, a circuit was completed, stopping the counter and permitting the output present to light up the lamp.

The random nature of the target was achieved by utilizing the unpredictability of quantum processes, i.e., the unpredictability of the time at which an electron is emitted by a Strontium 90 source. This source was arranged so that electrons arrived on a Geiger-Muller Tube placed near to it at an average rate of 10 per second. The oscillator was continually running, but it was gated so that the counter was only operated after the subject pressed his button. The four possible outputs then arose in rapid sequence during the interval between the subject pressing a button to signify his choice and the next electron emitted by the Strontium 90 source arriving at the Geiger-Muller tube. Randomness was dependent on the unpredictable time at which the electron was emitted. Following a delay of $1/10000$th of a second, the relevant lamp then lit up. Thus the target had not been decided at the time the subject pressed his button.

When the subject had pressed his button, a lamp lit showing him the correct answer, and when he *released* his button there was a delay of half a second, after which the counter again started running. The half-second delay enabled external recording equipment to be operated which indicated the target selected by the machine and the button pressed by the subject.

Electromagnetic counters in the machine registered the number of attempts and the number of hits. In each case two counters were provided. One gave a running total and could not be reset. The other one could be reset when required. These counters could be switched in or out of circuit and, thus, did not record every trial made on the machine.

The following safety features were built into Schmidt's machine:

1. More than one button could not be pressed at the same time and also operate to give a hit.

2. A millionth of a second after a button was pressed the other buttons were made inoperative until the cycle of operations was completed and all buttons had been released. If two were pressed within a millionth of a second, the mechanical counters became blocked, and the trial was not registered.

3. Mechanical reset counters were located on the front panel, but nonresettable counters provided a check on these. The machine could also be connected to a paper-tape puncher, which recorded details of buttons pressed and targets generated.

The resettable counters were usually reset after 100 trials, and the results written down by the experimenter. The nonresettable counters could be read at the beginning and end of a series of trials and compared with the readings recorded from the resettable counters. They could also be switched out of operation when not required.

Initially, Schmidt tested a large number of people "perhaps 100"—the number is not specified. The subject sat in front of the machine, the front panel of which contained the four pushbuttons and four corresponding lamps. The subject then tried to predict which lamp would light at each trial by pressing the relevant button. One of the four lamps then lit indicating the correct target, and the counters advanced to show the total number of trials made and the number of hits achieved.

Schmidt found that only a few persons seemed to be "outstandingly successful in predicting random numbers." Three of these persons took part in the first experiment.

The First Main Precognition Experiment

The tests were carried out in the subjects' homes. During tests the paper-tape puncher was connected and the electromechanical reset and nonreset counters for hits and trials were switched on. Between tests, the paper-tape puncher and the nonreset counters were disconnected, and the subjects were allowed to play with the machine.

It had been decided, in advance, to evaluate all the events recorded on tape and no others. The total number of trials to be made was specified in advance as being between 55,000 and 70,000. It is not clear why a precise number was not specified for each subject. In fact 63,066 trials were made.

Great care was said to be taken to work only under what seemed to be "psychologically favorable conditions." The number of trials to be made each day was determined by the subjects' and experimenters' mood and "availability." A single experimenter, Dr. Schmidt, took part. He was present at most of the tests, but in certain cases the subjects worked without an experimenter being present.

The paper punch was employed during all tests, and it was pointed out in the report that forging the records by the subject would have been extremely difficult, as it would have required advancing the nonreset counters by electrical impulses and the punching of properly coded holes into the paper tape.

The first subject (Mr. O. C.) was tested on eleven days between February 20 and March 9, 1967. Over this period there appear to have been consistently above-chance scores. In all, O. C. gained 5,928 hits in 22,569 trials as against the chance expectation score of 5,642.25 hits. The odds against chance of such a score are about 1,000,000 to 1.

The second subject (Mrs. J. B.) was tested on five days and produced 4,153 hits in 16,250 trials. This represents 90.5 more hits than expected by chance (odds about 8 to 1). The third subject (K. M. R.) achieved 6,377 hits in 24,247 attempts. This represented 315.25 hits above the chance level with odds against chance occurrence of around 100,000 to 1. Combining the results for the three subjects gave 16,458 hits in 63,066 trials. Such a result had odds against chance greater than a million to 1.

The results for the three subjects are shown in Table 18-1 where it will be seen that the scoring rate, for the three subjects combined, was such that about 1 extra hit above the chance level was obtained in every 100 trials.

The Second Main Precognition Experiment

In the second main experiment [4] one of the subjects (K.M.R.) was replaced by S.C. (the sixteen-year-old daughter of O.C.). In these tests the subject had the option either to predict which lamp would light next or to try to select a lamp which would not light, thus aiming at a low score on the machine. Whether to try for a high or low score was decided at the beginning of each session, and the two modes of guessing were recorded on the tape in different codes (details of which are not given), so that the computer could separate the two types of test.

Four sessions were held with subject O. C., who only tried for high scores, eleven sessions with J. B., who tried for both high and low scores, and six sessions with J. C., who tried for low scores only. It was decided in advance to make a total of either 20,000 or 40,000 trials. In fact 20,000 were made. The number of trials in which high or low scores were to be attempted was not specified in advance. The results were as in Table 18–2.

Table 18-1
Hits and above-chance odds achieved by three subjects in first main experiment

(Chance occurrence figures corrected for optional stopping)

Subject	Trials	Hits	Hits above chance	Odds against chance occurrence (approx.)
O. C.	22,569	5,928	285.75	27,000 : 1
J. B.	16,250	4,153	90.5	6.5 : 1
K. M. R.	24,247	6,377	315.25	94,000 : 1
Total	63,066	16,458	691.5	10^8 : 1

Table 18-2
Hits above chance level and successes achieved by
three subjects in second main experiment

Subject	Aim of subject	Trials	Hits above chance expectation	Succeses above chance expectation
O. C.	High score	5,000	+66	+66
J. B.	High score	5,672	+123	+123
J. B.	Low score	4,328	−126	+126
S. C.	Low score	5,000	−86	+86
Totals		20,000	−23	401

It will be seen that while the total hits—i.e., where the button depressed agreed with the target—were 23 below the chance expectation level (a purely chance result); the successes—i.e., including cases where the hits below chance were regarded as successes when the subject was aiming at scoring low—were 410 above the chance level (a result having odds of greater than 10^{10} against chance).

Precautions Necessary When Using a Machine

While the use of a machine eliminates some of the obvious causes of error in ESP research, e.g. nonrandomness of targets and errors in recording hits and misses—its use does not mean that all other experimental precautions can be dropped. Assuming for the moment that the machine was foolproof, there are several obvious features of the experiments that require investigation. In particular the use of a system in which the subject tried for high or for low scores requires special experimental safeguards.

Given a satisfactory machine with nonresettable counters permanently in circuit sealed up within it, that machine should show a significant excess of hits (or a deficiency, if it is used exclusively for attempts at low scores) after a period of use, provided it is only used either for the high or for the low-score condition. If, for example, the score registered on the machine after a period of use had a probability of 10^{-6} of having arisen by chance, such a result would be much more striking than the type of data so far produced by Schmidt.

In his second experiment the significance of the result was not revealed by the nonresettable counters inside the machine, since these showed only a surplus of 23 hits in 20,000 trials. The odds of ten thousand million to one, claimed as those appertaining to the result of the experiment, apply to data extracted from the machine on the print-out but selected according to whether the subject was trying to secure hits or misses.

While the tape-punch recording showed which type of attempt was being made, the data was not, so far as the report indicates, obtained on a continuous

Table 18-3
Clairvoyance experiments

Hits above chance level obtained
under high and low aim conditions for three subjects

Subject	Aim	Trials	Hits above chance level
D. W.	High	3,687	+56
V. H. and M. K.	High	542	−10
J. B. and R. L.	High	718	+8
O. C.	High	2,144	−54
Total		7,091	+108
D. W.	Low	2,381	−60
V. H. and M. K.	Low	2,576	−48
J. B. and R. L.	Low	250	+5
O. C.	Low	2,702	−49
Total		7,909	−152
Overall totals	High and low combined	15,000	−44

tape, nor were precautions taken to ensure that all those tapes were employed in the final analyses and checked against other records of counter readings. The presence of observers (or a second experimenter), the use of separate machines for high- and low-score attempts, the fixing of the exact dates and numbers of trials to be made by each subject, and the counterchecking of all records, were precautions which should have been included.

Clairvoyance Experiments

Rather than proceed further with the investigation of precognition or even to substantiate his data with the use of independent investigators, Schmidt next turned to clairvoyance.[5] He used the same type of machine, but this time the target—rather than being decided by a random number generator after the subject made his choice—was obtained from a prepared list of randomized targets punched on tape, one such target being available for each trial. The target had, therefore, been determined before the subject recorded his guess, although the preselected lamp remained unlit until a button was pressed.

The results shown in Table 18–3 had a remarkable similarity to those in the second precognition experiment. The total of 15,000 trials was specified but the total number of attempts using each condition (high or low scores) was not specified. Again subjects aimed at either a low or a high score but the number of attempts using each condition for each subject was not specified in advance.

The overall deficiency of hits recorded on the counters in the machine was 44 in 15,000 trials—indicating that the in-built counters did not provide evidence of having been used in an abnormal manner. The subject was not obtaining a significant number of hits on the correct target. Only when negative and positive deviations were combined as "hits" from data recorded on the external recording equipment were any peculiarities observed in the result.

Weaknesses in Design

The important experimental precautions in such a situation are again not the accuracy of counting hits (although this obviously must be accurate) but ensuring that:

1. Complete isolation into two groups aiming at high or low scores is made before the experiment is started and maintained unchanged and intact throughout the experiment. It would be preferable to use only one type of attempt in a particular experiment, so that a single machine could be employed with the score displayed on its nonresettable counters. It would in fact have been better to have employed two machines, one for high score and the other for low score attempts.

2. Records can in no way be changed, as, for example, changing the designation of a run from "high score" to "low score" after it had been recorded.

3. All attempts are included in the final assessment. This can best be done by employing separate machines with nonresettable counters as in 1, and keeping a close check on the cumulative counter readings for each session in addition to the readings on the nonresettable counters.

4. No single experimenter has complete control of the experimental conditions or of the records. If anyone wanted to rig such an experiment it would be easy to do so unless special precautions were taken using a second—or preferably several more—investigators.

Psychokinesis Experiments

Having dealt with precognition and clairvoyance, Schmidt moved on to psycho-kinesis.[6] The research again had obvious similarities to his earlier work, but now rather than suggest that his subjects were able to predict random events, he claimed that they influenced physical events.

Schmidt used a binary randomizer (similar to his earlier machine, employing radioactive material), in which one of two outputs present operated a panel of nine lamps (arranged in a circle), one of which was lit. The machine provided the two

Table 18-4
Psychokinesis experiments

Hits above chance level and odds against result arising
by chance for two subjects

Subject	Number of attempts	Aim	Hits	Hits above chance level
K. G.	6,400	High scores	3,360	+160
R. R.	6,400	Low scores	3,056	−144
Totals	12,800		6,416	+16

outputs in random order. One of the two types of output (call this +1) caused the light to move clockwise and the other (−1) to move counterclockwise. The apparatus was operated at about 1 jump per second. In a standard test run, the light started at the top of the circle, and the generator produced a sequence of 128 movements. The subject sat in front of the panel and attempted to force the light to move in a clockwise direction rather than counterclockwise. The outputs of the generator were reversed after each test run, so that if any systematic bias were present, it would not affect the overall result.

Preliminary tests by Schmidt with eighteen subjects showed a generally below-chance scoring rate. Three of the eighteen subjects obtained above-chance results, fifteen of them failed to do so—although the actual number giving a below-chance score—rather than a chance score—is not stated.

Schmidt then stated that he was mainly interested in testing whether there was an effect rather than whether it was in any particular direction. For the main experiment he used a team consisting of nine subjects who had scored below chance, together with a further six recruited later. With this team a total of 256 runs of 128 trials was made.

The result was that jumps of the light occurred significantly more often in the nondesired direction (50.9 percent of trials) than in the desired direction (49.1 percent of trials). In a total of 32,768 trials, clockwise movements gave a negative deviation of 129 hits. This result had odds of 1000 to 1 against arising by chance. When the machine was left running unattended, it was found that no systematic bias was present.

In further tests two subjects were employed one of whom (K. G.) had scored high in preliminary tests the other (R. R.) who had scored low. These subjects were tested over a ten-day period. The results have a strong similarity to those of Schmidt's earlier experiments. K. G. scored consistently high over the ten-day period, and R. R. consistently low, but combining the numbers of "hits" gives a chance result.

The machine itself again recorded on its in-built counters only an excess of 16 of one type of outcome in 12,800 trials—a result that does not indicate any external influence on its outputs.[7]

Weaknesses in Design

The two really important precautions in this experiment are, first, to ensure that all runs are included correctly in the statistical analysis, second, to ensure that there is no selection of data or alteration of the subject's aim (high or low scores). These were not discussed in the experimental report.

Looking at Schmidt's research on the three processes, precognition, clairvoyance, and psychokinesis, it emerges that with each process the overall result recorded on the machine, except in the first experiment, was not significantly different from chance. Only in the case of the first experiment on precognition with the three subjects (O. C., J. G., and K. M. R) was the data obtained in relation to a single type of outcome (high scores) and with a single type of subject (high scorer). But in this case the same machine was used for both the tests and for practice. While the paper punch was disconnected for practice runs, the internal nonresettable counters had to be left in circuit. The actual readings on these counters were not reported.

The significance attributed to the result emerged from an analysis of the results after classifying them into two categories. If a subject, or a series of subjects, could cause nonresettable counters in a foolproof machine to record scores having enormous antichance odds, this would provide far better evidence for ESP than data which has been extracted from sets of results obtained on a machine.

Summary of Weaknesses in Schmidt's Experiments on Humans

In general Schmidt's experiments are unsatisfactory for a number of reasons. These will be discussed under the following headings:

1. The experimental design.
2. Unsatisfactory features of the machine employed.
3. Inability to confirm the findings.

The experimental design

It becomes evident, when assessing Schmidt's experiments, that they are not adequately described in the experimental reports. Insofar as they can be assessed from the rather meager details given, the following weaknesses appear to be present in the experimental design:

1. The exact numbers and types of trial to be undertaken by each subject were not specified before tests were started. As the research proceeded, there was some attempt to specify the number of trials in advance, but an added complication

then arose of subjects *attempting to score* in one of two ways. The numbers of trials using each condition were not then specified.

2. The allocation into high-scoring and low-scoring runs, or into high-scoring and low-scoring subjects, provided obvious loopholes.

3. Subjects practiced on some occasions and carried out experimental runs on others using the same machine.

4. There was control of the subject through the use of the machine but little control of the experimenter. A reasonable experimental design must control the experimenter. Thus, as far back as 1938, it was agreed at the conference of the American Psychological Association that at least two investigators are necessary. Where a single investigator is present repetitions of the complete experiment by other investigators may serve a similar purpose, but since such attempts have not been successful in the case of Schmidt's experiments (see below), it is not possible to place any reliance on his findings. In order to control the experiment the following minimum precautions should have been taken.

a. At least one other experimenter should have been present.

b. The number of runs and the conditions for each run should have been specified in advance.

c. All forms employed, and tapes used in recording equipment, should have been of a uniform type and length. They should all have been serially numbered in advance of use. All forms and tapes should have been filed and registered by an independent person who should have been given back forms for filing immediately after the termination of each test and before they were scored.

d. Separate machines giving distinguishable printouts should have been employed for each type of test, i.e., high-scoring or low-scoring attempts and also for any practice on the part of the subject. One set of counters should have been nonresettable, and one set should have been wired permanently in circuit to record trials, hits, and also misses. Punched tapes should have been maintained and held by an independent person unaware of the main aims of the experiment who should have independently calculated the scores achieved by subjects. These should have been checked with scores noted by the investigator on special registered forms, maintained by an independent person, showing the numbers indicated on the resettable counters before and after each test run and with the nonresettable counters at the termination of the experiment.

e. The nonresettable counters should be permanently in circuit, with no means of switching them in or out.

The most remarkable feature of Schmidt's experiments is the manner in which, in the majority of cases, his results manage to exclude any safeguard conferred by using a machine.

A satisfactory machine where the selection of targets is random—or unpredictable at above the chance level—where checking of hits and misses is automatic and where adequate safeguards have been made to ensure that it is reliable is obviously necessary for ESP research.

If the series generated by the machine is truly random, a subject will, in the absence of ESP, be unable to operate such a machine to obtain consistently above-chance scores, thus the results will be independent of whether or not he obtains knowledge of results after each attempt. Given such a machine with counters sealed up inside it so that they cannot be tampered with, a potential psychic who could return the machine showing enormous above-chance scores on these counters would provide strong evidence for ESP.

Unsatisfactory features of the machine employed

The most obvious weakness in Schmidt's machine is that the results are in no case recorded positively inside the machine. They are only revealed after processing data obtained from the resettable counters in the machine or from the paper punch connected to it. While machines may be relatively foolproof, human beings seldom are. Thus, in the case of the clairvoyance experiments (see page 225), Schmidt finished up with two sets of figures, those where the subject aimed at high scores and those where he aimed at low scores. The machine was not involved in the allocation of the results of tests made on it into the two categories—high and low scores. The confidence to be placed on the experimental findings is dependent not only on the machine, which may be 100 percent efficient, but also on the arrangements made to ensure that the two categories of scores are decided before the tests are made, that they are not changed during the experiment, and that all records are included in the final assessment. If Schmidt had used two machines, his scores for high- and low-aiming runs could have been kept separate from the start. Nonresettable counters could have ensured that all attempts were recorded and some supervision of the use and recording of the counters would have instilled more confidence into readers of the reports than they are likely to have at present.

It will also be noted that in certain cases Schmidt was dealing not with direct observations, but with data that had already been processed. Thus, in Table 18-2, high-scoring subjects aiming at high scores gave a positive deviation and those aiming at low scores, a negative deviation. The negative and positive deviations are both then called *successes* and added together for purposes of statistical analysis. The fact that when positive and negative deviations are combined (maintaining their sign) they invariably give a purely chance score suggests that sampling from a common distribution may have taken place. It will be noted that similar arguments apply to many other experiments where contrasted groups are compared (e.g., sheep-goats, see Chapter 14).

If Schmidt wishes to convince skeptics, he will first have to ensure that his experiments are carried out under conditions where the result cannot have arisen through carelessness, error, or trickery on his part or that of his subjects. The use of a machine should largely eliminate the possibility of trickery on the part of the subject, but it does not appreciably affect the chances of the experimenter indulging in it.

Further difficulties with a machine of the type used by Schmidt might become apparent after thorough testing. The machine would have been better if the counter had been continually running and its state checked at the instant of the next electron arriving at the Geiger-Muller tube, rather than being gated. In addition the method of switching the counters in and out could raise difficulties. Thus, after a subject made his guess and the target had been decided, it would appear that the oscillator output was blocked until the subject made his next guess. Operation of the switch which put the counter in or out of circuit—by connecting it to the power supply—during this period would produce a further count on the associated electromagnetic counter.

There are many features in an electronic machine that require consideration and test before it can be judged foolproof, particularly where on/off, reset, or other control switches are accessible to the subject. It is mentioned in Schmidt's original report that a difficulty arose with his machine that enabled a subject to obtain above-chance scores which required a modification of the circuitry.

A further feature that has to be considered is the possibility of any bias being present in the electronic counter owing to very small differences in switching time. Schmidt made tests to check that bias was not present, but it is preferable that a machine should be constructed so that if any such bias arises, its effects will not be present in the numbers generated. In a machine built at Swansea for use in a student project, the four outputs from the counter (A, B, C, D) are connected to final outputs (A', B', C', D') through a switching system. After each number is generated, the outputs A, B, C, D are switched to a new arrangement of the final outputs A', B', C', D'. This is done systematically so that the possible arrangements arise equal numbers of times, and each counter output is connected to each final output an equal number of times in any multiple of four numbers generated.

Inability to confirm

In view of the inadequate experimental control in Schmidt's experiments, it is of interest to compare his results with those of other investigations in which a machine has been employed.

First, why are his results quite different from those obtained in the VERITAC experiment? It might be said that Schmidt's machine was dependent on the indeterminacy of quantum processes and that VERITAC was not. But if the difference in results is due to the difference in the manner in which the two machines generate a random number series, this would imply that Schmidt's subjects were influencing the quantum processes involved with his randomizer. In fact, Schmidt has reported positive results for clairvoyance with his machine when the random number series was not generated by the process involving quantum indeterminacy.

Referring to the Schmidt experiment, John Randall writes "In so far as it is humanly possible to prove anything in this uncertain world, the Schmidt experiments provide us with the final proof of the reality of both ESP and PK. There is now only one possible escape for the sceptic who wishes to avoid the reality of psi, and that is to believe that Schmidt deliberately falsified the whole series of experiments."[8]

Perhaps what has been written here will indicate reasons for questioning the proof supplied by Schmidt without implying that he need necessarily have been more than a careless experimenter who had little idea of the precautions necessary in an ESP experiment.

Schmidt's Cat

Following his success with human subjects, Schmidt turned to the area of animal behavior.[9] One cold winter's night, he placed his cat in a cold garden shed which was heated only by a 200 w. lamp. The temperature was around zero in the shed, and the cat tended to "settle down" immediately next to the lamp. Schmidt thought that perhaps the cat's "feeling of pleasure" when the lamp was lighted might be utilized to affect the binary random number generator. He connected up the lamp so that each time the generator produced a +1 output the lamp went on and each time it produced a −1 it went off. The purpose of the experiment was to see whether the cat's "feeling of pleasure" when the lamp was lighted might cause the lamp to light more than the expected 50 percent of the time. This would, in turn, require the machine to generate more +1's than −1's. The machine, in fact, operated a lamp from each output, but one of the lamps was always outside the shed in a box. The lamps were interchanged each day so that any bias of the machine, whereby it might be producing a surplus of +1's, was cancelled out.

According to Schmidt, when the cat was in the shed, the lamp tended to be on at above-chance level, and the cat had affected the random number generator to keep itself warm in some way unknown to physics. When the cat was not in the shed, the lamp was only on 50 percent of the time, showing that the random number generator was operating normally when the cat was not influencing it. The experiment was discontinued because it was said that the outside temperature had risen. If Schmidt's theory about the cat's "feeling of pleasure" was correct, the lamp would, presumably, stay off more than 50 percent of the time in warm weather when the cat wanted to keep cool.

Cockroach Experiments

These experiments were followed by others employing cockroaches as subjects. The animals received a shock or not according to the state of the randomizer. In this case the cockroaches, it seems, were unsuccessful in affecting the randomizer so as to avoid shock, but they caused it to produce 109 more shocks in 6,400 generated numbers than would be expected to arise by chance. Schmidt commented: "The magnitude of this deviation suggested that it might be a real effect, even though it raised the question of why a possible PK ability in cockroaches should work to their disadvantage." He did not consider the possibility that there might be any fault in his randomizer or method of data collection, or even that the result might have arisen by chance.

In a further experiment with cockroaches, Schmidt, after generating 25,600 randomized outputs giving shock or no shock, found that the number giving shock was 13,109, which was 309 less than chance expectation. This result has odds greater than 10,000 to one against arising by chance. Here again, the important question is whether these values, in toto, were obtained from unresettable counters on the machine without necessitating the recording and addition of separate batches of results from the machine. In addition, a means of cancelling out machine bias as described earlier would have been preferable rather than relying on tests made on the machine at some other time.

Other Animal Studies Employing Machines

Schmidt's experiments with animals have been supplemented with several other studies where targets are generated by a machine and where scoring of the responses made by the animals is also automatic. Until recently, the animal studies were claimed to provide the first repeatable demonstrations of ESP.

The basis for the investigations was an experiment reported by Duval and Montredon on precognition in mice.[10] In their experiment a mouse was placed in a testing cage which was divided into two compartments by a partition. The mouse could remain in one compartment or jump to the other compartment in order to avoid a shock which was administered at random to one of the two compartments.

Duval and Montredon reported three experiments in each of which the animals moved about in such a manner that they occupied the side receiving shock less often than the other side of the cage. Results in two experiments were stated to be significant at less than the .001 level, i.e., had odds of less than 1 in 1,000. It will be noted that the mice expended much energy jumping from one side of the cage to the other. Schmidt's cat would, presumably, have remained still and affected the randomizer.

In 1971, at the Parapsychology Laboratory, a group of investigators headed by W. L. Levy, Director of the Institute for Parapsychology, repeated these experiments and confirmed the findings.[11] In three successive experiments, they reported a statistically significant result. Further experiments followed.

In 1974, John Randall, discussing the animal research was able to list twelve experiments of this type, constituting all those he knew to have been carried out, each of which produced a significant positive result.

In July 1974 I wrote:

John Randall lists all experiments of this type known to have been performed. Each of these has produced a positive significant result. But of the 12 experiments he lists, three were reported by two "eminent" but anonymous French biologists: the remaining nine were conducted in the United States by Walter J. Levy and three co-workers. Levy has also found that fertilised chicken's eggs affect the randomiser so as to keep themselves warm in the same manner as Schmidt's cat.[12]

In August 1974, it was revealed that Levy had been caught cheating in an experiment, had admitted to having done so, and had been sacked from his post as Director of the Institute of Parapsychology.

According to a report in the *International Herald Tribune*, August 20, 1974, some of Levy's co-workers had noticed him hovering about one of the data-recording devices while experiments were in progress. A group of technicians arranged an independent method of recording the data with the result that "The technicians' recording device yielded data far less supportive of the theory that the rats possessed psychic ability than did Dr. Levy's data."

In the *Journal of Parapsychology*, where J. B. Rhine gave details of this episode, he wrote that it would be necessary to suspend judgment on all Levy's published work.[13] He also suggested that work carried out by Levy and confirmed in other laboratories should be evaluated entirely on the strength of the replicated work.

If these revelations of trickery had not arisen, discussion of the animal experiments would no doubt have occupied considerable space in this volume. It is likely that the most important criticism would have been, as implied in my review of Beloff's book, that the findings had not been confirmed by independent investigators. The incident again highlights the fact that automation in itself is of little value without adequate experimental design and control of the experimenters.

Notes

1. W. R. Smith, Everest F. Dagle, Margaret D. Hill, and John Mott Smith, *Testing for Extra Sensory Perception with a Machine*, Data Sciences Laboratory Project 4610, May 1963.
2. John Randall, *ibid*, p. 121.
3. Helmut Schmidt, *Anomalous Prediction of Quantum Processes by Some Human Subjects*, Boeing Scientific Research Laboratories Document D1. 82.0821, Plasma Physics Laboratory, February 1969.
4. Helmut Schmidt, "Precognition of a Quantum Process," *Journal of Parapsychology*, 33 (1969): 106.
5. Helmut Schmidt, "Clairvoyance Tests with a Machine," *Journal of Parapsychology*, 33 (1969): 305.

6. Helmut Schmidt, "A PK Test with Electronic Equipment," *Journal of Parapsychology*, 34 (1970): 176–87.
7. Helmut Schmidt, "Mental Influence on Random Events," *New Scientist*, 24 (June 1971): 757.
8. Randall, *ibid*, p. 131.
9. Helmut Schmidt, "PK Experiments with Animals as Subjects," *Journal of Parapsychology*, 34 (1970): 255–61.
10. P. Duval and E. Montredon (Pseudonyms), "ESP Experiments with Mice," *Journal of Parapsychology*, 32 (1968): 155–66.
11. W. J. Levy, L. A. Mayo, E. Andre and A. McRae, "Repetition of the French Precognition Experiments with Mice." *Journal of Parapsychology*, 35 (1971): 1–17.
12. C. E. M. Hansel, "Review of 'New Directions in Parapsychology'," *New Scientist*, July 25, 1974; see also W. J. Levy and E. Andre, "Possible PK by Young Chickens to Obtain Warmth," *Journal of Parapsychology*, 34 (1970): 303.
13. J. B. Rhine, "A New Case of Experimenter Unreliability," *Journal of Parapsychology*, 38 (1974): 218–55(b).

19
Psychical Research at SRI

Experiments using a machine performing essentially the same functions as that of Helmut Schmidt have been conducted by Russell Targ, Phyllis Cole and Harold Puthoff at the Stanford Research Institute (SRI)[1]. They have not published details of their investigations in a journal although the intention of doing so is stated in the report. Details of the experiments together with a critical evaluation have, however, been published by Martin Gardner in the *Scientific American*.[2] It appears that the research was funded by an $80,000 grant from NASA. Gardner comments: "The story of the failure of this expensive experiment is almost a paradigm of what has happened numerous other times in ESP research. High-scoring subjects are first identified by loosely controlled screening, then as their testing proceeds, under better (that is, more complex) controls, their psi powers mysteriously fade."

In these experiments, the aim was both to use a machine that would provide automatic generation and checking of targets and to give training on ESP recognition by providing knowledge of results after each trial. As stated in connection with VERITAC, such feedback cannot affect the success rate provided the target series is random. But it may be argued that if there is some degree of ESP ability present in the population, as suggested by Rhine and others, then subjects should learn to use this ability through knowledge of results so that their scoring rate becomes improved.

The machine showed four targets represented on 35 mm slides. After the subject had signaled his guess by pressing a button, the relevant slide lit up so that he could see whether he was correct or not, and in addition a bell sounded following a correct choice. The total hits and trials for each run were shown on counters on the front panel. The subject could also, if he desired, press a "pass" button and proceed to the next target without the machine recording a trial.

The machine was used to test clairvoyance by changing the target after the subject had made his choice and before he made his next attempt. Each run consisted of 25 trials. A record of runs, hits, and misses was maintained on special score sheets or, on some occasions, by employing a printout. Four series of experiments were reported in which the experimental conditions were varied.

Phase 0 (Pilot Study)

After about 100 trials had been run on the device by friends and fellow employees, two individuals were asked to act as subjects. Subject A_1 worked at home. The scores for each run were recorded on prepared score sheets by his father. Subject A_2 recorded his own data on the prepared score sheets, working the machine in the SRI Laboratory.

Under these conditions A_1, in making 9,600 guesses, averaged 26.06 hits per 100 trials (as against the chance expectation value of 25). The odds against this score arising by chance are about 120 to 1. Subject A_2 achieved a scoring rate of 30.5 with odds against chance of 500,000 to 1. Each subject's scoring rate improved as the tests proceeded.

Phase 1 Experiments

Phase 1 was intended to screen 145 volunteer subjects consisting of adults and children. They worked unsupervised in one of three laboratories, either at the Institute or in a school. During these tests the machine provided a printout on paper tape.

The group as a whole produced 105,890 hits in a total of 423,000 trials. This is not significantly above the chance expectation value of 105,750 hits.

One subject (A_3), however, had a scoring rate of 29.57 per 100 trials with odds against chance of greater than a million to one. One other subject had a scoring rate having odds of 200 to 1 against chance, and a further nine subjects had scores with odds of greater than 20 to 1 against chance. Except in the case of A_3, the results are not unexpected in view of the fact that 145 subjects were tested.

Phase 2 Experiments

The aim of Phase 2 was to carry out further, more rigorous tests with successful subjects. The conditions here were tightened up by having the printer located in the experimenter's office, remote from the subject. Twelve subjects who had done well in earlier experiments were tested (including subject A_3).

Under these new conditions, none of the twelve subjects who had been outstandingly successful in the previous experiment obtained a result that was significantly above the chance level. The investigators did not interpret the difference between this result and the earlier tests as indicating that anything untoward had occurred in the less rigorously conducted experiments. They thought that the difference in results might have been due to the fact that in the second experiment the subjects were aware that they were in a test situation. They state that their subjects uniformly complained that in the revised experimental conditions "it all felt different, being connected to a computer." However, in the Phase 2 experiment the printout was not in the same room as the subject, and he need not have been aware of its use. In the Phase 1 experiment the printout was creating a great deal of noise and was located in the room with the subject.

Phase 3 Experiments

Here the investigators stated that they wished to examine the hypothesis "that the more complex the observation system of a subject's performance, the more gross is the perturbance of his perceptual channel."

They thought that an unfamiliar experimenter, or the presence of a printout apparatus would have adverse effects on the subject. In Phase 3 they attempted to rehabilitate selected subjects' high scores by returning to the experimental conditions of subject A_1 in Phase 0. Here, it is stated, an observer seated with the subjects recorded the score at the end of each run of 25 trials. (In fact, in the earlier part of the report discussing Phase 0, *data collection,* it is stated that one of the two subjects "recorded his own data on the prepared score sheets.")

Seven subjects who had achieved significantly above-chance scores in the pilot study and Phase 1 (screening) experiments acted as subjects. A new subject also took part. In the Phase 3 experiments, there was an experimenter with the subject in sessions carried out both in his own home and in the SRI Laboratory.

Seven of these subjects now produced scores at the chance level (odds less than 20 to 1). The eighth subject (A_3) worked under different conditions. He, it seems, expressed a desire for "practice sessions at various points during the experiment." He specified, prior to any set of trials, when he wished to practice. His results are shown in Table 19-1.

Weaknesses in the Experiments

In general, these experiments show that in Phase 0 and 1, where the experimental conditions were relatively loose, a significant above-chance result was obtained that was mainly dependent on one subject (A_3). When conditions were tightened up, as in Phase 2, by placing the subject in another room and presumably under the supervision of an experimenter, the high scores were no longer obtained. After relaxing the conditions, subject A_3 again achieved a score having a low probability

Table 19-1
Scores obtained by Subject A_3 in practice and test sessions

	Presentation	Hits	Surplus	Odds against chance
Trials	2,500	697	+72	2,000 to 1
Practice	4,500	1,143	+ 8	4 to 1
Total	7,000	1,840	+90	148 to 1

of chance occurrence. This was not the total score recorded by the machine, but the score obtained after removing the scores made under practice conditions.

These experimental results are again of importance in showing that a testing machine in itself will not eliminate the possibility of error or trickery. Since subject A_3, and possibly others, obtained above-chance scores under phase 1 conditions but not under those of phase 2, a reasonable suggestion would be that the difference in the conditions was responsible for the difference in results obtained.

Targ and Puthoff state that one change made in Phase 2 was to place the "fairly noisy printer" where it was remote from the subjects. They thought that the clatter of the printer might have been a distraction. The result after moving the printer to another room was, however, to reduce scores to the chance level.

It should be noted that there was only one outstanding subject referred to as A_3 in the report. Under Phase 1 conditions, when he worked alone in the room with the printout, he obtained high scores. He was unable to maintain his impressive performance when the printout was moved to another room.

Since he was a scientist employed at SRI he may have been familiar with the operation of the printout apparatus. It would thus be essential to ensure that when he worked alone with the apparatus and obtained high scores, it was not possible for him to interfere with the apparatus or with the printout record.

Discussing Martin Gardner's criticisms in the *Scientific American* article, Targ and Puthoff point out that subjects made runs of 25 trials and that these trials were automatically printed on continuous fanfold paper tape, which carried a permanent record of every "trial, machine state, and trial number from 1 to 25 for each run." They state that after 8 to 10 runs the subject "would bring the continuous fanfold tape for entry into the experimental log." They claimed that the tapes were always delivered intact with all runs recorded.

An essential control feature of any experiment is to ensure that all records are preserved in the final assessment. With cumulative unresetable counters inside the machine, it is possible to take precautions to ensure that this is done. With a printout this is possible, provided there can be no selection of sheets handed to the experimenters—or included in the final report. This requires that all recording is done on a single, continuous uncut tape or that every run in the machine has a serial number which is preserved on a nonresetable counter within the machine and which is marked on the tape. This counter must indicate the serial number of every run made on the machine, after it is initially constructed and put into use. The final report must show that these serial numbers are continuous and account for all runs made on the machine. In the Pratt-Woodruff experiment (Chapter 11) this precaution was taken by having standard score sheets serially numbered in the office and maintained there after each subject had been tested. In the experimental session each subject's score sheet was inserted through a slit into a locked box by an experimenter, checked by the second experimenter at the end of each run. A further independent record was kept by each experimenter.

Targ and Puthoff appear to have been blissfully ignorant of the need for precautions to ensure that experimenters could not select data. It is necessary not only to embody such precautions in the experiments but also to have checks to ensure that any such features are rigorously adhered to during the course of the experiment. This requires that each experimenter is checked by a second experimenter and a record made each time a check is made.

Targ and Puthoff[3] state, in reply to Gardner's criticism, that the tapes were always delivered intact and not torn into "disconnected bits and pieces." But from their own descriptions, subjects took along the tape after they had torn it off the remainder of the reel contained in the machine. What precautions were taken to ensure that all runs made by the subject were included on the tape, that all tape torn off was handed in, and that it was all included when arriving at the final figures? In the absence of a predetermined number of runs, the subject could ensure that his record started and (or) finished with an above-chance score. The machine printed a cumulative trial number from beginning to end of a session. But switching the machine off and on again would presumably ensure that the subject could reject an unsatisfactory initial run or initial guesses and restart, since the counters were electronic, i.e., they would reset at switch off. The subject need not have included his first run until he had achieved one that was above chance.

In general, the criticisms of experimental procedure expressed in connection with Schmidt's experiments also apply to the SRI experiments. Although three investigators prepared the report, they do not appear to have been involved together in each test in a manner that would provide an adequate check either on each other or on the subjects.

Notes

1. R. Targ, Phyllis Cole, and H. Puthoff, "Development of Technique to Enhance Man/Machine Communication." Obtainable from the Stanford Research Institute, Menlo Park, California 94025. Final report covering period from April 15, 1973 to May 15, 1974.
2. Martin Gardner, "Mathematical Games. Concerning an Effort to Demonstrate Extra-Sensory Perception by Machine," *Scientific American* (November 1975): 113–18.
3. R. Targ and H. Puthoff, *Mind-Reach* (New York: Delacorte, 1977).

20
Telepathy in Dreams

The possibility of dreams being affected by telepathy has been investigated since 1960 by Dr. Montague Ullman, a New York psychiatrist. His work eventually led to the setting up of the Dream Research Laboratory at the Maimonides Medical Centre in Brooklyn, New York. Experiments made there by a team of investigators are claimed to provide conclusive evidence for ESP arising during dreaming.

The dream research reported in 1973 by Ullman, Stanley Krippner, and Alan Vaughan, in their book *Dream Telepathy*[1] has been said in the appendix to that book by Dr. Berthold Eric Schwartz, a Consultant Psychiatrist at the Brainwave Laboratory, Essex County Medical Center, New Jersey, to herald "the long awaited breakthrough and the beginning of a new era in parapsychology."

In their summary of experiments, Ullman, Krippner, and Vaughan give details of some ten investigations. Two of these were screening studies in which twelve subjects were tested for one night each in the attempt to find successful subjects for later research. In a single night's test the dreams of the subject were compared with a target viewed by another person to see whether there were signs of ESP. The main results reported in *Dream Telepathy* were obtained by eleven subjects, each tested for several nights. Of the ten experiments, seven are reported as having given a result with odds of up to 250 to 1 against arising by chance. Two of the experiments were conducted on subjects who had done well in screening tests but who then failed to give a significant result when retested. As the experiments proceeded, changes were introduced into the design, procedures, and the statistical analysis to make them more watertight, but the main features of the experiments are as described below.

The Basic Method

An agent concentrated on a picture and attempted to influence by telepathy a sleeping person so that his dreams would display features in common with the picture.

The subject slept in a special room situated at a distance of 96 feet from the room occupied by the agent. Electro-oculogram (EOG) electrodes were attached to his head. The EOG measures the potential difference between the retina at the back of the eye and the cornea. By placing electrodes on each side of the eye, its movements may be detected through the changes in potential arising between the electrodes. It affords a measure that can detect about 1° of lateral eye movement. Rapid eye movements have been found to arise during dreaming. Thus, by observing the subject's EOG, an experimenter in an adjoining room detected when he started to dream. He then alerted the agent so that he could concentrate on a randomly selected target picture. When the eye movements ceased, indicating that dreaming had ended, the experimenter was able to awaken the subject through an intercom system and obtain details of his dreams. The subject might be asked questions by the experimenter, after which he could go to sleep again. He might be re-awakened several times during the night in this manner. Next morning additional information was obtained from the subject in an interview conducted by the experimenter. Both the reports of the subject about his dreams and the interviews were taperecorded.

The results were evaluated in two ways. In the first method the subject was given eight pictures, one of which was the target picture that had been employed. He then compared each of these pictures with the dream material and decided which one fitted best, giving it the rank 1. Second best was given rank 2, and so on, until the eight pictures had been ranked 1-8 according to their correspondence to the dream.

The second method was to send transcripts of the dreams, together with the eight pictures used on the eight different nights, to independent outside judges who ranked, in order, each of the eight targets against the set of eight dream materials. Ranks 1-4 were then considered as hits, and ranks 5-8 as misses. If the dreams over an eight-night investigation were assessed in this manner, the chance expectation of hits was 4, since each target had an equal chance of being a hit or a miss. The odds against any score arising by chance could then be calculated.

Other methods of evaluation employing various forms of statistical method were employed in the earlier experiments. These were of dubious validity and will not be discussed further. The claims made for the experiments do not depend on these earlier types of evaluation, and the conclusions reached through their use are, in fact, unlikely to be very different from those when the method described above is employed.

The Experiment on Robert Van de Castle

In the most successful of the experiments, originally reported by Stanley Krippner and Montague Ullman,[2] the subject was Dr. Robert Van de Castle, a clinical psychologist and parapsychologist who had performed well in earlier exploratory tests. Over a series of eight nights, his dreams, when assessed against the targets by the independent judge, gave a hit against the target on each occasion, a result having odds of 256 to 1 against arising by chance. The main features and the procedure employed in this experiment are described below.

The targets employed were postcard-sized prints of famous paintings. One of the Dream Laboratory staff members (name not given) was designated the "Recorder" (R). He had the task of preparing duplicate sets of targets in the following manner. For each set he collected together 72 pictures and divided these into 9 target pools, each containing 8 pictures. Each target pool was given a code number, and each picture was given a separate number. R placed each art print into an opaque envelope, which he sealed and signed across the flap. He then covered his signature with transparent adhesive tape. The eight envelopes in each pool were then randomly assigned numbers 1-8. R placed the eight envelopes for each pool into a large opaque envelope, which was again signed and sealed as above. It was also marked with the code number. He then had a set of eight envelopes, each containing a target to be used by the agent during the experiment and also a second duplicate set of the targets to be used when checking the subject's dreams for their correspondence with the targets. R had no contact with the subject and returned to college shortly after the experiments started.

The aim of this part of the procedure was to ensure that the target pictures to be used with any subject were unknown to the subject, the agent, or the two experimenters.

The subject slept in the Dream Laboratory on eight successive nights. Three agents were employed for these eight sessions, the subject being allowed to choose the agent he was to work with on each night.

At the start of a session, the subject and agent engaged in informal conversation while the electrodes were being attached to the subject by one of the investigators (E). The subject then went to bed, and immediately afterwards, the agent, together with an experimenter, entered an office and selected a "random number." The agent then counted down through the stack of large envelopes containing the nine target pools until he reached that number. He then selected another "random number," and, after opening the large envelope, counted down through the eight smaller envelopes inside it in order to obtain the target. He gave the code number of the large envelope containing the pool of targets to the experimenter, who was with him, so that the duplicate pool of targets could be located for judging purposes in the morning.

The agent then went to his room which was situated 96 feet from the room in which the subject was sleeping. There he opened the envelope and extracted the target. According to the report, "he was encouraged to write down his associations, to visualize the picture, to concentrate upon it and to treat it in any other manner which would make its contents a dynamic part of his conscious processes."

During the night the experimenters in an adjoining room to the subject monitored the subject's sleep. When the rapid eye movements stage was reached, an experimenter signaled the agent by means of a one-way buzzer, so that he awakened and concentrated on the target. When rapid eye movements stopped, indicating that the dream had ended, the subject was awakened by means of the two way intercom. He then gave an account of his dreams after which he was asked a number of specific questions about them. The subject might be awakened several times in this manner during the night. After the final awakening, a postsleep interview with the subject was carried out in order to elicit any additional information.

When this was completed the subject was shown the pool of eight pictures and asked to try to identify the target. He then ranked each picture against his dreams in the manner already described. The taperecordings of the dream reports and interview were mailed to a transcriber, and the transcripts were used by an outside judge for a supplementary evaluation.

The outside judge ranked each of the eight target pictures used on the eight nights with Van de Castle against the set of eight nights' dreams. The target was, in fact, placed in the top half of the rankings for each night's dreams. This result has a probability of $(\frac{1}{2})^8$ of arising by chance, yielding odds of 256 to 1 against chance occurrence. The overall result of the experiment was thus claimed to provide evidence that the subject's dreams had been influenced by ESP.

First, consider the design of the experiments. It was important that only the agent should know the identity of the target and that its identity should not be revealed to anyone until both the subject and the judges had made their evaluations. But an experimenter appears to have been with the agent when he opened his target envelope. In the report it is stated that, before opening the envelope containing the target, *he was encouraged* to write down his associations, etc., and then *once this was done,* there was no way that A could communicate with E or with S without leaving his room and *breaching the conditions* of the experiment. (Italics mine.)

Attempted Confirmation of the Experiment

Replication of the experiment was attempted by Edward Belvedere of the Maimonides Laboratory and David Foulkes of the University of Wyoming.[3] Foulkes had not worked in parapsychology before but was well known for his work on orthodox aspects of dream research.

Five experimenters, E_1 to E_5, took part. They employed the same subject—Dr. Robert Van de Castle—as had taken part in the original experiment. The method employed was basically similar, but additional safeguards were introduced into the procedure. Only the essential differences in procedure will be described.

The material consisted of pictures from magazines. Ten groups of eight pictures were collected together and placed in small, sealed envelopes as in the earlier experiment. A duplicate set was also made. The small envelopes containing the target pictures were "randomly numbered" 1-8, and each pool of eight such targets was placed in a larger envelope, thus forming ten target pools, which were labeled A to J. This part of the procedure was carried out by E_1, who handed over one set of ten envelopes (each containing its pool of targets contained in smaller envelopes) to E_2. It is not completely clear what he did with the duplicate set at this point, since he is merely reported as handing over ten envelopes to E_2.

E_2 acted as "security officer." He stored these envelopes off the premises. On the evening of each experiment, he randomly selected one of the larger envelopes containing a target pool and took it to the laboratory.

At the laboratory the subject selected his own agent each night from a group of three young ladies. (The subject appeared to prefer female agents.) After the participants arrived at the laboratory, the agent watched E_3 attach the electrodes to the subject. E_4 then conducted the subject to his bedroom. When the subject was in bed, E_3 received the target pool from E_2—who only came to the laboratory after he had been given a signal from E_3 that the subject was in bed. E_3 *verified the signature and seal* and held the envelope for delivery to the agent when he was locked in his room for the night. E_3 then conducted the agent to her room, where he gave her the large envelope containing that night's target pool. The agent was instructed not to open the envelope until E_5 had delivered a slip bearing a randomly selected number indicating which of the eight potential targets (contained in the smaller numbered envelopes inside the large envelope) was to be the night's target. E_5 did not enter the room but pushed the slip under the door and then left the building. He retained a duplicate of each night's number, and *it was later* checked that the agent had opened the right envelope. E_5 selected his number with replacement so that the same number could arise more than once. E_2's numbers were selected without replacement so that a target pool would only be used once. (This feature could affect the statistical evaluation, but it is not of importance in the present discussion.)

The agent was situated in a suite of rooms well away on a different floor from the subject's room. The building was locked, the agent's door was locked, and tape seals were attached to the windows and door by E_3. Therefore, the agent could not leave her suite and return without detection.

The subject was locked in his room, and continuous polygraph monitoring was made, as well as monitoring through the intercom system. E_3 monitored the polygraph recordings from a control area next to the subject's bedroom. At the start of each period of rapid eye movements he signaled the agent via a one-way buzzer so that she could concentrate on the target. The agent indicated that she had received the signal by turning a switch which put on a light in the control room. At the end of the period of rapid eye movements, E_3 signaled E_4, who was in a room adjacent to the control area so that E_4 could awaken the subject. He also signaled the agent so that she would know that the dream period had ended. The agent indicated receipt of the message by turning off the switch that controlled the signal lamp in the control area. Details of dreams as reported by the subject were taperecorded and postdream interviews were carried out by E_4. After each report the subject was free to indicate any idea he had concerning the nature of the target.

The subject was awakened at 7 A.M. E_4 disconnected the electrodes from the subject. Meanwhile, E_2 had delivered the duplicate pool of targets to E_3 *who verified that the seal and signature were intact.* E_4 took these materials into the subject's room and placed the taperecorder there. The subject then ranked the targets for their similarity to his dreams—he could play back, if necessary, from the tape his own reports of the dreams which he had made during the night.

The agent was not released from her suite until the evaluations had been completed and the judgments were in E_4's hands. E_3 *checked the seals of the agent's suite* and also *checked that only one of the eight envelopes in the target pool had been opened.* He also *checked that the envelope opened corresponded to the number on the slip delivered by E_5 to the subject.* He then conducted the agent to the subject's room, where, in the presence of E_2, E_3, and E_4, the target was ascertained. E_3 *and E_5 later verified that the agent's random number sheets corresponded to those held by E_5.*

The correspondence between dreams and targets was assessed using the ranking procedure, by the subject, and also by independent outside judges.

Results

The finding was that neither the subject nor the judges matched dreams with targets at significantly above the chance level. The subject himself assigned three hits and five misses (i.e., one hit less than would be expected to arise by chance). Judge 1 also assigned three hits and five misses. Judge 2 assigned two hits and six misses, when judging only on the basis of the dreams, and four hits and four misses when also taking into account the subject's associations.

Foulkes and Belvedere concluded that their failure to confirm the result of the original experiment led to "two lines of enquiry." First, they asked, if ESP does not influence dreams, why did the original study produce above-chance results? Second, if the attempt at repetition was to be rejected as unsatisfactory, what features of the original study had been altered or omitted so as to interfere with the demonstration of a telepathic influence?

Approach I: If ESP does not exist why did the first experiment produce evidence for its existence?

Foulkes and Belvedere concluded that there were no flaws in the design of the original study. But this conclusion may be questioned. To the reader it may appear that a large number of additional and necessary precautions were taken in the second study, and insofar as these were not taken in the original study, it contained flaws. The most likely reason for a positive result in the first study in the absence of a positive result in the more carefully controlled study was surely the presence of a loophole in its design. It is, therefore, of interest to see what additional precautions were present in the second experiment and how the absence of these could have affected the freedom of action of those taking part in the investigations.

Consider the essential precautions necessary to ensure that no one taking part in the experiment, either intentionally or otherwise, could influence the result.

The agent.   Completely satisfactory methods of selecting the target and of isolating the agent should ensure that neither the subject nor experimenters could influence the result. Selection of the target had to be completely random—i.e., carried out in such a way that no one could predict which of the pool of targets would be selected. The experimenters had to be ignorant of the target and of anything about it, since they had contact with the subject.

It is unlikely, but not impossible, that a subject should be in collusion with one or more agents to fake the experiment. It is much more likely that an experimenter, through having some information about the targets, should unwittingly influence the subject when communicating with him during the night or during the matching of dreams and targets the following morning. In the repetition study, elaborate precautions were taken to ensure that the agent could not leave her room until the session was complete and that only the agent should know the target for the night. It is not evident, from the experimental report, that sufficient attention was paid to this aspect in the original experiment.

In the original experiment, a great deal depended on the activities of the two experimenters in charge. Since they were in two-way sensory contact with the subject, it was essential that they should be isolated from the agent. A separate person was employed for creating the target pools, who, it was stated, had no contact with the subject or agents, but it is not clear whether he maintained contact in any way with the experimenters. If an experimenter was with the agent when he opened the envelope containing the target picture, unless this experimenter was isolated from all others taking part until judging was completed, a serious weakness was present in the experimental design.

The subject.   It is claimed that the subject displayed knowledge that would normally only be available to him through transmission of information. It is, thus, necessary to ensure that the subject is isolated in such a manner that information cannot reach him through normal sensory channels.

This can be achieved in two ways:

1. by isolating the subject.
2. by arranging for selection of the target and viewing of the target by the agent to be done in such a manner that information about the target is confined to the agent, who is isolated from all sensory contact with other individuals.

Isolation of the subject was not complete in either experiment since the investigators communicated with him through an intercom system before and after he reported his dream. It was, thus, essential for the experimenters to be as carefully isolated as the subject. There would, in fact, appear to be little point in permitting discussion with the subject during the experiment or of having any form of communication with him other than the EOG monitor and a signal (such as a bell) to awaken him.

Target selections.   Precautions need to be taken when allocating targets to envelopes.

1. Envelopes should be completely "opaque," so that a target cannot be seen by strong light or by rendering the envelope transparent.
2. The envelopes to be used by the agent should be randomly numbered *after* the pictures are sealed inside by some other person who could have no knowledge of the contents. (These numbers were not required for the duplicate set.) This other person merely saw eight similar envelopes and assigned numbers 1-8 to them at random. It was essential to ensure that the agent did not decide which of the eight targets was used. It was only for this reason that it was necessary to number the envelopes containing the targets.

It should be noted that a target can easily be concealed so that no particular person can have knowledge of it. If there are five investigators, the first investigator places the targets into eight similar envelopes, shuffles them, and seals them. He hands these to the second experimenter, who places these at random into eight slightly larger envelopes, and so on. Each of the investigators can ensure that none of his fellows nor himself has any information as to the location of the targets. Numbers 1-8 may then be placed randomly only on the outside envelopes, or omitted, and the agent left free to choose any one envelope. (It would be quite evident if the agent opened more than one envelope.)

During the experiment it was not essential, in view of the assessment procedure employed, for the eight possible targets to be unknown to the subject. The experimental procedures might have been simplified by letting him know the targets since this has been done in most other ESP tests. For example, both Rhine's and Soal's subjects knew the identities of five possible targets from which the target was selected for each trial.

The experimental conditions would have been improved if the same precautions had been taken to isolate the two experimenters, E_3 and E_4, from each other and from the subject, as were employed with the agent. The experimental report does not make it clear, in fact, whether communication between E_3 and E_4 was limited to the signal with which E_3 signaled E_4 to initiate the awakening of the subject at the termination of rapid eye movements.

The agent signaled to the experimenter E_3, by means of a switch, to show that she had awakened after hearing the buzzer telling her to concentrate on the target. This signaling system might have been omitted since it could have been employed to transmit information from the agent to E_3. The presence of E_1, E_2, and E_5 was not sufficient to stop E_3, E_4, and the agent influencing the experiment if they so desired.

Complete isolation of the subject, except for a buzzer to awaken him after his dream, until after the targets had been judged against the dreams would have been preferable, since the post-dream interviews seemed to serve no useful purpose and omission of any discussion between the experimenter and subject was desirable.

An excellent feature of the replication experiment was that each of the precautions taken was later checked as part of the procedure. There is no mention of this being done in the original experiment.

Approach II: If ESP exists, what were the changes in the second experiment that resulted in lack of results?

This is the second approach suggested by Foulkes and Ullman. It should be noted that the failure to replicate is typical of other ESP experiments reported in the past. When an experiment is carried out to check an initial experiment, it may be expected that improvements, extra safeguards, or improved care in conducting the experiment will be introduced. This is particularly likely if an outside person, who is not a parapsychologist, is included among the testing personnel.

Two features of any experiment are of particular importance:

1. The method or design employed.
2. The procedure adopted during the conduct of the experiment.

If a replication experiment is conducted using an identical *method* to the first experiment, it is still possible for changes in procedure to bring about a different result. The replication experiment of Foulkes and Belvedere had features incorporated in the design to ensure that an exact procedure was followed. (See italicized passages in description of the procedure.)

The presence of a new and critical experimenter, not part of an established team, is likely to ensure that careful attention is paid to exact procedure. An experiment is likely to be conducted in a less informal atmosphere than has been customary, particularly if the stranger is taking some interest in the conduct of the experiment.

If the lack of evidence for ESP in the second experiment was due to tightening up of method and procedure, and if ESP only manifests itself in loosely designed and conducted tests, it becomes impossible to provide experimental evidence for its existence. Perhaps the most important feature of the second experiment was the presence of a new member of the team who was not strongly committed to establishing a case for ESP.

The two "lines of inquiry," suggested by Foulkes and Belvedere, would be better rephrased so as to reflect on the observations rather than on inferences made from them:

1. If the experimental conditions do not permit information that could affect the subject's dreams to reach him, why did the first experiment indicate a gain of information by the subject in relation to the target?
2. What were the differences between the two experiments that were responsible for the difference in results?

The main differences were, first, that extra precautions were taken in the second experiment to ensure that the identity of the target card could be known only to the agent until the matching procedure was completed; second, that a new investigator was present; and third, checks were incorporated into the experimental design to ensure that each part of the procedure was fully adhered to.

Further Studies

Other studies at the Dream Laboratory employed experimental conditions less rigorous than those in the experiment described above. Thus, in an early study, the agent sometimes monitored the polygraph for a short period of time to relieve the experimenter. In another experiment, called the second Erwin study, where Dr. William Erwin acted as subject, it was decided that, in addition to the target picture, the agent would be provided with "props" that were supposed to reinforce the impact of the painting on the agent. The props consisted of objects such as toy soldiers and a boxing glove (used with a picture of a boxing match). The objects were placed in a box which was available to the subject together with the target picture.

Ullman and Krippner report that they set their staff in search of "multi-sensory" materials to accompany the pool of ten art prints. Thus, it was likely that a number of people, including the investigators, had some idea of the types of pictures in the target pool.

In an experiment reported by Krippner, Honorton, and Ullman, together with R. E. L. Masters and Jean Houston of the Foundation for Mind Research in New York,[4] the agent viewed audiovisual programs in a "sensory bombardment" chamber and attempted to influence the subject's dreams. The agent was situated in Masters and Houston's laboratory, fourteen miles from the subject, who was situated in the Maimonides Laboratory. Eight subjects were each tested for one night.

The dreams for each night were ranked against a list of six possible "audio visual programs," Ranks 1, 2, and 3 were then considered to be hits and ranks 4, 5, and 6 as misses. Using this procedure 8 hits and 0 misses were obtained, a result having odds of 256 to one against arising by chance. (Each set of dreams had a probability of ½ of being judged a hit. The probability of obtaining 8 hits was thus $(\frac{1}{2})^8 = 1/256$)

Attempted Replication

An attempt to replicate this experiment using the original subject was made by Foulkes and Belvedere,[5] in conjunction with the original investigators. Again there was failure to confirm the result obtained in the original experiment.

The main differences in the replication experiment were, first, that the subject was situated 2,000 miles from the agent in Wyoming rather than 14 miles away; second, the experimental procedure was tightened up.

Summary

Looking at the dream research as a whole, it is clear that over a period of twelve years, some twelve investigations have been carried out, in which experimental conditions have varied considerably and gradually become more rigorous, but positive results have not been obtained under rigorous experimental conditions. It was, moreover, possible on two occasions for a successful subject to be retested with a further outside investigator present. In one case, the original investigators were also present, but in neither case was the result of the earlier experiment confirmed.

The dream studies have features in common with other ESP research. It was claimed that the subject's dreams were affected by telepathy, but this did not manifest itself in any definite fashion. A number of dreams were checked against a number of targets. There might have been no apparent connection between any of the dreams and any of the targets, but the judge was required to rank them in order of similarity. The judge was acting like the percipient in a card-guessing experiment. It was as necessary to isolate him from any possible sources of information as it was to isolate the percipient and agent in a card-guessing experiment.

Precautions were taken to exclude the possibility of information being transmitted by normal means, but the original precautions did not appear to be adequate. When additional precautions were taken, above-chance scores were no longer obtained.

According to Foulkes and Belvedere, the extra precautions in the replication experiment inhibited the ESP powers of their subject; but it is more logical to assume that these precautions removed a source of experimental error that was responsible for the result of the first experiment.

Notes

1. M. Ullman, S. Krippner, and A. Vaughan, *Dream Telepathy* (New York: Macmillan, 1973). (Foreword by Murphy Gardner).
2. M. Ullman and S. Krippner, *Dream Studies and Telepathy—An Experimental Approach,* Parapsychology Monograph, number 12 (New York: Parapsychology Foundation, 1970), p. 99.
3. E. Belvedere and D. Foulkes, "Telepathy and Dreams: A Failure to Replicate," *Perceptual and Motor Skills,* 33 (1971): 783–89.
4. S. Krippner, C. Honorton, M. Ullman, R. Masters and J. Houston, "A Long-Distance 'Sensory Bombardment' Study of ESP in Dreams," *Journal of the American Society for Psychical Research,* 65 (1971): 468–75.
5. D. Foulkes, E. Belvedere, R. Masters, J. Houston, S. Krippner, C. Honorton, and M. Ullman, "Long-Distance 'Sensory Bombardment' ESP in Dreams: A Failure to Replicate," *Perceptual and Motor Skills,* 35 (1972): 731–34.

21

The Challenge of Chance

The last major experiment reported in Britain was carried out by the Oxford biologist, Professor Sir Alister Hardy, together with Mr. Robert Harvie, a psychology graduate of London University,[1] over a period of a week at the Caxton Hall, London. The experiments were, basically, telepathy tests, in which the main part of an audience of about 200 persons saw a drawing of some object (the target) while a group of subjects, isolated from the main audience in cubicles, attempted to draw it.

The Caxton Hall Experiment

The essential features of the main experiment were as follows. In the center of the hall, towards the back, a block of twenty cubicles had been constructed out of black-out material on light metal frames. Occupants of the cubicles were screened at the front and sides. A group of 20 persons drawn from the audience, sat in the cubicles, while the remaining members of the audience viewed a series of target pictures displayed on the stage at the front of the hall. The "percipients," inside the cubicles, attempted to draw pictures corresponding to the targets. After ten targets had been attempted, the twenty percipients were replaced by a further group from the audience. This process was continued until each member of the audience had had a turn at being a percipient.

In this way, a total of 2,200 drawing attempts was obtained. These were checked against the targets, and the number of hits established. In a "control experiment" the judges matched drawings against targets other than those being displayed when the drawings were made.

Hardy and Harvie found evidence for ESP neither in their group as a whole nor in the individual results from their 220 subjects. The number of drawings resembling targets was no greater in the experimental group than in the control experiment. They claimed, however, that the subjects, while showing no ability for telepathy, displayed "coincident thoughts." Drawings made by different percipients of a particular target, while not resembling the target, resembled each other more often than theory indicated. If this were so, it would appear that one form of telepathy had been replaced by another. The subjects, instead of telepathizing the thoughts of members of the audience, were telepathizing each other's thoughts.

Hardy and Harvie did not, however, interpret their result in this way. With Arthur Koestler, they published details of the experiments in *The Challenge of Chance,* maintaining that their findings supported the general theme that events—in this case, thoughts—arise simultaneously without there being a common causal factor. They claimed that "coincident thoughts" arose in adjoining booths and that percipients who were not in adjoining booths did not have coincident thoughts.

But very little attention was paid in the experiments to eliminating auditory cues. These might seem to afford a more likely cause of the simultaneous thoughts than some new property of nature. Moreover, communication need only have arisen about once in every 100 trials for the observed effect to come about. The investigators mentioned in their report that they had stressed the importance of everyone "remaining absolutely silent . . . not to allow oneself to make even the slightest involuntary sound such as a sigh or gasp of surprise or a little laugh . . . which might indicate something of the nature of the drawing being displayed." The *guessers* may not have thought that they could disclose anything about the targets since they could not see them, and according to the original aim of the experiment they were in no position to affect telepathy scores; but they were certainly in a position to produce coincidental thoughts.[2]

In fact, there is little point in pursuing this matter further since the investigators, when counting the number of coincidences to be used in their statistical test, counted the number of drawings resembling any other drawing.[3] Thus if Drawing A resembled Drawing B, B also resembled A, and two resemblances were counted. The two observations were not independent. They should have counted the number of pairs of drawings judged alike—and also triplets, quadruplets, etc.—thus obtaining approximately half the numbers of cases for the χ^2 test that they employed. If their data are analyzed correctly, a lower significance level is obtained than the one they claimed.[4] Only an approximation is possible from their reported data, but this gives a probability value of .09. Thus, their effect is hardly worth any further investigation.

Dispensing with the Percipient

A second experiment to demonstrate quirks in probability theory was carried out by Mr. Harvie. At Duke University, in the early 1930s, J. B. Rhine discovered that it was unnecessary to have an agent—or transmitter in ESP tests—since the guesser did just as well under clairvoyance conditions when the targets were not seen by any other person (Chapter 8). Harvie went a stage further in his experiment: he also dispensed with the percipient. He compared 49,600 digits from tables of "random numbers" representing guesses, item by item, with the same number of digits in other series of "random numbers" produced by computers (representing targets). The number of "hits" detected (4,749) was less than chance expectation (4,960). Such a result has odds greater than 1,000 to 1 against arising by chance.

Harvie was obviously aware that during his Herculean task of making 49,600 comparisons he might have missed one or two hits, but he pointed out that an independent comparison of *4,000 guesses* and targets by a colleague gave results *"substantially* in accordance with mine but with some minor discrepancies which suggested that I had indeed erred towards missing out possible coincidences."(Italics mine) He did not give actual figures, and he did not mention having made any independent check of the 4,000 guesses and targets to see whether his colleague's figures could be confirmed.

The Caxton Hall experiment represents an attempt to test a large sample of subjects—mostly believers in ESP. It was conducted in an informal friendly manner by believers in ESP. It revealed no evidence for ESP by the group or by any single individual. It also failed to provide any clear evidence for "coincidental thoughts."

The Roots of Coincidence

The idea of synchronicity had been discussed by Arthur Koestler in his book *The Roots of Coincidence*.[5]

According to Koestler, synchronicity is responsible for coincidences arising in everyday life and for quirks in probability theory. Koestler claims that such coincidences may be due to an underlying acausal principle in nature. He gives examples in which he finds it difficult to reconcile indeterminancy at the microscale of subatomic physics with orderly prediction at the macro-scale and suggests that there is a basic flaw or inadequacy in the current concepts of chance and randomness, which calls for some additional hypothesis to account for the spontaneous emergence of "order from disorder."

As an example, according to Koestler "—the point in time at which a radioactive atom will disintegrate is totally unpredictable, . . . and yet it does have a hidden relationship with the rest of the world, because the "half-life period" of any grain of a radio active substance . . . is precisely fixed and predictable. . . ." In his contribution to *The Challenge of Chance*, Robert Harvie produces a similar example. He writes, "thus although in a collection of, say, one million nuclei of the same kind, it is impossible to say exactly when any one of them will disintegrate, we know that after a time equivalent to the half-life only half a million will survive unchanged."

Koestler and Harvie seem to be implying that while it is not possible to know when a radioactive atom will disintegrate, a collection of atoms somehow synchronizes its activities so that after a precisely fixed period of time exactly half of the atoms will still be intact.

Difficulty arises in Koestler's use of the word "precisely." If the "grain of radioactive material consisted of one atom, it would have no half-life period. The half-life period becomes more exactly specifiable (in terms of a mean and standard deviation) as the number of atoms constituting the "grain" increases. It can never be numerically precise in view of the indeterminate behavior of individual atoms.

Harvie's "half million" constitutes the most likely number to survive, but it is unlikely that exactly that number will survive in a particular sample, just as it becomes increasingly unlikely, as we increase the number of pennies tossed, that exactly half will turn up heads.

If we deal in precise and exact numbers, Koestler's paradox assumes a different form. Thus, a single penny can result in two different end-states, but 1,000,000 pennies can result in $2^{1,000,000}$ different end-states. It is also much more likely that tossing two pennies will result in exactly one head and one tail than that tossing a million pennies, will result in exactly 500,000 heads and 500,000 tails. In general, at the macro level the end-state is less certain than at the micro level. Koestler is, of course, not concerned with precise end-states, but with properties at the macro-level in which a large number of end-states are, for the purposes of the observer, equivalent.

Koestler is particularly concerned with the problem of explaining how orderly patterns emerge at the macroscopic level that are dependent on chance or unpredictable events at the microscopic level; or of how large numbers of unpredictable events can lead to more or less predictable averages.

He quotes three cases. These are concerned with the number of reports of dogs biting people each day in New York, with the numbers of people murdered in England and Wales, and with the numbers of cavalry horses administering fatal kicks to soldiers in the German army of the last century.

Dogs Biting People

Koestler quotes the figures given in Column 2, Table 21–1, from the New York City Department of Health of the average number of reports per day of dogs biting people seriously enough to be reported in 1955. He notes that the average daily number of bites remains at a relatively stable value between 72.4 and 75.3.

Murders in England and Wales

Koestler has also noted that murderers in England and Wales "displayed the same respect for the law of statistics" as dogs did when biting people. He gives the figures shown in Table 21–2, Column 2, for the average number of murders per million of the population over successive decades.

Table 21-1
Average number of reports per day of dogs biting people

Year	Average number of reports per day	Cases per year
1955	75.3	27,484.5
1956	73.6	26,864
1957	73.5	26,827.5
1958	74.5	27,192.5
1959	72.4	26,426

It should be noted that the figures Koestler gives in both the above examples are not observed numbers of cases, but average values. The number of dogs biting a person can be obtained from Column 2 of Table 21–1, by multiplying the values reported by 365. These figures are shown in Column 3. Similarly an approximation to the actual numbers of murders committed in each ten-year period can be obtained by multiplying the figures in Column 2 of Table 21–2 by 40 (the population of England and Wales being approximately 40 million). These figures are shown in Column 3.

Variability in the figures in Column 3 will be expected owing to a large number of unpredictable factors. Given a sufficient number of such features, some acting one way others the other, the values will be unpredictable, and display chance fluctuations. Where a single factor is operating at a sufficiently high level—say a very hot summer—it might produce a change in the figures that is not averaged out among the other factors.

The figures in both tables display these variations. Thus, for a sample obtained from a large population of events having a low frequency of occurrence, the standard deviation may be estimated as $\sqrt{N}$ where N is the number of cases arising in the sample. A difference in the number from one year to the next of 2 standard deviations has odds of arising by chance of 1 in 20. Thus, both sets of figures suggest some variability. In the case of Table 21-1, the figures for 1956 are 620 less than those for 1955 whilst the standard deviation is about 165, giving a

Table 21-2
Average murders per million of population

Year	Average murders per million population	Actual murders	Standard deviation
1920–29	3.84	154	12.41
1930–39	3.27	131	11.45
1940–49	3.92	157	12.53
1950–59	3.3	132	11.49
1960–69	3.5	140	11.83

difference more than 3.5 standard deviations with odds of about 1 in 2500 of arising by chance.

The average values for each year will obviously vary much less than the individual values from which they are derived. But from Column 3, it is seen that the amount of variability is larger than might be expected from a purely chance event. Koestler should be surprised that the statistics he quotes are not less variable than they are from year to year if his murderers are busy making up their yearly quota.

Fatal Kicks in the German Army

Koestler's other case concerns a similar statistical reliability in the number of "cavalry horses administering fatal kicks to soldiers in the German army of the last century; they were apparently guided by the so-called Poisson equation of probability theory." Koestler is referring to data originally discussed by R. A. Fisher in his book *Statistical Methods for Research Workers*.[6] There Fisher gives data originally obtained by Bortkewitch from the records of 10 army corps over a period of twenty years, giving 200 samples in all. The number of deaths arising in each sample was noted. In some samples there were no deaths, in others 1, 2, or more. The observed frequencies with which 0, 1, 2, etc., deaths occurred in the 200 samples considered were then compared with the theoretical figures, assuming a fatal horse kick being a random (unpredictable) event having a very low probability of arising.

Fisher showed that a remarkably close fit was obtained between these figures and those expected on the basis of the Poisson distribution. The features in the data that puzzle Koestler arise because he considered not the actual numbers of cases, but values derived from them.

When considering the statistics of fatal kicks in the German army, Koestler is not concerned with *which* cavalry horses guided by the so-called Poisson equation of probability theory, administered fatal kicks to German soldiers, but with *how many* soldiers got kicked.

Notes

1. A. Hardy, R. Harvie, and A. Koestler, *The Challenge of Chance: Experiments and Speculations* (London: Hutchinson, 1973).
2. C. E. M. Hansel "Baffling Coincidences?" Review *New Scientist,* December 27, 1973, p. 919; A. Hardy and R. Harvie, Correspondence *New Scientist,* January 24, 1974, p. 219.
3. C. E. M. Hansel, Challenge of Chance Correspondence *New Scientist,* February 7, 1974, p. 366.
4. *Ibid.*
5. A. Koestler, *The Roots of Coincidence* (London: Hutchinson, 1972). (Postscript by Renee Hayes.)
6. R. A. Fisher, *Statistical Methods for Research Workers,* Oliver and Boyd, eds. (Edinburgh, 1944), p. 55

22
The Miracle Men

From time to time an individual hits the headlines with some new and miraculous feat which is attributed to his psychic powers. A small number of such men have maintained their reputations over considerable periods of time, but most of them create a brief sensation and then fade into oblivion. The four cases considered here are all active at the present time, and they have each been tested under what are claimed to be strict test conditions. Each of them is claimed to possess paranormal abilities.

The first of these, Gerard Croiset, has acted as a professional clairvoyant in Holland for a number of years and claims to have assisted the police in solving crimes. He was extensively studied by Professor W. H. C. Tenhaeff, formerly Director of the Institute of Parapsychology at the University of Utrecht.

The second case is that of Pavel Stepanek. He is possibly the sole surviving high-scoring subject at card guessing, although he has not been tested with the normal ESP cards. He has taken part in experiments for some seventeen years, and his feats have been described in *Nature,* the leading British science periodical.

The third case is that of a former Chicago bell-hop, Edward Serios, who claims to be able to cause photographs to appear on a photographic film by gazing into the camera and impressing the image onto the film. While others have been able to duplicate his feats using normal means, Serios is still regarded as having psychic abilities by parapsychologists.

The fourth case, Uri Geller, clearly deserves a chapter to himself. Although offering a limited repertoire, he is possibly the most colorful and best-publicized psychic since Eusapia Palladino. He has also survived examination in a scientific laboratory without being exposed as bogus, although he was unable to perform there his most spectacular feat—bending a teaspoon.

Gerard Croiset

Croiset has become well known through the writings of Professor W. H. C. Tenhaeff and also through newspaper accounts appearing at regular intervals all over the world that publicize his feats in assisting—or claiming to assist—the police in solving crime. The following is an example, which was reported in an article "Crime Busting with ESP," by Jack Harrison Pollack in *This Week* magazine on February 26, 1961.

> An early success in this case I checked in the Parapsychology Institute and Dutch police files. On December 5, 1946, a pretty blond 21-year old girl was returning home at 5:45 P.M. along a quiet country road near Wierden, Holland. Suddenly a man *leaped out from behind a stone warehouse,* and assaulted her, hitting her on the *neck and arms* with a hammer. Before he disappeared into the dark, she was able to wrench the hammer away from him.
>
> *Police contacted Dr. Tenhaeff, who came to the station,* bringing Gerard Croiset, one of his team of paragnosts. Because the *girl was in the hospital,* Croiset didn't see her. Instead he picked up the hammer, his large hand squeezing the handle as *police* watched skeptically. Croiset concentrated.
>
> 'He is tall and dark, about 30 years old, and has a somewhat deformed left ear,' said the paragnost. 'But this hammer doesn't belong to him. Its owner was a man of about 55 whom the criminal visits often at a small white cottage . . . near here. It is one of a group of three cottages, all the same.'
>
> *The deformed left ear was a key clue.* Several months later the police picked up a tall, dark 29-year-old man on another morals charge. His *badly scarred and swollen left ear* led to questioning about the first attack. Finally, he admitted assaulting the girl with the hammer. He said he had *borrowed it from a friend, who, the police discovered, lived in a white cottage on the edge of town, with two others just like it on either side.*
>
> Dr. Tenhaeff's files bulge with such cases. Each is documented with a recording or stenographic transcript of the prediction, and with statements confirming its accuracy from witnesses and police. [italics added.][1]

I sent this account to the police at Wierden asking whether they could verify that the account agreed with data in their files. I received in reply the following letter from the burgomaster, E. D. Maaldrink.

Wierden, March 22, 1961.

Dear Sir,

With a great interest and even still greater astonishment, I read your letter of March 9th. How is it possible that a simple story can be mutilated in such a way! Maybe the answer is simple: when someone desires to see something special, after a certain time he will see it, even if it is not there.

Your letter was directed to me, as in Holland the burgomaster is normally also head of the local police, and so I'll try to answer it. My English grammar being rather poor, I do beg you to take the freedom of interrogating me about questions which are not described clear enough.

When the story began on December 5th, 1946, I was already burgomaster of the town of Wierden, Overijessel, Holland.

The whole community at whose head I have the honour and the pleasure to stand, has about 15,000 inhabitants, and contains two villages: Wierden with 6000 inhabitants, and Enter with 4000, the rest of the people living as farmers round about in the country.

So the young girl, indeed good-looking, lived with her family in a farm, about three kilometers from the village of Wierden.

In the evening of the fifth of December she returned home on her bicycle by a sand-road, with a big box of cardboard held in one hand, with a sugar-cake, as it was the evening of the national homely feast of Santa-Claus.

Being about 700 meters from her house she was indeed assaulted by a man. He did *not* leap from behind a stone storehouse. In the neighborhood there is not any building to be found.

The man hit her twice with a hammer on the head, *not* on the neck and arms.

Then he saw the light of another bicycle, which was nearing and fled away on his own cycle, leaving the wounded young girl and his hammer.

The girl was transported to her home and it was *not* necessary to bring her to an hospital.

The policemen of course did all their best to find the man, but without any result in the beginning.

After a few days there circulated the name of a certain young man, called K. Who called the name first, is not clear.

He was married since a year and a few months and his wife had a first baby.

It seems the name was mentioned because some people had noticed that he had committed or tried to commit exhibitional acts.

The truth hereabout we could not find out. As you know most people don't like to talk about such facts.

The only spur was the hammer. To find the owner it was showed behind the window of a grocer's shop in the midst of Wierden, but nobody seemed to recognise it.

Then after several weeks, perhaps even six, I received the visit of an elderly sort of landlord, who lives at a country place, not far from the spot where the assault was committed.

The family had as a girl-servant the sister of the attacked young girl and this girl did not dare to turn home when she was not guided by the landlord.

The last was of course rather annoyed about these trips every evening and asked me if I would allow him to take the hammer to Mr. Croiset and ask him information.

So happened. I don't know yet exactly who belonged to the party which visited Mr. Croiset, then living at Enschede.

And unhappily I don't neither know if the visit was beforehand announced to him. The last thing is in this kind of matter very important as later turned out.

About the hammer Croiset told that it had been behind a big window. In fact it had been behind the window of the grocer.

Further that the owner of the hammer or the owner of the window had a disease of the aerial ways. Indeed the grocer has bronchitis.

About the performer of the assault he told that he lived in a small house, rather similar to the houses of the two neighbours, with a stone well behind it.

When you believe in Telepathy, you can imagine that the policeman, who was present, thought at that moment about the rather likely house of Mr. K. and that Mr. Croiset felt this!

Further he told that it was a young person, but anybody will give young men greater chance to do such silly things than elder men. Mr. K. was born December 16th 1919.

And the man would have a deformed ear and a ring with a blue stone in it.

The police could do nothing with these communications. Mr. K. had two normal ears and when he might possess a ring with a blue stone, he seemed never to wear it.

So one month after another passed on without any result for the Wierden police.

Then in the early springtime 1947 Mr. K. was arrested near the town of Almelo (which lies only five kilometers from Wierden) while committing the act of exhibitionism.

He was tried for several hours by our police and at the end he confessed.

We even yet don't know who was the owner of the hammer. This morning one of my policemen asked him, but Mr. K. refuses to tell us, so we suppose he has stolen it.[2]

Pollack said that he had checked the case in the Dutch police files. I wrote to *This Week* pointing out discrepancies in the account and asking that details of the police files consulted should be stated. My letter was not published, but from the reply received from Pollack, it would appear that the nearest he got to a police file was to see the burgomaster's original letter to Tenhaeff in the files at the Parapsychology Institute. Unless he read Dutch, that would have meant little to him.

I received two further communications about this story, the first from a Dutch parapsychologist, P. B. Otterwanger, who for years has cast a critical eye on the activities of parapsychologists in Holland. He confirmed what the burgomaster had told me and stated that other cases reported by Pollack in his article were equally misleading.

Croiset lived at Enschede, less than seventeen miles from Wierden and at one time worked as delivery boy for a grocer there. It is possible, therefore, that he knew of the grocer in whose window the hammer had been displayed and that he had heard about the crime. Thus, if all the information he gave had turned out to be true, it need have surprised no one.

It is of interest that the newspaper account introduced details that were lacking in Tenhaeff's account. Tenhaeff's report was accurate, but he did not mention that Mr. K. was suspected from the start by the police or that some of Croiset's remarks turned out to be wrong. He reported that the girl was hit on the head. He did not note the stone storehouse. He made no mention of the girl being in the hospital. And did not mention that Croiset could say nothing of value until after he had been told that the hammer had been used in a case of attempted murder.

The Wierden story appeared again in a 1961 article in *Maclean's* magazine, "First Report on Extra-Sensory Powers among Canadians," by Sidney Katz. It had by then undergone further changes.

> One of Dr. Tenhaeff's most gifted psychics, it is said, described the unknown assailant of a pretty blonde as a tall, dark man of thirty with a deformed left ear. He went on to state that the weapon used was a hammer borrowed from a friend who lived in a small white cottage, which is one of a group of three white cottages. This information, according to one report, was enough for the police to make an arrest.[3]

Katz's account is typical of the type of story that emerges after a series of repetitions.

At the present time, mediums or clairvoyants claim to assist the police in the detection of criminals, and in some countries the police have utilized their services and made decisions as a result of their advice. Dr. F. Brink, who, as a Dutch Police Inspector, investigated the activities of parapsychologists in their attempts to assist the Dutch police in solving crimes, has sent me an article he published in the *International Criminal Police Review*. It is of great interest to see how a trained investigator reacted to the artfulness of the mediums and the tests he applied to test their claims. His conclusion was that while such persons were sporadically consulted, the police had, to his knowledge, never derived any help from their supposed powers of clairvoyance.

Brink described investigations he made of four clairvoyants, one of whom was very well known. These tests involved handing photographs to them of objects or people. Some were from police files and others were of persons or things with no connection with the police. Letters of an abusive nature, anonymous letters, and such things as weapons, knives, and keys were also handed to the clairvoyants. Such objects are referred to as "inductive material." Of them, Brink said:

> The several tests were marked by a diversity of procedure and circumstances. Those made during a period of over one year have not evinced anything that might be regarded as being of actual use to police investigation. Whether the relevations made by the clairvoyants had been inspired by any of the things, transmitted by way of inductive material, or by photos, of which as many as

twenty-four had been occasionally given to them for the same purpose, the results invariably proved to be nil. . . .

Another remarkable feature of the clairvoyant's manner of performance—which is bound to strike anyone who is listening in to the reproduction of their revelations, registered by a tape recorder—is that clairvoyants appear to favour the habit of expressing the greater majority of their remarks, communications and conclusions in the interrogative form. Even though they should know, or at least presume, that they cannot expect a direct answer from the experimenter addressed in that manner, they persistently indulge in this habit.

In this connection it is worth noting that in the event of any of their feelers, in the form of tentative questions, such as, "May it be possible that————" being answered in the affirmative, they will instantly make the experimenter feel that they have scored a hit, by saying "I told you so, didn't I?" thus creating the impression that their particular mode of speech should be regarded as an instance of knowing, really, and not of probing.

In those cases where the experimenter is not responsive to this form of enticement, it will nevertheless be hard to control involuntary reactions produced by the sensorimotor process, and showing emotional effects, such as mimic gestures, muscular contradiction, etc. It is practically impossible to restrain these unconscious reactions, especially in the case of a person who is confronted with a continuous flow of questions.[4]

Croiset is still active in Holland. In 1973, I was invited by Eric Twiname of the British Broadcasting Corporation to take part in a program where I was required to discuss experiments carried out in a Pharmacology Laboratory in Holland on Croiset. Details of the experiments were supplied to me before the program.

It appeared that Tenhaeff had approached Dr. G. H. van Leeuwen President of Enzypharm n.v., to conduct experiments on the effect exerted by Croiset on animals and drugs that he handled. In the resulting experiments, it was claimed that Croiset had influenced a solution of nickel chloride so that its absorption characteristics for light, as measured on a Beckman spectrophotometer changed over a period of five days after Croiset had exerted his influence. Copies of the print-out taken on successive days were supplied to me from which it was clear that the overall transmission as recorded by the instrument had increased greatly. In fact, at the wavelength giving maximum transmission, it recorded a transmission of more than 100 percent. Thus, either the instrument was not set up properly, or else the nickel chloride had started emitting light.

It was claimed that the second experiment showed that when Croiset handled mice of a type that tended to produce tumors after lactation, the mice produced more tumors than similar mice that had not been handled. There was, however, in this case more to follow. If Croiset handled a syringe containing a substance that reduced the rate of tumor formation, the solution lost its therapeutic properties. In this experiment, the data was so confused that it was difficult to unravel precisely what had happened. However, I prepared my comments but had very little time given me in which to voice my criticisms. When the program *"GERARD CROISET: More Things in Heaven and Earth,"* was broadcast, most of what I had said was cut out altogether. Details of the experiments do not appear to have been published since.

Croiset still claims to assist the police in Holland and elsewhere. His son, Gerard Croiset, also claims to have clairvoyant powers, and it is sometimes difficult to decide from the reports which member of the family business is involved. Between them, they must give advice in so many cases that an outstanding success should eventually materialize.

I have encountered three such cases arising locally and have heard of others.

A case was reported in the Manchester *Evening Post* of December 7, 1963, where it was stated that Croiset had given details of what he believed were the movements of a missing boy on the day he had disappeared. He had "seen" the boy near the town square with a man about thirty-two years old, 5 ft. 5 in. tall, with brown hair. The man lived or worked in a particular street. He named a park and a part of the town where a railway bridge passed over a road and river.

The following account appeared in *The Guardian* of March 27, 1965, under the heading *Clairvoyants "body in canal" vision fails:*

Four police frogmen searched 150 yards of the murky Bridgewater Canal yesterday at a spot where a Dutch clairvoyant claimed they would find a woman's body. But there was no trace of Mrs. Martha Hardy, aged 73, a widow of Starkey Street, Heywood, who disappeared 16 months ago.

Her daughter, Mrs. Margaret Burton, aged 50, a former 'GI bride' who has flown from America to investigate her mother's disappearance, said: 'I am grateful to the police because this stretch has not been searched before, but I did not expect anything because I do not believe in clairvoyants.'

In the 95 minutes they searched the 8 ft. deep stretch at Stretford, where the canal crosses the Mersey, the frogmen brought up a kettle, a football, and an old sock.

The spot had been delineated by Mr. Gerard Croiset, aged 57, in Utrecht after he studied maps and a pair of Mrs. Hardy's gloves. A Lancashire County police spokesman said the suggestion was 'remotely feasible.'

Since moving to Swansea, I have noticed a further case arising about twelve miles away, in the town of Neath. The following extract is from the *South Wales Evening Post* of November 15, 1974:

Startling revelations about the deaths of the three Neath girls who were brutally murdered more than 12 months ago have been made by a world famous Dutch psychic who claims to have extra-sensory perception.

Gerard Croiset, junior, had here been at work. He described a man between thirty-nine and forty, just under six feet, heavily built and with a large mouth, with brown hair graying at the sides and a graying moustache. Whether Croiset's prognostications were correct or not is not known since the crime is still unsolved.

Pavel Stepanek

In 1962, Milan Ryzl, a biochemist at the Institute of Biology at the Czechoslovack Academy of Science in Prague started investigations on a subject, Pavel Stepanek, who was claimed to have ESP powers comparable to those of the high-scoring subjects discovered by Rhine in his heyday.[5] The method employed in the initial experiments was as follows:

An observer was given a pile of envelopes together with cards, one side white, the other green. The observer placed the cards into the envelopes with either the white or the green side uppermost. The envelopes were then given to Stepanek, who judged whether the card inside the envelope had its white side or its green side uppermost. A statistical analysis revealed that he was correctly allocating the envelopes into the two categories at well above the chance level.

In 1965, I suggested that clues due to warping of the cards might be responsible for this result. This would be due to shrinkage on the side of the card that had been colored. It was noted that when the experiment was carried out by Dr. John Beloff, a psychologist from Edinburgh University who supplied his own cards, Stepanek's extrasensory abilities had deserted him.

In October 1968, a paper was published in *Nature*[6] in which further evidence for Stepanek's clairvoyant powers was revealed. The authors, seven in all, were from the Universities of Virginia, Amsterdam, Tasmania, Lund, and the Psychical Research Foundation, Durham, North Carolina. It appeared that, in 1965, Stepanek lost the ability to say which way up the cards were inside the envelopes. But around the same time, he developed a new ability. He now tended to call *white* to a particular *envelope*, irrespective of whether the card inside it was one way up or the other. It was decided that Stepanek was now using ESP to discriminate between the envelopes.

A series of eighteen experiments was then conducted in which the envelopes—now referred to as covers—were placed inside further envelopes—referred to as jackets. For some reason the green and white cards were still placed inside the covers, although they did not appear to contribute anything to what was going on.

In the first three experiments, the covers were exposed to Stepanek's view, in the remaining fifteen, they were placed inside the jackets. In the first five experiments, ten covers, each containing a card, were used. After the fifth experiment, the number of covers was reduced from ten to eight, and after the seventh experiment, it was further reduced to four. In each reduction covers were retained that had given the most positive results in earlier tests. One cover in particular (no. 15/16) appeared to give excellent results, and data for this cover was presented in the article in *Nature*.

The general procedure was as follows: The covers were randomized "outside the subject's sight," and the prepared stack of four to ten covers—normally inside their jackets—were placed in front of Stepanek. He then judged each in turn, placing it aside into a new stack as he did so. The experimenter recorded Stepanek's guesses and then recorded the targets from the order of the jackets in the pile at the end of the run.

Various changes were introduced as the series of experiments proceeded. After series 7 the targets were randomized by one experimenter using random number tables and another experimenter conducted the testing.

In series 1, where Pratt was the only experimenter, Stepanek responded to cover 13/16 by saying *white* eighty-six times and *green* fourteen times. According to the report "This consistency of choice showed that he somehow recognised this cover as an object regardless of which side was presented upward." It will be noted, however, that Stepanek was attempting to say whether a card inside the cover was white or green side up and this he appears to have been unable to do. Each time he came to cover 15/16 among the stack of ten covers, he tended to judge that the card inside it was *white* side up, without being correct at above the chance level.

In series 2, the contents of cover 15/16 were interchanged with those of another cover for which Stepanek had tended to call *green*. Stepanek seemed to be unaffected by this and continued to call *white* more often than *green* to cover 15/16.

After series 3, the covers were placed inside the further envelopes, referred to as jackets. These were made of two sheets of cardboard cut from manilla file jackets stapled together on three sides. The open side of the jacket always pointed away from Stepanek. The tendency for cover 15/16 to produce the call *white* from Stepanek continued.

In series 6, the cards, covers, and jackets were interchanged randomly before each run. The effect was found to be dependent only on the covers.

In series 7, Stepanek was observed by two Czeck citizens, a psychologist, and a government official. For the first time his performance deteriorated markedly, although he still scored at above the chance level on cover 15/16.

A number of other changes were introduced, the most important being:

1. Before series 9, in which the number of covers used was four, "the open ends of the four covers were closed up by taping onto them a folded piece of cardboard." High scores were obtained by Stepanek.
2. Before series 11, "several cotton balls were inserted between the two layers of the jackets." The investigators wished to ensure that any irregularities in the shapes of the covers, inside the jackets could not be transmitted through the jackets. High scores were still observed.
3. After thirty runs of series 12, the covers were made equal in weight within a limit of variation of 0.1 gm. High scores continued.

4. In series 12, a third experimenter was present who watched Stepanek closely on each trial to see that he did not glimpse an edge or corner of the enclosed cover. This had no appreciable affect on Stepanek's performance.

5. In series 14, the *jacket* sides were stapled together throughout their entire length, including the fourth side. Stepanek's ability to say *white* to cover 15/16 now abruptly disappeared. But in series 15—where presumably the same precautions were taken—it made a brief reappearance. After that, in the remaining three series—16, 17, and 18—it was no longer in evidence. Now, however, according to the report, a new feature emerged. "There was a shift in the pattern of response that yielded statistical significance (p. 001). This was a consequence of the subject's tendency in that session to associate one color with one side of the cover and the other color with the other side."

Looking at the experiments in general, Stepanek not only touched, but handled, the covers or the jackets containing the covers throughout. The investigators did not report the fact that Stepanek was unsuccessful when objects he was attempting to identify were placed inside rigid boxes rather than cardboard covers, although such a result had been reported by another investigator.

Stepanek had full view of the jackets. Tests are not reported in which he was screened both from the object he was handling and from the experimenter. In many of the tests, he was merely required to identify a particular cover, but this fact appears to have escaped the attention of the investigators.

It is clear from other research, such as that of S. G. Soal on a music hall artist, Marion (see p. 36), that it is necessary to take the same precautions with an experimenter who is present with a subject as it is with the subject to ensure that he will not have information about a target. It may appear strange that Stepanek's ability should desert him in series 14, when the fourth jacket side was stapled to exclude the possibility of his "glimpsing an edge or corner of the enclosed cover," because in the previous experiment, the fourth side was facing away from him. But, while it is difficult to see how the addition of a few extra staples should have affected Stepanek's extra sensory powers, they could have prevented the experimenter from seeing inside the jackets and voluntarily or involuntarily transmitting information to Stepanek.

It is not clear from the report whether a precaution once introduced into an experiment was thereafter retained for all later tests. Thus in experiment 6, the cards, covers, and jackets were changed before each run. This was a necessary precaution, since if a cover remained in the same jacket throughout, it would not be possible to say whether Stepanek was identifying the cover or the jacket. But, in experiment 14, when staples were placed for the first time into the fourth side of the jackets, the staples had, presumably, to be removed and reinserted after each four trials—i.e., a total of 100 times—in order to change the covers and cards. Stepanek was unsuccessful in this experiment, but were the precautions of changing the contents of the jackets and of stapling them retained for the four remaining experiments? If so, the staples would have had to be removed and replaced a further 300 times. If the precautions were not taken, the statistical evaluation of the results would have been affected, since Stepanek would have been discriminating between one of four jackets on each trial. If the precautions were not taken after experiment 14, it would appear that Stepanek was successful, provided it was possible for him or for some other person to glimpse "an edge or corner of the enclosed covers."

It is difficult to believe that the investigators did not ask themselves whether Stepanek's performance depended on his handling or seeing the materials. But no tests are reported in which he was kept out of contact with the jackets. Discussing the article in *Nature*,[7] I asked whether such an experiment ever took place or whether Stepanek had refused to perform under such conditions. No reply was forthcoming.

A further unsatisfactory feature of the experiments was that one investigator, J. G. Pratt, was present on each occasion when an above-chance result was obtained. The necessity of successful subjects being tested by independent investigators has been repeatedly stressed in the past. It is clearly necessary, where a series of experiments is carried out by various investigators headed by a main investigator, that the result should be confirmed in the absence of the main investigator. Preferably, the result should be confirmed by an independent team of *critical* investigators.

It may be asked why *Nature* should publish such unsatisfactory material. At the end of the article, it was stated in an editorial comment that it had been sent to two referees. One of these recommended that it should not be published (this was, in fact, myself), while the other thought that it should be published, with the comment, "I cannot fault the author's claim to have effectively eliminated all normal counterhypotheses."

Ted Serios

One of the more sensational miracle men emerged in 1967. He was brought to public attention by a psychiatrist, Jules Eisenbud, M.D., in a book, *"The World of Ted Serios."*[8] Eisenbud gave details of what are optimistically described on the dust jacket as "two years of well-controlled experimentation" in which, "not only was every safeguard taken against the possibility of deception, conscious or unconscious," but also the participation of scientists was sought.

According to the same dust jacket, John Beloff, Lecturer in Psychology at Edinburgh University claimed that thoughtography was "likely to prove the most remarkable paranormal phenomenon of our time," and C. J. Ducasse, Professor of Philosophy, Emeritus, Brown University, declared that Eisenbud's book was "decidely important and merits wide attention from scientists and from the thinking public." Marie Coleman Nelson, editor of the *Psychoanalytic Review* went even further and was quoted as saying that it "represents the most significant contribution to our knowledge of mental processes since Freud's discovery of psychoanalysis." In addition, she thought that "its revolutionary implications call for a searching re-examination of the conceptual foundations of science."

The basic feature of Serios' performance was that he held a Polaroid Land camera fitted with an electronic flash and loaded by Dr. Eisenbud or some other person, so that it pointed at himself. After releasing the shutter, a photograph would be obtained—on rare occasions—not of Serios but of some other object, which, it was claimed, Serios had put there by the power of thought. The photograph was usually out of focus and indistinct, and in one instance was found to correspond with an illustration in a book owned by Serios.

A feature noted by the investigators was that Serios used what he called a "gismo"—a small tube which he fashioned out of wrapping paper to help him focus his psychic powers. The gismo was held against the camera lens in a most suspicious manner, but according to Eisenbud, it had been closely examined and was not capable of producing the photograph.

Large numbers of photographs were taken, many of which contained no unusual features. But on some of them an image was apparent. In some other cases the picture came out black all over, indicating that the film had not been exposed—which Serios called a "blackie"—or white all over, indicating that it had been fully over exposed all over its area—which Serios called a "whitie." It appears that Serios was not successful with a thin layer of masking tape covering the lens, but he managed to produce a picture when the lens of the camera was removed.

Unusual features of the photographs were, first, the appearance of something that was not present in the field of view and, second, the fact that the image which should have been there in view of the direction in which the camera was pointing, was absent.

In *The World of Ted Serios,* Eisenbud discusses the possibility of various forms of trick photography having been used. He points out that a transparency could be held an inch or so from the camera lens, with an auxilliary lens placed against the lens. But he comes to the conclusion that the sleight of hand required to operate a system of this nature and escape detection would not be within the capacity of Serios. In addition, Serios, it appears, could operate at distances of more than six feet from the camera.

The Popular Photography Investigation

In 1967, *Popular Photography* magazine formed a research team to visit Serios in Denver, where he lived with Dr. Eisenbud and his family. The team consisted of David B. Eisendrath, Jr., who was a working industrial and scientific photographer, a contributing editor of *Popular Photography,* and a magician of professional skill; Charles Reynolds, a professional film maker, head of the Photography Department of the School of Visual Arts in New York City, who was also a skilled magician, accompanied by a well-known professional magician who remained anonymous.

The investigating committee did not witness thoughtography, since when they were present, Serios's powers deserted him. But following the investigation, it was possible for them to state in *Popular Photography* "To the satisfaction of at least three experts in photography or legerdemain, the authors of this article have proved that there is a relatively simple way to produce images on Polaroid Land film without psychic power or ability."[9]

The method they suggested was similar to that discussed by Eisenbud, but with the components mounted in a unit which fitted inside the gismo. It contained a lens of short focal length—about one inch—with the transparency mounted a suitable distance away to project an image through the lens of the camera. This special gismo was substituted during the performance. Eisenbud had thought that any substitution would be difficult, but the experiments were full of incidents, with long periods when nothing was happening except Serios's histrionics and his demonstrations of his ability to dispose of large quantities of alcoholic refreshment and still remain upright.

The Morning After

After the Eisendrath—Reynolds report was published in 1967, Serios either lost his thoughtographic abilities or they underwent a radical change. According to Eisenbud, "the structured phase" of thoughtography came to an abrupt end in June 1967.[10] Eisenbud also revealed that in 1964 Serios had shown him how to obtain images using an eighth inch wide planoconvex lens made from the tip of a flashlight bulb, with a small transparency mounted on the flat side of the lens. Serios, it appears, had learned the trick while employed in the research laboratories of Borg-Warner near Chicago. Eisenbud appears to have kept to himself what Serios had told him until after Eisendrath and Reynolds made their report.

A further observation made by Eisenbud and reported in his book on Serios was that at an early point in the tests, Ted had showed him the gismo he was using. It consisted of a cylinder with its ends covered in cellophane. Inside one end under the cellophane was a piece of film negative covered with stove blacking. He did not report whether there was any image on the negative under the stove blacking.

How Did Serios Do It?

Taking into account the information given by Eisenbud after the event, it is considered that Serios probably employed more than one technique, suiting the method to the experimental conditions. Using the lens from a flashlamp bulb in the manner described by Serios, it is possible to make a device less than one eighth inch deep that will fit into the lens barrel of the camera or which can be mounted by pushing it over the lens barrel in the manner that a filter is mounted. It can incorporate its own transparency, or the transparency can be held against the camera lens with the attachment already fitted to the lens.

The gismo is mainly employed to fit and remove the device on the camera and to act as a blind, diverting suspicion. Thus, the gismo is initially held against the camera lens enabling the attachment inside it to be pushed onto the lens. The gismo is removed and, if necessary, made available for inspection. The gismo is then placed against the lens while the shutter is released and afterwards taken away with the attachment gripped inside it. The attachment is then transferred to the other hand or dropped into the lap.

With the attachment once in place, it is merely necessary to hold·a piece of film bearing the pictures to be thoughtographed against the camera lens mount. The film can contain a number of different pictures, since each will occupy less than one eighth inch square on the film. If the camera is to be held by some other person, a device is fitted with its own transparency mounted in it. The device would be about one half inch in diameter and one eighth inch deep. For cameras other than the normal Polaroid 95 model used, a device would be held against the lens inside the gismo.

Practical Thoughtography

To construct a device of this nature, a flashlamp bulb of the type used in miniature torches is first left to soak in methylated spirit. The glass part can then be detached from the base, after crushing the base with a pair of pliers. The unwanted glass is "nibbled" away with the pliers, leaving the lens. This is mounted into a hole of suitable size, drilled in a circular disc, about one eighth inch thick. A filter mount may then be used, or an attachment made with a lathe, that will slide into the lens mount of the camera. For experimental purposes, in order to see the image produced and to determine the positioning of the transparency from the lens, a 35mm film projector may be used as a light source. This is shone from a distance of about a foot into the lens of a reflex camera. A 6 x 6 twin lens reflex is ideal for this purpose as the viewfinder part of the camera can be employed.

The only difficult part of the construction is the making of a suitable lens mount. Eisenbud mentions that when Serios first arrived in Denver, his worldly possessions included; sets of tools, a miniature lathe, and parts of model trains. This would constitute a suitable beginner's kit.

Transparencies may be constructed by placing diagrams from books on a large board which is photographed at a distance of six or more feet. After preparing a positive by contact, this may be cut up either into a circle to fit into the device, or into a larger circle—say 1 inch diameter with a number of different diagrams on it.

Notes

1. J. H. Pollack, "Crime Busting with ESP," *This Week* Magazine, February 26, 1961.
2. In a letter to the author. Printed by permission of E. D. Maaldrink.

3. S. Katz, "First Report on Extra Sensory Perception," *Maclean's*, July 29, 1961, p. 44.
4. F. Brink, "Parapsychology and Criminal Investigation," *International Criminal Police Review*, 134 (January 1960): 8.
5. M. Ryzl and J. G. Pratt, "A Further Confirmation of Stabilised ESP Performance in a Selected Subject," *Journal of Parapsychology*, 27, 2 (June 1963): 74–83.
6. J. G. Pratt, I. Stevenson, W. G. Roll, J. G. Bloin, G. L. Meinsma, H. H. J. Keil, and N. Jacobson, "Identification of Concealed Randomised Objects through Acquired Response Habits of Stimulus and Word Association," *Nature*, 220 (October 5, 1968).
7. C. E. M. Hansel, "ESP: Deficiencies of Experimental Method," *Nature*, 221 (March 22, 1969): 1171–72.
8. J. Eisenbud, *The World of Ted Serios: 'Thoughtographic' Studies of an Extraordinary Mind*, (New York: Morrow, 1967).
9. D. B. Eisendrath, Jr. and C. Reynolds, "An Amazing Weekend with the Amazing Ted Serios," *Popular Photography*, October 1967.

23
Uri Geller
at SRI

The best known of the professed psychics of the last ten years has been the magician Uri Geller. By means of simple tricks and a persuasive tongue, he has managed to convince a large part of the public, and a few gullible scientists, of his ability to bend various items of cutlery, to draw pictures concealed in envelopes, and to cause clocks to start and to stop.

Geller is, by training, a professional stage conjurer, who at one time toured the music halls of Israel. According to the London *Daily Mail,* in January, 1971, "a Berrsheba magistrate ruled that Geller was guilty of breach of contract in that he employed sleight of hand on stage, instead of the telepathy which he had promised in his publicity material. The magistrate ordered him to pay costs and repay the price of the tickets to the member of the audience who had sued after seeing the show."[1]

On November 23, 1973, Geller achieved instant fame in Britain after appearing in "The Dimbleby Talk-In" on BBC television. This program would normally be expected to command a large audience, but, on that particular occasion, the number of male viewers, especially, was no doubt even greater than usual since it followed immediately after the "Miss World" competition.

Geller took second spot, following tests on a water-diviner, the results of which were not revealed, presumably because he made a *miss*. Geller's performance was relatively simple compared with that of the average stage magician. He bent a spoon, started a watch which the audience was informed had not previously been operating, and drew a picture corresponding to one that had been drawn by some other person before the program.

But the public appeared to have been influenced by two things: first, the impressive things said about Geller by David Dimbleby including the fact that he had been investigated at the Stanford "Think Tank," and, second, the fact that Geller claimed to be a psychic rather than a magician. The public was, no doubt, also later affected by the reports made by many science correspondents in the press, who contributed to the deception, by their inability to observe and report accurately, incidents in which they were involved with Geller or to give complete and, therefore, accurate information to the public.

Geller's most publicized feat was his bending of a spoon before the television cameras. Anyone can perform this trick with very little practice. One or two forks are prepared beforehand by gripping one end in a vice and bending the other end backwards and forwards until the spoon is almost, but not quite, coming apart. These spoons are mixed with others on a tray, care being taken that they can be identified when required. Holding the fingers over the weak point on the spoon, as Geller did, the process of bending and breaking the spoon is completed before the audience. A few days after the television program, I was able to do this in front of an audience without any difficulty. Geller's performance appears to have been similar in every respect, insofar as the mechanical aspects of bending the spoon were concerned, although, no doubt, performed with much greater skill.

Tests at the Stanford Research Institute

A great deal of information has been published about Geller's background and the way he performs his tricks. It is not intended to add to this extensive literature, but the tests carried out at the Stanford Research Institute have received very little detailed examination, other than in statements from *Nature* itself indicating that they were considered by referees to be not very carefully controlled but worth publishing. These experiments will be considered here because they have been said to provide experimental evidence for ESP ability on Geller's part.

The Stanford Research Institute was founded in 1946 by Stanford University and a group of individuals to provide research services to business, individual foundations, and the government. The Research Institute was legally separated from the University in 1970 and is now wholly independent. The two physicists— Russell Targ and Harold Puthoff—who carried out the investigation, had strong interests in parapsychology and had carried out research on various psychical matters together in the past, including their tests on ESP with a machine (see p. 237).

The Nature Report on Uri Geller

The most important fact to emerge in Targ and Puthoff's article in *Nature* is that they were unable to obtain evidence that Geller could bend metal objects in the manner he had claimed. They comment at the end of their article:

It has been widely reported that Geller has demonstrated the ability to bend metal by paranormal means. Although metal bending by Geller has been observed in our laboratory we have not been able to combine such observations with adequately controlled experiments to obtain data sufficient to support the paranormal hypothesis.''[2]

Since metal bending is the only item in Geller's repertoire that differs from other routine stage acts, it may be assumed that, initially, Targ and Puthoff were mainly interested in this phenomenon. To check whether a man can bend a spoon without using finger pressure should present no difficulty. The absence of any details of the experiments attempted by Targ and Puthoff is presumably due either to Geller's failure to bend objects or to his refusing to submit to being tested under reasonable test conditions. He could have acted in this manner because he knew full well that his claims were fraudulent. If Geller took part in any tests and failed to produce evidence for his paranormal abilities, the details of the experiments should have been given no less fully than if he had succeeded. In addition, the conditions under which he refused to make an attempt and those in which he was willing to do so should have been revealed.

A fact that emerges from the *Nature* article is that, when Geller made himself available for scientific tests at SRI, he was unable to provide evidence to support his claims. But Targ and Puthoff do not appear to have been interested in finding out whether Geller was a fraud or not, but only in providing evidence for Geller's ability to bend metal by psychic means.

According to a report in *The New Scientist*[3] by Dr. Joseph Hanlon who had visited the SRI laboratories, Targ and Puthoff spent most of their time investigating metal bending and conducted several unsuccessful tests that have not been reported. Hanlon also stated that a film made at SRI, but available only by renting to universities and research organizations, showed five tests, but only one of these was considered acceptable by the time a report was submitted.

Remote Viewing

In *Nature*, Targ and Puthoff stated that they had investigated "the ability of certain people·to describe graphical material or remote scenes shielded against ordinary perception, and that they had conducted their experiments with sufficient control, utilizing visual, acoustic and electrical shielding to ensure that all conventional paths of sensory input were blocked. They gave details of three series of experiments in which Geller took part.

Series 1 Experiments: Drawing Concealed Targets

Geller made attempts on 13 occasions (described as *Experiments 1–13*) to draw a concealed target drawing. The tests took place between 4th August, and 10th August, 1973.

All 13 experiments, except nos. 4 and 5, were conducted with Geller inside a shielded room. This consisted, in the case of experiments 1–4 and 6–10, of a double-walled steel room (dimensions not stated) normally used at SRI for EEG research and, in the case of experiments 11, 12, and 13, a double-walled, copper-screen, Faraday cage. The steel-walled room was locked by means of inner and outer doors, each of which was fitted with a refrigerator-type locking mechanism. A one-way audio monitor was used to monitor Geller during the tests. This enabled him to communicate with the experimenters, who were outside the room, but it did not enable the experimenters to talk back to Geller.

It is stated that, at the beginning of the experiment, "either Geller or the experimenters entered a shielded room, so that from that time forward Geller was at all times visually, acoustically and electrically shielded from personnel and material at the target location. Only following Geller's isolation from the experimenters was a target chosen and drawn."

Two features emerge from the above statement:

1. The process of deciding a target appears to have consisted of first obtaining a word designating a drawable object and then drawing it.
2. This procedure was sometimes varied. Thus, we read: "In Experiment 5, the person to person link was eliminated by arranging for a scientist outside the

Table 23-1
Conditions and results for experiments 1–13 of series 1

Experiment	Conditions	Target selection	Geller's position in relation to screened room	Outcome
1	Experimenters knew the target	First drawable word from the dictionary	Inside	Poor
2			Inside	Good
3			Inside	Poor
4			Outside	Good
5	Experimenters did not know the target	Outside person selected	Outside	No drawing attempted
6			Inside	
7			Inside	
8	Experimenters saw the target	Prepared set of drawings	Inside	Good
9			Inside	Fair
10			Inside	Good
11	Experimenters saw the target	Picture on cathode ray tube	Inside*	Good
12		Picture stored in memory	Inside*	Poor
13		Picture on screen at zero intensity	Inside*	Fair

*Screened room consisted of Faraday cage.

usual experimental group to draw a picture, lock it in the shielded room before Geller's arrival at the SRI and leave the area. Geller was then led by the experimenters to the shielded room and asked to draw the picture located inside the room.'' On these occasions, neither Geller nor the experimenters were presumably inside the screened room.

It is, then, likely that only in Experiment 5, when Geller was outside the screened room, were Targ and Puthoff inside it. Three different methods were used for selecting the target:

1. Opening a dictionary at random and choosing the first word that could be drawn (for Experiments 1–4).
2. "Targets blind to experimenters and subject, prepared independently by SRI scientists outside the experimental group" (following Geller's isolation) and provided to the experimenters during the course of the experiment (Experiments 5–7, 11–13).
3. Selecting from a target pool created in advance and "designed to provide data concerning information content for use in testing specific hypotheses" (Experiments 8–10).

These conditions for the experiments, insofar as they can be reconciled with the descriptions given in the article, are tabulated in Table 23–1.

Geller's task was to produce with pen on paper a line drawing similar to the one drawn at the target location. He either passed, if he felt he could not succeed, or produced a drawing which was collected before he was permitted to see the target.

Experiments 11–13 were carried out at a different location. Geller was now isolated in the double-walled, copper-screen, Faraday cage, fifty-four meters from the computer room in which the targets were located. The targets were chosen following Geller's isolation "by computer laboratory personnel not otherwise associated with either the experiment or Geller, and the experimenters and subject were kept blind as to the contents of the pool."

It is not clear whether the experimenters who were unaware of the target pool became aware of the target after it had been chosen for each experiment. Details are not given of any precautions taken to ensure that the target remained secret. In Experiment 11, the target was drawn on the face of a cathode-ray tube display screen. For Experiment 12, a picture was drawn and stored in the computer memory; For Experiment 13, the picture was drawn on the face of the cathode-ray tube, and the display intensity was turned off so that the picture was not visible.

Results of Series 1 Experiments

Some of Geller's drawings and the corresponding targets are shown in Table 23–1. It will be observed that in several cases there is no doubt that Geller was obtaining information about the targets by some means or other. In his report in *The New Scientist,* Hanlon classified Geller's various attempts as poor, fair, or good. These classifications are shown in Column 5 of Table 23–1.

The most important feature to emerge from the series as a whole is that Geller was at all times able to make a drawing having some degree of resemblance to the target except in the case of Experiments 5, 6 and 7. The main feature of the experimental conditions for these three experiments, not present in the remaining experiments, was that only then were conditions such that the targets were likely to have remained unknown to the experimenters or to any other persons present.

Features Emerging from the Series 1 Experiments

It is far easier to test whether a person is capable of gaining information about graphical material without employing known senses (clairvoyance) than to test whether he can gain information about another person's thoughts (telepathy). In the same way, clairvoyance tests with cards are easier than telepathy tests since only a single subject—the receiver—is involved. In a clairvoyance test, it is only necessary to ensure that *no one* knows the identity of the target until the drawing has been made. Precautions to guard against a second person transmitting information to the percipient are unnecessary since no other person has information to transmit.

The elaborate precautions taken by Targ and Puthoff to screen their subject, e.g., "the Faraday cage providing 120 dB attenuation for plane wave radio frequency radiation over a range of 15 KH2 to GHz. For magnetic fields, attenuation is 68 dB at 15 KH2 and decreases to 3 dB at 60H" . . . was only of interest in the event of someone being able to signal to Geller by electromagnetic radiation.

While any precautions that can assist in eliminating trickery are desirable, it is doubtful whether they were necessary if other aspects of the experimental situation had been devised with more care. By keeping the target secret, i.e., unknown to anybody, no such precautions would have been necessary. While it is doubtful whether Geller was effectively screened (even from all forms of electromagnetic communication), a target drawing can certainly be screened from the known sensory channels, making it impossible for anyone, even given a laboratory of instruments, to send information about it. Screening the subject merely results in his being largely unsupervised during the tests.

A stage magician can impress an audience with his extraordinary powers, provided he operates under his own conditions. But there are very simple precautions, avoided by the magician but used in everyday life, that ensure the secrecy of a target. If this were not so, card games such as bridge would require complex screening procedures.

If a subject is attempting to describe a concealed picture, the particular picture he is attempting to draw has to be defined, but no one need know its identity. The subject may, for example, be asked to draw a picture similar to the one contained inside the package placed in front of him. If the particular package is one drawn at random from a large number of similar packages, it is a relatively simple matter to arrange that the target inside is unknown to any person.

The relatively foolproof methods of randomizing, i.e., producing an unpredictable result, or of keeping the identities of objects secret, such as with playing cards, rely on the fact that a method of randomization (shuffling) is employed that ensures a particular card's identity being kept secret. The most expert card manipulator knows that if he employs a standard pack of playing cards and shuffles it in an orthodox manner, he can then draw a card and he himself be quite unaware of its identity. He can also stipulate a variety of conditions under which neither he nor anyone else can know a card's identity.

It would have been a simple matter to test Geller under such conditions, since an independent person could have been asked to select a target from a set in such a manner that he could not know its identity. The target could then have remained unknown until Geller had completed his drawing. In the event that Geller required some other person to see the target, this other person could have been locked in the sealed room (with the audio link removed), where he would open and inspect his target, ensuring that no other person could see it even if they were gazing through a window in the wall.

These conditions were present to some extent in experiments (5, 6, and 7), when an outside person made a drawing and locked it in a laboratory, where it remained until after Geller made his drawing. If this outside person had not known which particular drawing he was locking in the room, and if the precautions were sufficient to ensure that no one could obtain sight of the drawing after it was locked inside the room, Geller would have had difficulty displaying his paranormal abilities. In that event, he would not attempt to make a drawing under the conditions imposed in Experiments 5, 6, and 7.

For Experiments 8–10, the target was selected from "a target pool," decided upon in advance, and "designed to provide data concerning information content for use in testing specific hypotheses." This is all that is reported about this method of target selection. It is not revealed: (1) how many items were in the target pool; (2) how they were prepared; (3) how a particular target was selected and whether its identity was known only to the person who drew it or to a large number of people. It is merely stated "Only following Geller's isolation from the experimenters was a target chosen and drawn." It thus would appear that the "target pool" consisted of a list of words designating possible targets rather than a collection of drawings and that the actual drawing was made after Geller was isolated. Thus, at least one person, and possibly several persons, knew the identity of the target.

When a drawing is made, it is possible for another person present to obtain information about it in numerous ways, e.g., by watching the top of the pencil or from the impressions left on the pad. Were any precautions taken to ensure that the drawings were made under conditions where they, and the word designating the target, would remain known only to a single person selecting the word and making the drawing?

In Experiments 11–13, the target had to be drawn on the face of the cathode-ray tube. The location of the experimenters is not stated. They were, presumably, in the same room as the computer and cathode-ray screen on which the drawing was made. It is stated that they were "kept blind as to the contents of the target pool." Were they kept blind as to the target itself? The targets could hardly have been completely private, since they were drawn on the cathode-ray tube. No mention is made of the personnel present in the room or in the building.

The New Scientist Report on Geller

At the time that Targ and Puthoff's article appeared in *Nature, The New Scientist*, which had also taken an active interest in metal bending, devoted a large amount of space to a report by Dr. Joseph Hanlon entitled "Uri Geller and Science." This gave the results of a *New Scientist* investigation and included a large amount of factual data, including details of various episodes in Uri Geller's checkered career. It also included a section describing the Stanford Research Institute's investigations, in which considerably more detail became apparent about the conditions under which Geller was tested than was given in the *Nature* article.

It emerged that Geller had been at SRI several times over an eighteen-month period starting in November 1972. Targ and Puthoff, two experienced parapsychologists, had received an $80,000 grant from NASA, originally given for their work on testing and training clairvoyance with a machine (see page 237). Further funds were received from wealthy individuals, including ex-astronaut Edgar Mitchell.

Series III experiments, in which Geller guessed the face uppermost of a die, had already been carried out in November 1972, when Dr. Wilbur Franklin of Kent State University was also present to assist with the experiments. Series I experiments with concealed drawings took place nine months later, in August 1973. It is not made clear why the series were not numbered in chronological order.

Hanlon observed that the drawings produced by Geller and published in the Targ and Puthoff *Nature* article seemed to be based on the words that would be used to describe the target rather than either the target word or the target drawing. This is a most interesting observation, since in a fake telepathy act, it is difficult to transmit details of a picture consisting of a random pattern of lines by means of a code, but it is easy to transmit details of a drawing of an object, provided it can be named (see the Smith-Blackburn experiment). Two features had to be kept secret: (1) the word and (2) the drawing corresponding to the target word. It is thus possible that the word rather than the picture became known to Geller. In fact, it is possible that Geller's drawings resemble words that might be used to describe what an observer thinks a second person is drawing when he watches the movements on his pencil. Thus, in Experiment 1, the target word was "firecracker. The target when being drawn would consist of two parallel vertical lines followed by a circle forming the top of the firework. The observer might think that a circle had been drawn of larger diameter than the distance allowed by the vertical lines.

According to Hanlon, "the Targ-Puthoff paper fails to communicate the circus atmosphere that surrounded all of the tests with Geller." He quotes Targ as having commented, "deliberately or accidentally Geller manipulates the experiments to a degree of chaos where he feels comfortable and where we feel uncomfortable. Then he bends something."

Hanlon gives several examples to indicate that the experiments at SRI were conducted in a highly lackadaisical manner. The laxity of control was conducive to error but favorable to Geller if he wished to indulge in any trickery. Hanlon suggested that Geller may have used a device patented by his sponsor, Dr. Andrija Puharich, in the form of a midget radio receiver concealed in a tooth. The device would convert "electromagnetic signals to electric signals modulated at audio frequency and impart the electrical signals to the nerve endings of the tooth for transmission to the brain." While such a device is hardly likely to operate in the way intended in the patent—and more likely to generate toothache—it could result in a signaling system in which bursts of pain (toothache) or its absence would constitute a binary code.

However, it is known that radio-type receivers have been used in stage magic for many years, and yet no precautions appear to have been taken to search Geller. Hanlon pointed out that two small pieces of evidence supported his suggestion. First, Geller's drawings were representations of words: second, Paharich had told Hanlon that, before an experiment, Uri should be "properly examined" for hidden devices. He then suddenly added, "But I know Uri will not submit to excessive examination like total body X-radiation." Hanlon pointed out that SRI had employed shielded rooms, but, after taking expert advice, he doubted whether these would screen all forms of electromagnetic signals.

From impressions gained of the conduct of the experiments, Geller could have had a radio receiver available on his person without any difficulty and without having to have it concealed in a tooth. It would, in fact, have been a relatively simple matter for the investigators to "jam" any transmitter, but it is considered unlikely that Geller need have had assistance from any such device.

A further important point that arises in Hanlon's paper is that Geller had an inseparable companion called Shipi Strang with him in the U.S. No details are given of the personnel present at each experiment or in other rooms in the building, and no mention is made of Strang's whereabouts. But if he—a professional conjuror's assistant—was anywhere in the building, it is of the greatest importance to know where he was and what he was doing.

How Could Geller Have Discovered the Target?

At this point, the keen student of parapsychology should turn back to Chapter 4 and compare Smith and Blackburn's performance with Geller's in the Series I experiments. Smith was perhaps not screened as adequately as Geller, but in 1882 screening against radio devices was hardly necessary. In some ways, however, Smith was better screened than Geller, since observers could see around the pile of blankets covering him. Observers were not situated all around the screened room in which Geller was isolated or in adjoining rooms to ensure that no assistant of Geller's could interfere with the screened room in any way. Smith could indulge in activity under his blankets, but he could not move about. Geller was quite free to walk around. Just as the blanket assisted Smith, enabling him to use the luminous slate without being observed, so also the screened room may have been of assistance to Geller.

How could one transmit information to a man in a double-walled steel box. Consider the following possibilities:

1. Tap the side of the box with a hammer (or something lighter) and ensure, if necessary, that the person inside has his ear (or a stethoscope) pressed against the interior wall. A single tap is all that might be required.

2. Drill a small hole (say $1/16''$) straight through the two walls, at a convenient point. Signal by means of a light through the hole, or wire up a light bulb on the outside of the box so that it could be controlled at a distance and seen by the occupant of the room through the hole.

3. Signal by modulating the interior light. (Geller presumably had to have some illumination in order to make his drawing.) This could be done by inserting a resistor at any point in the wiring to the light and signaling by pressing a button, shorting out the resistor.

4. Provide an auditory signal via the ventilation system, or modulate the sound created by the ventilation system by blocking and unblocking its outlet.

5. Make a drawing or write down a description or word, and push it through a suitable aperture.

There are numerous possible ways of transmitting information, but the above methods are sufficient for the present discussion.

It might appear difficult to transmit information rapidly enough to signal the nature of an object using methods 1–4. However, this difficulty could be easily overcome. In the experiments it appears that Geller, when inside his sealed room, took "a few minutes to half an hour" to produce his drawing. During this time, he was monitored by a one-way audio system, so that those outside the room could hear Geller, but he could not receive messages from them.

Details are not given of what Geller did or said during the time he was attempting to draw the target. But the importance of complete sensory isolation— in the event of the target being known—may become evident by considering the manner in which a medium is guided by the responses of a sitter. Consider the following possibility.

Geller, in his sealed room, indulges in a monologue uttering words or the names of objects in the manner that mediums make vague suggestive utterances and utter cue words in the hope of obtaining a response from their clients (see p. 266). His words are heard in the experimenters' room on the one-way intercommunication system. It is possible that a confederate could hear them in the experimenters' room via the one-way intercom or directly through the walls of the room. He could also do so by being elsewhere in the building, for example, by bugging the room in which Geller was situated or the room in which the experimenters were listening to the intercom. The assistant in league with Geller has only now to transmit a simple binary message to let the subject know when he is on the right track. A single tap on the wall, floor, or ceiling of the box following a particular word is enough to tell Geller that he is getting warm; two taps would designate a direct hit.

John Taylor, Professor of Applied Mathematics, King's College, University of London, who claimed to have himself discovered a number of juvenile metal benders, gave further details of the SRI experiments in the London *Observer*.[4] There he stated that the possibility of Geller "receiving any clues was zero," and he attributed this zero possibility to the fact that Geller was electrically screened. But does he really think that if someone had kicked the door of the screened room, Geller would not have heard him?

Taylor stated that when Geller made his first test (Experiment 1), the word chosen from the dictionary was "fuse," and Geller drew a "firecracker." He also stated that Geller said he saw a cylinder with a noise coming out of it. Geller's drawing was similar to the target but represented a drum rather than a firework. Taylor stated that, on the occasion when Geller drew a bunch of grapes, the word chosen was "bunch." Geller then said he saw drops of water coming out of the picture, after which he mentioned "purple circles." Taylor noted, "He then drew a bunch of grapes, exactly the same in number, 24, as the original drawing and of nearly identical shape." Were these the only utterances made by Geller, others being off the mark? Since Geller was making utterances that could be heard on the intercom while he was isolated in the screened room, it was necessary to isolate him from any possible feedback cue.

The precautions taken by Targ and Puthoff in some cases were an advantage to Geller. The audio-monitor system would have been better removed. Rather than isolate Geller in the screened room, an experimenter could have been with him to observe what he was up to. Rather than employ a screened room, a jamming device could have been available. This put into operation following any initial success would have indicated whether or not a transmitter was being employed.

Series 2 Experiments: Drawing Pictures Unseen by an Agent

The second series of experiments was conducted in order to see if it was necessary for some person to know the target picture in order for Geller to become aware of it.

Here 100 target pictures were drawn beforehand by an SRI artist and sealed by other SRI personnel in double envelopes containing black cardboard. The 100 targets were divided randomly into groups of 20. On each of the three days of the experiment, a different group of 20 targets was used. Throughout the series, Geller "declined to associate any envelope with a drawing that he made, expressing dissatisfaction with the existence of such a large pool." His results gave no evidence for anything other than guesswork.

Series 3 Experiments: Guessing the Uppermost Face on a Die

The third series, described as "a simpler experiment," tested Geller's ability to know which face was uppermost on a ¾-inch die contained in a 3 × 4 × 5 inch steel box. The box was vigorously shaken by one of the experimenters and placed on the table, so that, presumably, no one present knew the face that was uppermost on the die inside the box. Geller then wrote down his guess. In ten attempts, Geller passed twice and was successful on the remaining eight occasions (three 2's, one 4, two 5's and two 6's). He thus scored hits on the eight occasions on which he made an attempt. The odds against this result arising by chance are greater than a million to one.

It will be noted that in Series 3 experiments Geller was "successful" although no other person knew the target. In Series 1 experiments, he was successful, provided some person present knew the target, and in Series 2, he was not successful when no other person knew the target.

These experiments with the die, although called Series 3, were carried out in 1972 at the start of the investigations at SRI. The extremely impressive result was obtained under easily controlled conditions, and the whole experiment comprising eight attempts by Geller could have taken less than half an hour. What happened next? After eight attempts, why not a few more? Did Geller feel tired and want to go to bed? The experiments were conducted at the start of the eighteen-month period when Geller was at SRI. Is it conceivable that, having obtained such a remarkable result, the investigators should drop this form of experiment completely?

In their book *Mind Reach*, Targ and Puthoff state that "these ten trials were the only ten, and were not selected out of a longer run." Since it is incomprehensible that, after this result, the experiment should be dropped completely it would appear likely that Geller refused to participate in any further tests.

The reaction of any normal person in such an experiment would surely be to wonder if a trick had been employed, particularly if he is dealing with a professional magician. He would then ask for further trials in which he would tighten up the experimental conditions, perhaps initially keeping Geller out of reach of the box. But there is no mention of this having been done.

If Geller's performance was genuine, it would be possible to produce overwhelming evidence for clairvoyance very rapidly and thus save large amounts of money—such as the $80,000 contributed by NASA. Two professional magicians—James Randi in the U.S. and David Berglas in the U.K.—have offered large rewards to Geller if he can give a genuine psychical performance. Why has he not spent half an hour convincing them? If he is not a fraud, all he would require would be a few dice.

   Although professional magicians are loathe to reveal the "modus operandi" of their profession, a number of accounts have been published to indicate possible methods employed by Geller in the various tricks in his repertoire. In particular James Randi,[5] the eminent American magician, has divulged details of various techniques, and Uria Fuller[6]—a fictitious magician—has provided a most amusing and instructive account of how he went psychic and, with the aid of two assistants, Schlepi and Ms. ———, gave demonstrations similar to those of Geller.

Notes

1. *London Daily Mail,* November 26, 1973.
2. Russell Targ and Harold Puthoff, "Information Transmission under Conditions of Sensory Shielding," *Nature,* 251, 5476 (October 18, 1974): 602–7.
3. Joseph Hanlon, "Uri Geller and Science," *The New Scientist,* 64, 919: 170–85.
4. John Taylor, *The Observer,* April 6, 1975, pp. 20–28.
5. James Randi (The Amazing Randi), *The Magic of Uri Geller* (New York: Ballantine, 1975).
6. Uriah Fuller, *Confessions of a Psychic* (Karl Fulves, Box 433, Teaneck, NJ 07666).

24
Mind-Reach

In their article in *Nature* describing Uri Geller's ability to draw concealed targets, Targ and Puthoff also gave details of experiments on "remote viewing." This they defined as the ability of some individuals to perceive, and to be able to describe what they would see if they were located at some distant location. They reported tests on a subject, Pat Price, an ex-police commissioner who had, it appears, in the past used this ability to track down suspects. Further details of these and other experiments are described in their book *Mind-Reach*,[1] and in other published articles.[2]

When Price first phoned to offer his services, Puthoff gave him the co-ordinates on the map of the area on the East Coast that Targ was visiting at that time. Three days later, he received from Price five pages of description, which included such features as descriptions of buildings, details of equipment in the buildings, names from desks, and a list of labelings on file folders locked in a secret cabinet. According to Targ and Puthoff, the descriptions were "essentially correct."

Price also sent them data concerning various situations that he gathered-in during his nightly "scans." Much of this, it seems, related to political or military issues. After confirmations started to come in, Price was invited to participate in a "rigorous investigation" of his abilities. He then agreed to take part in experiments at SRI.

At SRI, Price took part in remote-viewing experiments in which he had to describe target locations situated a few miles from the SRI laboratories. These experiments, described in *Nature* and with slight variations in other sources, were conducted as follows.

The subject was supervised by one experimenter (call him E_1). The second experimenter (call him E_2) was in charge of a team of two to four co-experimenters, who were called the "Target Demarcation Team." A Division Director at SRI who was not otherwise associated with the experiment had "chosen" a set of twelve target locations clearly differentiated from each other and within thirty minutes driving time of SRI. *Sets of traveling orders* were then prepared and kept in his safe.

During each experiment, E_2 left E_1 with the subject and then obtained a set of traveling orders from the Division Director, who picked one of these at random from the safe for each experiment. E_2 then set off with the demarcation team, which started viewing the target area thirty minutes after leaving the subect and E_1. Fifteen minutes was then allowed, during which time the subject described what he thought the target area looked like into a tape recorder and made drawings. The experimenter E_1 was with the subject while he did this and encouraged him to "clarify" his descriptions where he thought it necessary.

After the demarcation team had returned, an "informal comparison" was made of the subjects' descriptions and the target site. The subject was then taken to see the target site.

When nine experiments, each with a single target, had been conducted in this manner over a period of days, the descriptions and drawings made by Price together with a list of the target locations were given to independent judges. The judges visited the target locations, and each judge chose what he considered to be the best fitting description for each target. A description that matched best with the target constituted a hit. A ranking procedure was also employed using another judge in which each description was ranked against each target.

Under these conditions, Price scored at well above the chance level. The five judges gave a total of 24 hits against a total of 45 (5×9), which was the maximum possible. In the *Nature* article, it is stated that the probability of this result arising by chance is 8×10^{-10}. This constitutes an elementary statistical error, since each judge matched the same set of drawings and descriptions against the nine targets. Given a set of targets and descriptions that happen to match in a particular way, any number of judges is likely to place them in approximately the same matchings. The probability is not changed by getting more and more judges to make more or less the same judgments.

Features of the Experimental Design

With this general design, it is important to know precisely how the targets were chosen and what instructions were given to the person making the selection. Were the targets to be well-known places in the vicinity which the subject might have seen? Were they to have easily recognizable features differentiating the one from the other, i.e., not to include more than one church, one tower, one lake, one radio telescope, etc. Why were twelve targets selected, and only nine used? Was the number of experiments decided beforehand?

The fact that Price saw the target location at the end of each experiment must have raised some difficulties. For example, anyone acting as a subject in a similar experiment carried out in Paris (France), seeing the Eiffel Tower after the first test, would omit it as a possibility for subsequent tests. Given, say, twenty differentiating features, the mere ommission of some of these for a particular target would increase the possibility of achieving a hit in a mass of descriptive material that could apply in part to almost any target.

A vulnerable feature of the design lies in the fact that experimenter E_1 was with the subject urging him on. How was this done? Did he interrupt Price when in full flow and ask him to elaborate a point, or did he ask him to add detail to a feature in a drawing? While E_1 did not know the target locations, he knew a good deal about the likely targets in the vicinity. The fact that he was with the subject and in a position to affect his responses increased the experimental safeguards required.

In fact, it transpires that there were more obvious reasons for the result achieved by Price. In a letter in *Nature* August 17, 1978,[3] David Marks and Richard Kamman from the Department of Psychology, Otago University, New Zealand, revealed that Marks had visited SRI and attempted to rank the original descriptions given by Price against the target locations. Only five of the transcripts and locations were treated in this manner, since details of the remaining four had already been published and would have been seen by Marks.

Marks and Kamman reported:

Although not stated in the original reports the judges were provided with a listing of targets in the correct (original) sequence. In addition, careful examination of the transcripts indicated that a large number of cues were available indicating the position of a transcript in the series; for example: (1) Price expresses apprehension and an inability to do this kind of experiment (Target 1); (2) a reference is made to the fact that this experiment is the "second place of the day" (Target 2); (3) a reference is made to "yesterday's two targets"; (4) Targ says encouragingly, "Nothing like having three successes behind you" and mentions the nature reserve visited the day before (Target 4); (5) Price refers to the Marina which was the fourth target (Target 7)." Using these, and other, cues I was able to match the five transcripts correctly with a rank of one giving a sum of ranks of five (p 0.0005) (ref. 4). In this procedure it should be noted that I had never visited any of the five locations but completed the task solely on the basis of cues contained in the transcripts."

Marks and Kamman concluded:

Until remote viewing can be confirmed in conditions which prevent sensory cueing the conclusions of Targ and Puthoff remain an unsubstantiated hypothesis. Our own experiments on remote viewing under cue-free conditions have consistently failed to replicate the effect."

Precognitive Remote Viewing

Experiments similar to those of Targ and Puthoff on remote viewing have been reported by J. B. Bisaha and B. J. Dunne of Mundelein College, Chicago.[4] Their experiment was in many ways similar to that of Targ and Puthoff, but they were testing for *precognitive* remote viewing. Their subject described scenes that were not chosen or viewed until after his descriptions had been completed.

Seven subjects took part, a pair of them being selected each day for use with a particular target. In all, seven tests were made using seven different targets. In four tests the subjects were in the same building but in different rooms and supervised by an observer. In the remaining three tests the subjects were at different locations approximately ten miles apart and, it would appear, unsupervised.

When the subjects started generating their descriptions, the experimenter left the area. He had with him ten envelopes that had been randomly selected from a target pool of over a hundred targets consisting of locations in the city and suburbs of Chicago. It is not clear whether the target pool consisted of over a hundred sealed *envelopes* containing targets or whether it was a *list* from which ten targets were randomly selected. In addition, the method of obtaining a random choice is not stated. The experimenter departed at the time that the subjects started their descriptions. He then drove around for twenty minutes, at the end of which time he chose a number 1–10 by blindly selecting one of the ten sheets bearing numbers 1–10 from a container. He then counted down through the envelopes until he came to the target location for that day. He arranged that he would arrive at the location fifteen minutes later and stayed there for fifteen minutes taking photographs and making notes. The choice of target was thus made five minutes after the subects had completed their descriptions and the experimenter arrived at the target location twenty minutes after the subjects had completed their descriptions.

The descriptions given by the subjects were split into two batches A and B, each containing a description made by one of the subjects in relation to each target. Six independent judges were employed. Two of them ranked descriptions in batch A against the photos and descriptions given by the experimenter of the targets. Two more judges ranked the descriptions in batch B. The remaining two judges ranked the subjects' descriptions in batch A against those in batch B. Results indicating precognitive remote viewing were obtained with antichance odds of around 200 to one. In terms of straight hits, i.e., where a description made on a particular day was ranked first against the target for that same day, the results were Judge 1, 2 hits; Judge 2, 5 hits; Judge 3, 3 hits; Judge 4, 1 hit. Thus there was considerable disagreement between the two judges as to what constituted the best hit among the descriptions.

Bisaha and Dunne give examples to indicate the accuracy of the subjects' descriptions. Thus, where the target was a railway station, one subject's description included, a railway station, railway lines, and other features, but whereas one judge placed this description first, the other judge only gave it a second ranking. Thus other descriptions probably contained references to stations and railway lines. It is thus likely that the example given was a fragment of a much longer description describing many different features, so that each description would be likely to have something in common with each target. But there is little point picking out the accurate details to impress the reader unless the amount of inaccurate detail is also mentioned.

The description of their experiment given by Bisaha and Dunne makes no mention of essential experimental controls and a large number of questions arise about their procedure.

1. Why were ten targets randomly selected and only seven of them used?

2. Why were subjects numbered S_4 to S_7? What happened to Subjects S_1, S_2, and S_3?

3. How were the ten targets randomly selected from the pool of over one hundred targets? What form did the pool take?

4. When the sheet bearing a number 1–10 was drawn from the container to decide the target, was it replaced in the container? What check was made to see that the experimenter went to the target that had been selected in this manner?

5. When the experimenter arrived back from viewing the target, did he keep details of the targets secret until all the judging had been completed? Did the experimenter reveal the identity of the target to anyone else, or talk to others involved in the experiment? What did he do with the photographs and notes he had made? Who developed the photographs?

6. What precautions were taken to ensure that the whole of the subjects' descriptions and drawings were included for judging? Were the descriptions edited in any way? Were descriptions made on a different tape each day? How were these taperecordings kept until judging was completed? Was the *date* recorded on each tape so that no mix-up could arise? When judges ranked the decriptions "blind," it would appear essential that the dates on which the targets were viewed and the dates on which descriptions were made should be unknown to them until rankings were completed. Was this control exercised? It may be observed that in Targ and Puthoff's experiment the order in which targets were viewed was available to the judges.

7. What were the duties of each experimenter? Was more than one experimenter involved? Who were the observers who were sometimes present with the subjects? What were the names of the subjects?

8. Where a great deal of descriptive material is written down that could apply in part to a large number of different targets, part of the material may be influenced by contemporary events, i.e., events in the news that day or television programs. The same may apply to descriptions made by the experimenter (agent) of the target area. Was any account taken of this possibility? If the experimenter had been in conversation with a subject, a common element may similarly be established that could reflect in the descriptions made on the following day. Were subjects kept isolated from each other and from others taking part in the experiments?

These experiments were both inadequately reported and too loosely controlled to serve any useful function. They indicate the importance of giving complete details of every control feature. Lessons could have been learned by the investigators from studying the later dream research experiments. An important feature in any experimental report is that the names of both experimenters and subjects should be stated, since the subjects themselves may exercise control of the experiment by reading the experimental report and reporting any divergences from the stated procedure.

Other Findings Reported in Mind Reach

Targ and Puthoff report a number of other tests in *Mind Reach* conducted under various experimental conditions. In some of these tests, subjects were able, according to Targ and Puthoff, to identify places, objects, and drawings without any other person viewing them. Why, then, did they complicate their main experiment on remote viewing by having not only an agent, but a team of viewers, as part of the experiment? Uri Geller had identified the face uppermost on a die inside a steel box to their complete satisfaction. No other person had seen the die. Pat Price had already demonstrated his remarkable powers when identifying remote geographical locations and labelings on files in a secret cabinet when, presumably, there was no one gazing at them.

In general, subjects tested by Targ and Puthoff displayed exceptional abilities in some tests that were not maintained under strict conditions. Their subjects behaved as did the high-scoring subjects in the early days of card guessing. Their psychic powers were inhibited by more rigorous test conditions. Just as it would have been a simple matter to establish whether any one of Rhine's high-scoring subjects was genuine or bogus, so it should be a simple matter to determine whether a subject can identify the positions of dice in a steel box, describe remote locations in detail, or identify labelings on file covers in a secret cabinet.

Notes

1. R. Targ and H. Puthoff, *Mind Reach: Scientists Look at Psychic Ability* (New York: Delacorte/Eleanor Friede, 1977).
2. H. E. Puthoff and R. Targ, "A Perceptual Channel for Information Transfer over Kilometer Distances: Historical Perspective and Recent Research," *Proceedings of the IEEE*, 64, 3 (March 1976); R. Targ, H. E. Puthoff, and E. C. May, *State of the Art in Remote Viewing Studies at SRI* (Stanford Research Institute).
3. D. Marks, R. Kamman, "Information Transmission in Remote Viewing Experiments." *Nature*, 274 (August 17, 1971).
4. J. P. Bisaha and B. J. Dunne, *Multiple Subjects and Long Distance Precognitive Remote Viewing* (Chicago: Mundelein College).

25

Summary to Part Three

During the past fifteen years, marked changes have arisen in the methods of investigation employed in ESP research, but little has been done to provide the *conclusive* experiment. One exception has been the work at the Maimonides Dream Research Laboratory, where attempts have been made to confirm results with an independent investigator present and with improved experimental conditions.

If there had been any real effect to investigate, the animal research could have led to conclusive forms of experimentation and to the repeatable demonstration; but here much time and effort would have been spared if independent investigators had been employed for each of the attempted replications of the original experiment. As it is, thanks must go to the laboratory technicians, who displayed a critical attitude singularly lacking in the parapsychologists involved in the research.

The investigations using machines could have led to conclusive forms of experimentation if some attention had been paid to the design, method, and procedure employed. In addition, the results reported would have been far more impressive if the investigators had examined one thing at a time. The introduction of high and low scorers and the fact that practice runs were made on the same machines as were used for the tests made the experiments vulnerable and largely offset the advantages of employing a machine to keep track of the scores.

The most marked change in the last fifteen years has been the cessation of tests using ESP cards and a return to earlier methods in which complex drawings or scenes were employed as targets. This has been accompanied by a change from a situation where the subject chooses from a number of known alternative targets to one in which he makes a relatively free response with no knowledge of what is contained in the target. Both the British research conducted in the Caxton Hall and the American research with dreams and remote scenes was of this nature. The results reported for these experiments had relatively small odds against chance occurrence.

This raises a further problem, since some parapsychologists have assumed that a number of results of this nature can collectively provide conclusive evidence for ESP. Under certain conditions this might be so, but these conditions have not been obtained in ESP experiments to date. Thus R. A. Fisher has written

> In order to assert that a natural phenomenon is experimentally demonstrable we need, not an isolated record, but a reliable method of procedure. In relation to the test of significance, we may say that a phenomenon is experimentally demonstrable when we know how to conduct an experiment which will rarely fail to give us a statistically significant result.[1]

The Criterion of Significance

In the case of experiments in which the result has low antichance odds, it is necessary to exercise care in interpreting the results of statistical tests of significance. If a result is reported to be significant at the $p = .01$ level, i.e., having odds of a hundred to one against arising by chance, this implies that the theoretical fraction of cases giving the same number of hits or more would be .01 in a large number of similar experiments where the targets were matched by some process of random selection. If a result is significant at the .01 level and this result is not due to chance but to information reaching the subject, it may be expected that by making two further sets of trials the antichance odds of one hundred to one will be increased to around a million to one, thus enabling the effects of ESP—or whatever is responsible for the original result—to manifest itself to such an extent that there will be little doubt that the result is not due to chance.

It may be argued that when a result is published with antichance odds of a hundred to one, two further experiments carried out by other investigators, each giving these odds, could result in overall antichance odds of a million to one. But there are dangers in assuming that three separate experiments of this nature provide evidence to compare with a single experiment achieving odds of a million to one. If the original experiment happened to have arisen by chance and a hundred investigators seek to confirm the result, one of them may well do so by chance, and several are likely to produce confirmations at the .05 confidence level (i.e., having antichance odds of twenty to one). These investigators are more likely to submit their results for publication and more likely to get them accepted than the remaining investigators. But if the original result was due to chance, it is unlikely that it will be maintained as the number of observations is increased.

Consider the case of an experiment that can be completed in three days. An investigator who carries out two such experiments a week will complete about a hundred experiments over a period of a year. It is likely that one of these will give a result significant at the $p = .01$ level. Adopting a criterion of significance of $p = .000001$ (i.e., odds of one in a million), the same investigator is only likely to produce a significant result, in the absence of ESP, once in 10,000 years. With a hundred investigators working away at experiments, such a result would only be expected to arise once in a century.

Parapsychologists are well aware of the danger of selecting results from a large number of observations. They are unlikely to go on repeating an experiment until a significant result emerges. But ESP experiments are seldom repeated in their original form. A large number of experiments may be regarded as different from each other although they are all testing for ESP because there are differences in method and procedure.

The danger of drawing conclusions about the existence of ESP from a number of different experiments that each yield a positive result is similar to the problem of deciding whether a large number of unusual experiences reported as arising in everyday life can indicate the operation of ESP. Every person has hundreds of experiences every day. Let each person in a population of 300 million have, say, ten experiences each day, the total number of experiences in a year will then be around 10^{12}. Thus the one in ten thousand million chance coincidence will be expected to arise about a hundred times during the year. Some of these experiences may be reported, but most of the remaining events will remain unnoticed and be forgotten. If extraordinary coincidences never were reported it would be even more remarkable than the fact that they arise from time to time.

Difficulties Arising with Complex Targets

The return to the telepathy condition with complex pictures and objects as targets in the dream studies and remote viewing experiments has made experiments difficult to control for scoring and interpretation of the results. Whereas it is a simple matter to decide what is a hit and what is a miss in card guessing, this is not so when using complex pictures. The role of the judge, and the precautions necessary to ensure that he or she has no information to affect the decisions, becomes as important as controlling the subject in card guessing tests. In addition, the number of persons who can affect the result in remote viewing is increased, making control more difficult; the interval of twenty-four hours between tests on single targets also raises difficulties, since the subject and personnel taking part cannot be confined to a laboratory until all tests are completed.

While parapsychologists have been reluctant to repeat any of the earlier *conclusive* experiments, they also have seemed loathe to incorporate features emerging from findings of those experiments into their experiments. Recent research could have been greatly simplified and made more effective had the claimed discoveries from earlier work been incorporated into these later experiments. This could have been done first by employing clairvoyance and precognitive conditions rather than telepathy, and second, by getting the subject to choose from a fixed number of known targets rather than having a free choice.

Clairvoyance Conditions

Under clairvoyance conditions the target can be completely secret to everyone involved in the experiment—except to the subject exercising any supposed ESP ability. This removes many of the difficulties arising when designing the experiment. Rhine claimed that the clairvoyance condition was as effective as the telepathy condition. Targ and Puthoff also claimed their more impressive results with Pat Price and with Uri Geller under this condition.

Precognitive Conditions

In the experiments reported by Bisaha and Dunne it is claimed that similar results to those reported by Targ and Puthoff in *Mind Reach* are obtained under precognitive conditions. Since in their experiment the person who is to view the target does not arrive on the scene until after the percipient has completed his description, further difficulties in design are overcome. Under precognitive clairvoyance conditions, the target merely has to be selected after the subject has made his descriptions. The real target can remain secret inside its envelope.

Fixed Choice Targets

When a subject attempts to guess one of five possible targets, it is a simple matter to decide whether he has secured a hit or not, but with the targets employed in remote viewing experiments this is far from being the case. Difficulties arise, first, in deciding what is a hit and what is a miss, and second, in knowing the extent to which there is true random selection of targets and how the procedures for selecting targets can affect the scores.

In the card guessing experiments the subject merely has to select from a small number of possible targets, all of which are well-known to him. Employing the same method with remote viewing, a fixed number of locations, all well-known to the subject and identified by a name, could be used as targets. The subject would then have to name which target the agent was viewing or would be viewing in ten minutes' time. He could, alternatively, merely point to one of a number of pictures depicting the possible targets. It might be expected that a recognition task would be easier for the subject than his having to describe the target, both from the findings with card guessing experiments and also from the study of recall and recognition tests in the study of sensory perception and memory.

Thus when pushed to a logical conclusion, the results claimed from recent ESP research point to simple methods of testing that would have avoided many of the difficulties present in the reported experiments.

The Possibility of ESP

In recent years there has been some discussion of the argument put forward in *ESP: A Scientific Evaluation,* where I suggested that when examining experiments claiming to establish ESP—or any other new and a priori unlikely process—it is best, first, to assume that ESP is impossible and then to seek some explanation to account for the results in terms of well established processes. Making an initial assumption of impossibility does not rule out the possibility of ESP, it merely provides an approach that is necessary if the experiment is to be critically examined and one that is also likely to save time. It is an approach dependent on the principle of "Occam's razor" that has proved useful in science generally. Adopting this approach, it eventually may be necessary to make the alternative assumption—that ESP is possible. If Uri Geller, for example, really could predict the fall of a die correctly eight times in eight attempts and if he could repeat this demonstration many times before independent critical experimenters, the assumption of impossibility would eventually have to be rejected.

I did not assume that the first approach should necessarily constitute the eventual conclusion, or that there are no new processes awaiting discovery that might require revisions in existing knowledge. This, however, has been the interpretation of some parapsychologists, and in order to criticize it, they have produced their own version of what I have written on the matter. Thus in their book, *Mind Reach,* and in an article,[2] Targ and Puthoff produced the following quotation that they attributed to me: "In view of the a priori arguments against it *we know in advance* that telepathy, etc., cannot occur." The reference given was to *ESP: A Scientific Evaluation* in which these words do not appear.

The same quotation also appeared in a book review by Philip Toynbee in the London *Observer* on October 8, 1967. The review was of *Science and ESP,*[3] edited by J. R. Smythies. Toynbee had obtained the quotation from a chapter contributed by Sir Cyril Burt, who had attributed it to me. Burt's reference to the quotation read: "C. E. M. Hansel, 'Experiments on Telepathy in Children,' *British Journal of Statistical Psychology* 13, 175–78, cf. *idem, New Scientist* V (1959): 459 ff." But the statement does not appear in either of these references.[4]

What I actually wrote, in reply to an article by Burt on the Jones Boys,[5] in the *British Journal of Statistical Psychology* was

In the philosophical sense *any* proposition has a cetain probability of being true. But *telepathy either can occur or cannot occur.* When examining the experiments, it is not unreasonable to assume that telepathy cannot occur in view of the a priori arguments against it; in fact a vast amount of experimental work has failed to give a satisfactory demonstration of its occurrence. If, in the case of an experiment which we are examining in this way, we find our original assumption is untenable, then we are quite free to make any other assumption to account for what happens.

In his article Burt produced several quotations that he accredited to me, but which he had concocted himself. In one case, however—and only one—he quoted my actual words: "we know that there must be some explanation of the trick which involves only natural processes." He omitted to mention that this statement was made in my article in the *New Scientist*[6] where I was discussing the attitude we adopt when we see a lady apparently being sawn in half by a conjurer.

Parapsychology, together with the occult and pseudosciences in general, has received increasing publicity in the mass media. Thus the British Broadcasting Corporation, once known for its accuracy, reliability, impartiality, and its aim (in the words of Lord Reith) of "educating by stealth," today provides horoscopes as a daily service both for adults and children. Programs on parapsychology appear to aim at sensationalism rather than at providing exact facts and authoritative opinion. Uri Geller received wide television coverage on his initial appearance and the public was misled into thinking that he was providing a demonstration of abilities established as authentic by scientists. No attempt was made to rectify the damage done by this program when further facts about Uri Geller became available.

The Ghosts of Borley

A further tendency that is becoming apparent is for discredited claims of the past to be revived for the benefit of the public. Criticism soon becomes forgotten. Thus one of the most sensational cases in the history of psychical research was the haunting of Borley Rectory, the "most haunted house in England." This house was owned by the late Harry Price, who at one time was recognized as Britain's chief publicizer of psychical matters. He wrote two books about Borley that became best sellers, *The Most Haunted House in England* in 1940[7] and *The End of Borley Rectory* in 1946.[8] From 1940 on Borley became well-known through newspapers, magazines, and radio programs. Then in 1956 E. J. Dingwall and K. M. Goldney of the Society for Psychical Research, together with T. H. Hall, published the findings of their five-year investigation which included data from Price's correspondence, obtained after his death.[9] The report was a complete demolition of the whole case for psychical events at Borley. Following publication of the report it appeared to be accepted by most people and by the Society for Psychical Research that Borley had been accounted for and that Harry Price was a liar and a fraud.

However, with the passage of time the Borley affair has been resuscitated. Mr. Harvey Crane in the *News Chronicle* of April 11, 1959 referred to Dingwall, Goldney, and Hall as "the scoffers who accused Harry Price, the greatest of ghost seekers, of rigging the whole legend.'' The matter was again revived in 1962, in an independent television program ''About Religion.'' After this, popular demand increased for Price's two books, which had to be reprinted, and further television programs appeared.

Following an increasing tendency to discredit the evidence indicating that Harry Price had faked events at Borley, Trevor Hall has now published the results of his detailed investigation of Price.[10] In this book *In Search of Harry Price* he indicates that not only was Borley Rectory ''one of the most complex frauds ever perpetrated, but that Price himself, in almost everything that he said or wrote about himself was no less fraudulent.'' This brilliant and devastating analysis of the life and writings of Harry Price should finally have laid the ghosts of Borley to rest, but most of the experiments and other evidence for ESP is far from dead. In their endless quest, the majority of parapsychologists are reluctant to drop a single iota of what they claim to be evidence for the paranormal. Card testing experiments are largely a thing of the past—presumably because they do not work—but the findings from those experiments are still reported in the literature as part of the supposed ''science'' of parapsychology.

Perhaps the most important development during this last period has been the setting up of a Committee for the Scientific Investigation of Claims of the Paranormal chaired by Paul Kurtz, professor of philosophy at the University of Buffalo. The aim of the committee is to combat the publicity given to occultism and pseudoscience, and to attempt to ensure that information given about these topics does not misrepresent the views of orthodox science. The committee publishes a periodical called *The Skeptical Inquirer* that serves as an antidote to the distorted claims provided by press and television. In particular, it can rapidly disseminate information to science writers, a number of whom have already reported the activities and views of the committee to the general public.

A further valuable source of information and discussion has appeared in the form of *The Zetetic Scholar*. This originally was a newsletter giving details of developments and publications in areas of the occult and pseudoscience, circularized by Marcello Truzzi, professor of sociology at East Michigan University. It now appears in the form of a periodical, and its aim is to enhance communication between proponents and their critics and to provide informed discussion on the various claims.

Notes

1. R. A. Fisher, *The Design of Experiments* (Edinburgh: Oliver and Boyd, 1942).
2. H. E. Puthoff and R. Targ, ''A Perceptual Channel for Information Transmission Over Kilometer Distances: Historical Perspective and Recent Research.'' *Proceedings of the IEEE* 64 No. 3, (1976).

3. J. R. Smythies, Ed., *Science and ESP* (London: Routledge and Kegan Paul), p. 75.
4. C. E. M. Hansel, "Experiments on Telepathy in Children: A Reply to Sir Cyril Burt," *British Journal of Statistical Psychology* 13 (1960): 175–78; C. E. M. Hansel, "Experiments on Telepathy," *New Scientist* 5 (1959): 459.
5. C. Burt, "Experiments on Telepathy in Children: Critical Notice." *British Journal of Statistical Psychlogy* 12 (1959): 99.
6. Hansel, "Experiments on Telepathy."
7. H. Price, *"The Most Haunted House in England"* (London: Longmans Green).
8. H. Price, *The End of Borley Rectory* (London: George Harrop, 1946).
9. E. J. Dingwall, K. M. Goldney, and T. H. Hall, *The Haunting of Borley Rectory: A Critical Survey of the Evidence* (London: 1956).
10. T. H. Hall, *In Search of Harry Price* (London: Duckworth, 1978).

PART FOUR

26
Conclusions

Is ESP Possible?

ESP can only be possible if there are new, and at present unknown, processes and properties of matter that permit it to take place. If such processes are nonexistent, ESP is impossible. Thus more fundamental than the question "does ESP exist?" is the question "is ESP possible?" If there were no living person who could demonstrate ESP, it might still be a possibility, just as radio communication was a possibility in the 12th century, although no one at that time had the necessary knowledge and materials to use it for communication purposes. Either ESP investigators are attempting to prove that human beings can do something that is possible, or else they cannot hope to provide proof for ESP, since what they seek to demonstrate is fundamentally impossible.

A great deal of experimental work has failed to provide a clear case for the existence of ESP, but at least two facts have been established: first, subjects trying to guess targets have obtained scores that cannot be attributed to chance; second, some of those taking part in ESP experiments have cheated to produce high scores.

The first fact cannot be disputed. Results such as those obtained by Hubert Pearce or the Jones boys need no statistical analysis for the purpose of establishing that something was happening during the experiments other than pure guesswork. The second fact—that those taking part in experiments sometimes cheat—is known from admissions of trickery. The first two major experiments in Great Britain, on the Creery sisters and on Smith and Blackburn, involved eight subjects:

seven admitted to cheating, and the other cheated according to his partner in the act. Strong evidence is now available to indicate that Soal interfered with his target sheets. His experiments on the Welsh schoolboys in 1955–57 involved two subjects, both of whom admitted to cheating after being caught in the act. It would be remarkable if such attempts to assist the natural course of events ceased altogether between the years 1882 and 1956. In fact, close examination of the most spectacular findings in parapsychology—where the possibility of other forms of error is not evident—invariably points to some form of trickery as an alternative to ESP. To the skeptic, psychical research seems as much a history of how the artful can mislead the innocent as it is a reflection of any more esoteric activity.

Cheating in one form or another is one of the most common of human activities. If it never occurred, much of the expense and complication of modern life would be avoided. The paperwork involved in accounting and auditing—tickets, bills, counterfoils, invoices—would no longer be necessary. Games, examinations, competitions, and numerous such activities would be simplified. On the other hand, it is unlikely that more than a small number of experiments on ESP are affected by cheating, since the investigator does his or her best to ensure that subjects cannot cheat and, no doubt, usually succeeds. The majority of parapsychologists are likely to have sufficient faith in the reality of ESP to believe that it will manifest itself without outside aid. It may then seem strange to the reader that so much space has been given here to the matter of trickery. Why, in the case of each of the so-called conclusive experiments discussed in Part Two, should trickery invariably emerge as a likely alternative to ESP?

One reason is that an experiment is not classified as conclusive unless the known causes of experimental error have been eliminated in its design. None of the experiments in Part Three, giving high antichance odds, could thus be considered as being in this category. If a trick is used in an experiment, it might be expected to produce an impressive result having large odds against arising by chance and, if the experiment is of the "conclusive" category, trickery would be the only alternative explanation to ESP. Thus, the process by which conclusive experiments are weeded out will also bring to light experiments in which a trick has been used.

A trick also involves a trickster. The following remarks made by George R. Price are very relevant.

The wise procedure, when we seek to evaluate the probability of fraud, is to try to ignore all vague, psychological criteria and base our reasoning (i) on such evidence as would impress a court and (ii) on purely statistical considerations. And here we must recognise that we usually make a certain gross statistical error. When we consider the possibility of fraud, almost invariably we think of particular individuals and ask ourselves whether it is possible that this particular man, this Professor X, could be dishonest. The probability seems small, but the procedure is incorrect. The correct procedure is to consider that we very likely would not have heard of Professor X at all except for his psychic findings. Accordingly, the probability of interest to us is the probability of there having been anywhere in the world, among its more than two billion inhabitants, a few people with the desire and ability to produce false evidence for the supernatural.[1]

There is one psychological criterion, however, that even a court of law would regard as impressive. That is the question of motive. Why should people go to all the trouble of entering into complicated conspiracies merely to deceive their fellows? It should first be noted that there are many cases of known trickery in science where the motive is not clear. The Piltdown skull discovered in 1912 at first appeared to be an important piece of evidence in the history of man's development, and involved the tricksters in a lot of work for little apparent gain.

However, in the case of many individuals acting as subjects in parapsychology, there is often a very clear motive. Mediums at one time in the United States were said to constitute the second highest paid profession open to women, and even where monetary gain is not involved, there may be the desire to impress people or to gain prestige. In addition, there is the desire present in most investigations to provide evidence to support their beliefs. In the case of each of the major ''conclusive'' experimental investigations to which a chapter has been given in Part Two of this book, there is a possible monetary or prestige motive for trickery.

In the early 1930s during the Depression, students at Duke University who acted as subjects in ESP experiments were paid an hourly wage for their services. If Pearce was paid to act as a subject, he had every incentive to continue in that capacity. The Pratt-Woodruff experiment was a continuation of work started by Woodruff that constituted part of the requirement for a higher degree. The Soal-Goldney experiment gained Soal his doctorate of science at London University and followed many years of patient investigation in which no evidence for ESP had been established. Mrs. Stewart was paid for her services. The Jones boys earned large rewards for high scores.

Parapsychologists are themselves to blame for the emphasis that has to be placed on cheating when considering their work. In science generally it is likely that investigators at times indulge in underhanded activities, but their experiments are shown up when other scientists fail to duplicate their results. In such cases it is not necessary to hold a long postmortem on the earlier experiment; it is just forgotten. However, parapsychologists—or at least some of the more vociferous of them—by denying the necessity of a result being confirmed by repetition, make it essential that each experiment be examined in detail to ensure that the result could not have been caused by cheating.

It is often difficult to discuss the possibility of cheating objectively. Parapsychologists tend to present their critics with a *fait accompli*. A similar situation would arise in orthodox science if a chemist reported an experimental result that contradicted all the previous research findings and theories of his fellow chemists, together with the statement ''Either this finding must be accepted as valid or else you must accuse me of being a cheat and a liar. Do you accept it?'' In such circumstances, orthodox chemists might feel diffident about openly expressing their doubts. They might, however, repeat the experiment to see whether they got the same result. If they failed to confirm the result, they would not go into a long discussion about whether the original investigator was a liar or a cheat. They would just take any further experimental reports from the same source with a grain of salt.

The trickster often has been assisted by the investigator's overwhelming confidence in his ability to detect trickery. Observers, however careful, must be prepared to make mistakes. But in psychical research many of the investigators have considered themselves infallible. Soal claimed that boys of the caliber of Glyn and Ieuan could never hope to deceive him. A series of "foolproof experiments" have been produced that invariably contain flaws permitting trickery to take place.

If a trick is used in an experiment, this fact might be expected to make itself apparent in the course of further research. But parapsychologists have erected a system that aids the trickster and at the same time preserves experimental findings. During the course of the investigation of many of the reported ESP experiments, it would have been possible to check whether tricks were being used by conducting further tests after improving the conditions. Following Uri Geller's successful predictions of the position of the die in the steel box, further tests could have removed any suspicion that the result was due to a trick. No magician can operate under laboratory conditions where he has to follow instructions and give a performance on demand unless the investigators are grossly incompetent. But such further tests are not made if the investigators are so convinced of the reality of ESP and of their ability to eliminate trickery that they discount its possibility.

Survival Characteristics of ESP

Scientists in general have been little influenced by philosophers who strive to inform them about the methodology and logic of their subject. Science has a basic methodological principle that is self-generating. It was not formulated by anybody, but it has the same empirical basis and underlying logic as the principle of natural selection in evolution. Investigators are continually producing reports of their experimental findings that may be classified, for convenience, as good or bad. The good ones survive because they are confirmed in further research. The bad ones are forgotten because they cannot be confirmed. Science advances through a process of natural selection. New findings become targets for criticism: they must be confirmed by critics under their own experimental conditions. It then soon becomes clear when a finding should be rejected.

If anyone invents a pseudoscience in which this principle ceases to operate, the result soon becomes apparent, for the new "science" fails to have predictive value and leads to more and more findings and theories that are incompatible with orthodox science. This is what has happened in parapsychology. When critics fail to confirm ESP, this is not accepted as a reason for dropping the subject; on the contrary, belief in the reality of ESP is so strong that the principle of repeatability has been rejected or rendered impotent by the invoking of new processes which are claimed as subsidiary characteristics of the phenomenon. Thus, given a high-scoring subject, it would in the normal course of events be only a matter of time before every critic could be silenced, but these subjects cease to achieve high scores when tested by critics. Extrasensory perception only manifests itself before uncritical investigators.

Again, Rhine and Pratt have observed,

> Another major difficulty can be seen in the fact that some experimenters after a period of earlier success in obtaining extrachance results in PSI experiments have proved less effective in their later efforts. In such instances something apparently has been lost that was once a potent factor. The element most likely to change under prolonged testing would seem to be the quality of infectious enthusiasm that accompanies the initial discoveries of the research worker.[2]

Rhine continues: "Those who never succeed at all may, of course, be suspected of not ever having felt such contagious or communicable interest as would help to create a favorable test environment for their subjects." In other words, experimenters fail to confirm their own results, and a further subsidiary characteristic emerges: ESP is affected by the mental state of the person investigating it. If fresh characteristics are postulated in this manner, it is possible to survive almost any form of criticism. An experimental result cannot be confirmed or refuted, since ESP does not operate in front of critics. After tightening up his experimental conditions, an investigator cannot disclaim the findings of his earlier work; failure in later work merely reveals that he has lost his enthusiasm!

Since the chief characteristic of the exploratory stage, according to the statement of Rhine and Pratt given on page 24, is that the investigator carries out his work "without being burdened with too much precautionary concern," failure to confirm earlier work is likely to arise when the investigator graduates from the exploratory stage to one where he takes more care with his work. After an investigator becomes burdened with concern, his precautions will, presumably, be against error and trickery rather than against ESP. It may be assumed that any change in his experimental results is due to the effectiveness of his precautions.

A Revised Approach

In 1965 there were signs that the arguments put forward to support the work on ESP were changing. In 1961 Rhine and Pratt suggested that the case for ESP does not, after all, depend on conclusive experiments, but on general features that emerge from the whole mass of studies, conclusive or inconclusive; it is as if quantity can make up for quality when the latter has been found lacking. They wrote:

> The body of fact in parapsychology is like a many-celled organism. Its strength is that of a growth-relationship, consisting not only of the com-

pounding of one cell with another, but also of the many lawful interrelations that emerge in the growing structure. Going back as Hansel has done, with a one-cell perspective, to fix attention on some incomplete stage of development within a single experimental research is hard to understand in terms of healthy scientific motivation.[3]

But what is the point of presenting conclusive experiments for the consideration of the scientific world if they cannot be criticized? How can an experiment be criticized until it has first been isolated? If experiments are to be considered en masse, will not data be contaminated with results such as those obtained with the Creery sisters, Smith and Blackburn, and others? As soon as criteria are set up by means of which experiments are selected or rejected, it becomes necessary to isolate each experiment to see whether it satisfies those criteria.

Moreover, what precisely are the "lawful interrelations" within the body of fact in parapsychology to which Rhine refers? To date, not a single lawful interrelation appears to have been established. How, for example, does distance affect extrasensory perception? The relationship between scoring rate and distance is completely chaotic, apparently dependent on the investigator, the subject, and the experimental conditions. If it were possible to give a standardized test for ESP to different groups of subjects, systematically varying factors such as age, nationality, intelligence, previous practice, distance, and so on, some lawful interrelations might eventually be expected to reveal themselves. But each of the reported investigations yields a result that has little relationship to any of the others.

Extrasensory perception is not a fact, but a theory put forward to account for high scores obtained during the course of experiments. Parapsychologists have made such observations under a diversity of research conditions from which a number of facts emerge. If these facts can be related to one another by a theory that enables any one to be deducible from knowledge of the others, that theory has some value and plausibility. Predictions might then be made of what will happen in further experiments so that the theory can be tested further. However, a theory that fails to account for a variety of facts and that cannot predict what will happen in further tests is of no value.

If some facts gleaned from the literature on ESP are assembled, they might appear as follows:

1. Subjects, when attempting to guess card symbols, have obtained scores that cannot be attributed to chance.

2. Some of those taking part in ESP experiments have indulged in trickery.

3. Subjects who obtain high scores cannot do so on all occasions.

4. Subjects tend to lose their ability to obtain high scores. This loss often coincides with publication of an experimental result.

5. A successful subject may be unable to obtain high scores when tested by a critical investigator.

6. Some investigators often observe high scores in the subjects they test; others invariably fail to observe such scores.

7. A subject may obtain high scores under one set of experimental conditions and fail to do so under other experimental conditions.

8. No subject has ever demonstrated an ability to obtain consistently high scores when the test procedure is mechanized to the extent that he or she can repeat the exceptional performance when the experimenter is changed.

Assuming that ESP exists, fact 1 is directly applicable. Fact 2 is not relevant to such a hypothesis. Facts 3 and 4 are not predictable but could be said to provide further information about ESP: that is, it appears to be spasmodic and temporary. The remaining facts (5–8) are not predictable, and in the case of any other supposed process investigated by psychologists, would throw doubt on its authenticity. These facts can only be explained by invoking subsidiary characteristics of ESP.

Assuming ESP does not exist, fact 1 is directly applicable to a hypothesis predicting trickery. Fact 2 demonstrates that such a hypothesis is correct in the case of certain experiments. The remaining facts (3–8) are all predictable from what is well-known about trickery.

Lawful relationships can readily be seen among the facts when they are interpreted in accordance with the hypothesis of trickery (or other causes of experimental error). Thus, for example, from fact 7 it might be predicted that those experimental conditions that eliminate the possibility of trickery will also be the ones in which high scores do not arise. This is confirmed by fact 8, and also by examining the experimental conditions under fact 7 in which high scores have, and have not, been observed. Thus, the set of facts given above display lawful interrelationships when interpreted in terms of the hypothesis of trickery, but they are difficult to reconcile with a hypothesis based on the existence of ESP.

A number of other facts could be added to the above list to which neither the hypothesis of trickery nor that of ESP would be applicable. This is to be expected, since a great deal of research—both in parapsychology and elsewhere—has revealed the manner in which high scores can arise from experimental error.

The conclusions stated above are those reached in 1965. Although the experiments now take a different form they are essentially similar in nature to those of the past. In 1965 I suggested that experiments carried out by the VERITAC team of investigators might be used as a model for further research. This suggestion was misinterpreted, and no further research has been published employing such a model. It requires (1) a team of investigators, (2) a suitable laboratory and apparatus, (3) a systematic experimental procedure, and (4) the possibility that duplicative tests can be conducted under the original experimental conditions. In addition, it is necessary for the investigators to be continually vigilant and on the watch for flaws in the experimental procedure.

If definite conclusions are to be drawn, an essential of such research is that very large samples of individuals be tested When investigating any human ability it is necessary to obtain some idea of its distribution among the population, and, in the case of an ability peculiar to some people, to find individuals having the ability. The Society for Psychical Research has carried out one such screening test for ESP and found it to be nonexistent in their sample. Other surveys have been made on radio and television shows, from which nothing appears to have emerged, presumably because television producers lose interest when there is nothing sensational to report.

I make the following suggestion to indicate a way to screen large numbers of the public at negligible expense. Booths would be placed in large stores throughout the country, in which members of the public could test their ESP ability for a modest fee and hope to obtain large monetary rewards rather in the manner that they compete on slot machines. In this case, however, rather than gambling they would hope to use ESP to improve their chances of winning. The machines would pay according to the calculated chance odds, retaining a small percentage for running costs—or for a contribution to some worthwhile cause.

The testing machine, rather like a telephone booth, would be on full view to the public with suitable displays and flashing lights to indicate how the occupant was progressing. A large jackpot would take the form of a ticket, and when the winner cashed it in, details of the successful client could be obtained, and a record would be maintained in the machine of each competitor's score over a fixed number of runs (perhaps 10 p per 25 trials). This would enable any successful subjects to be contacted if necessary.

No doubt some large chain store would welcome the opportunity to attract large numbers of the public and to contribute to the cause of scientific enquiry. Good evidence would eventually be obtained of the ESP scoring ability, at least in those members of the public interested enough to compete.

Alternatively, the television producers who seek to attract audiences with sensational programs about the paranormal might do better by arranging mass screening tests in which members of the public could be persuaded to compete. The first ten successful attempts at a concealed target received would entitle the persons involved to appear in the studio and participate in further tests—perhaps matched against celebrities such as Uri Geller or Bernard Levin.

After 100 years of research, not a single individual has been found who can demonstrate ESP to the satisfaction of independent investigators. For this reason alone it is unlikely that ESP exists. But this empirical finding confirms the theoretical viewpoint of psychologists that sensory information is required to provide the causal link between objects and events in the environment and events in the brain that determine perception.

In this research a number of properties of ESP are assumed to have been discovered Since if ESP is nonexistent these properties are also nonexistent, only utter confusion can exist if the findings from the experiments are retained. The aim of parapsychology should be to produce one individual who can give a reliable and repeatable demonstration of ESP.

In the event such an individual is found, confirmation by independent investigators could easily be arranged. If parapsychologists were to undertake systematic forms of investigation and eliminate all that is not confirmed beyond all doubt, they would have a better chance of revealing any new human abilities that may exist.

Notes

1. G. R. Price, *Science* (1955), p. 363.
2. Rhine and Pratt, *Parapsychology*, p. 132.
3. Rhine and Pratt, *Journal of Parapsychology* (1961), p. 94.

Suggestions for Further Reading

Critical Assessments

Newcomb, Simon, Modern Occultism, *Nineteenth Century,* 1909.

Gardner, Martin, *Fads and Fallacies in the name of Science,* New York, Dover Publications, Inc. 1957.

Rawcliffe, D. H. *Illusions and Delusions of the Supernatural and the Occult,* New York, Dover Publications, Inc., 1959.

Price, G. R. *Science and the Supernatural,* Science, no. 122, 1955.

General Reviews of Experiments (mainly uncritical)

Pratt, J. A., Rhine, J. B., Smith, M. Burke, and Stuart, Charles E., *Extra-Sensory Perception after Sixty Years,* Boston: Bruce Humphries, Publishers, 1940.

Soal, S. G., and Bateman, F. *Modern Experiments in Telepathy,* London: Faber & Faber Ltd., 1954.

Beloff, John (ed.), *New Directions in Parapsychology,* London: Ekek Science, 1974.

Randall, John L. *Parapsychology and the Nature of Life.* London: Souvnir Press, 1975.

Wolman, Benjamin B. (ed.), *Handbook of Parapsychology,* New York: Van Nostrand, 1977.

Early History of Psychical Research

Hall, Trevor H., *The Strange Case of Edmund Gurney,*London: Gerald Duckworth, 1974.

Spiritualism

Rinn, J. F. *Searchlight on Psychical Research,* London: Rider 7 Co., 1954.
Hall, Trevor H., The Spritualists: *The Story of William Crookes and Florence
   Cooke,* London: Gerald Duckworth, 1962.

Ghosts

Dingwall, E. J., Goldney, K. M. and Hall, Trevor H., *The Haunting of Borley
   Rectory: A Critical Survey of the Evidence,* London: 1956.
Hall, Trevor H., *Search for Harry Price,* London: Gerald Duckworth, 1978.

Index